A·N·N·U·A·L E·D·I·T·I·O·N·S

Sociology

Thirty-first Edition

02/03

EDITOR

Kurt Finsterbusch

University of Maryland, College Park

Kurt Finsterbusch received a bachelor's degree in history from Princeton University in 1957 and a bachelor of divinity degree from Grace Theological Seminary in 1960. His Ph.D. in sociology, from Columbia University, was conferred in 1969. Dr. Finsterbusch is the author of several books, including *Understanding Social Impacts* (Sage Publications, 1980), *Social Research for Policy Decisions* (Wadsworth Publishing, 1980, with Annabelle Bender Motz), and *Organizational Change as a Development Strategy* (Lynne Rienner Publishers, 1987, with Jerald Hage). He is currently teaching at the University of Maryland, College Park, and, in addition to serving as editor for *Annual Editions: Sociology*, he is also editor of *Annual Editions: Social Problems*, McGraw-Hill/Dushkin's *Taking Sides: Clashing Views on Controversial Social Issues*, and *Sources: Notable Selections in Sociology*.

McGraw-Hill/Dushkin

530 Old Whitfield Street, Guilford, Connecticut 06437

Visit us on the Internet
http://www.dushkin.com

Credits

1. **Culture**
   Unit photo—© 2002 by Cleo Freelance Photography.
2. **Socialization and Social Control**
   Unit photo—Courtesy of Cheryl Greenleaf.
3. **Groups and Roles in Transition**
   Unit photo—Courtesy of McGraw-Hill/Dushkin.
4. **Stratification and Social Inequalities**
   Unit photo—© 2002 by Sweet By & By/Cindy Brown.
5. **Social Institutions: Issues, Crises, and Changes**
   Unit photo—Courtesy of Pamela Carley.
6. **Social Change and the Future**
   Unit photo—© 2002 by Sweet By & By/Cindy Brown.

Copyright

Cataloging in Publication Data
Main entry under title: Annual Editions: Sociology. 2002/2003.
1. Sociology—Periodicals. 2. United States—Social conditions—1960—Periodicals.
I. Finsterbusch Kurt, comp. II. Title: Sociology
ISBN 0–07–250648–2   658'.05   ISSN 0277–9315

Thirty-First Edition

Cover image © 2002 PhotoDisc, Inc.
Printed in the United States of America   234567890BAHBAH5432   Printed on Recycled Paper

To the Reader

In publishing ANNUAL EDITIONS we recognize the enormous role played by the magazines, newspapers, and journals of the public press in providing current, first-rate educational information in a broad spectrum of interest areas. Many of these articles are appropriate for students, researchers, and professionals seeking accurate, current material to help bridge the gap between principles and theories and the real world. These articles, however, become more useful for study when those of lasting value are carefully collected, organized, indexed, and reproduced in a low-cost format, which provides easy and permanent access when the material is needed. That is the role played by ANNUAL EDITIONS.

The new millennium has arrived with difficult new issues such as how to deal with new levels of terrorism, while many of the old issues remain unresolved. There is much uncertainty. Almost all institutions are under stress. The political system is held in low regard because it seems to accomplish so little, to cost so much, and to focus on special interests more than on the public good. The economy is in a recession in the short term, and in the long term it suffers from foreign competition, trade deficits, economic uncertainties, and a worrisome concentration of economic power in the hands of relatively few multinational corporations. Complaints about the education system continue, because grades K–12 do not teach basic skills well and college costs are too high. Health care is too expensive, many Americans lack health care coverage, and some diseases are becoming resistant to our medicines. The entertainment industry is booming, but many people worry about its impact on values and behavior. News media standards seem to be set by the tabloids. Furthermore, the dynamics of technology, globalization, and identity groups are creating crises, changes, and challenges. Crime rates have declined somewhat, but they are still at high levels. The public is demanding more police, more jails, and tougher sentences, but less government spending. Government social policies seem to create almost as many problems as they solve. Laborers, women, blacks, and many other groups complain of injustices and victimization. The use of toxic chemicals has been blamed for increases in cancer, sterility, and other diseases. Marriage and the family have been transformed, in part by the women's movement and in part by the stress that current conditions create for women who try to combine family and careers. Schools, television, and corporations are commonly vilified. Many claim that morality has declined to shameful levels. Add to all this the problems of population growth, ozone depletion, and global warming, and it is easy to be pessimistic. Nevertheless, crises and problems also create opportunities.

The present generation may determine the course of history for the next 200 years. Great changes are taking place, and new solutions are being sought where old answers no longer work. The issues that the current generation faces are complex and must be interpreted within a sophisticated framework. The sociological perspective provides such a framework. It expects people to act in terms of their positions in the social structure, the political,

economic, and social forces operating on them, and the norms that govern the situation.

Annual Editions: Sociology 02/03 should help you to develop the sociological perspective that will enable you to determine how the issues of the day relate to the way society is structured. The articles provide not only information but also models of interpretation and analysis that will guide you as you form your own views. In addition, both the *topic guide* and the *World Wide Web* pages can be used to further explore the book's topics.

This thirty-first edition of *Annual Editions: Sociology* emphasizes social change, institutional crises, and prospects for the future. It provides intellectual preparation for acting for the betterment of humanity in times of crucial change. The sociological perspective is needed more than ever as humankind tries to find a way to peace, prosperity, health, and well-being that can be maintained for generations in an improving environment. The numerous obstacles that lie in the path of these important goals require sophisticated responses. The goals of this edition are to communicate to students the excitement and importance of the study of the social world and to provoke interest in and enthusiasm for the study of sociology.

Annual Editions: Sociology depends upon reader response in order to develop and change. You are encouraged to return the postage-paid *article rating form* at the back of the book with your opinions about existing articles, recommendations of articles you think have sociological merit for subsequent editions, and advice on how the anthology can be made more useful as a teaching and learning tool.

Kurt Finsterbusch

Kurt Finsterbusch

Editor

Dedicated to Ned and Katia Ramsay as they not only adapt to the changing world around them but also contribute to it.

Contents

UNIT 1
Culture

Four selections consider what our culture can learn from primitive peoples, what forces are shaping today's cultures and lifestyles, and the impact of crises on culture.

UNIT 2
Socialization and Social Control

Five articles examine the effects of social influences on childhood, personality, and human behavior with regard to the socialization of the individual.

The concepts in bold italics are developed in the article. For further expansion, please refer to the Topic Guide and the Index.

UNIT 3
Groups and Roles in Transition

Six articles discuss some of the social roles and group relationships that are in transition in today's society. Topics include primary and secondary groups and the re-evaluation of social choices.

The concepts in bold italics are developed in the article. For further expansion, please refer to the Topic Guide and the Index.

UNIT 4
Stratification and Social Inequalities

Eight selections discuss the social stratification and inequalities that exist in today's society with regard to the rich, the poor, blacks, and gender issues.

The concepts in bold italics are developed in the article. For further expansion, please refer to the Topic Guide and the Index.

UNIT 5
Social Institutions: Issues, Crises, and Changes

Nine articles examine several social institutions that are currently in crisis. Selections focus on the political, economic, and social spheres, as well as the overall state of the nation.

The concepts in bold italics are developed in the article. For further expansion, please refer to the Topic Guide and the Index.

The concepts in bold italics are developed in the article. For further expansion, please refer to the Topic Guide and the Index.

The concepts in bold italics are developed in the article. For further expansion, please refer to the Topic Guide and the Index.

Topic Guide

This topic guide suggests how the selections in this book relate to the subjects covered in your course. You may want to use the topics listed on these pages to search the Web more easily.

On the following pages a number of Web sites have been gathered specifically for this book. They are arranged to reflect the units of this *Annual Edition*. You can link to these sites by going to the DUSHKIN ONLINE support site at *http://www.dushkin.com/online/*.

ALL THE ARTICLES THAT RELATE TO EACH TOPIC ARE LISTED BELOW THE BOLD-FACED TERM.

Abortion
30. Seeking Abortion's Middle Ground

African Americans
20. Racism Isn't What It Used to Be
21. Where Bias Begins: The Truth About Stereotypes

AIDS
31. Death Stalks a Continent

Capitalism
18. Corporate Welfare
27. Twilight of the Corporation
28. Work, Work, Work, Work!

Children and childhood
2. The Mountain People
5. Boys Will Be Boys
10. The American Family
11. Should You Stay Together For the Kids?
21. Where Bias Begins: The Truth About Stereotypes
29. Schools That Develop Children

Community
2. The Mountain People
8. The Secrets of Gun Violence in America
14. Demand for Density? The Functions of the City in the 21st Century
15. Does the Internet Strengthen Community?
26. Where the Public Good Prevailed
29. Schools That Develop Children
35. Feeling the Heat: Life in the Greenhouse
40. Community Building: Steps Toward a Good Society

Corporate welfare
18. Corporate Welfare

Crime
3. More Moral
7. Preventing Crime: The Promising Road Ahead
8. The Secrets of Gun Violence in America
9. The War on Addiction

Culture
1. Modernization's Challenge to Traditional Values: Who's Afraid of Ronald McDonald?
2. The Mountain People
3. More Moral
5. Boys Will Be Boys
6. Born to Be Good?
10. The American Family
12. Now for the Truth About Americans and Sex
13. The Betrayal of the American Man
22. The Past and Prologue
26. Where the Public Good Prevailed
28. Work, Work, Work, Work!
29. Schools That Develop Children
30. Seeking Abortion's Middle Ground

Demography
33. 16 Impacts of Population Growth
34. The Alien Payoff

Discrimination
20. Racism Isn't What It Used to Be
21. Where Bias Begins: The Truth About Stereotypes
22. The Past and Prologue
23. Violence Against Women

Drugs
9. The War on Addiction

Ecology
2. The Mountain People
33. 16 Impacts of Population Growth
35. Feeling the Heat: Life in the Greenhouse
36. Grains of Hope
37. The Secret Nuclear War

Economy
16. Still the Land of Opportunity?
17. Are the Rich Cleaning Up?
18. Corporate Welfare
27. Twilight of the Corporation
28. Work, Work, Work, Work!
41. Across the Great Divide

Education
29. Schools That Develop Children

Employment
20. Racism Isn't What It Used to Be
22. The Past and Prologue
28. Work, Work, Work, Work!

Family and marriage
2. The Mountain People
3. More Moral
10. The American Family
11. Should You Stay Together For the Kids?

Future
27. Twilight of the Corporation
32. The Future of Religion in America
33. 16 Impacts of Population Growth
35. Feeling the Heat: Life in the Greenhouse
36. Grains of Hope
37. The Secret Nuclear War
38. Unmasking Bioterror
40. Community Building: Steps Toward a Good Society
41. Across the Great Divide

Gender roles
5. Boys Will Be Boys
10. The American Family
13. The Betrayal of the American Man

World Wide Web Sites

The following World Wide Web sites have been carefully researched and selected to support the articles found in this reader. The easiest way to access these selected sites is to go to our DUSHKIN ONLINE support site at *http://www.dushkin.com/online/*.

AE: Sociology 02/03

The following sites were available at the time of publication. Visit our Web site—we update DUSHKIN ONLINE regularly to reflect any changes.

General Sources

Library of Congress
http://www.loc.gov

Examine this extensive Web site to learn about resource tools, library services/resources, exhibitions, and databases in many different subfields of sociology.

Social Science Information Gateway (SOSIG)
http://sosig.esrc.bris.ac.uk

SOSIG is an online catalog of Internet resources relevant to social science education and research. Resources are selected by librarians or subject specialists.

Sociological Tour Through Cyberspace
http://www.trinity.edu/~mkearl/index.html

Prepared by Michael Kearl at Trinity University, this extensive site provides essays, commentaries, data analyses, and links on death and dying, family, the sociology of time, social gerontology, social psychology, and more.

UNIT 1: Culture

American Studies Web
http://www.georgetown.edu/crossroads/asw/

This eclectic site provides links to a wealth of resources on the Web related to American studies: gender studies, environment, race, and more. It is of great help when doing research in demography, genealogy, and population studies.

Anthropology Resources Page
http://www.usd.edu/anth/

Many cultural topics can be accessed at this site from the University of South Dakota. Click on the links to find information about differences and similarities in values and lifestyles among the world's peoples.

Human Rights and Humanitarian Assistance
http://www.etown.edu/vl/humrts.html

Through this part of the World Wide Web Virtual Library, you can conduct research into a number of human-rights topics in order to gain a greater understanding of issues affecting indigenous peoples in the modern era. The site also provides links to many other subjects related to sociology.

Sociology Library
http://www.library.upenn.edu/resources/subject/social/sociology/ sociology.html

A number of indexes of cultural and ethnic studies, criminology, population, and demographics are provided on this Web site.

UNIT 2: Socialization and Social Control

Crime Times
http://www.crime-times.org

This interesting site lists research reviews and other information regarding causes of criminal, violent, and psychopathic behavior. It is provided by the Wacker Foundation, publishers of *Crime Times.*

Ethics Updates/Lawrence Hinman
http://ethics.acusd.edu

This site provides both simple concept definition and complex analysis of ethics, original treatises, and sophisticated search-engine capability. Subject matter covers the gamut, from ethical theory to applied ethical venues. There are many opportunities for user input.

National Institute on Drug Abuse (NIDA)
http://165.112.78.61/

Use this site index of the National Institute on Drug Abuse for access to NIDA publications and communications, information on drugs of abuse, and links to other related Web sites.

Sexual Assault Information Page
http://www.cs.utk.edu/~bartley/saInfoPage.html

This invaluable site provides dozens of links to information and resources on a variety of sexual assault–related topics, including child sexual abuse, date rape, incest, secondary victims, and offenders. It also provides some material of interest in the pornography debate.

UNIT 3: Groups and Roles in Transition

The Gallup Organization
http://www.gallup.com

Links to an extensive archive of public opinion poll results and special reports on a huge variety of topics related to American society are available on this Gallup Organization home page.

Grass-Roots.org
http://www.iglou.com/why/ria.htm

Grass-roots.org offers this site as part of its program called Reinvesting in America (its effort to help people fight hunger and poverty in their communities). Various resources and models for grassroots action are included here.

The North-South Institute
http://www.nsi-ins.ca/ensi/index.html

Searching this site of the North-South Institute—which works to strengthen international development cooperation and enhance gender and social equity—will help you find information on a variety of issues related to social transitions.

PsychNet/American Psychological Association
http://www.apa.org/psychnet/

By exploring this site, you will be able to find links to an abundance of articles and other resources related to interpersonal relationships throughout the life span.

www.dushkin.com/online/

SocioSite: Feminism and Woman Issues
http://www.pscw.uva.nl/sociosite/TOPICS/Women.html

Open this enormous sociology site of the University of Amsterdam's Sociological Institute to gain insights into a number of issues that affect both men and women. It provides biographies of women through history, an international network for women in the workplace, links in gay studies, affirmative action, family and children's issues, and much more. Return to the site's home page for many other sociological links.

UNIT 4: Stratification and Social Inequalities

American Scientist
http://www.amsci.org/amsci/amsci.html

Investigating this Web site of the *American Scientist* will help students of sociology to access a variety of articles and to explore issues and concepts related to race and gender.

Joint Center for Poverty Research
http://www.jcpr.org

Finding research information related to poverty is possible at this site. It provides working papers, answers to FAQs, and facts about who is poor in America. Welfare reform is also addressed.

Patterns of Variability: The Concept of Race
http://www.as.ua.edu/ant/bindon/ant101/lectures/race/race1.htm

This site provides a handy, at-a-glance reference to the prevailing concepts of race and the causes of human variability since ancient times. It can serve as a valuable starting point for research and understanding into the concept of race.

The Urban Institute
http://www.urban.org/welfare/overview.htm

The Urban Institute offers lengthy discussions of issues related to welfare and its reform. This page starts with the assertion that "No one likes the current welfare system."

UNIT 5: Social Institutions: Issues, Crises, and Changes

International Labour Organization (ILO)
http://www.ilo.org

ILO's home page leads to links that describe the goals of the organization and summarizes international labor standards and human rights. Its official UN Web site locator can point to many other useful resources.

IRIS Center
http://www.iris.umd.edu

The project on Institutional Reform and the Informal Sector (IRIS) aims to understand transitional and developing economies. Examine this site to learn about research into government institutions and policies that help to promote successful economic change in the global age.

Marketplace of Political Ideas/University of Houston Library
http://info.lib.uh.edu/politics/markind.htm

Here is a collection of links to campaign, conservative/liberal perspectives, and political-party sites, including General Political, Democratic, Republican, and Third-Party sites.

National Center for Policy Analysis
http://www.ncpa.org

Through this site, you can reach links that provide discussions of an array of topics that are of major interest in the study of American politics and government from a sociological perspective, including regulatory policy, affirmative action, and income.

National Institutes of Health (NIH)
http://www.nih.gov

Consult this site for links to extensive health information and scientific resources of interest to sociologists from the NIH, one of eight health agencies of the Public Health Service.

UNIT 6: Social Change and the Future

Gil Gordon Associates
http://www.gilgordon.com

This site consolidates a wide variety of information from around the world on the subject of telecommuting, teleworking, the virtual office, alternative officing, and related topics.

National Immigrant Forum
http://www.immigrationforum.org/index.htm

This pro-immigrant organization offers this site to examine the effects of immigration on the U.S. economy and society. Click on the links for discussion of underground economies, immigrant economies, and other topics.

Terrorism Research Center
http://www.terrorism.com/index.shtml

The Terrorism Research Center features definitions and original research on terrorism, counterterrorism documents, a comprehensive list of Web links, and monthly profiles of terrorist and counterterrorist groups.

United Nations Environment Program (UNEP)
http://www.unep.ch

Consult this home page of UNEP for links to environmental topics of critical concern to sociologists. The site will direct you to useful databases and global resource information.

William Davidson Institute
http://www.wdi.bus.umich.edu

The William Davidson Institute at the University of Michigan Business School is dedicated to the understanding and promotion of economic transition. Consult this site for discussion of topics related to the changing global economy and the effects of globalization in general.

We highly recommend that you review our Web site for expanded information and our other product lines. We are continually updating and adding links to our Web site in order to offer you the most usable and useful information that will support and expand the value of your Annual Editions. You can reach us at: *http://www.dushkin.com/annualeditions/*.

UNIT 1
Culture

Unit Selections

1. **Modernization's Challenge to Traditional Values: Who's Afraid of Ronald McDonald?** Ronald Inglehart and Wayne E. Baker
2. **The Mountain People**, Colin M. Turnbull
3. **More Moral**, David Whitman
4. **The Final Freedom**, Alan Wolfe

Key Points to Consider

- What do you think are the core values in American society?

- What are the strengths and weaknesses of cultures that emphasize either cooperation or individualism?

- What is the relationship between culture and identity?

- What might a visitor from a primitive tribe describe as shocking and barbaric about American society?

 **Links: www.dushkin.com/online/**
These sites are annotated in the World Wide Web pages.

The ordinary, everyday objects of living and the daily routines of life provide a structure to social life that is regularly punctuated by festivals, celebrations, and other special events (both happy and sad). These routine and special times are the stuff of culture, for culture is the sum total of all the elements of one's social inheritance. Culture includes language, tools, values, habits, science, religion, literature, and art.

It is easy to take one's own culture for granted, so it is useful to pause and reflect on the shared beliefs and practices that form the foundations for our social life. Students share beliefs and practices and thus have a student culture. Obviously the faculty has one also. Students, faculty, and administrators share a university culture. At the national level, Americans share an American culture. These cultures change over time and especially between generations. As a result, there is much variety among cultures across time and across nations, tribes, and groups. It is fascinating to study these differences and to compare the dominant values and signature patterns of different groups.

The two articles in the first subsection deal with traditional cultures that are under considerable stress today. In the first the authors study the differences between the cultures of rich and poor countries using an ambitious cross-national survey. The peoples of poor countries are more anchored in traditions and less imbued with secular/rational values or involved in self-expression. The study also clearly shows some of the important effects that economic development has on culture. The second article, by Colin Turnbull, reports how the Ik tribe of Africa suffered the loss of its tribal lands and was forced to live in a harsh environment. When a society's technology is very primitive, its environment has a profound impact on its social structure and culture. We would expect, therefore, that such a momentous change in the tribe's environment would require some interesting adaptations. The change that occurred, however, was shocking. Literally all aspects of life changed for the tribe's members in a disturbingly sinister way. Moreover, the experience of this tribe leads Turnbull to question some of the individualistic tendencies of America.

In the next subsection, David Whitman attacks the moral decline thesis. He shows that most moral indicators have improved in the last 25 years. Drug and alcohol use, heavy drinking and drunk driving, cheating on taxes, political corruption, and crime have declined noticeably. Controlling for inflation charitable giving has increased 50 percent. Church attendance and religion-based behavior have not declined. Though a few are negative, the positive direction of most moral indicators and the vast im-

provement on some social issues, such as discrimination, lead Whitman to conclude that America is more moral today than it was 25 years ago.

In the final article of this subsection, Alan Wolfe identifies some of the unique aspects of American culture. Perhaps the most prominent aspect is the high degree of moral freedom that Americans claim. They do not seek freedom from morality but the freedom to choose their own morality. They are often criticized as immoral because they are not responsive to many traditional morals, but they do try to live morally.

Modernization's Challenge to Traditional Values: Who's Afraid of Ronald McDonald?

"Modernization" means "Americanization" to many who fear a coming McWorld. But a study by two social researchers indicates that traditional values will keep most countries from becoming clones of the United States.

By Ronald Inglehart and Wayne E. Baker

The World Values Survey—a two-decade-long examination of the values of 65 societies coordinated by the University of Michigan's Institute for Social Research—is the largest investigation ever conducted of attitudes, values, and beliefs around the world. This study has carried out three waves of representative national surveys: the first in 1981–1982, the second in 1990–1991, and the third in 1995–1998. The fourth wave is being completed in 1999–2001. The study now represents some 80% of the world's population. These societies have per capita GNPs ranging from $300 to more than $30,000. Their political systems range from long-established stable democracies to authoritarian states.

The World Values Survey data have been used by researchers around the world for hundreds of publications in more than a dozen languages. Studies that have been based on the data cover a wide range of topics, including volunteerism in Europe, political partisanship and social class in Ireland, democratization in Korea, liberalization in Mexico, future values in Japan, and the religious vote in Western Europe.

This article examines the relationship between cultural values and economic globalization and modernization: What impact does economic development have on the values of a culture, and vice versa? Is a future "McWorld" inevitable?

Rich Values, Poor Values

The World Values Survey data show us that the world views of the people of rich societies differ systematically from those of low-income societies across a wide range of political, social, and religious norms and beliefs. The two most significant dimensions that emerged reflected, first, a polarization between *traditional* and *secular-rational* orientations toward authority and, second, a polarization between *survival* and *self-expres-*

sion values. By *traditional* we mean those societies that are relatively authoritarian, place strong emphasis on religion, and exhibit a mainstream version of preindustrial values such as an emphasis on male dominance in economic and political life, respect for authority, and relatively low levels of tolerance for abortion and divorce. Advanced societies, or *secular-rational*, tend to have the opposite characteristics.

A central component of the survival vs. self-expression dimension involves the polarization between materialist and postmaterialist values. Massive evidence indicates that a cultural shift throughout advanced industrial society is emerging among generations who have grown up taking survival for granted. Values among this group emphasize environmental protection, the women's movement, and rising demand for participation in decision making in economic and political life. During the past 25 years, these values have become increasingly widespread in almost all advanced industrial societies for which extensive time-series evidence is available.

Economic development brings with it sweeping cultural change, some modernization theorists tell us. Others argue that cultural values are enduring and exert more influence on society than does economic change. Who's right?

One goal of the World Values Survey is to study links between economic development and changes in values. A key question that we ask is whether the globalization of the economy will necessarily produce a homogenization (or, more specifically, an Americanization) of culture—a so-called "McWorld."

In the nineteenth century, modernization theorists such as Karl Marx and Friedrich Nietzsche made bold predictions about the future of industrial society, such as the rise of labor and the decline of religion. In the twentieth century, non-Western societies were expected to abandon their traditional cultures and assimilate the technologically and morally "superior" ways of the West.

Clearly now, at the start of the twenty-first century, we need to rethink "modernization." Few people today anticipate a proletarian revolution, and non-western societies such as East Asia have surpassed their Western role models in key aspects of modernization, such as rates of economic growth. And few observers today attribute moral superiority to the West.

Two Dimensions of Cross-Cultural Variation

1. Traditional vs. Secular-Rational Values
   Traditional values emphasize the following:
   • God is very important in respondent's life.
   • Respondent believes it is more important for a child to learn obedience and religious faith than independence and determination.
   • Respondent believes abortion is never justifiable.
   • Respondent has strong sense of national pride.
   • Respondent favors more respect for authority.
   Secular-Rational values emphasize the opposite.
2. Survival vs. Self-Expression Values
   Survival values emphasize the following:
   • Respondent gives priority to economic and physical security over self-expression and quality of life.
   • Respondent describes self as not very happy.
   • Respondent has not signed and would not sign a petition.
   • Respondent believes homosexuality is never justifiable.
   • Respondent believes you have to be very careful about trusting people.
   Self-Expression values emphasize the opposite.

Source: World Values Survey (http://wvs.isr.umich.edu)

On the other hand, one core concept of modernization theory still seems valid: Industrialization produces pervasive social and cultural consequences, such as rising educational levels, shifting attitudes toward authority, broader political participation, declining fertility rates, and changing gender roles. On the basis of the World Values Surveys, we believe that economic development has systematic and, to some extent, predictable cultural and political consequences. Once a society has embarked on industrialization—the central element of the modernization process—certain changes are highly likely to occur. But economic development is not the *only* force at work.

In the past few decades, modernization has become associated with *post*-industrialization: the rise of the knowledge and service-oriented economy. These changes in the nature of work had major political and cultural consequences, too. Rather than growing more materialistic with increased prosperity, postindustrial societies are experiencing an increasing emphasis on quality-of-life issues, environmental protection, and self-expression.

While industrialization increased human dominance over the environment—and consequently created a dwindling role for religious belief—the emergence of postindustrial society is stimulating further evolution of prevailing world views in a different direction. Life in postindustrial societies centers on services rather than material objects, and more effort is focused on communicating and processing information. Most people spend their productive hours dealing with other people and symbols.

Thus, the rise of postindustrial society leads to a growing emphasis on self-expression. Today's unprecedented wealth in advanced societies means an increasing share of the population grows up taking survival for granted. Their value priorities shift from an overwhelming emphasis on economic and physical security toward an increasing emphasis on subjective well-being and quality of life. "Modernization," thus, is not linear—it moves in new directions.

How Values Shape Culture

Different societies follow different trajectories even when they are subjected to the same forces of economic development, in part because situation-specific factors, such as a society's cultural heritage, also shape how a particular society develops. Recently, Samuel Huntington, author of *The Clash of Civilizations* (Simon & Schuster, 1996), has focused on the role of religion in shaping the world's eight major civilizations or "cultural zones": Western Christianity, Orthodox, Islam, Confucian, Japanese, Hindu, African, and Latin American. These zones were shaped by religious traditions that are still powerful today, despite the forces of modernization.

Distinctive cultural zones persist two centuries after the industrial revolution began.

Other scholars observe other distinctive cultural traits that endure over long periods of time and continue to shape a society's political and economic performance. For example, the regions of Italy in which democratic institutions function most successfully today are those in which civil society was relatively well developed in the nineteenth century and even earlier, as Robert Putnam notes in *Making Democracy Work* (Princeton University Press, 1993). And a cultural heritage of "low trust" puts a society at a competitive disadvantage in global markets because it is less able to develop large and complex social institutions, Francis Fukuyama argues in *Trust: The Social Virtues and the Creation of Prosperity* (Free Press, 1995).

The impression that we are moving toward a uniform "McWorld" is partly an illusion. The seemingly identical McDonald's restaurants that have spread throughout the world actually have different social meanings and fulfill dif-

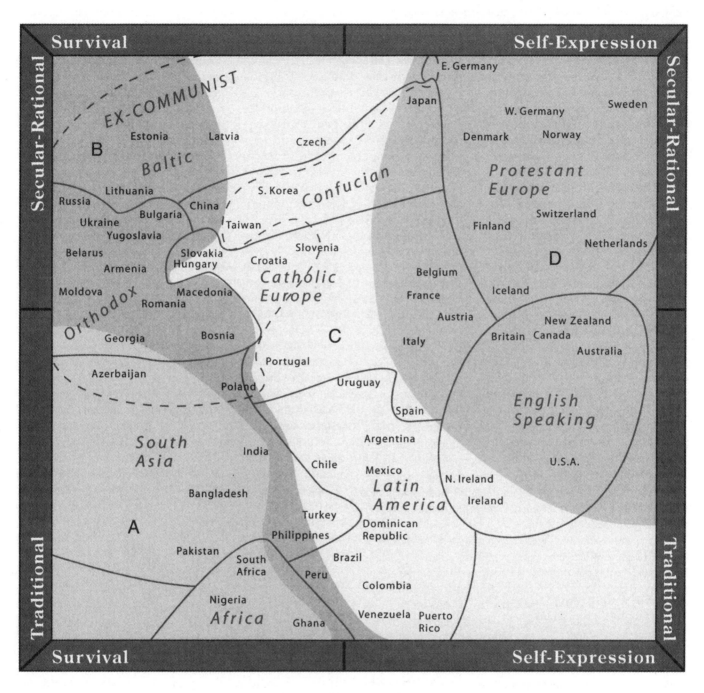

Less than $2,000 GNP per capita   A   C $5,000 to $15,000 GNP per capita

$2,000 to $5,000 GNP per capita   B   D   More than $15,000 GNP per capita

ferent social functions in different cultural zones. Eating in a McDonald's restaurant in Japan is a different social experience from eating in one in the United States, Europe, or China.

Likewise, the globalization of communication is unmistakable, but its effects may be overestimated. It is certainly apparent that young people around the world are wearing jeans and listening to U.S. pop music; what is less apparent is the persistence of underlying value differences.

Mapping and Predicting Values

Using the 1995–1998 wave of the World Values Survey, we produced a map of the world's values, showing the locations of 65 societies on the two cross-cultural dimensions—traditional vs. secular-rational values and survival vs. self-expression values.

What the map shows us is that cross-cultural variation is highly constrained. That is, if the people of a given society place a strong emphasis on religion, that society's relative position on many other variables can be predicted—such as attitudes toward abortion, national pride, respect for authority, and child-drearing. Similarly, survival vs. self-expression values reflect wide-ranging but tightly correlated clusters of values: Materialistic (survival-oriented) societies can be predicted to value maintaining order and fighting inflation, while postmaterialistic (self-expression-oriented) societies can be predicted to value freedom, interpersonal trust, and tolerance of outgroups.

Economic development seems to have a powerful impact on cultural values: The value systems of rich countries differ systematically from those of poor countries. If we superimpose an income "map" over the values map, we see that all 19 societies with an annual per capita GNP of over $15,000 rank relatively high on both dimensions, placing them in the upper right-hand corner. This economic zone cuts across the boundaries of the Protestant, ex-Communist, Confucian, Catholic, and English-speaking cultural zones.

On the other hand, all societies with per capita GNPs below $2,000 fall into a cluster at the lower left of the map, in an economic zone that cuts across the African, South Asian, ex-Communist, and Orthodox cultural zones. The remaining societies fall into two intermediate cultural-economic zones. Economic development seems to move societies in a common direction, regardless of their cultural heritage. Nevertheless, distinctive cultural zones persist two centuries after the industrial revolution began.

Of course, per capita GNP is only one indicator of a society's level of economic development. Another might be the percentage of the labor force engaged in the agricultural sector, the industrial sector, or the service sector. The shift from an agrarian mode of production to industrial production seems to bring with it a shift from traditional values toward increasing rationalization and secularization.

But a society's cultural heritage also plays a role: All four of the Confucian-influenced societies (China, Taiwan, South Korea, and Japan) have relatively secular values, regardless of the proportion of their labor forces in the industrial sector. Conversely, the historically Roman Catholic societies (e.g., Italy, Portugal, and Spain) display relatively traditional values when compared with Confucian or ex-Communist societies with the same proportion of industrial workers. And virtually all of the historically Protestant societies (e.g., West Germany, Denmark, Norway, and Sweden) rank higher on the survival/self-expression dimension than do all of the historically Roman Catholic societies, regardless of the extent to which their labor forces are engaged in the service sector.

We can conclude from this that changes in GNP and occupational structure have important influences on prevailing world views, but traditional cultural influences persist.

Religious traditions appear to have had an enduring impact on the contemporary value systems of the 65 societies. But a society's culture reflects its entire historical heritage. A central historical event of the twentieth century was the rise and fall of a Communist empire that once ruled one-third of the world's population. Communism left a clear imprint on the value systems of those who lived under it. East Germany remains culturally close to West Germany despite four decades of Communist

rule, but its value system has been drawn toward the Communist zone. And although China is a member of the Confucian zone, it also falls within a broad Communist-influenced zone. Similarly, Azerbaijan, though part of the Islamic cluster, also falls within the Communist superzone that dominated it for decades.

The Deviant U.S.

The World Value Map clearly shows that the United States is a deviant case. We do not believe it is a prototype of cultural modernization for other societies to follow, as some postwar modernization theorists have naively assumed. The United States has a much more traditional value system than any other advanced industrial society.

On the traditional/secular-rational dimension, the United States ranks far below other rich societies, with levels of religiosity and national pride comparable to those found in developing societies. The United States does rank among the most advanced societies along the survival/self-expression dimension, but even here it does not lead the world. The Swedes and the Dutch seem closer to the cutting edge of cultural change than do the Americans.

Modernization theory implies that as societies develop economically their cultures tend to shift in a predictable direction. Our data supports this prediction. Economic differences are linked with large and pervasive cultural differences. But we find clear evidence of the influence of long-established cultural zones.

Do these cultural clusters simply reflect economic differences? For example, do the societies of Protestant Europe have similar values simply because they are rich? No. The impact of a society's historical-cultural heritage persists when we control for GDP per capita and the structure of the labor force. On a value such as *interpersonal trust* (a variable on the surival / self-expression dimension), even rich Catholic societies rank lower than rich Protestant ones.

Within a given society, however, Catholics rank about as high on *interpersonal trust* as do Protestants. The shared historical experience of given nations, not individual personality, is crucial. Once established, the cross-cultural differences linked with religion have become part of a national culture that is transmitted by the educational institutions and mass media of given societies to the people of that nation. Despite globalization, the nation remains a key unit of shared experience, and its educational and cultural institutions shape the values of almost everyone in that society.

The Persistence of Religious and Spiritual Beliefs

As a society shifts from an agrarian to an industrial economy and survival comes to be taken for granted, traditional religious beliefs tend to decline. Nevertheless, as the twenty-first century opens, cleavages along religious lines remain strong. Why has religion been so slow to disappear?

History has taken an ironic turn: Communist-style industrialization was especially favorable to secularization, but the collapse of Communism has given rise to pervasive insecurity—

and a return to religious beliefs. Five of the seven ex-Communist societies for which we have time-series data show rising church attendance.

Throughout advanced industrial societies we see two contrasting trends: the decline of attendance at religious services on the one hand, and on the other the persistence of religious beliefs and the rise of spirituality. The need for answers to spiritual questions such as why we are here and where we are going does not die out in postindustrial society. Spiritual concerns will probably always be part of the human outlook. In fact, in the three successive waves of the World Values Survey, concern for the meaning and purpose of life became *stronger* in most advanced industrial societies.

Conclusion: Whither Modernization?

Economic development is associated with pervasive, and to an extent predictable, cultural changes. Industrialization promotes a shift from traditional to secular-rational values; postindustrialization promotes a shift toward more trust, tolerance, and emphasis on well-being. Economic collapse propels societies in the opposite direction.

Economic development tends to push societies in a common direction, but rather than converging they seem to move along paths shaped by their cultural heritages. Therefore, we doubt that the forces of modernization will produce a homogenized world culture in the foreseeable future.

Certainly it is misleading to view cultural change as "Americanization." Industrializing societies in general are not becoming like the United States. In fact, the United States seems to be a deviant case: Its people hold much more traditional values and beliefs than do those in any other equally prosperous society. If any societies exemplify the cutting edge of cultural change, it would be the Nordic countries.

Finally, modernization is probabilistic, not deterministic. Economic development tends to transform a given society in a predictable direction, but the process and path are not inevitable. Many factors are involved, so any prediction must be con-

---

Modernization and McDonald's

McDonald's restaurants have become a dominant symbol of the globalization of the economy and target of the wrath of globalization's many opponents. But local values still wield great influence on culture, so don't look for McWorld to emerge anytime soon, say social researchers Ronald Inglehart and Wayne E. Baker.

---

tingent on the historical and cultural context of the society in question.

Nevertheless, the central prediction of modernization theory finds broad support: Economic development is associated with major changes in prevailing values and beliefs. The world views of rich societies differ markedly from those of poor societies. This does not necessarily imply cultural convergence, but it does predict the general direction of cultural change and (insofar as the process is based on intergenerational population replacement) even gives some idea of the rate at which such change is likely to occur.

In short, economic development will cause shifts in the values of people in developing nations, but it will not produce a uniform global culture. The future may *look* like McWorld, but it won't feel like one.

About the Authors

Ronald Inglehart is professor of political science and program director at the Institute for Social Research, University of Michigan, Ann Arbor, Michigan 48106. E-mail RFI@umich.edu. The World Values Survey Web site is http://wvs.isr.umich.edu/.

Wayne E. Baker is professor of organizational behavior and director of the Center for Society and Economy, University of Michigan Business School, and faculty associate at the Institute for Social Research. He may be reached by e-mail at wayneb@umich.edu; his Web site is www.bus.umich.edu/cse.

This article draws on their paper "Modernization, Cultural Change, and the Persistence of Traditional Values" in the American Sociological Review (February 2000).

The Mountain People

Colin M. Turnbull

In what follows, there will be much to shock, and the reader will be tempted to say, "how primitive, how savage, how disgusting," and, above all, "how inhuman." The first judgments are typical of the kind of ethno- and egocentricism from which we can never quite escape. But "how inhuman" is of a different order and supposes that there are certain values inherent in humanity itself, from which the people described here seem to depart in a most drastic manner. In living the experience, however, and perhaps in reading it, one finds that it is oneself one is looking at and questioning; it is a voyage in quest of the basic human and a discovery of his potential for inhumanity, a potential that lies within us all.

Just before World War II the Ik tribe had been encouraged to settle in northern Uganda, in the mountainous northeast corner bordering on Kenya to the east and Sudan to the north. Until then they had roamed in nomadic bands, as hunters and gatherers, through a vast region in all three countries. The Kidepo Valley below Mount Morungole was their major hunting territory. After they were confined to a part of their former area, Kidepo was made a national park and they were forbidden to hunt or gather there.

The concept of family in a nomadic society is a broad one; what really counts most in everyday life is community of residence, and those who live close to each other are likely to see each other as effectively related, whether there is any kinship bond or not. Full brothers, on the other hand, who live in different parts of the camp may have little concern for each other.

It is not possible, then, to think of the family as a simple, basic unit. A child is brought up to regard any adult living in the same camp as a parent, and age-mate as a brother or sister. The Ik had this essentially social attitude toward kinship, and it readily lent itself to the rapid and disastrous changes that took place following the restriction of their movement and hunting activities. The family simply ceased to exist.

It is a mistake to think of small-scale societies as "primitive" or "simple." Hunters and gatherers, most of all, appear simple and straightforward in terms of their social organization, yet that is far from true. If we can learn about the nature of society from a study of small-scale societies, we can also learn about human relationships. The smaller the society, the less emphasis there is on the formal system and the more there is on interpersonal and intergroup relations. Security is seen in terms of these rela-

tionships, and so is survival. The result, which appears so deceptively simple, is that hunters frequently display those characteristics that we find so admirable in man: kindness, generosity, consideration, affection, honesty, hospitality, compassion, charity. For them, in their tiny, close-knit society, these are necessities for survival. In our society anyone possessing even half these qualities would find it hard to survive, yet we think these virtues are inherent in man. I took it for granted that the Ik would possess these same qualities. But they were as unfriendly, uncharitable, inhospitable and generally mean as any people can be. For those positive qualities we value so highly are no longer functional for them; even more than in our own society they spell ruin and disaster. It seems that, far from being basic human qualities, they are luxuries we can afford in times of plenty or are mere mechanisms for survival and security. Given the situation in which the Ik found themselves, man has no time for such luxuries, and a much more basic man appears, using more basic survival tactics.

Turnbull had to wait in Kaabong, a remote administration outpost, for permission from the Uganda government to continue to Pirre, the Ik water hole and police post. While there he began to learn the Ik language and became used to their constant demands for food and tobacco. An official in Kaabong gave him, as a "gift," 20 Ik workers to build a house and a road up to it. When they arrived at Pirre, however, wages for the workers were negotiated by wily Atum, "the senior of all the Ik on Morungole."

The police seemed as glad to see me as I was to see them. They hungrily

asked for news of Kaabong, as though it were the hub of the universe. They had a borehole and pump for water, to which they said I was welcome, since the water holes used by the Ik were not fit for drinking or even for washing. The police were not able to tell me much about the Ik, because every time they went to visit an Ik village, there was nobody there. Only in times of real hunger did they see much of the Ik, and then only enough to know that they were hungry.

The next morning I rose early, but even though it was barely daylight, by the time I had washed and dressed, the Ik were already outside. They were sitting silently, staring at the Land Rover. As impassive as they seemed, there was an air of expectancy, and I was reminded that these were, after all, hunters, and the likelihood was that I was their morning's prey. So I left the Land Rover curtains closed and as silently as possible prepared a frugal breakfast.

Atum was waiting for me. He said that he had told all the Ik that Iciebam [friend of the Ik] had arrived to live with them and that I had given the workers a "holiday" so they could greet me. They were waiting in the villages. They were very hungry, he added, and many were dying. That was probably one of the few true statements he ever made, and I never even considered believing it.

There were seven villages in all. Village Number One was built on a steep slope, and even the houses tilted at a crazy angle. Atum rapped on the outer stockade with his cane and shouted a greeting, but there was no response. This was Giriko's village, he said, and he was one of my workers.

"But I thought you told them to go back to their villages," I said.

"Yes, but you gave them a holiday, so they are probably in their fields," answered Atum, looking me straight in the eye.

At Village Number Two there was indisputably someone inside, for I could hear loud singing. The singing stopped, a pair of hands gripped the stockade and a craggy head rose into view, giving me an undeniably welcoming smile. This was Lokelea. When I asked him what he had been singing about, he answered, "Because I'm hungry."

Village Number Three, the smallest of all, was empty. Village Number Four had only 8 huts, as against the 12 or so in Lokelea's village and the 18 in Giriko's. The outer stockade was broken in one section, and we walked right in. We ducked through a low opening and entered a compound in which a woman was making pottery. She kept on at her work but gave us a cheery welcome and laughed her head off when I tried to speak in Icietot. She willingly showed me details of her work and did not seem unduly surprised at my interest. She said that everyone else had left for the fields except old Nangoli, who, on hearing her name mentioned, appeared at a hole in the stockade shutting off the next compound. Nangoli mumbled toothlessly at Losike, who told Atum to pour her some water.

As we climbed up to his own village, Number Five, Atum said that Losike never gave anything away. Later I remembered that gift of water to Nangoli. At the time I did not stop to think that in

this country a gift of water could be a gift of life.

Atum's village had nearly 50 houses, each within its compound within the stout outer stockade. Atum did not invite me in.

A hundred yards away stood Village Number Six. Kauar, one of the workers, was sitting on a rocky slab just outside the village. He had a smile like Losike's, open and warm, and he said he had been waiting for me all morning. He offered us water and showed me his own small compound and that of his mother.

Coming up from Village Number Seven, at quite a respectable speed, was a blind man. This was Logwara, emaciated but alive and remarkably active. He had heard us and had come to greet me, he said, but he added the inevitable demand for tobacco in the same breath. We sat down in the open sunlight. For a brief moment I felt at peace.

After a short time Atum said we should start back and called over his shoulder to his village. A muffled sound came from within, and he said, "That's my wife, she is very sick—and hungry." I offered to go and see her, but he shook his head. Back at the Land Rover I gave Atum some food and some aspirin, not knowing what else to give him to help his wife.

I was awakened well before dawn by the lowing of cattle. I made an extra pot of tea and let Atum distribute it, and then we divided the workers into two teams. Kauar was to head the team building the house, and Lokelatom, Losike's husband, was to take charge of the road workers.

While the Ik were working, their heads kept turning as though they were expecting something to happen. Every now and again one would stand up and peer into the distance and then take off into the bush for an hour or so. On one such occasion, after the person had been gone two hours, the others started drifting off. By then I knew them better; I looked for a wisp of smoke and followed it to where the road team was cooking a goat. Smoke was a giveaway, though, so they economized on cooking and ate most food nearly raw. It is a curious hangover from what must once have been a moral code that Ik will offer food if surprised in the act of eating, though they now go to enormous pains not to be so surprised.

I was always up before dawn, but by the time I got up to the villages they were always deserted. One morning I followed the little *oror* [gulley] up from *oror a pirre'i* [Ravine of Pirre] while it was still quite dark, and I met Lomeja on his way down. He took me on my first illicit hunt in Kidepo. He told me that if he got anything he would share it with me and with anyone else who managed to join us but that he certainly would not take anything back to his family. "Each one of them is out seeing what he can get

for himself, and do you think they will bring any back for me?"

Lomeja was one of the very few Ik who seemed glad to volunteer information. Unlike many of the others, he did not get up and leave as I approached. Apart from him, I spent most of my time, those days, with Losike, the potter. She told me that Nangoli, the old lady in the adjoining compound, and her husband, Amuarkuar, were rather peculiar. They helped each other get food and water, and they brought it back to their compound to eat together.

I still do not know how much real hunger there was at that time, for most of the younger people seemed fairly well fed, and the few skinny old people seemed healthy and active. But my laboriously extracted genealogies showed that there were quite a number of old people still alive and allegedly in these villages, though they were never to be seen. Then Atum's wife died.

Atum told me nothing about it but kept up his demands for food and medicine. After a while the beady-eyed Lomongin told me that Atum was selling the medicine I was giving him for his wife. I was not unduly surprised and merely remarked that that was too bad for his wife. "Oh no," said Lomongin, "she has been dead for weeks."

It must have been then that I began to notice other things that I suppose I had chosen to ignore before. Only a very few of the Ik helped me with the language. Others would understand when it suited them and would pretend they did not understand when they did not want to listen. I began to be forced into a similar isolationist attitude myself, and although I cannot say I enjoyed it, it did make life much easier. I even began to enjoy, in a peculiar way, the company of the silent Ik. And the more I accepted it, the less often people got up and left as I approached. On one occasion I sat on the *di* [sitting place] by Atum's rain tree for three days with a group of Ik, and for three days not one word was exchanged.

The work teams were more lively, but only while working. Kauar always played and joked with the children when they came back from foraging. He used to volunteer to make the two-day walk into Kaabong and the even more tiring

two-day climb back to get mail for me or to buy a few things for others. He always asked if he had made the trip more quickly than the last time.

Then one day Kauar went to Kaabong and did not come back. He was found on the last peak of the trail, cold and dead. Those who found him took the things he had been carrying and pushed his body into the bush. I still see his open, laughing face, see him giving precious tidbits to the children, comforting some child who was crying, and watching me read the letters he carried so lovingly for me. And I still think of him probably running up that viciously steep mountainside so he could break his time record and falling dead in his pathetic prime because he was starving.

Once I settled down into my new home, I was able to work more effectively. Having recovered at least some of my anthropological detachment, when I heard the telltale rustling of someone at my stockade, I merely threw a stone. If when out walking I stumbled during a difficult descent and the Ik shrieked with laughter, I no longer even noticed it.

Anyone falling down was good for a laugh, but I never saw anyone actually trip anyone else. The adults were content to let things happen and then enjoy them; it was probably conservation of energy. The children, however, sought their pleasures with vigor. The best game of all, at this time, was teasing poor little Adupa. She was not so little—in fact she should have been an adult, for she was nearly 13 years old—but Adupa was a little mad. Or you might say she was the only sane one, depending on your point of view. Adupa did not jump on other people's play houses, and she lavished enormous care on hers and would curl up inside it. That made it all the more jump-on-able. The other children beat her viciously.

Children are not allowed to sleep in the house after they are "put out," which is at about three years old, four at the latest. From then on they sleep in the open courtyard, taking what shelter they can against the stockade. They may ask for permission to sit in the doorway of their parents' house but may not lie down or sleep there. "The same thing applies to old people," said Atum, "if they can't build a house of their own and, of course, *if* their children let them stay in their compounds."

I saw a few old people, most of whom had taken over abandoned huts. For the first time I realized that there really was starvation and saw why I had never known it before: it was confined to the aged. Down in Giriko's village the old ritual priest, Lolim, confidentially told me that he was sheltering an old man who had been refused shelter by his son. But Lolim did not have enough food for himself, let alone his guest; could I... I liked old Lolim, so, not believing that Lolim had a visitor at all, I brought him a double ration that evening. There was rustling in the back of the hut, and Lolim helped ancient Lomeraniang to the entrance. They shook with delight at the sight of the food.

When the two old men had finished eating, I left; I found a hungry-looking and disapproving little crowd clustered outside. They muttered to each other about wasting food. From then on I brought food daily, but in a very short time Lomeraniang was dead, and his son refused to come down from the village above to bury him. Lolim scratched a hole and covered the body with a pile of stones he carried himself, one by one.

Hunger was indeed more severe than I knew, and, after the old people, the children were the next to go. It was all quite impersonal—even to me, in most cases, since I had been immunized by the Ik themselves against sorrow on their behalf. But Adupa was an exception. Her madness was such that she did not know just how vicious humans could be. Even worse, she thought that parents were for loving, for giving as well as receiving. Her parents were not given to fantasies. When she came for shelter, they drove her out; and when she came because she was hungry, they laughed that Icien laugh, as if she had made them happy.

Adupa's reactions became slower and slower. When she managed to find food—fruit peels, skins, bits of bone, half-eaten berries—she held it in her hand and looked at it with wonder and delight. Her playmates caught on quickly; they put tidbits in her way and watched her simple drawn little face wrinkle in a smile. Then as she raised her

hand to her mouth, they set on her with cries of excitement, fun and laughter, beating her savagely over the head. But that is not how she died. I took to feeding her, which is probably the cruelest thing I could have done, a gross selfishness on my part to try to salve my own rapidly disappearing conscience. I had to protect her, physically, as I fed her. But the others would beat her anyway, and Adupa cried, not because of the pain in her body but because of the pain she felt at the great, vast, empty wasteland where love should have been.

It was *that* that killed her. She demanded that her parents love her. Finally they took her in, and Adupa was happy and stopped crying. She stopped crying forever because her parents went away and closed the door tight behind them, so tight that weak little Adupa could never have moved it.

The Ik seem to tell us that the family is not such a fundamental unit as we usually suppose, that it is not essential to social life. In the crisis of survival facing the Ik, the family was one of the first institutions to go, and the Ik as a society have survived.

The other quality of life that we hold to be necessary for survival—love—the Ik dismiss as idiotic and highly dangerous. But we need to see more of the Ik before their absolute lovelessness becomes truly apparent.

In this curious society there is one common value to which all Ik hold tenaciously. It is *ngag*, "food." That is the one standard by which they measure right and wrong, goodness and badness. The very word for "good" is defined in terms of food. "Goodness" is "the possession of food," or the "*individual* possession of food." If you try to discover their concept of a "good man," you get the truly Icien answer: one who has a full stomach.

We should not be surprised, then, when the mother throws her child out at three years old. At that age a series of *rites de passage* begins. In this environment a child has no chance of survival on his own until he is about 13, so children from age bands. The junior band consists of children between three and seven, the senior of eight- to twelve-year-olds. Within the band each child seeks another close to him in age for defense against the older children. There friendships are temporary, however, and inevitably there comes a time when each turns on the one that up to then had been the closest to him; that is the *rite de passage*, the destruction of that fragile bond called friendship. When this has happened three or four times, the child is ready for the world.

The weakest are soon thinned out, and the strongest survive to achieve leadership of the band. Such a leader is eventually driven out, turned against by his fellow band members. Then the process starts all over again; he joins the senior age band as its most junior member.

The final *rite de passage* is into adulthood, at the age of 12 or 13. By then the candidate has learned the wisdom of acting on his own, for his own good, while acknowledging that on occasion it is profitable to associate temporarily with others.

One year in four the Ik can count on a complete drought. About this time it began to be apparent that there were going to be two consecutive years of drought and famine. Men as well as women took to gathering what wild fruits and berries they could find, digging up roots, cutting grass that was going to seed, threshing and eating the seed.

Old Nangoli went to the other side of Kidepo, where food and water were more plentiful. But she had to leave her husband, Amuarkuar, behind. One day he appeared at my *odok* and asked for water. I gave him some and was going to get him food when Atum came storming over and argued with me about wasting water. In the midst of the dispute Amuarkuar quietly left. He wandered over to a rocky outcrop and lay down there to rest. Nearby was a small bundle of grass that evidently he had cut and had been dragging painfully to the ruins of his village to make a rough shelter. The grass was his supreme effort to keep a home going until Nangoli returned. When I went over to him, he looked up and smiled and said that my water tasted good. He lay back and went to sleep with a smile on his face. That is how Amuarkuar died, happily.

There are measures that can be taken for survival involving the classical institutions of gift and sacrifice. These are weapons, sharp and aggressive. The object is to build up a series of obligations so that in times of crisis you have a number of debts you can recall; with luck one of them may be repaid. To this end, in the circumstances of Ik life, considerable sacrifice would be justified, so you have the odd phenomenon of these otherwise singularly self-interested people going out of their way to "help" each other. Their help may very well be resented in the extreme, but is done in such a way that it cannot be refused, for it has already been given. Someone may hoe another's field in his absence or rebuild his stockade or join in the building of a house.

The danger in this system was that the debtor might not be around when collection was called for and, by the same token, neither might the creditor. The future was too uncertain for this to be anything but one additional survival measure, though some developed it to a fine technique.

There seemed to be increasingly little among the Ik that could by any stretch of the imagination be called social life, let alone social organization. The family does not hold itself together; economic interest is centered on as many stomachs as there are people; and cooperation is merely a device for furthering an interest that is consciously selfish. We often do the same thing in our so-called "altruistic" practices, but we tell ourselves it is for the good of others. The Ik have dispensed with the myth of altruism. Though they have no centralized leadership or means of physical coercion, they do hold together with remarkable tenacity.

In our world, where the family has also lost much of its value as a social unit and where religious belief no longer binds us into communities, we maintain order only through coercive power that is ready to uphold a rigid law and through an equally rigid penal system. The Ik, however, have learned to do without coercion, either spiritual or physical. It seems that they have come to a recognition of what they accept as man's basic selfishness, of his natural determination to survive as an individual before all else. This they consider to be man's basic right, and they allow others to pursue that right without recrimination.

In large-scale societies such as our own, where members are individual beings rather than social beings, we rely on law for order. The absence of both a common law and a common belief would surely result in lack of any community of behavior; yet Ik society is not anarchical. One might well expect religion, then, to play a powerful role in Icien life, providing a source of unity.

The Ik, as may be expected, do not run true to form. When I arrived, there were still three ritual priests alive. From them and from the few other old people, I learned something of the Ik's belief and practice as they had been before their world was so terribly changed. There had been a powerful unity of belief in Didigwari—a sky god—and a body of ritual practice reinforcing secular behavior that was truly social.

Didigwari himself is too remote to be of much practical significance to the Ik. He created them and abandoned them and retreated into his domain somewhere in the sky. He never came down to earth, but the *abang* [ancestors] have all known life on earth; it is only against them that one can sin and only to them that one can turn for help, through the ritual priest.

While Morungole has no legends attached to it by the Ik, it nonetheless figures in their ideology and is in some ways regarded by them as sacred. I had noticed this by the almost reverential way in which they looked at it—none of the shrewd cunning and cold appraisal with which they regarded the rest of the world. When they talked about it, there was a different quality to their voices. They seemed incapable of talking about Morungole in any other way, which is probably why they talked about it so very seldom. Even that weasel Lomongin became gentle the only time he talked about it to me. He said, "If Atum and I were there, we would not argue. It is a good place." I asked if he meant that it was full of food. He said yes. "Then why do Ik never go there?" "They do go there." "But if hunting is good there, why not live there?" "We don't hunt there, we just go there." "Why?" "I told you, it is a good place." If I did not understand him, that was my fault; for once he was doing his best to communicate something to me. With others it was the same. All agreed that it was "a good place." One added, "That is the Place of God."

Lolim, the oldest and greatest of the ritual priests, was also the last. He was not much in demand any longer, but he was still held in awe, which means kept at a distance. Whenever he approached a *di*, people cleared a space for him, as far away from themselves as possible. The Ik rarely called on his services, for they had little to pay him with, and he had equally little to offer them. The main things they did try to get out of him were certain forms of medicine, both herbal and magical.

Lolim said that he had inherited his power from his father. His father had taught him well but could not give him the power to hear the *abang*—that had to come from the *abang* themselves. He had wanted his oldest son to inherit and had taught him everything he could. But his son, Longoli, was bad, and the *abang* refused to talk to him. They talked instead to his oldest daughter, bald Nangoli. But there soon came the time when all the Ik needed was food in their stomachs, and Lolim could not supply that. The time came when Lolim was too weak to go out and collect the medicines he needed. His children all refused to go except Nangoli, and then she was jailed for gathering in Kidepo Park.

Lolim became ill and had to be protected while eating the food I gave him. Then the children began openly ridiculing him and teasing him, dancing in front of him and kneeling down so that he would trip over them. His grandson used to creep up behind him and with a pair of hard sticks drum a lively tattoo on the old man's bald head.

I fed him whenever I could, but often he did not want more than a bite. Once I found him rolled up in his protective ball, crying. He had had nothing to eat for four days and no water for two. He had asked his children, who all told him not to come near them.

The next day I saw him leaving Atum's village, where his son Longoli lived. Longoli swore that he had been giving his father food and was looking after him. Lolim was not shuffling away; it was almost a run, the run of a drunken man, staggering from side to side. I called to him, but he made no reply, just a kind of long, continuous and horrible moan. He had been to Longoli to beg him to let him into his compound because he knew he was going to die in a few hours, Longoli calmly told me afterward. Obviously Longoli could not do a thing like that: a man of Lolim's importance would have called for an enormous funeral feast. So he refused. Lolim begged Longoli then to open up Nangoli's *asak* for him so that he could die in *her* compound. But Longoli drove him out, and he died alone.

Atum pulled some stones over the body where it had fallen into a kind of hollow. I saw that the body must have lain parallel with the *oror*. Atum answered without waiting for the question: "He was lying looking up at Mount Meraniang."

Insofar as ritual survived at all, it could hardly be said to be religious, for it did little or nothing to bind Icien society together. But the question still remained: Did this lack of social behavior and communal ritual or religious expression mean that there was no community of belief?

Belief may manifest itself, at either the individual or the communal level, in what we call morality, when we behave according to certain principles supported by our belief even when it seems against our personal interest. When we call ourselves moral, however, we tend to ignore that ultimately our morality benefits us even as individuals, insofar as we are social individuals and live in a society. In the absence of belief, law takes over and morality has little role. If there was such a thing as an Icien morality, I had not yet perceived it, though traces of a moral past remained. But it still remained a possibility, as did the existence of an unspoken, unmanifest belief that might yet reveal itself and provide a basis for the reintegration of society. I was somewhat encouraged in this hope by the unexpected flight of old Nangoli, widow of Amuarkuar.

When Nangoli returned and found her husband dead, she did an odd thing: she grieved. She tore down what was left of their home, uprooted the stockade, tore up whatever was growing in her little field. Then she fled with a few belongings.

Some weeks later I heard that she and her children had gone over to the Sudan and built a village there. This migration was so unusual that I decided to see whether this runaway village was different.

Lojieri led the way, and Atum came along. One long day's trek got us there. Lojieri pulled part of the brush fence aside, and we went in and wandered around. He and Atum looked inside all the huts, and Lojieri helped himself to tobacco from one and water from another. Surprises were coming thick and fast. That households should be left open and untended with such wealth inside… That there should have been such wealth, for as well as tobacco and jars of water there were baskets of food, and meat was drying on racks. There were half a dozen or so compounds, but they were separated from each other only by a short line of sticks and brush. It was a village, and these were homes, the first and last I was to see.

The dusk had already fallen, and Nangoli came in with her children and grandchildren. They had heard us and came in with warm welcomes. There was no hunger here, and in a very short time each kitchen hearth had a pot of food cooking. Then we sat around the central fire and talked until late, and it was another universe.

There was no talk of "how much better it is here than there"; talk revolved around what had happened on the hunt that day. Loron was lying on the ground in front of the fire as his mother made gentle fun of him. His wife, Kinimei, whom I had never seen even speak to him at Pirre, put a bowl of fresh-cooked berries and fruit in front of him. It was all like a nightmare rather than a fantasy, for it made the reality of Pirre seem all the more frightening.

The unpleasantness of returning was somewhat alleviated by Atum's suffering on the way up the stony trail. Several times he slipped, which made Lojieri and me laugh. It was a pleasure to move rapidly ahead and leave Atum gasping behind so that we could be sitting up on the *di* when he finally appeared and could laugh at his discomfort.

The days of drought wore on into weeks and months and, like everyone else, I became rather bored with sickness and death. I survived rather as did the young adults, by diligent attention to my own needs while ignoring those of others.

More and more it was only the young who could go far from the village as hunger became starvation. Famine relief had been initiated down at Kasile, and those fit enough to make the trip set off. When they came back, the contrast between them and the others was that between life and death. Villages were villages of the dead and dying, and there was little difference between the two. People crawled rather than walked. After a few feet some would lie down to rest, but they could not be sure of ever being able to sit up again, so they mostly stayed upright until they reached their destination. They were going nowhere, these semianimate bags of skin and bone; they just wanted to be with others, and they stopped whenever they met. Perhaps it was the most important demonstration of sociality I ever saw among the Ik. Once they met, they neither spoke nor did anything together.

Early one morning, before dawn, the village moved. In the midst of a hive of activity were the aged and crippled, soon to be abandoned, in danger of being trampled but seemingly unaware of it. Lolim's widow, Lo'ono, whom I had never seen before, also had been abandoned and had tried to make her way down the mountainside. But she was totally blind and had tripped and rolled to the bottom of the *oror a pirre'i;* there she lay on her back, her legs and arms thrashing feebly, while a little crowd laughed.

At this time a colleague was with me. He kept the others away while I ran to get medicine and food and water, for Lo'ono was obviously near dead from hunger and thirst as well as from the fall. We treated her and fed her and asked her to come back with us. But she asked us to point her in the direction of her son's new village. I said I did not think she would get much of a welcome there, and she replied that she knew it but wanted to be near him when she died. So we gave her more food, put her stick in her hand and pointed her the right way. She suddenly cried. She was crying, she said, because we had reminded her that there had been a time when people had helped each other, when people had been kind and good. Still crying, she set off.

The Ik up to this point had been tolerant of my activities, but all this was too much. They said that what we were doing was wrong. Food and medicine were for the living, not the dead. I thought of Lo'ono. And I thought of other old people who had joined in the merriment when they had been teased or had a precious morsel of food taken from their mouths. They knew that it was silly of them to expect to go on living, and, having watched others, they knew that the spectacle really was quite funny. So they joined in the laughter. Perhaps if we had left Lo'ono, she would have died laughing. But we prolonged her misery for no more than a few brief days. Even worse, we reminded her of when things had been different, of days when children had cared for parents and parents for children. She was already dead, and we made her unhappy as well. At the time I was sure we were right, doing the only "human" thing. In a way we *were*—we were making life more comfortable for ourselves. But now I wonder if the Ik way was not right, if I too should not have laughed as Lo'ono flapped about, then left her to die.

Ngorok was a man at 12. Lomer, his older brother, at 15 was showing signs of strain; when he was carrying a load, his face took on a curious expression of pain

that was not physical pain. Giriko, at 25 was 40, Atum at 40 was 65, and the very oldest, perhaps a bare 50, were centenarians. And I, at 40, was younger than any of them, for I still enjoyed life, which they had learned was not "adult" when they were 3. But they retained their will to survive and so offered grudging respect to those who had survived for long.

Even in the teasing of the old there was a glimmer of hope. It denoted a certain intimacy that did not exist between adjacent generations. This is quite common in small-scale societies. The very old and the very young look at each other as representing the future and the past. To the child, the aged represent a world that existed before their own birth and the unknown world to come.

And now that all the old are dead, what is left? Every Ik who is old today was thrown out at three and has survived, and in consequence has thrown his own children out and knows that they will not help him in his old age any more than he helped his parents. The system has turned one full cycle and is now self-perpetuating; it has eradicated what we know as "humanity" and has turned the world into a chilly void where man does not seem to care even for himself, but survives. Yet into this hideous world Nangoli and her family quietly returned because they could not bear to be alone.

For the moment abandoning the very old and the very young, the Ik as a whole must be searched for one last lingering trace of humanity. They appear to have disposed of virtually all the qualities that we normally think of as differentiating us from other primates, yet they survive without seeming to be greatly different from ourselves in terms of behavior. Their behavior is more extreme, for we do not start throwing our children out until kindergarten. We have shifted responsibility from family to state, the Ik have shifted it to the individual.

It has been claimed that human beings are capable of love and, indeed, are dependent upon it for survival and sanity. The Ik offer us an opportunity for testing this cherished notion that love is essential to survival. If it is, the Ik should have it.

Love in human relationships implies mutuality, a willingness to sacrifice the

self that springs from a consciousness of identity. This seems to bring us back to the Ik, for it implies that love is self-oriented, that even the supreme sacrifice of one's life is no more than selfishness, for the victim feels amply rewarded by the pleasure he feels in making the sacrifice. The Ik, however, do not value emotion above survival, and they are without love.

But I kept looking, for it was the one thing that could fill the void their survival tactics had created; and if love was not there in some form, it meant that for humanity love is not a necessity at all, but a luxury or an illusion. And if it was not among the Ik, it meant that mankind can lose it.

The only possibility for any discovery of love lay in the realm of interpersonal relationships. But they were, each one, simply alone, and seemingly content to be alone. It was this acceptance of individual isolation that made love almost impossible. Contact, when made, was usually for a specific practical purpose having to do with food and the filling of a stomach, a single stomach. Such contacts did not have anything like the permanence or duration required to develop a situation in which love was possible.

The isolation that made love impossible, however, was not completely proof against loneliness, I no longer noticed normal behavior, such as the way people ate, running as they gobbled, so as to have it all for themselves. But I did notice that when someone was making twine or straightening a spear shaft, the focus of attention for the spectators was not the person but the action. If they were caught watching by the one being watched and their eyes met, the reaction was a sharp retreat on both sides.

When the rains failed for the second year running, I knew that the Ik as a society were almost certainly finished and that the monster they had created in its place, that passionless, feelingless association of individuals, would spread like a fungus, contaminating all it touched. When I left, I too had been contaminated. I was not upset when I said good-bye to old Loiangorok. I told him I had left a sack of *posho* [ground corn meal] with the police for him, and I said I would send money for more when that ran out.

He dragged himself slowly toward the *di* every day, and he always clutched a knife. When he got there, or as far as he could, he squatted down and whittled at some wood, thus proving that he was still alive and able to do things. The *posho* was enough to last him for months, but I felt no emotion when I estimated that he would last one month, even with the *posho* in the hands of the police. I underestimated his son, who within two days had persuaded the police that it would save a lot of bother if he looked after the *posho*. I heard later that Loiangorok died of starvation within two weeks.

So, I departed with a kind of forced gaiety, feeling that I should be glad to be gone but having forgotten how to be glad. I certainly was not thinking of returning within a year, but I did. The following spring I heard that rain had come at last and that the fields of the Ik had never looked so prosperous, nor the country so green and fertile. A few months away had refreshed me, and I wondered if my conclusions had not been excessively pessimistic. So, early that summer, I set off to be present for the first harvests in three years.

I was not surprised too much when two days after my arrival and installation at the police post I found Logwara, the blind man, lying on the roadside bleeding, while a hundred yards up other Ik were squabbling over the body of a hyena. Logwara had tried to get there ahead of the others to grab the meat and had been trampled on.

First I looked at the villages. The lush outer covering concealed an inner decay. All the villages were like this to some extent, except for Lokelea's. There the tomatoes and pumpkins were carefully pruned and cleaned, so that the fruits were larger and healthier. In what had been my own compound the shade trees had been cut down for firewood, and the lovely hanging nests of the weaver birds were gone.

The fields were even more desolate. Every field without exception had yielded in abundance, and it was a new sensation to have vision cut off by thick crops. But every crop was rotting from sheer neglect.

The Ik said that they had no need to bother guarding the fields. There was so much food they could never eat it all, so why not let the birds and baboons take some? The Ik had full bellies; they were good. The *di* at Atum's village was much the same as usual, people sitting or lying about. People were still stealing from each other's fields, and nobody thought of saving for the future.

It was obvious that nothing had really changed due to the sudden glut of food except that interpersonal relationships had deteriorated still further and that Icien individualism had heightened beyond what I thought even Ik to be capable of.

The Ik had faced a conscious choice between being humans and being parasites and had chosen the latter. When they saw their fields come alive, they were confronted with a problem. If they reaped the harvest, they would have to store grain for eating and planting, and every Ik knew that trying to store anything was a waste of time. Further, if they made their fields look too promising, the government would stop famine relief. So the Ik let their fields rot and continued to draw famine relief.

The Ik were not starving any longer; the old and infirm had all died the previous year, and the younger survivors were doing quite well. But the famine relief was administered in a way that was little short of criminal. As before, only the young and well were able to get down from Pirre to collect the relief; they were given relief for those who could not come and told to take it back. But they never did—they ate it themselves.

The facts are there, though those that can be read here form but a fraction of what one person was able to gather in under two years. There can be no mistaking the direction in which those facts point, and that is the most important thing of all, for it may affect the rest of mankind as it has affected the Ik. The Ik have "progressed," one might say, since the change that has come to them came with the advent of civilization to Africa. They have made of a world that was alive a world that is dead—a cold, dispassionate world that is without ugliness because it is without beauty, without hate because it is without love, and without any realization of truth even, because it simply is. And the symptoms of change in our own society indicate that we are heading in the same direction.

Those values we cherish so highly may indeed be basic to human society but not to humanity, and that means that the Ik show that society itself is not indispensable for man's survival and that man is capable of associating for purposes of survival without being social. The Ik have replaced human society with a mere survival system that does not take human emotion into account. As yet the system i[s] imperfect, for although survival is assured, it is at a minimal level and there is still competition between individuals. With our intellectual sophistication and advanced technology we should be able to perfect the system and eliminate competition, guaranteeing survival for a given number of years for all, reducing the demands made upon us by a social system, abolishing desire and consequently that ever-present and vital gap between desire and achievement, treating us, in a word, as individuals with one basic individual right—the right to survive.

Such interaction as there is within this system is one of mutual exploitation. That is how it already is with the Ik. In our own world the mainstays of a society based on a truly social sense of mutuality are breaking down, indicating that perhaps society as we know it has outworn its usefulness and that by clinging to an outworn system we are bringing about our own destruction. Family, economy, government and religion, the basic categories of social activity and behavior, no longer create any sense of social unity involving a shared and mutual responsibility among all members of our society. At best they enable the individual to survive as an individual. It is the world of the individual, as is the world of the Ik.

The sorry state of society in the civilized world today is in large measure due to the fact that social change has not kept up with technological change. This mad, senseless, unthinking commitment to technological change that we call progress may be sufficient to exterminate the human race in a very short time even without the assistance of nuclear warfare. But since we have already become individualized and desocialized, we say that extermination will not come

15

in our time, which shows about as much sense of family devotion as one might expect from the Ik.

Even supposing that we can avert nuclear holocaust or the almost universal famine that may be expected if population keeps expanding and pollution remains unchecked, what will be the cost if not the same already paid by the Ik? They too were driven by the need to survive, and they succeeded at the cost of their humanity. We are already beginning to pay the same price, but we not only still have the choice (though we may not have the will or courage to make it), we also have the intellectual and technological ability to avert an Icien end. Any change as radical as will be necessary is not likely to bring material benefits to the present generation, but only then will there be a future.

The Ik teach us that our much vaunted human values are not inherent in humanity at all but are associated only with a particular form of survival called society and that all, even society itself, are luxuries that can be dispensed with. That does not make them any less wonderful, and if man has any greatness, it is surely in his ability to maintain these values, even shortening an already pitifully short life rather than sacrifice his humanity. But that too involves choice, and the Ik teach us that man can lose the will to make it. That is the point at which there is an end to truth, to goodness and to beauty, an end to the struggle for their achievement, which gives life to the individual and strength and meaning to society. The Ik have relinquished all luxury in the name of individual survival, and they live on as a people without life,

without passion, beyond humanity. We pursue those trivial, idiotic technological encumbrances, and all the time we are losing our potential for social rather than individual survival, for hating as well as loving, losing perhaps our last chance to enjoy life with all the passion that is our nature.

Anthropologist Colin M. Turnbull, author of The Forest People *and* The Lonely Africans, *went to study the Ik of Uganda, who he believed were still primarily hunters, in order to compare them with other hunting-and-gathering societies he had studied in totally different environments. He was surprised to discover that they were no longer hunters but primarily farmers, well on their way to starvation and something worse in a drought-stricken land.*

From *Intellectual Digest,* April 1973. © 1972 by Colin M. Turnbull. Reprinted by permission of Simon & Schuster.

America's moral non-decline.

MORE MORAL

By David Whitman

By the time the Lewinsky scandal erupted, three out of four Americans already believed that moral values had weakened in the past quarter-century. Now, thanks to Bill Clinton's Oval Office high jinks, the case that moral standards are eroding seems stronger than ever. In his new bestseller *The Death of Outrage*, William Bennett argues that the lack of public outcry over the president's adultery and prevarication is but one more sign that people's "commitment to long-standing American ideals has been enervated." Al Gore would disagree with Bennett's analysis of Clinton, but he, too, believes that "there is indeed a spiritual crisis in modern civilization."

Yet, for all the bipartisan hand-wringing about moral decline, there is surprisingly little evidence that Americans *act* more immorally today than they did a quarter-century ago. In fact, just the opposite seems to be true—as even a few conservatives are beginning to concede. In the current issue of the right-leaning magazine *The American Enterprise*, editor-in-chief Karl Zinsmeister urges fellow conservatives not "to accuse the American people of becoming morally rotten. Especially when there exist abundant data suggesting that the residents of our land are actually becoming *less* morally rotten." It is still true, of course, that millions of citizens continue to err and sin, and that the culture now has a surfeit of coarseness, from noxious rap lyrics to the "Jerry Springer Show." But, if one looks beyond the anecdotes, the picture of how people behave is unexpectedly encouraging.

Compared with their predecessors of a quarter-century ago, Americans today are less likely to drink to excess, take drugs, rely on the dole, drive drunk, or knowingly evade paying taxes. They give more money to charity and spend as much or more time in church. And they are more likely than their predecessors to do good Samaritan work among the poor, sick, and elderly. Despite fears of random violence, FBI reports suggest that

fewer people were murdered by strangers in 1997 (2,067) than in 1977 (about 2,500), even though the U.S. population grew by 47 million during that time. The dramatic drop in the number of Americans victimized by murder, burglary, and theft represents another well-known illustration of moral progress, but there are many more.

For example, Americans now donate significantly more money to charity than they did a generation ago, as Everett Carll Ladd, director of the Roper Center for Public Opinion Research, documents in a forthcoming book. Adjusted for inflation, Americans gave about $525 per adult to charity in 1996. That is 50 percent more than Americans on average donated in 1970 ($349) and roughly triple what people gave in 1950 ($179). Starting in 1977, pollsters also began regularly asking adults whether they were involved in charity or social services, such as helping the poor, the sick, or the elderly. The ranks of those participating roughly doubled from 26 percent in 1977 to 54 percent in 1995. Volunteer work by college students is up, too. In 1998, 74 percent of college freshmen had done volunteer work the preceding year, the highest such figure since researchers started tracking it in 1984.

Charity has often gone hand in hand with religion, so perhaps it is not surprising to learn that religious faith, too, is not in decline. On the contrary, America remains a deeply religious nation, with a reinvigorated evangelical movement. In 1997, the Gallup Poll replicated one of its earliest surveys on Americans' religious practices from 1947. The 50-year update found that the same percentage of Americans pray (90 percent), believe in God (96 percent), and attend church once a week. One of the few differences between the two eras was that Americans were actually more likely to give grace or give thanks aloud in 1997 than in 1947 (63 percent compared with 43 percent).

Both adults and teens are now as likely to belong to a church or synagogue as their counterparts were 25 years ago, and they attend religious services a bit more often. Two months ago, at the start of December, 42 percent of adults reported attending a service at a church or synagogue the previous week—a tad higher than the 40 percent or so who said they had attended services in 1972, 1950, and 1940. As the political scientist Seymour Martin Lipset writes in his book *American Exceptionalism*, "Religious affiliation and belief in America are much higher in the twentieth century than in the nineteenth, and have not decreased in the post–World War II era."

While everyone "knows" that cheating on tests has exploded in recent decades, the few studies that have looked at trends over time suggest a different picture. A 1996 analysis by Donald McCabe and Linda Klebe Trevino of Rutgers University at nine state universities did find that cheating on tests and exams increased significantly from 1963 to 1993. But serious cheating on written work, such as plagiarism and turning in work done by others, had declined slightly, leading the researchers to conclude that "the dramatic upsurge in cheating heralded by the media was not found."

Cheating on taxes also appears to be no worse than in the recent past. Since 1973, the Internal Revenue Service has tracked the "voluntary compliance rate," a figure used to describe the percentage of total tax liability that individuals and corporations pay voluntarily. In 1992, the voluntary compliance rate for the individual income tax was roughly 83 percent, a hair higher than in 1973.

As for another vice—drug use—Americans seem to be doing better, not worse. Use of illicit drugs peaked in 1979, when 14.1 percent of the population reported having used an illicit drug the previous month, more than double the 1997 figure of 6.4 percent. Cocaine use peaked in 1985; Americans were four times as likely to use cocaine then as they are today. The trends are similar among high school seniors (though marijuana use has risen since 1992).

At the same time, heavy alcohol consumption, binge drinking, and drunken driving have all declined. Heavy alcohol use—defined as having five or more drinks on the same occasion on each of five or more days in the previous months—at its lowest point since 1985, when the federal government first started tracking the figure. In 1985, 8.3 percent of the population were heavy drinkers compared with 5.4 percent in 1997, a drop of about a third. The decline in drunken driving has been equally marked. In 1997, the number of people killed in alcohol-related crashes dropped to less than 40 percent of all traffic fatalities for the first time since the government started tracking this statistic in 1975. Americans consumed about as much alcohol per person in 1995 as in 1945—and drank substantially less than in 1970.

For all the talk of scandal, and despite the official statistics, political corruption seems to be waning, too. In 1996, 952 individuals were indicted in federal prosecutions for public corruption, more than triple the number in 1975. Yet most historians believe the apparent rise in corruption stems from the proliferation of special prosecutors and inspector generals, not from a real upsurge in unethical conduct. New disclosure rules, government intercessions in allegedly corrupt unions, a law enforcement crackdown on the mob, the disappearance of Tammany Hall–style urban political machines and "good-time Charlie" governors, and a more watchful press all seem to have reduced bribes, hush money, and other blatant types of political corruption. Even William Bennett concedes in *The Death of Outrage* that "in general, politics today is less corrupt than perhaps at any point in American history."

Granted, not all the news on the moral front is good. One institution that undeniably weakened in the past quarter-century is the family. Since the early '70s, out-of-wedlock childbearing has skyrocketed. Child abuse and neglect have risen, too—thanks mainly to the advent of crack—and most noncustodial parents still don't pay their child support.

Yet other much-lamented changes in family life do not really demonstrate a rise (or fall) in collective virtue. The surge in divorce suggests that Americans now lack a sense of commitment, but most divorced couples do not think they are acting immorally—more often, they think they have done the right thing by ending a troubled marriage. Many couples similarly defend cohabitation, once deemed to be "living in sin," as a sensible trial run at marriage.

Some moral behavior that has improved in the past quarter-century, particularly the reduction in criminality and drug-taking, is still worse today than it was in the 1950s. But, even when stacked up against the "good ol' days," there are plenty of signs of moral progress. In the 1950s, well over half of the nation's black population lived under almost apartheid-like conditions through much of the South. Millions of women faced sexual discrimination and were denied the right to pursue a calling of their own. Society treated the elderly shabbily, with more than one in three living in poverty (compared with one in ten today). The disabled faced blatant, ugly bigotry, as did homosexuals.

Why hasn't the news about moral progress reached the public? In part, the reason is that it is often thought that people were more moral in earlier eras. Back in 1939, a Gallup Poll showed that 62 percent of the population believed that Americans were happier and more contented in the horse-and-buggy days; a survey taken by Elmo Roper two years earlier found that half of the population felt religion was then losing its influence on American life as well.

But part of the explanation for the public disbelief is that Americans experience an "optimism gap." When members of the public voice distress about family breakdown they are almost always referring to other people's families. Yet the vast majority of citizens do not have serious moral qualms about themselves or their families. Surveys show that most people think they are more moral than the average American, and members of the public repeatedly describe their own families as happy ones with strong ties.

In 1997, *U.S. News & World Report* conducted a revealing survey of 1,000 adults who were asked to rate the chances that various celebrities would one day get into heaven. Topping the list of famous people bound for heaven was Mother Teresa, who had not yet died. Nearly 80 percent of those polled thought it likely that the Nobel Peace Prize winner would one day get her wings. But the survey's most startling finding was that the individuals voted most likely to get into heaven were, well, those being polled. Eighty-seven percent felt that they were heaven-bound, compared with 79 percent who thought the same of Mother Teresa.

Most Americans, in short, hold a generous opinion of their own morals, even while they remain acutely aware of others' failings. But, if Americans can convince themselves that they are bound for heaven, it may also be time to acknowledge that the rest of the nation is not making a beeline for purgatory.

DAVID WHITMAN is a senior writer at *U.S. News & World Report* and the author of *The Optimism Gap: The I'm OK—They're Not Syndrome and the Myth of American Decline* (Walker and Company).

The Final Freedom

The 19th century was about economic freedom. The 20th century was about political freedom. This century will be about Americans deciding for themselves what's moral and what's not.

By Alan Wolfe

Should I lie or tell the truth? Is my marriage vow binding? Ought I give in when temptation calls? To whom are my obligations strongest? To answer such questions, Americans have traditionally relied on time-tested moral rules, usually handed down by a supreme being, that command obedience and punish defiance. Now we live in an age of moral freedom, in which individuals are expected to determine for themselves what it means to lead a good and virtuous life. We decide what is right and wrong, not by bending our wills to authority, but by considering who we are, what others require and what consequences follow from acting one way rather than another.

This country has always experienced freedom, but only recently has it discovered moral freedom. In the 19th century, principles of economic liberty were instrumental in creating a society in which the right to own property, to hire workers and to manufacture and dispose of goods was accepted as the most productive way for a society to create and distribute its wealth. This was followed, in the 20th century, by the spread of political freedom. By century's end, the idea that people had a right to vote and to run for office—and that such a right could not be denied them on the basis of ownership of property, race or gender—had become so widely accepted that no society could be considered good unless its political system was organized along democratic lines.

Although political freedoms are enormously important, they are restricted to one sphere of human activity: obtaining and exercising political power. The same is true of economic freedom, which, by definition, is limited to such essential, but also essentially mundane, matters like the buying and selling of commodities. Moral freedom involves the sacred as well as the profane; it is freedom over the things that matter most. The ultimate implication of the idea of moral freedom is not that people are created in the image of a higher authority. It is that any form of higher authority has to tailor its commandments to the needs of real people. It cannot be surprising that Americans made a best seller out of a book—actually three books—called "Conversations With God."

Even the most traditional Americans have been touched by the spread of moral freedom. Born-again Christians generally do not believe that people should be free to live as they choose, especially when they choose what evangelicals consider sinful: homosexuality, for example, or premarital sex. Yet evangelicals are also people who often reject the religion of their upbringing, opt for start-up churches and prefer to home-school their children, giving them more in common than they realize with gays and lesbians who have redefined marriage and family and founded houses of worship that serve their own spiritual needs. Conservative millionaires may vote Republican because they believe America lost its Christian standards under Bill Clinton, but they probably obtained their millions living by rules of corporate loyalty, equity and honesty that Christians generations ago would have called sinful.

MORAL FREEDOM IS SO RADICAL AN IDEA, SO DISturbing in its implications, that it has never had much currency among any but a few of the West's great moral theorists. Even those who made passionate arguments in defense of freedom in general did not extend their arguments to moral freedom. Indeed, the common position among most Western thinkers has been to argue the necessity for moral constraint as a precondition for freedom in all other aspects of life. This was most true of conservatives who justified the received authority of church, prince, law or nature. But it was also true of liberal thinkers like John Locke and Immanuel Kant, for whom liberty made sense only when shaped by pre-existing religious or ethical commandments. Timeless, transcendental, absolute—morality stood in the sharpest possible contrast to freedom, which was transient, inconsistent and dependent on mere circumstance. Even in America, despite the celebratory individualism of an Emerson or a Whitman, the idea of moral freedom made little sense until very recent times. When Franklin Roosevelt in 1941 announced the four freedoms—of speech, of worship, from want, from fear—moral freedom was not among them. When, in 1957, the United States Supreme Court finally got around to talking about sexual freedom—calling sex "a great and mysterious force in human life," which was "a subject of absorbing interest"—it did so in the context of upholding a conviction for violating obscenity laws.

In the 1960's and 1970's, for the first time in American history, a number of thinkers began to take the idea of moral freedom seriously, and enough people paid them attention to mount a significant challenge against moral authority. Reviewing the history of religion in America since the first Spanish and French settlements, the historian Sidney Ahlstrom concluded that "only in the 1960's would it become apparent that the Great Puritan Epoch in American history had come to an end." If nothing is so powerful as an idea whose time has come, the idea of moral freedom, when it finally came, was powerful enough, at least for a time, to sweep all before it.

Because moral freedom is so new an idea, it inevitably arouses opposition. There is a widespread feeling that the legacy of the 1960's has been corrosive to the American social fabric. Disrespectful of established authority, cut off from tradition, unattached to family or faith, Americans, we have been repeatedly told, embraced moral freedom only to experience painful results. To discover whether such charges resonate among Americans themselves, I assembled a research team and spent the last couple of years talking with people from all walks of life about what it means to lead a good and virtuous life. We concentrated on four virtues that have been praised by theologians and philosophers for their moral seriousness: honesty, loyalty, forgiveness and self-discipline. Are critics of our condition right to worry that we no longer believe in the old-fashioned virtues that once made us great? Or should we celebrate the arrival of moral freedom for the same reasons we have come to accept economic and political freedom: society is better off when people decide for themselves the right thing to do rather than have it decided for them by others?

We need not, and should not, take the thoughts of ordinary Americans as the final word on our condition. But, as the reaction to recent events ranging from the school shootings in Santee, Calif., to the presidential pardons demonstrate, there is moral talk aplenty in America; if talk about morality were only a measure of morality, we would be hearing about a moral surplus, not a moral deficit. The least

we can do, before we stand up to preach, is to listen to what Americans have to say.

"THERE'S NOTHING LIKE LOADING A FEW coffins," a retired Air Force officer told us of his service in Vietnam. "It turned my life around." Now working as a substitute teacher and occasional lecturer outside Dayton, Ohio, he worries that his country recently has become too soft and self-indulgent. "The wonderful thing about democracy and capitalism is that they lead to the good life, as Aristotle would want us to have it," he says. But the problem "is that we tend to lose focus on the virtues," the most important of which are "hard work, dedication and sacrifice."

As much as this man's views resonate with ideas of America's decline from a more virtuous age, his defense of self-discipline was decidedly uncommon among our respondents. "You can be disciplined in a bad way," said one woman in Tipton, Iowa. "You work 70, 80 hours a week, ignoring your family. I don't think that is good self-discipline." Good self-discipline makes room for obligations to others. In a paradoxical way, it also involves obligations to the self. Many people told us that the person who indulges from time to time is more likely to be productive than the obsessive workaholic.

St. Augustine wrote that it is always wrong to lie. But the people with whom we spoke believe that you are under a greater obligation to be honest to a friend than to a stranger—and that you are under no obligation at all to be honest to someone who is dishonest to you. Honesty is not a one-size-fits-all virtue. Many of the gay men with whom we spoke in San Francisco did not believe in loyalty to their sexual partners, but, determined not to hide their sexual orientation, were among the most passionate believers in honesty. Other respondents felt that there are times when honesty can be a vice. "You know," said a San Francisco therapist, "people say terrible things and then they go, 'Well, I was just being honest.'" In her view, a person of good character would rank sensitivity to others higher than honesty to them.

Whatever the virtue, Americans will be more practical than principled. An engineer in Silicon Valley talked about the problem of marital loyalty as if he were tinkering with a stubborn software program: "Is it irretrievably broken or can you patch it up? Was there a basis for the marriage in the first place? Is there a basis for working together as part of a team to move ahead from where you are and ignore the past?" A divorced woman in Hartford believes in forgiveness, not out of a recognition that even sinners may nonetheless be good in the eyes of God, but "because when we don't forgive, it holds us back, it eats away at us."

As they decide for themselves the best way to live, people can and do consult traditional sources of moral wisdom. Our respondents mentioned not only popular television programs and self-help books but also the example of Jesus Christ, philosophers from Plato and Aristotle to

Kant and William James, novelists like F. Scott Fitzgerald, Jane Austen and Alexander Solzhenitsyn and theologians including Teilhard de Chardin and Rabbi Hillel. Still, listening to their reasoning gives a certain credibility to those who argue that contemporary Americans have too much freedom for their own good. Our respondents are guided by subjective feelings more than they are by appeals to rational, intellectual and objective conceptions of right and wrong. They do not think that virtue consists in subsuming their needs and desires to the authority of tradition. Indeed, some of them are not even sure that virtuous is what they want to be. Without firm moral instruction, Americans approach the virtues gingerly. They recognize their importance but reinvent their meaning to make sense of the situations in which they find themselves.

> **Americans make a pretty clear distinction between moral choice and unboundedness. The former, they usually insist, is something worth having. The latter, most of them feel, is something worth avoiding.**

Just because Americans may be living "after virtue"—to use the evocative words of the moral philosopher Alasdair MacIntyre—does not, however, mean that they are living before vice. Both conservatives and liberals see a direct link between the 1960's and now. From the point of view of those aghast at what the 1960's have bequeathed us, one mistake—the wrong drug or, later, the wrong sex partner—and life itself could be threatened. From the point of view of those who embraced the social changes of that time, one too many concessions to established institutions of authority, and freedom itself could be sacrificed. Yet for the people with whom we spoke, the 1960's—understood as a political movement designed to challenge the status quo in favor of revolutionary transformations in lifestyle—barely exist. Even in San Francisco, despite the fact that we asked people questions about the most morally contentious issues of the day, only a couple of our respondents reflected on what the tumultuous events of those years meant for them and for their country.

The debate over the 1960's confuses two different phenomena. One is the freedom to choose how to live. The other is the freedom to consider oneself unbound by moral rules. The Americans with whom we have spoken make a pretty clear distinction between choice and unboundedness. The former, they usually insist, is something worth having. And the latter, most of them feel, is something

worth avoiding. When Americans think of the kind of moral anarchy and irresponsibility that conservatives associate with the excesses of the 1960's, they do not think about their own lives but about the wild lives of Hollywood celebrities, the self-centered actions of corporations and the dishonesty exhibited by politicians.

Moderate in economics and politics, our respondents are, for the most part, moderate in morality. The great bulk of them no longer adhere to traditional ideas about virtue and vice, but neither do they live as moral libertines. They do not take their marriage vows as binding under all circumstances and for all time, but they often approach the question of divorce in a morally serious way, reserving it as an option when the price of excessive loyalty is unwanted cruelty toward spouse or child. They are not as loyal as they once were in the workplace, but only after being provoked into that position by extensive, and often ruthless, disloyalty on the part of their employers. In their effort to find balance in all things, they forgive to get on with life but do not forget wrongs done to them and do not relativize away acts they consider evil.

THE CONCEPT OF MORAL FREEDOM CORRESPONDS to a deeply held populist suspicion of authority and a corresponding belief that people know their own best interest. Historically, populist impulses expressed themselves in politics; Americans distrusted elites, especially those whose power appeared to rest on breeding and connections, in favor of appeals to the common man. Now that same populist sensibility extends to all kinds of institutions; if Americans have learned to obtain a second opinion concerning their medical condition, they are also likely to seek additional opinions concerning their moral condition. As radical an idea as this may seem to those once issued commands and expected to obey them, second-opinion morality seeks to work with, not against, the institutions that make social life possible.

In an age of moral freedom, moral authority has to justify its claims to special insight. Religion offers the best window into the ways such justifications are likely to take place. More and more Americans are redefining God to suit their own tastes and inclinations: Christian ministers who draw upon the Jewish tradition, Reform Jews seeking gender-inclusive language and Americans of all faiths who borrow from every religion and none simultaneously. Whatever emerges from the efforts on the parts of so many Americans to redefine their faith, it is unlikely to resemble Jonathan Edwards's Northampton, the urban parishes of 1950's Catholicism, the revival meetings of Billy Sunday or synagogue life on the Lower East Side.

Yet the desire of so many Americans to have a greater say in the moral choices they make is anything but a bitter renunciation of religion. It is more likely to take the form of a prayer that someone in a position of religious authority will take them seriously as individuals with minds and desires of their own. Far from being secular humanists, Americans want faith and freedom simultaneously. That would seem like an odd combination to Europeans, for whom faith has often meant dogma and freedom has often meant dissent. But it suggests that in America, religious institutions will not break under the weight of moral freedom but bend, as many of them have bent already, to accommodate themselves to the freedom of moral choice to which Americans have increasingly grown accustomed.

What is true of religious institutions applies to other institutions like schools, if from the opposite direction. In the spirit of the 1960's, educational reformers began to advocate radical changes in education, proposing that schools should stop disciplining students, encourage free-form expression and individual creativity, de-emphasize honors classes and tracking and find new ways to teach such subjects as math and history. In extreme versions of educational reform, moral anarchy rather than moral freedom seemed to be the operating principle, as if schooling itself ought to be abolished. So powerful were the forces behind educational reform that in most established school districts, one version or another of educational reform produced schools that no longer resembled the strict, segregated, vocational and prayer-infused institutions of the 1950's.

Americans today want second opinions about both what and how their children learn in schools. Resisting the influence of liberal school administrators with as much determination as they resist the messages of conservative religious moralists, those who support greater school choice through vouchers and charter schools see freedom of choice as a way of encouraging greater institutional responsibility. Those who continue to support public schooling often express a desire for higher standards and an insistence on the value of teaching character. If American schools move in a more "conservative" direction toward discipline, it will be for the same reasons that churches move in a more "liberal" direction of therapeutic inclusion. After anarchy, moral freedom can be a requirement for re-establishing authority.

In a time of moral freedom, no institution will be able to stick its head in the sand and pretend that the people who approach it for advice and guidance can be treated as supplicants. Morality has long been treated as if it were a fixed star, sitting there far removed from the earthly concerns of real people, meant to guide them to the true and the beautiful. In the contemporary world, however, people experience in their own lives many situations for which traditional conceptions of morality offer little guidance: what do you do when the pursuit of one virtue conflicts with another? How do you apply moral precepts to situations unforeseen by those religious and philosophical traditions developed for another time and place? Can seemingly unambiguous moral principles be capable of multifaceted interpretations? Faced with such real-world conflicts, many Americans will say, as did one of our respondents in San Antonio: "Somebody can't make you do something you don't want to do. You know, you draw your own guidelines."

No matter how strong their religious and moral beliefs, nearly all people will encounter situations in which they will feel such a need to participate in interpreting, applying and sometimes redefining the rules meant to guide them. Are they somehow less moral if they do? Telling them that they are will cut no ice with a gay couple determined to legalize their union in an era of widespread heterosexual divorce, with women who find that a too-early marriage stultifies their desire to become more autonomous later in life or with religious believers who find that the best way to express one's faith in God is to reject traditional denominations.

Because we can never know what freedom will bring in its wake, defenders of social order have never been all that comfortable with any of the forms taken by freedom in the modern world. Economic freedom did not create a hoped-for society of independent yeomen but a regime of mass consumption. Political freedom did not result in active and enlightened civic participation but in voter apathy. In a similar way, moral freedom is highly unlikely to produce a nation of individuals exercising their autonomy with the serious and dispassionate judgment of Immanuel Kant. Yet moral freedom is as inevitable as it is impossible. Critics of America's condition insist on the need to return to the morality of yesterday, but it may be better, given its inevitability, to think of moral freedom as a challenge to be met rather than as a condition to be cured.

Alan Wolfe is the director of the Boisi Center for Religion and American Public Life at Boston College. His new book, "Moral Freedom," from which this essay is adapted, will be published next month by W.W. Norton.

UNIT 2

Socialization and Social Control

Unit Selections

Key Points to Consider

- What are the major differences between the ways that boys and girls are socialized?

- How can the ways in which children are socialized in America be improved?

- Why is socialization a lifelong process?

- What are the principal factors that make people what they are?

- What are the major ways to reduce crime in the United States, and how effective are they?

- How do you explain the increase in Columbine-type shootings?

- How should the drug problem be dealt with?

 **Links: www.dushkin.com/online/**
These sites are annotated in the World Wide Web pages.

Crime Times
http://www.crime-times.org

Ethics Updates/Lawrence Hinman
http://ethics.acusd.edu

National Institute on Drug Abuse (NIDA)
http://165.112.78.61/

Sexual Assault Information Page
http://www.cs.utk.edu/~bartley/saInfoPage.html

Why do we behave the way we do? Three forces are at work: biology, socialization, and the human will or internal decision maker. The focus in sociology is on socialization, which is the conscious and unconscious process whereby we learn the norms and behavior patterns that enable us to function appropriately in our social environment. Socialization is based on the need to belong, because the desire for acceptance is the major motivation for internalizing socially approved attitudes and behaviors. Fear of punishment is another motivation. It is utilized by parents and institutionalized in the law enforcement system. The language we use, the concepts we apply in thinking, the images we have of ourselves, our gender roles, and our masculine and feminine ideals are all learned through socialization. Socialization may take place in many contexts. The most basic socialization takes place in the family, but churches, schools, communities, the media, and workplaces also play major roles in the process.

The first subsection deals with issues concerning the basic influences on the development of our character and behavior patterns. Barbara Kantrowitz and Claudia Kalb review the latest research on child development and compare the development of boys and girls, but with an emphasis on boys because boys have been slighted in the research of previous decades. The authors conclude that "boys and girls really are from two different planets," and that boys are commonly misunderstood. It is normal for them to have "an abundance of energy and the urge to conquer," but they usually are penalized by adults for these traits. Nevertheless, they hold each other to norms of masculinity and toughness. In the second article, Celia Kitzinger seeks to explain why people are so good. Is it because they are rewarded for being good? Is it because people have a natural feeling of empathy that allows them to enjoy the pleasure and suffer the pain of others? Or does the answer lie in the human capacity for moral reasoning of which we are so proud? Kitzinger's answer to each question is "yes, in part." The more basic answer, however, is social pressure, which urges us to be good. At times it also urges us to be bad.

The next subsection deals with crime, law enforcement, and social control—major concerns today because crime and violence seem to be out of control. The first article in this subsec-

tion, "Preventing Crime: The Promising Road Ahead," tries to find out what works and what does not work in preventing crime. Gene Stephens looks at over 500 studies of crime prevention programs and finds that many popular programs have little or no effect.

The next article deals with the issue of gun violence, which is a major problem. In 1998, 30,708 Americans died from bullets (compared to 83 in Japan), of whom 17,424 were suicides, 12,102 were murdered, and 866 were unintentionally shot. Why does such carnage exist only in the United States? Its existence reveals flaws in American institutions. The politics of gun regulation or lack thereof is part of the explanation of why this problem persists. But the deeper question is why are people, especially children, so much more into violence now than a generation ago? According to Richard F. Corlin, the answer is computer games, videos, and the media. The final article in this section deals with a major aspect of the crime problem—drugs. The movie "Traffic" revealed the horrors of drug addiction and the drug war. Much crime is drug-related, and some commentators argue that legalizing narcotics would eliminate much crime. Jonathan Alter, however, says legalization will not happen nor will America eliminate the supply through its war on drugs. The answer that is currently being emphasized is reducing demand, largely through the treatment of drug addiction. For criminals, the treatment is often mandatory, with imprisonment for those who refuse it.

Boys will be Boys

Developmental research has been focused on girls; now it's their brothers' turn. Boys need help, too, but first they need to be understood.

BY BARBARA KANTROWITZ AND CLAUDIA KALB

IT WAS A CLASSIC MARS-VENUS ENCOUNTER. Only in this case, the woman was from Harvard and the man—well, boy—was a 4-year-old at a suburban Boston nursery school. Graduate student Judy Chu was in his classroom last fall to gather observations for her doctoral dissertation on human development. His greeting was startling: he held up his finger as if it were a gun and pretended to shoot her. "I felt bad," Chu recalls. "I felt as if he didn't like me." Months later and much more boy-savvy, Chu has a different interpretation: the gunplay wasn't hostile—it was just a way for him to say hello. "They don't mean it to have harsh consequences. It's a way for them to connect."

The Wonder (and Worry) Years

There may be no such thing as *child* development anymore. Instead, researchers are now studying each gender's development separately and discovering that boys and girls face very different sorts of challenges. Here is a rough guide to the major phases in their development.

Boys

0-3 years At birth, boys have brains that are 5% larger than girls' (size doesn't affect intelligence) and proportionately larger bodies—disparities that increase with age.

4-6 years The start of school is a tough time as boys must curb aggressive impulses. They lag behind girls in reading skills, and hyperactivity may be a problem.

Age 1	2	3	4	5	6	7

Girls

0-3 years Girls are born with a higher proportion of nerve cells to process information. More brain regions are involved in language production and recognition.

4-6 years Girls are well suited to school. They are calm, get along with others, pick up on social cues, and reading and writing come easily to them.

7-10 years While good at gross motor skills, boys trail girls in finer control. Many of the best students but also nearly all of the poorest ones are boys.

11-13 years A mixed bag. Dropout rates begin to climb, but good students start pulling ahead of girls in math skills and catching up some in verbal ones.

14-16 years Entering adolescence, boys hit another rough patch. Indulging in drugs, alcohol and aggressive behavior are common forms of rebellion.

8	9	10	11	12	13	14	15	16

7-10 years Very good years for girls. On average, they outperform boys at school, excelling in verbal skills while holding their own in math.

11-13 years The start of puberty and girls' most vulnerable time. Many experience depression; as many as 15% may try to kill themselves.

14-16 years Eating disorders are a major concern. Although anorexia can manifest itself as early as 8, it typically afflicts girls starting at 11 or 12; bulimia at 15.

SOURCES: DR. MICHAEL THOMPSON, BARNEY BRAWER. RESEARCH BY BILL VOURVOULIAS—NEWSWEEK

Trouble Spots: Where Boys Run Into Problems

Not all boys are the same, of course, but most rebel in predictable patterns and with predictable weapons: underachievement, aggression and drug and alcohol use. While taking chances is an important aspect of the growth process, it can lead to real trouble.

When Johnny Can't Read

Girls have reading disorders nearly as often as boys, but are able to overcome them. Disability rates, as identified by:

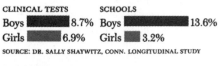

CLINICAL TESTS	SCHOOLS
Boys 8.7%	Boys 13.6%
Girls 6.9%	Girls 3.2%

SOURCE: DR. SALLY SHAYWITZ, CONN. LONGITUDINAL STUDY

Suicidal Impulses

While girls are much more likely to try to kill themselves, boys are likelier to die from their attempts.

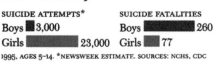

SUICIDE ATTEMPTS*	SUICIDE FATALITIES
Boys 3,000	Boys 260
Girls 23,000	Girls 77

1995, AGES 5–14. *NEWSWEEK ESTIMATE. SOURCES: NCHS, CDC

Binge Drinking

Boys binge more on alcohol. Those who had five or more drinks in a row in the last two weeks:

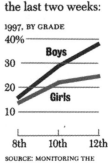

1997, BY GRADE

SOURCE: MONITORING THE FUTURE STUDY

Aggression That Turns to Violence

Boys get arrested three times as often as girls, but for some nonviolent crimes the numbers are surprisingly even.

Arrests of 10- to 17-year-olds: ■ Boys ■ Girls

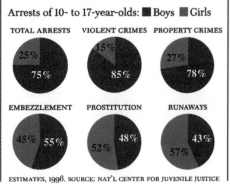

TOTAL ARRESTS	VIOLENT CRIMES	PROPERTY CRIMES
25% / 75%	15% / 85%	27% / 78%
EMBEZZLEMENT	PROSTITUTION	RUNAWAYS
45% / 55%	52% / 48%	57% / 43%

ESTIMATES, 1996. SOURCE: NAT'L CENTER FOR JUVENILE JUSTICE

Eating Disorders

Boys can also have eating disorders. Kids who used laxatives or vomited to lose weight:

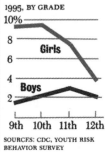

1995, BY GRADE

SOURCES: CDC, YOUTH RISK BEHAVIOR SURVEY

Researchers like Chu are discovering new meaning in lots of things boys have done for ages. In fact, they're dissecting just about every aspect of the developing male psyche and creating a hot new field of inquiry: the study of boys. They're also producing a slew of books with titles like "Real Boys: Rescuing Our Sons From the Myths of Boyhood" and "Raising Cain: Protecting the Emotional Life of Boys" that will hit the stores in the next few months.

What some researchers are finding is that boys and girls really are from two different planets. But since the two sexes have to live together here on Earth, they should be raised with special consideration for their distinct needs. Boys and girls have different "crisis points," experts say, stages in their emotional and social development where things can go very wrong. Until recently, girls got all the attention. But boys need help, too. They're much more likely than girls to have discipline problems at school and to be diagnosed with attention deficit disorder (ADD). Boys far outnumber girls in special-education classes. They're also more likely to commit violent crimes and end up in jail. Consider the headlines: Jonesboro, Ark.; Paducah, Ky.; Pearl, Miss. In all these school shootings, the perpetrators were young adolescent boys.

Even normal boy behavior has come to be considered pathological in the wake of the feminist movement. An abundance of physical energy and the urge to conquer— these are normal male characteristics, and in an earlier age they were good things,

even essential to survival. "If Huck Finn or Tom Sawyer were alive today," says Michael Gurian, author of "The Wonder of Boys," "we'd say they had ADD or a conduct disorder." He says one of the new insights we're gaining about boys is a very old one: boys will be boys. "They are who they are," says Gurian, "and we need to love them for who they are. Let's not try to rewire them."

Indirectly, boys are benefiting from all the research done on girls, especially the landmark work by Harvard University's Carol Gilligan. Her 1982 book, "In a Different Voice: Psychological Theory and Women's Development," inspired Take Our Daughters to Work Day, along with best-selling spinoffs like Mary Pipher's "Reviving Ophelia." The traditional, unisex way of looking at child development was profoundly flawed, Gilligan says: "It was like having a one-dimensional perspective on a two-dimensional scene." At Harvard, where she chairs the gender-studies department, Gilligan is now supervising work on males, including Chu's project. Other researchers are studying mental illness and violence in boys.

While girls' horizons have been expanding, boys' have narrowed, confined to rigid ideas of acceptable male behavior no matter how hard their parents tried to avoid stereotypes. The macho ideal still rules. "We gave boys dolls and they used them as guns," says Gurian. "For 15 years, all we heard was that [gender differences] were all about socialization. Parents who raised their kids through that period said in the end, 'That's not true. Boys and girls can be

awfully different.' I think we're awakening to the biological realities and the sociological realities."

But what exactly is the essential nature of boys? Even as infants, boys and girls behave differently. A recent study at Children's Hospital in Boston found that boy babies are more emotionally expressive; girls are more reflective. (That means boy babies tend to cry when they're unhappy; girl babies suck their thumbs.) This could indicate that girls are innately more able to control their emotions. Boys have higher levels of testosterone and lower levels of the neurotransmitter serotonin, which inhibits aggression and impulsivity. That may help explain why more males than females carry through with suicide, become alcoholics and are diagnosed with ADD.

The developmental research on the impact of these physiological differences is still in the embryonic stage, but psychologists are drawing some interesting comparisons between girls and boys (chart). For girls, the first crisis point often comes in early adolescence. Until then, Gilligan and others found, girls have an enormous capacity for establishing relationships and interpreting emotions. But in their early teens, girls clamp down, squash their emotions, blunt their insight. Their self-esteem plummets. The first crisis point for boys comes much earlier, researchers now say. "There's an outbreak of symptoms at age 5, 6, 7, just like you see in girls at 11, 12, 13," says Gilligan. Problems at this age include bed-wetting and separation anxiety. "They don't have the language or experience" to articulate it fully, she says, "but the feelings are no less intense." That's why Gilligan's student Chu is studying preschoolers. For girls at this age, Chu says, hugging a parent goodbye "is almost a nonissue." But little boys, who display a great deal of tenderness, soon begin to bury it with "big boy" behavior to avoid being called sissies. "When their parents drop them off, they want to be close and want to be held, but not in front of other people," says Chu. "Even as early as 4, they're already aware of those masculine stereotypes and are negotiating their way around them."

It's a phenomenon that parents, especially mothers, know well. One morning last month, Lori Dube, a 37-year-old mother of three from Evanston, Ill., visited her oldest son, Abe, almost 5, at his nursery school, where he was having lunch with his friends. She kissed him, prompting another boy to comment scornfully: "Do you know what your mom just did? She kissed you!" Dube acknowledges, with some sadness, that she'll have to be more sensitive to Abe's new reactions to future public displays of affection. "Even if he loves it, he's getting these messages that it's not good."

There's a struggle—a desire and need for warmth on the one hand and a pull toward independence on the other. Boys like Abe are going through what psychologists long ago declared an integral part of growing up: individualization and disconnection from parents, especially mothers. But now some researchers think that process is too abrupt. When boys repress normal feelings like love because of social pressure, says William Pollack, head of the Center for Men at Boston's McLean Hospital and author of the forthcoming "Real Boys," "they've lost contact with the genuine nature of who they are and what they feel. Boys are in a silent crisis. The only time we notice it is when they pull the trigger."

No one is saying that acting like Rambo in nursery school leads directly to tragedies like Jonesboro. But researchers do think that boys who are forced to shut down positive emotions are left with only one socially acceptable outlet: anger. The cultural ideals boys are exposed to in movies and on TV still emphasize traditional masculine roles—warrior, rogue, adventurer—with heavy doses of violence. For every Mr. Mom, there are a dozen Terminators. "The feminist movement has done a great job of convincing people that a woman can be nurturing and a mother and a tough trial lawyer at the same time," says Dan Kindlon, an assistant professor of psy-

chiatry at Harvard Medical School. "But we haven't done that as much with men. We're afraid that if they're too soft, that's all they can be."

And the demands placed on boys in the early years of elementary school can increase their overall stress levels. Scientists have known for years that boys and girls develop physically and intellectually at very different rates (time-line). Boys' fine motor skills—the ability to hold a pencil, for example—are usually considerably behind girls. They often learn to read later. At the same time, they're much more active—not the best combination for academic advancement. "Boys feel like school is a game rigged against them," says Michael Thompson, coauthor with Kindlon of "Raising Cain." "The things at which they excel—gross motor skills, visual and spatial skills, their exuberance—do not find as good a reception in school" as the things girls excel at. Boys (and girls) are also in academic programs at much younger ages than they used to be, increasing the chances that males will be forced to sit still before they are ready. The result, for many boys, is frustration, says Thompson: "By fourth grade, they're saying the teachers like girls better."

A second crisis point for boys occurs around the same time their sisters are stumbling, in early adolescence. By then, say Thompson and Kindlon, boys go one step further in their drive to be "real guys." They partake in a "culture of cruelty," enforcing male stereotypes on one another. "Anything tender, anything compassionate or too artistic is labeled gay," says Thompson. "The homophobia of boys in the 11, 12, 13 range is a stronger force than gravity."

Boys who refuse to fit the mold suffer. Glo Wellman of the California Parenting Institute in Santa Rosa has three sons, 22, 19 and 12. One of her boys, she says, is a "nontypical boy: he's very sensitive and caring and creative and artistic." Not surprisingly, he had the most difficulty growing up, she says. "We've got a long way to go to help boys… to have a sense that they can be anything they want to be."

In later adolescence, the once affectionate toddler has been replaced by a sulky stranger who often acts as though torture would be preferable to a brief exchange of words with Mom or Dad. Parents have to try even harder to keep in touch. Boys want and need the attention, but often just don't know how to ask for it. In a recent national poll, teenagers named their parents as their No. 1 heroes. Researchers say a strong parental bond is the most important protec-

tion against everything from smoking to suicide.

For San Francisco Chronicle columnist Adnir Lara, that message sank in when she was traveling to New York a few years ago with her son, then 15. She sat next to a woman who told her that until recently she would have had to change seats because she would not have been able to bear the pain of seeing a teenage son and mother together. The woman's son was 17 when his girlfriend dumped him; he went into the garage and killed himself. "This story made me aware that with a boy especially, you have to keep talking because they don't come and talk to you," she says. Lara's son is now 17; she also has a 19-year-old daughter. "My daughter stalked me. She followed me from room to room. She was yelling, but she was in touch. Boys don't do that. They leave the room and you don't know what they're feeling." Her son is now 6 feet 3. "He's a man. There are barriers. You have to reach through that and remember to ruffle his hair."

With the high rate of divorce, many boys are growing up without any adult men in their lives at all. Don Elium, coauthor of the best-selling 1992 book "Raising a Son," says that with troubled boys, there's often a common theme: distant, uninvolved fathers, and mothers who have taken on more responsibility to fill the gap. That was the case with Raymundo Infante Jr., a 16-year-old high-school junior, who lives with his mother, Mildred, 38, a hospital administrative assistant in Chicago, and his sister, Vanessa, 19. His parents divorced when he was a baby and he had little contact with his father until a year ago. The hurt built up—in sixth grade, Raymundo was so depressed that he told a classmate he wanted to kill himself. The classmate told the teacher, who told a counselor, and Raymundo saw a psychiatrist for a year. "I felt that I just wasn't good enough, or he just didn't want me," Raymundo says. Last year Raymundo finally confronted his dad, who works two jobs—in an office and on a construction crew—and accused him of caring more about work than about his son. Now the two spend time together on weekends and sometimes go shopping, but there is still a huge gap of lost years.

Black boys are especially vulnerable, since they are more likely than whites to grow up in homes without fathers. They're often on their own much sooner than whites. Black leaders are looking for alternatives. In Atlanta, the Rev. Tim McDonald's First Iconium Baptist Church just chartered a Boy Scout troop. "Gangs are so prevalent because guys want to belong to something," says McDonald. "We've got to give them something positive to belong to." Black educators like Chicagoan Jawanza Kunjufu think mentoring programs will overcome the bias against academic success as "too white." Some cities are also experimenting with all-boy classrooms in predominantly black schools.

Researchers hope that in the next few years, they'll come up with strategies that will help boys the way the work of Gilligan and others helped girls. In the meantime, experts say, there are some guidelines. Parents can channel their sons' energy into constructive activities, like team sports. They should also look for "teachable moments" to encourage qualities such as empathy. When Diane Fisher, a Cincin-

nati-area psychologist, hears her 8- and 10-year-old boys talking about "finishing somebody," she knows she has mistakenly rented a violent videogame. She pulls the plug and tells them: "In our house, killing people is not entertainment, even if it's just pretend."

Parents can also teach by example. New Yorkers Dana and Frank Minaya say they've never disciplined their 16-year-old son Walter in anger. They insist on resolving all disputes calmly and reasonably, without yelling. If there is a problem, they call an official family meeting "and we never leave without a big hug," says Frank. Walter tries to be open with his parents. "I don't want to miss out on any advice," he says.

Most of all, wise parents of boys should go with the flow. Cindy Lang, 36, a full-time mother in Woodside, Calif., is contin-

ually amazed by the relentless energy of her sons, Roger Lloyd, 12, and Chris, 9. "You accept the fact that they're going to involve themselves in risky behavior, like skateboarding down a flight of stairs. As a girl, I certainly wasn't skateboarding down a flight of stairs." Just last week, she got a phone call from school telling her that Roger Lloyd was in the emergency room because he had fallen backward while playing basketball and school officials thought he might have a concussion. He's fine now, but she's prepared for the next emergency: "I have a cell phone so I can be on alert." Boys will be boys. And we have to let them.

With KAREN SPRINGEN *in Chicago,* PATRICIA KING *in San Francisco,* PAT WINGERT *in Washington,* VERN E. SMITH *in Atlanta and* ELIZABETH ANGELL *in New York*

Born ^{to} **be good?**

What motivates us to be good, bad or indifferent towards others?
Celia Kitzinger examines the psychology of morality.

MANY of us, much of the time, act to benefit others. There are small kindnesses of everyday life—like holding open a door, sharing food or expressing compassion for someone in distress. Things so ordinary that we simply take them for granted.

We are pleased, but not particularly surprised that people commonly care for sick relatives, give money to help famine victims, donate blood to hospitals, or volunteer to assist at hospices. At times what people do for others is truly spectacular. In the US, Lenny Skutnik risked his life diving into the icy waters of the Potomac River to save an airline crash victim; in Nazi Europe many people risked their lives in offering protection to Jews. In both mundane and exceptional ways people often act to help others—which is why psychologists describe human beings not just as 'social' but also as 'pro-social' animals.

But why do people spend so much time and money and effort on others, when we could keep it all for ourselves? One argument is that self-interest lies at the root of all superficially 'moral' behaviour. According to sociobiologists, we are biologically driven towards those forms of altruism—caring for our families, for example—which improve the survival of our genes.[1] Moral actions are simply automatic and instinctive, of no greater or lesser significance than the behaviour of a

mother bird putting her own life at risk leading a predator away from her chicks. Helping people who are not genetically related to us can also be in the best interest of our genes if it sets up the expectation that we—or those who share our genes—will be helped in turn.

There are many subtle ways in which helping others can offer rewards which serve our self-interest. These include the praise of onlookers; gratitude from the person being helped; the warm glow of knowing we have done a good deed; and the benefit of avoiding guilt, shame or punishment. Most people agree that some good behaviour can be attributed to self-interest. But is that all there is?

In an ingenious set of experiments, a group of psychologists set out to test the idea that empathy—the ability to imagine ourselves in the place of another and to feel their emotions—can result in genuine altruism.[2] Subjects were encouraged to be empathetic while watching a 'worker' who they believed was reacting badly to a series of uncomfortable electric shocks. They were then given a chance to help the worker by receiving the shocks themselves. If helping were only self-serving egoism, then people who felt empathy for the victim would simply want to escape from the upsetting experience. But researchers found that those with strong em-

pathetic feelings volunteered to take the worker's place, even when told they that they could leave immediately if they refused. The researchers also found that high-empathy people, who were deprived of the opportunity to help, felt just as good when someone else helped instead. This suggests that the offer to help reflected a genuine wish to relieve the victim's suffering, rather than a desire for praise from other people. So it looks as if the cynical view that even good actions have selfish motives may well be wrong. Empathy is common in very small children who often respond to another's distress with crying and sadness, and may attempt to comfort them with a hug or a cuddly toy. Some psychologists believe that behaviour like this signals the start of moral development.[3]

Although empathy may be an important component of moral behaviour, morality cannot rely on empathy alone because this emotion is too circumscribed and partial. It can also lead us to make unfair decisions—taking sides in a dispute, for example. Another explanation for why people behave well is that they are motivated not by emotions but by reasoned moral principles. This is what Lawrence Kohlberg proposes in his 'cognitive-development model' theory.[4] Children, he says, begin at a 'preconventional' level in which they see morality in relation to obedience and punishments from adults. At the second, 'conventional' level, reached in late childhood or early adolescence, they are oriented first to pleasing and helping others and later to maintaining the existing social order. At the third and highest stage of moral development—reached by only a small proportion of adults—people begin to define moral values and principles such as human dignity, justice, universal human rights. According to this theory, morality is a matter of cognitive (not emotional) development: it matters not one whit whether we care about or empathize with other people so long as we respect their rights as human beings.

> *These people were not sadists or psychopaths. They were ordinary people*

Some critics, notably feminist psychologist Carol Gilligan, have challenged the theory as sexist: men may favour abstract theoretical notions of rights and justice, but women, she says, are more likely to construct morality rooted in their sense of connection with other people, a morality of care and empathy.[5] Others criticize the ethnocentrism of the model, pointing out that Kohlberg has elevated to the highest stage of moral development precisely those views most likely to be held by white, middle-class, educated North Americans.[6]

It's more likely that moral behaviour comes about in a variety of ways: sometimes we may act well in the hope of rewards; other times good behaviour may be motivated by empathy; sometimes it is the outcome of reasoned moral arguments. Crucially, though, neither strong feelings of empathy nor high moral principles guarantee that people will behave well. There is often a gap between moral beliefs and moral action—between how people think and hope they would behave in a situation and how they actually do behave. Some of the classic studies of psychology were prompted by situations in which people failed to act in accordance with their moral values.

In the 1960s a young woman named Kitty Genovese was murdered by a man who raped and stabbed her repeatedly for half an hour in front of 38 residents of a respectable New York City neighbourhood. Nobody went to help her. Only one person finally called the police, after she was dead. This incident prompted a flood of research into what became known as the 'bystander effect' which examined why people don't intervene when others are in pain or in danger.[7] Sometimes people fail to intervene out of callousness or indifference. But more often they fail to act in spite of what they feel they should do, and then feel ashamed afterwards. Why is this?

A common finding is that people are uncertain how to behave because, unsure about what they are seeing, they conform with the behaviour of others, who are equally unsure. Emergencies are rare events which happen suddenly and unexpectedly. How can we know that an emergency is real and is not a prank, a game, or a film being produced? The safest thing is to sit tight and wait to see how others react. If nobody else does anything, then people worry about making fools of themselves. A large group can stand by and do nothing, each lulled into thinking that there is no need to act, each waiting for someone else to make the first move. What looks like callous indifference is actually fear of what other people will think if they make an inappropriate response in an ambiguous situation.

Someone in Kitty Genovese's situation is less likely to be helped if many people are watching than if only one person witnesses the attack. For example, subjects asked to wait in a room before being interviewed heard a woman in the next room apparently fall, hurt herself, and cry out in distress. Of those waiting alone, 70 per cent went to help her, compared with only 7 per cent of those waiting with a stranger who did nothing. Today's altruist may be tomorrow's passive bystander; it all depends on the social situation because people tend to behave in accordance with socially prescribed roles rather than as individuals.

In a well-known study by Stanley Milgram, subjects were recruited through newspaper advertisements for what was described as 'an experiment in learning'. They were seated in front of a shock machine that could administer up 450 volts to the 'learner', a man strapped into a chair.[8] Each time the 'learner' made a mistake the subject had to pull a lever to give him an electric shock, increasing the voltage each time. (In fact, the lever was a dummy, and the 'learner' was acting out his response). At 150 volts the learner started shouting. At 180 volts, he cried out in pain and pleaded

to be released. At 300 volts he screamed with pain and yelled about his heart condition. Later still there was only deathly silence. If subjects wanted to stop giving shocks, the experimenter said only 'the experiment requires that you continue'. No threats, no incentives to go on, just the order. Under these conditions—and contrary to the predictions of psychiatrists who had guessed that virtually no-one would obey to the end—nearly two-thirds of subjects delivered the full range of shocks, proceeding beyond the levers marked 'Danger: Severe Shock' to the ones marked 'XXX'.

These people were not sadists or psychopaths. They were ordinary people who believed that you shouldn't hurt others, who often showed empathy for the learner, and who disliked what they were ordered to do. Virtually all of them complained to the experimenter and asked for permission to stop giving shocks. But when ordered to continue the majority did as they were told. As Milgram says: 'With numbing regularity, good people were seen to knuckle under the demands of authority and perform actions that were callous and severe.' Women were as likely as men to deliver shocks up to maximum intensity.

What all these studies illustrate is the extent to which moral behaviour is a social, not an individual issue. In thinking about why people fail to offer help, why they behave punitively, or why they inflict pain on others, we often resort to explanations which depend on individual characteristics—their personal religious beliefs, their capacity for empathy, their understanding of moral principles, or the kind of upbringing they had. But these explanations overlook the key role of social context. The frightening truth uncovered by these classic psychological studies is that it is not too difficult to set up situations in which most of us behave worse than we could have thought possible, out of conformity, fear of what others might think, loss of individual identity or obedience to authority.

The traditional view of moral behaviour is that people are intrinsically selfish beings whose natural anti-social impulses have been curbed by social structures designed to promote obedience to authority, law and order. An alternative possibility is that people are fundamentally pro-social beings, whose ability to act on altruistic impulses and moral principles is sometimes inhibited by precisely these social pressures. At the very least it is obvious that this is sometimes true, and that we need to develop ways of recognizing and challenging those social pressures which result in apathetic or cruel behaviour in our everyday lives.

Notes

1. Richard Dawkins, *The Selfish Gene,* OUP 1976.

2. CD Batson, *The Altruism Question,* Erlbaum Associates 1991.

3. C Zahn-Waxler & M Radke-Yarrow, 'The Development of Altruism' in N Eisenberg-Berg (ed.) *The Development of Prosocial Behaviour,* Academic Press 1986.

4. L Kohlberg, *The Philosophy of Moral Development,* Harper and Row 1981.

5. C Gilligan, *In a Different Voice,* Harvard University Press 1982.

6. EEL Simpson, 'Moral Development Research: A Case Study of Scientific Cultural Bias', *Human Development 17,* 1974.

7. B Latané & JM Draley, *The Unresponsive Bystander. Why doesn't he help?* Appleton-Century-Croft 1970.

8. S Milgram, 'Some Conditions of Obedience and Disobedience to Authority', *Human Relations 18,* 1965.

Celia Kitzinger teaches psychology at the University of Loughborough, England.

From *New Internationalist,* April 1997, pp. 15-17. © 1997 by New Internationalist Publications, Ltd. Reprinted by permission.

Preventing Crime: The Promising Road Ahead

Careful assessments of crime-prevention programs are revealing what really works. Crime problems could be drastically reduced in the years ahead.

By Gene Stephens

Street crime in America dropped to historically low levels by the end of the 1990s, according to the Department of Justice. The debate over the cause of this decrease has spurred an empirical search for answers. Some say the decrease is due to more police on the streets and tougher laws, but others believe that community initiatives and crime-prevention programs are behind it. Finding the answers will be critical to the public's safety in the twenty-first century.

Probably the best explanation for the decrease in crime lies in the budding success of the long-dormant "weed and seed" movement envisioned in the 1960s by now-famous criminologist James Q. Wilson. In his *Public Interest* article "Broken Windows," Wilson said neighborhoods in decline were places where the residents had lost hope and pride, where police rarely came except to make arrests, and where offenders could commit crimes almost with impunity.

Wilson suggested that the formula for change was to "weed" out the immediate problem—drug deal-ers and addicts, public drunks, thieves, street hustlers, and thugs—by crackdowns and arrests, using even minor offenses (loitering, vagrancy, spitting on the sidewalk, jaywalking) to "sweep" the streets clean. After "weeding," the government must then "seed" the community with programs that assist residents in keeping their communities crime free. Such programs might include enterprise zones to bring in jobs, day care, and health clinics. Depending on the character and needs of the neighborhood, drug rehabilitation, after-school centers, tutors, mentors, and many other activities might be required.

Wilson's ideas were embraced by federal officials in the late 1970s and 1980s. He even prepared a series of videos and publications for the National Institute of Justice (NIJ). Weed and seed money flowed from the U.S. Department of Justice to state and local officials, but congressional strings required more weeding than seeding. The "get tough" legislators at federal and state levels supported longer, mandatory sentences for law violators and built more prisons and jails to hold them. They also encouraged courts to give adult sentences to juveniles as a "deterrent."

Drug addicts were singled out in particular for harsh treatment; by 1999, more than two-thirds of federal prison inmates and 25% of all state prisoners were serving time for drug charges. Drug-prevention efforts were little more than the well-known "Just Say No" motto.

"Get tough" policies also led to "justice" issues, as research indicates most arrests and convictions come from information and/or testimony from "snitches"—usually offenders seeking money or dropped charges or lessened penalties in exchange for their "helping" police and prosecutors.

Finally, after an alarming increase in street violence in the late 1980s and early 1990s, the "seed" idea received increased attention, primarily through the Problem-Oriented Policing and Community-Oriented Policing movement. As the Justice Department began loosening strings on funding, success stories abounded in communities that developed programs to prevent crime rather than just suppress it. Soon, the

Justice Department was praising government-community partnerships, circulating model programs, and funding crime-prevention efforts.

What Works

In a July 1998 research briefing, NIJ reviewed major findings of a two-year, congressionally mandated, scientific examination of over 500 crime-prevention programs. Completed by a University of Maryland-led team of researchers, the study provides guidance for communities struggling with crime, with the caveat that, since this is the first study of its kind, the evaluations are based on "minimally adequate evidence." (The complete study can be found online at www.preventingcrime.org.)

The shortest list in the report, unfortunately, was of what works: For families, frequent home visits to infants by trained nurses and other helpers reduced child abuse and other injuries. For children under age five, attending preschool or being visited at home weekly by a teacher decreased their chances of being arrested later in life, at least through their teen years. Family therapy and parent training to deal with delinquent and at-risk pre-adolescents lessened risk factors for delinquency, such as aggression and hyperactivity.

In schools, clearly communicated rules, reinforcement of positive behavior, and school-wide initiatives (such as anti-bullying campaigns) reduced crime and delinquency. Lifeskills training such as problem solving, self-control, and stress management were also successful. Behavior-modification programs to train or coach thinking skills diminished substance abuse in high-risk youth.

Ex-offender job training for older males cut down on repeat offenses, while nuisance abatement suits or threats against landlords for failing to address drug problems on their premises reduced drug dealing and crime in privately owned rental housing.

Extra police patrols in high-crime "hot spots" such as nightclubs, bars, and "hangouts" curtailed crime in these areas. Monitoring high-risk repeat offenders with special units lessened their time on the street and their opportunities to commit more crimes by returning them to prison earlier. Arresting employed domestic abusers reduced repeat abuse (probably because of the threat of losing employment).

Incarcerating hard-core serious offenders prevented crimes they would have committed if on the streets, but researchers warn of diminishing returns for incarcerating less active or less serious offenders. Rehabilitation efforts worked if they were "appropriate to their risk factors"; both adults and juveniles receiving such treatment were less likely to re-offend. Even in-prison drug treatment in "therapeutic community programs" minimized repeat offending after release.

What Doesn't Work

The "doesn't work" list was longer:

Gun-buyback programs and inner-city community mobilization against crime were found ineffective. Guns could be easily obtained in other communities, and inner-city residents feared getting involved because the criminals might retaliate.

In schools, counseling not only failed to abate substance abuse and delinquency, but even increased it in some instances. Experimental psychologists could explain this seemingly illogical phenomenon: Attention-starved children often turn to drugs and delinquency, and counseling (attention) simply reinforces the behavior.

A surprise to many was that the original DARE curriculum—17 lessons taught in fifth and sixth grades by a uniformed police officer—failed to cut down on drug abuse. Since this finding, many DARE programs have been experimenting with follow-up programs at higher grade levels and have employed full-time

School Resource Officers to monitor and help students daily.

Summer jobs and short-term job training programs for at-risk youth failed to decrease crime, as did job training in place of prosecution for adult offenders. This agrees with earlier research (partially by this author) which found that job training and jobs alone could not overcome the multitude of problems facing at-risk youth and offenders.

Possibly most surprising to police was that the highly touted centerpiece of crime-prevention programs, Neighborhood Watch, failed to diminish burglary or other targeted crimes. However, the data was primarily from high-crime areas "where voluntary participation often fails." In other evaluations, Neighborhood Watch was found to be successful, but only when initiated and sustained by citizen groups. Police-initiated efforts were not sustained by residents.

One cause for alarm at a time when more youths are being arrested and treated harshly was the finding that "arrests of juveniles for minor offenses cause them to become more delinquent in the future than if police exercise discretion and merely warn them or use other alternatives to formal charging." The finding that "scared straight" programs (which bring minor juvenile offenders to visit maximum security prisons to see the severity of conditions there) can actually increase crime by these children should also raise a warning flag. Other research agrees, causing experts to conclude that keeping juveniles far away from the criminal-justice system is the best strategy for preventing crime. The system should be reserved for incorrigible or dangerous juvenile offenders.

Increased arrests of drug dealers were unsuccessful in deterring crime. Drug dealing was so fluid that police enforcement could not curtail it for more than a few days.

Correctional boot camps using a traditional military basic-training approach failed to lessen repeat offending, and "shock probation"—short periods of incarceration followed by probation/parole—did not prove any more effective than direct placement under community supervision. In fact, community supervision alone was usually more effective, as it avoids contact with the stigmatizing effects of imprisonment.

Neither home detention with electronic monitoring nor intensive supervision on probation was found to be any more effective in decreasing repeat offending than standard community supervision. If these results hold up under further study, then these expensive programs can be scrapped. The new electronic monitoring by global positioning satellite (which allows the client to go to school, work, therapy, as well as home) may prove more effective.

What's Promising

The "promising" list was the longest and most useful portion of the research findings:

Gang monitoring has proven tricky: Community workers, probation officers, and police have been able to reduce gang violence so long as they don't increase gang cohesion; if they do, gang crime increases, the study found.

Community-based mentoring and after-school recreation programs have shown promise of diminishing crime and substance abuse. Community-initiated programs appear more likely than government-created programs to be sustained. Big Brothers/Big Sisters, for example, has the expertise and experience that government efforts lack.

Shelters for battered women were likely to lessen repeat victimization, but only if the women took steps beyond staying in the shelter, such as seeking counseling, education, or job training.

"Schools within schools" programs that group students into smaller units for increased supportive interaction and flexibility in instruction abated drug abuse and delinquency in some locations. Improved classroom management and

innovative instructional techniques have also helped.

Both Job Corps, an intensive residential program for at-risk youth, and prison-based vocational programs for adult offenders have shown promise, probably because they provide not only long-term training but also preparation for entering the workplace.

Enterprise zones, which give tax-break incentives to employers and thereby provide jobs in high unemployment neighborhoods, reduced high crime risk factors such as high-school dropout and parental unemployment. So did dispersing public-housing residents out of the inner city and into suburban areas.

A potpourri of solutions have been deemed promising in places of business, neighborhoods, and schools. For example, street closures, barricades, and rerouting can reduce numerous street crimes in neighborhoods. Probably most promising here is a staple of Community-Oriented Policing programs, in which officers use "problem-solving analysis, addressed to the specific crime situation" such as drug dealing in a public housing project or burglary in a neighborhood.

Finally, combining monetary fines with other penalties might curtail repeat offenses. This finding supplements earlier studies in European countries where fines are attached to almost all offenses. Europeans have discovered that material losses will deter crime more effectively than will short sentences or community supervision.

The researchers were careful to avoid any sweeping conclusions from this first review of crime-prevention programs. However, to sum up, it appears that early intervention and proactive prevention programs show the most promise, along with close monitoring and arrests of hardcore offenders and at "hot spot" locations. Long-term, individual training and treatment are effective for those already at risk or in trouble. Beyond this, community-initiated programs fare better than government-created efforts, and government partner-

ships with existing, established programs are more effective than new government programs.

Other Assessments

At least two other assessments of crime-prevention efforts support the findings reviewed above.

The first crime-prevention textbook based entirely on scientific research, *The Prevention of Crime: Social and Situational Strategies* by Dennis P. Rosenbaum, Arthur J. Lurigio, and Robert C. Davis (Wadsworth Publishing, 1996) reviewed the plethora of prevention approaches and assessed their usefulness. In some cases, researchers found individual safety and community safety at odds. For example, a person carrying a gun in a high-crime neighborhood was slightly safer, but the added gun on the street placed the neighborhood at greater risk.

Another Justice Department agency— the Office of Juvenile Justice and Delinquency Prevention— offers a taxonomy of strategies to cope with gun violence. Its report, "Promising Strategies to Reduce Gun Violence," recommends programs similar to those mentioned already. These include rallies to highlight awareness of the problem, in-school mentoring and conflict resolution programs, gang and drug prevention initiatives, parenting skills programs, and job training for at-risk youth. (Visit http://ojjdp.ncjrs.org for more information.)

A New Model for Crime Prevention

Programs that can significantly reduce crime are emerging, but citizens must accept these new strategies, and communities must take control of the process from start to finish.

Community-oriented policing requires partnerships between all public and private agencies in the jurisdiction as well as active participation by community residents. Under ideal conditions, citizens lead the effort to analyze neighborhood needs and set priorities for dealing with crime-breeding situations. Thus, community policing is a philosophy rather than a set of specific tactics; each community must determine its own agenda and create its own plan and programs. However, successful efforts have several common principles:

- The community is involved in planning and supervision of police operations.
- Decision making shifts from standard operating procedures to creative, responsible action determined by the street officer.
- Crime-control methods—imposed authority, intimidation, demand for compliance, reaction to crime—are replaced by (or at least secondary to) prevention methods: establishing trust, sharing power, seeking out and alleviating problems that cause crime.

Several problems must be overcome for this approach to become the model for the twenty-first century. First, *creating* community is often necessary. Neighbors are often strangers; they are either transient or so busy that they don't socialize. Police must first identify and develop community leadership and then arrange social activities to begin the cohesion process.

Second, police recruitment and training must be improved. The high-school diploma remains the only educational requirement in a majority of departments, and training is centered on how to make an arrest, fire a gun, drive a car in pursuit, etc. Clearly the needs of community-oriented policing demand a better educated officer who desires to serve the public. Such officers must be trained in organization, communication, mediation, cooperation skills, and creative problem solving.

In addition, the professional pride of the police will have to be kept in check if community-policing efforts are to be successful. Clearly, police

need to learn to share power. Police traditionally have been "the law" at the street level and are not used to having outsiders determine the way they do their job. Known for clannishness, police are now being asked to accept direction from others.

A final issue is that police are charged with protecting constitutional rights while doing their job. Thus, if there is a consensus in a community to trample on the rights of a minority group to protect the majority, community-oriented police officers must use their mediation skills to redirect the decision-making process toward legal solutions.

Restorative Justice

Even the best proactive efforts of a community and police will not be enough to prevent crime in all situations. When crime does occur, restorative justice offers a proactive alternative to the current reactive and retributive courts and corrections systems, especially those in the juvenile justice process.

Restorative justice is not yet a well-developed alternative system; it has emerged piecemeal over the past three decades—from a few community mediation-arbitration programs starting in the 1970s, to growing use of community service and restitution as alternatives to incarceration, to greater attention to rehabilitation of offenders. Through the National Institute of Justice and many private and public agency efforts nationwide, the connections are being made to provide a coordinated system.

The philosophical principles underlying restorative justice hold that crime is an offense against human relationships, not governments. The first priority is to assist victims, and the second priority is to restore community to the degree possible. The offender has responsibilities to the victim and the community, and the community has responsibility to reclaim and reconcile with the offender as the debt is paid.

Weeding and Seeding in New York City

For much of the last decades of the twentieth century, Americans saw New York City as the epitome of urban decay—dirty, unsafe, and crime ridden. Many New Yorkers agreed: they huddled behind locked doors, afraid to walk the streets or ride the subways.

But in the latter half of the 1990s, the city made a dramatic turnabout—leading an urban renaissance with a huge decrease in street crime, revival of street life, and provision of safe, clean public transportation.

Crime decreased in New York because of a well-orchestrated "weed and seed" operation.

Weeding included shutting down criminal activity by using informants and task forces to "weed" communities of predators, addicts, and petty offenders, and keeping criminals out by temporarily monitoring communities 24-hours-a-day via barricading streets, stopping vehicles, checking pedestrians, and padlocking dwellings where illegal activity was found.

Seeding, carried out simultaneously, included improving quality of life by fixing potholes, removing graffiti and garbage, installing better street lights, and encouraging residents to organize tenant associations and block groups. To keep the gains from eroding, officers stayed involved with citizens on their beats and played an active role in assisting residents.

NYPD officer Garry McCarthy, initiator of the Model Block Programs, summed it up: "All this changed the neighborhood—and the cops. We stand on a corner and interact with people. No more hostile stares from either side."

While police confrontations and shootings actually decreased during this period, a few cases led to large demonstrations against the most flagrant of the weeding tactics. "Get tough" tactics alone cannot provide safety among freedom-loving people. "Weed" and "seed" tactics must be balanced.

—Gene Stephens

When fully developed, the restorative-justice process will begin with arbitration and mediation to determine the details of the incident. Often there is some blame on both sides, such as in an argument that escalates into an assault. The parties involved agree on an acceptable solution, or the arbiter makes the decision for them. The offender must make restitution to the victims and to the community and must apologize face-to-face. Offenders may be given drug treatment, tutoring, or vocational training in order to help them live lawfully in the community. Ideally, the victim, offender, and community are satisfied that justice has been done; peace is restored.

The Promise of Success

There are, of course, several obstacles that must be overcome to achieve acceptance of this model of community-oriented policing and restorative justice. The criminal justice establishment is a huge, multibillion-dollar complex. Many involved in it are comfortable and secure. They use fear to keep taxpayers' money flowing in.

Being asked to alleviate fear, identify and assist potential offenders, alleviate community ills, and share power with many other groups has led to high levels of resistance among police officers. For example, after the disastrous shoot-out following a Hollywood, California, bank robbery in 1997, police departments across the country cited the higher firepower of the robbers over police as undeniable evidence that police must have better weaponry. A new federal law allowed police to acquire automatic weapons, tanks, aircraft, and other high-tech gadgetry. SWAT teams were revitalized and expanded. (Even some university police established SWAT units.)

While it may be heresy to say this, the Hollywood incident should have redoubled efforts to ferret out and address the problems that led to the robbery and shootout in the first place. No one wins when "good" guys and "bad" guys accelerate their firepower in the community.

It seems, however, that the Community-Oriented Policing—Restorative Justice movement is strong enough to withstand resistance. Even those most opposed are often converted after seeing the successes—reduced crime, reduced fear, and revitalized communities. Consider the story of a Texas police officer:

> You know, years ago I came off a farm in South Texas and took a job as a city police officer. In my mind, I knew who the bad guys were, and I found a lot of fellow officers who felt the same way. We were out to rid society of these parasites. I policed this way for 15 years, and then a new chief came in and started this new-fangled community policing. He put me in a storefront precinct in a downtown district and had me walking a beat. I was so mad, I just sulked the first year. Well that got old, so I began to talk to people on my beat. After a while I learned they were much like me—concerned about their children, worried about drugs, upset about daily problems. As a police officer I had learned how to deal with many of these problems, and pretty soon I found myself referring these people to agencies that could help. For the first time in my career I feel like something other than a human garbage collector. Before, I rode around in my car all day and jumped out to grab what I considered human garbage. Now, I see people as just that—people. And the fact I can help them makes me feel good about myself and my job.

Gene Stephens is a professor in the College of Criminal Justice, University of South Carolina, and editor of *The Police Futurists*. He is contributing editor on criminal justice for THE FUTURIST. His address is University of South Carolina, Columbia, South Carolina 29208. E-mail stephens-gene@sc.edu.

Originally published in the November 1999 issue of *The Futurist*. Used with permission from the World Future Society, 7910 Woodmont Avenue, Suite 450, Bethesda, MD 20814. Telephone: 301/656-8274; Fax: 301/951-0394; http://www.wfs.org. © 1999.

The Secrets Of Gun Violence In America

WHAT WE DON'T KNOW IS KILLING US

Address by RICHARD F. CORLIN, *President, American Medical Association*
Delivered to the 2001 Annual Meeting, Chicago Hilton Hotel and Towers, Chicago, Illinois, June 20, 2001

Thank you for joining me tonight. It's my great pleasure to introduce to you the friends, colleagues and family members, without whom, I would not have made it here tonight. And without whose presence, this wouldn't be a special evening for me.

I grew up in East Orange, New Jersey in the 1940's and 1950's. My high school was a mosaic of racial and ethnic diversity—equal numbers of blacks and whites, some Puerto Ricans, and a few Asians. We'd fight among ourselves from time to time—sometimes between kids of the same race, sometimes equal opportunity battles between kids of different races and nationalities. Our fights were basically all the same: some yelling and shouting, then some shoving, a couple of punches, and then some amateur wrestling. They weren't gang fights—everyone but the two combatants just stood around and watched—until one of our teachers came over and broke it up.

My old high school reminds me a little of "West Side Story" only without the switchblades or a Leonard Bernstein score. And there were no Sharks or Jets. Remember, those were the days of James Dean and Elvis Presley. Nobody pulled out a gun—none of us had them and no one even thought of having one. The worst wound anyone had after one of those fights was a split lip or a black eye.

It was just like kids have always been—until today. Back then, no parents in that town of mostly lower-middle class blue collar workers had to worry that their children might get shot at school, in the park or on the front stoop at home. But then again, that was also a time when we thought of a Columbine as a desert flower, not a high school in Littleton, Colorado.

Even in my first encounter with medicine, when I was only 14 years old and got a summer job at Presbyterian Hospital in Newark, New Jersey, there were no guns. I worked on what was called the utility team—moving patients back to their own rooms after surgery, starting IVs, taking EKGs and passing N-G tubes. I told them I wanted to be a doctor and—unbelievably at the age of 14—they let me help the pathologist perform autopsies. I was so excited about helping with the autopsies that I used to repeat the details to my Mom and Dad over dinner. Before long, they made me eat by myself in the kitchen.

When I was old enough to get a driver's license, I got a job working as an emergency room aide and ambulance driver at Elizabeth General Hospital. In all that time, in five summers of working in two center city hospitals—in the recovery room, in the morgue, in the emergency room and driving the ambulance—I never saw even one gunshot victim.

Today, it's very different. Guns are so available and violence so commonplace that some doctors now see gunshot wounds every week—if not every day. It's as if guns have replaced fists as the playground weapon of choice. The kids certainly think so. In a nationwide poll taken in March after two students were shot to death at Santana High School near San Diego, almost half of the 500 high school students surveyed said it wouldn't be difficult for them to get a gun. And one in five high school boys said they had carried a weapon to school in the last 12 months. One in five. Frightening, isn't it?

I began by telling you how I grew up in a world without guns. That has changed for me—as it has for so many Americans. Recently, the violence of guns touched me personally. Not long ago, Trish, one of our office staff members in my practice—a vibrant, hard-working young woman from Belize—was gunned down while leaving a holiday party at her aunt's home in Los Angeles.

Trish had done nothing wrong—some might say that she was in the wrong place at the wrong time—but I don't buy into that. Here was a woman who was where she should be—leaving a relative's home—when she was gunned down. Someone drove down the street randomly firing an assault weapon out the car window, and he put a bullet through her eye. Trish lingered in a coma for eight days—and then she died, an innocent victim of gun violence.

With the preponderance of weapons these days, it comes as no surprise that gun violence—both self-inflicted and against others—is now a serious public health crisis. No one can avoid its brutal and ugly presence. No one. Not physicians. Not the public. And most certainly—not the politicians—no matter how much they might want to.

Let me tell you about part of the problem. In the 1990s, the CDC had a system in place for collecting data about the results of gun violence. But Congress took away its funding, thanks to heavy lobbying by the anti-gun control groups. You see, the gun lobby doesn't want gun violence addressed as a public health issue. Because that data would define the very public health crisis that these powerful interests don't want acknowledged. And they fear that such evidence-based data could be used to gain support to stop the violence. Which, of course, means talking about guns and the deaths and injuries associated with them.

We all know that violence of every kind is a pervasive threat to our society. And the greatest risk factor associated with that violence—is access to firearms. Because—there's no doubt about it—guns make the violence more violent and deadlier.

Now my speech today is not a polemic. It is not an attack on the politics or the profits or the personalities associated with guns in our society. It isn't even about gun control. I want to talk to you about the public health crisis itself—and how we can work to address it; in the same way we have worked to address other public health crises such as polio, tobacco, and drunk driving.

At the AMA, we acknowledged the epidemic of gun violence when—in 1987—our House of Delegates first set policy on firearms. The House recognized the irrefutable truth that "uncontrolled ownership and use of firearms, especially handguns, is a serious threat to the public's health inasmuch as the weapons are one of the main causes of intentional and unintentional injuries and death." In 1993 and 1994, we resolved that the AMA would, among other actions, "support scientific research and objective discussion aimed at identifying causes of and solutions to the crime and violence problem."

Scientific research and objective discussion because we as physicians are—first and foremost—scientists. We need to look at the science of the subject, the data, and—if you will—the micro-data, before we make a diagnosis. Not until then can we agree upon the prognosis or decide upon a course of treatment.

First, let's go straight to the science that we do know. How does this disease present itself? Since 1962, more than a million Americans have died in firearm suicides, homicides and unintentional injuries. In 1998 alone, 30,708 Americans died by gunfire:

- 17,424 in firearm suicides
- 12,102 in firearm homicides
- 866 in unintentional shootings

Also in 1998, more than 64,000 people were treated in emergency rooms for non-fatal firearm injuries.

This is a uniquely American epidemic. In the same year that more than 30,000 people were killed by guns in America, the number in Germany was 1,164, in Canada, it was 1,034, in Australia 391, in England and Wales 211, and in Japan, the number for the entire year was 83.

Next, let's look at how the disease spreads, what is its vector, or delivery system. To do that, we need to look at the gun market today. Where the hard, cold reality is—guns are more deadly than ever. Gun manufacturers—in the pursuit of technological innovation and profit—have steadily increased the le-

thality of firearms. The gun industry's need for new products and new models to stimulate markets that are already oversupplied with guns—has driven their push to innovate. Newer firearms mean more profits. With the American gun manufacturers producing more than 4.2 million new guns per year—and imports adding another 2.2 million annually—you'd think the market would be saturated.

But that's why they have to sell gun owners new guns for their collections—because guns rarely wear out. Hardly anyone here is driving their grandfather's 1952 Plymouth. But a lot of people probably have their grandfather's 1952 revolver. So gun manufacturers make guns that hold more rounds of ammunition, increase the power of that ammunition, and make guns smaller and easier to conceal.

These changes make guns better suited for crime, because they are easy to carry and more likely to kill or maim whether they are used intentionally or unintentionally. In fact, one of the most popular handgun types today is the so-called "pocket rocket:" a palm-sized gun that is easy to conceal, has a large capacity for ammunition and comes in a high caliber.

The Chicago Tribune reported that the number of pocket rockets found at crime scenes nationwide almost tripled from 1995 to 1997. It was a pocket rocket in the hands of a self-proclaimed white supremacist that shot 5 children at the North Valley Jewish Community Center and killed a Filipino-American postal worker outside of Los Angeles in August of 1999.

Now, we don't regulate guns in America. We do regulate other dangerous products like cars and prescription drugs and tobacco and alcohol—but not guns. Gun sales information is not public. Gun manufacturers are exempt by federal law from the standard health and safety regulations that are applied to all other consumer products manufactured and sold in the United States.

No federal agency is allowed to exercise oversight over the gun industry to ensure consumer safety. In fact, no other consumer industry in the United States—not even the tobacco industry—has been allowed to so totally evade accountability for the harm their products cause to human beings. Just the gun industry.

In a similar pattern to the marketing of tobacco—which kills its best customers in the United States at a rate of 430,000 per year—the spread of gun-related injuries and death is especially tragic when it involves our children. Like young lungs and tar and nicotine—young minds are especially responsive to the deadliness of gun violence.

Lieutenant Colonel Dave Grossman, a West Point professor of psychology and military science, has documented how video games act as killing simulators, teaching our children not just to shoot—but to kill. Grossman, who calls himself an expert in "killology," cites as evidence the marksmanship of the two children, aged 11 and 13, in the Jonesboro, Arkansas shootings in 1998. Both shooters were avid video game players. And just like in a video game—they fired off 27 shots—and hit 15 people. Killing four of their fellow students—and a teacher. Such deadly accuracy is rare and hard to achieve—even by well-trained police and military marksmen.

I want you to imagine with me a computer game called "Puppy Shoot." In this game puppies run across the screen. Using a joystick, the game player aims a gun that shoots the puppies. The player is awarded one point for a flesh wound, three points for a body shot, and ten points for a head shot. Blood spurts out each time a puppy is hit—and brain tissue splatters all over whenever there's a head shot. The dead puppies pile up at the bottom of the screen. When the shooter gets to 1000 points, he gets to exchange his pistol for an Uzi, and the point values go up.

If a game as disgusting as that were to be developed, every animal rights group in the country, along with a lot of other organizations, would protest, and there would be all sorts of attempts made to get the game taken off the market. Yet, if you just change puppies to people in the game I described, there are dozens of them already on the market—sold under such names as "Blood Bath," "Psycho Toxic," "Redneck Rampage," and "Soldier of Fortune." These games are not only doing a very good business—they are also supported by their own Web sites. Web sites that offer strategy tips, showing players how to get to hidden features, like unlimited ammunition, access more weapons, and something called "first shot kill," which enables you to kill your opponent with a single shot.

We do not let the children who play these games drive because they are too young. We do not let them drink because they are too young. We do not let them smoke because they are too young. But we do let them be trained to be shooters at an age when they have not yet developed their impulse control and have none of the maturity and discipline to safely use the weapons they are playing with. Perhaps worst of all, they do this in an environment in which violence has no consequences. These kids shoot people for an hour, turn off the computer—then go down for dinner and do their homework.

We need to teach our children from the beginning that violence does have consequences—serious consequences—all the time. Gunfire kills 10 children a day in America. In fact, the United States leads the world in the rate at which its children die from firearms. The CDC recently analyzed firearm-related deaths in 26 countries for children under the age of 15—and found that 86 percent of all those deaths—occurred in the United States.

If this was a virus—or a defective car seat or an undercooked hamburger—killing our children, there would be a massive uproar within a week. Instead, our capacity to feel a sense of national shame has been diminished by the pervasiveness and numbing effect of all this violence.

We all are well aware of the extent of this threat to the nation's health. So why doesn't someone do something about it? Fortunately, people are. People we know, people we don't know, and people we have only heard about are working hard to abolish the menace of gun violence—of all forms of violence—from the American scene. Some of them are with us tonight.

One of them is Elizabeth Kagan, the newly inaugurated president of our AMA Alliance. Elizabeth will head the Alliance campaign for Safe Gun Storage.

Another is Dr. William Schwab, chief of trauma surgery at the University of Pennsylvania in Philadelphia. He is truly one of the heroes in this battle. His work has shown us just the kind of information we really need to reduce this violence. We are extremely pleased that he has agreed to be one of our ongoing advisors in this activity.

These are the people who stand and deliver when it comes to educating the nation about the threat of gun violence. Elizabeth and Bill, will you please stand? They certainly deserve a hand.

Elizabeth and Bill will be with us through the evening, and I urge as many of you as possible to spend a few minutes with them. They came here because they understand that gun violence in the United States is a problem that is bigger than every one of us. And the blood in America's streets—and classrooms—is a problem for all of us.

I was gratified when—earlier today—Terry Hillard, Superintendent of the Chicago Police Department, stopped by to join me in talking with reporters. We discussed the importance of data collection and how the physician community can work together with law enforcement to tackle this important issue of gun violence.

The question remains, what are we—the physician community—going to do about it? I can tell you first what we're not going to do. We're not going to advocate changing or abolishing the Second Amendment to the Constitution. We really don't have to, to make our point.

The gun lobby loves to use the Second Amendment as a smokescreen—to hide the reality of the damage that guns do—and to prevent our looking any deeper into the facts and statistics of that damage. We've all heard that tired old statement: Guns don't kill people—people kill people. But how does that explain these facts? A gun kept in the home for self-defense is 22 times more likely to be used to kill a family member or a friend than an intruder. The presence of a gun in the home triples the risk of homicide—and increases the risk of suicide fivefold.

And listen to this quote: "... the Second Amendment has been the subject of one of the greatest pieces of fraud, I repeat the word fraud, on the American people by special interest groups that I have ever seen in my lifetime. The very language of the Second Amendment refutes any argument that it was intended to guarantee every citizen an unfettered right to any kind of weapon. Surely the Second Amendment does not remotely guarantee every person the constitutional right to have a Saturday night special or a machine gun. There is no support in the Constitution for the argument that federal and state governments are powerless to regulate the purchase of such firearms."

These are the words of a respected conservative jurist, the late Chief Justice of the Supreme Court, Warren Burger.

As I said, our mission is not to abolish all guns from the hands of our fellow citizens. We're not advocating any limitations on hunting or the legitimate use of long guns, or for that matter, any other specific item of gun control. And we won't even be keeping a scorecard of legislative victories against guns in Congress and in the statehouses.

Why not? Because all these well-intentioned efforts have been tried by good people—and they have not met with success. Instead, they have been met with a well-organized, aggressive protest against their efforts by powerful lobbies in Washington and at the state and community levels. We—the American Medical Association—are going to take a different route—not just calls for advocacy—but for diplomacy and for statesmanship and for research as well. And make no mistake about this: We will not be co-opted by either the rhetoric or the agendas of the public policy "left" or "right" in this national debate about the safety and health of our citizens.

One of the ways we will do this is—to help assemble the data. Current, consistent, credible data are at the heart of epidemiology. What we don't know about violence—and guns—is literally killing us. And yet, very little is spent on researching gun-related injuries and deaths.

A recent study shows that for every year of life lost to heart disease, we spend $441 on research. For every year of life lost to cancer, we spend $794 on research. Yet for every year of life lost to gun violence, we spend only $31 on research—less than the cost of a taxi ride here from the airport.

That's bad public policy. It's bad fiscal policy. And it certainly is bad medical policy. If we are to fight this epidemic of violence, the Centers for Disease Control must have the budget and the authority to gather the data we need. As I mentioned earlier, the CDC's National Center for Injury Prevention and Control researched the causes and prevention of many kinds of injuries. But in the mid-90's the gun lobby targeted the NCIPC—and scored a bulls eye when Congress eliminated its funding. It wasn't a lot of money—just $2.6 million—budget dust to the Federal government. But it meant the difference between existence and extinction for that project.

Just think—gun injuries cost our nation $2.3 billion dollars in medical costs each year—yet some people think $2.6 million dollars is too much to spend on tracking them. Every dollar spent on this research has the potential to reduce medical costs by $885.

The CDC is intent on doing its job and is now heading up the planning for a National Violent Death Reporting System—coordinated and funded at the federal level—and collecting data at the state level. Because knowing more about the who, what, when, where, why and how of violent homicides, suicides, and deaths—will help public health officials, law enforcement, and policy makers prevent unnecessary deaths.

We must further insist that such a system be expanded to cover data about non-fatal gunshot injuries so that we can prevent these as well. Such a system of data collection and analysis has already helped us address another national epidemic—motor vehicle fatalities. Prompting preventive measures like mandatory seat belt laws, air bags, improved highway signage, and better designed entry and exit ramps—not the confiscation of cars. The establishment of a National Violent Death and Injury Reporting System would help us establish similar preventive measures against violence. And help us fill in all the blanks about violent death and injury in America. Including such basics as:

- How do kids with guns get their weapons?
- Do trigger locks work?
- What can we do to reduce accidental, self-inflicted gun injuries?
- What are the warning signs of workplace or school shootings?

- During which hours of the week and in what specific parts of town (down to individual blocks—not just neighborhoods) do the shootings occur?
- Do we need to work with Police Departments to change patrolling patterns based on these data?
- And finally, the realization that the answers to these questions are apt to be different from one town to the next.

Today, we can't answer these questions—because we are not allowed to collect the data. Collecting and considering the facts isn't a matter of opinion or politics, it's essential. It's a matter of working with other committed leaders to get the job done.

The good news is that we have HELP—the Handgun Epidemic Lowering Plan—with membership of 130 organizations including the AMA, and, among others, the Rehabilitation Institute of Chicago, and the Minnesota Department of Health. We also have the Surgeon General's National Strategy for Suicide Prevention, released last month, which also supports the National Violent Death Reporting System.

We will not advocate any changes at all based on urban legend, anecdote or hunch. We will only base our conclusions on evidence-based data and facts. It's just good, common sense—the kind of solid epidemiology that has been brought to bear on other public health hazards—from Legionnaire's Disease to food-borne illnesses to exposure to dioxin or DDT. Trustworthy science that can help us prevent harm before it happens. For, as we physicians know, prevention is usually the best cure.

One of the giants of American medicine, Dr. William Osler, proposed using preventive medicine against serious public health threats like malaria and yellow fever. And the tools he advocated—education, organization and cooperation—sound like a pretty good definition of diplomacy to me. We will put these same tools to use in removing the threat of gun violence from our society.

As we have in the past, we have already sought the cooperation of the American Bar Association—and we are grateful that our invitation has been accepted. We will be working with the ABA on their Forum on Justice Improvements, taking place this October in Washington D.C. The forum, set up by their Justice Initiatives Group, will focus on gun violence.

We are being advised by a panel of physicians and other experts, who have worked long and hard in tackling the many-headed monster of gun violence and its grisly outcomes. They have welcomed our involvement in this issue and look forward to a newly configured playing field with allies that command such clout as the ABA and the AMA.

People have told me that this is a dangerous path to follow. That I am crazy to do it. That I am putting our organization in jeopardy. They say we'll lose members. They say we'll be the target of smear campaigns. They say that the most extremist of the gun supporters will seek to destroy us. But I believe that this is a battle we cannot not take on.

While there are indeed risks—the far greater risk for the health of the public, for us in this room, and for the AMA, is to do nothing. We, as physicians, and as the American Medical Association, have an ethical and moral responsibility to do this—as our mission statement says—"to promote the science

41

and art of medicine and the betterment of public health." If removing the scourge of gun violence isn't bettering the public health—what is? As physicians, we are accustomed to doing what is right for our patients—and not worrying about our comfort, ease or popularity. Our goal is to help cure an epidemic, not to win a victory over some real or imagined political enemy. Anyone who helps us in this fight is an ally—anyone.

We don't pretend to have all the answers. Nor do we expect the solution to be quick—and we certainly don't expect it to be easy. In fact, I am certain that we will not reach the solution during my term as your president. But, together as the American Medical Association—guided by our stated mission—we recognize our obligation to contribute our voice, our effort and our moral imperative to this battle. And we will.

Almost a century ago, in his book Confessio Medici, Stephen Paget, the British physician and author, referred to medicine as a divine vocation. This is part of what he said:

"Every year young people enter the medical profession… and they stick to it… not only from necessity, but from pride, honor, and conviction. And Heaven, sooner or later, lets them know what it thinks of them. This information comes quite as a surprise to them… that they were indeed called to be doctors.… Surely a diploma… obtained by hard work… cannot be a summons from Heaven. But it may be. For, if a doctor's life may not be a divine vocation, then no life is a vocation, and nothing is divine."

We are here today as the guardians of that divine vocation and as such are dedicated to do what is right, whether or not it is comfortable, whether or not it is easy, and whether or not it is popular. Stephen Paget, you can rest well tonight. Your divine vocation is in good hands. We will guard it well. We will live up to our mission—we will do what is right.

Thank you.

From *Vital Speeches of the Day,* August 1, 2001, pp. 610-615. © 2001 by City News Publishing Company, Inc.

SPECIAL REPORT

THE WAR ON ADDICTION

ABUSE IN AMERICA: Fresh research and shifting views of treatment are opening new fronts in a deadly struggle.

By Jonathan Alter

MAYBE YOU'VE SEEN THE MOVIE: DAD, AN OHIO judge and the nation's new drug czar, needs a cocktail to "take the edge off." Mom has her own youthful history with drugs and scoffs at Dad's suggestion that she was just "experimenting." Their 16-year-old daughter, a lovely straight-A student at a fancy private school, starts freebasing cocaine, then turns tricks to pay for her habit.

Whatever happens next month at the Oscars, the movie "Traffic" is a cinematic IV injection—a jolting reminder of the horrors of drugs and the drug war. After a campaign in which both parties all but ignored the drug issue, director Steven Soderbergh manages the nearly impossible feat of illuminating a national debate without taking sides (both reformers and hard-liners like the movie), beyond attaching a patina of hopelessness to the whole issue.

Actually, the future may not be quite as bleak as the film suggests. While policy revolutions—like legalizing narcotics or somehow eradicating supply—are pipe dreams, change is coming to the world of addiction and drug policy. Voters in several states are far ahead of the politicians, approving ballot initiatives that offer more treatment options. "Drug courts" that allow judges to impose substance-abuse treatment in place of jail have grown fiftyfold since the mid-1990s, part of a new understanding that, even with frequent relapses, treatment is much less expensive for society than prison and interdiction. All of the former drug czars as well as the man rumored to be President Bush's choice for the job, retired Col. James McDonough, stress treatment and demand-

side reduction as their first priority, though the funding decisions have yet to catch up to the new rhetoric.

More broadly, this relatively peaceful interlude in the nation's drug history (half as many regular drug users as in 1979 and the crack epidemic ebbing) offers a rare chance to rethink old approaches not just to renewed threats like heroin but to the mother of all abused substances—alcohol. Science is yielding clues about the "hedonic region" of the brain, while breakthrough medications and greater understanding of the mental-health problems that underlie many addictions are giving therapists new tools.

DRUG CULTURES
Stars become inmates; generals decry war. Even Hollywood can't write an ending to the substance-abuse story.

Addiction is hardly an American affliction, but it sometimes looks that way. The master narrative of public life these days seems to be all about abuse and recovery, with inner demons replacing outer enemies or forces of nature as the dramatic foils of choice. After leaving drug rehab, Jennifer Capriati stages an improbable tennis comeback to win the Australian Open. Robert Downey Jr. relapses once again, a haunting symbol of the limits of treatment. The departing president of the United States appears to have been addicted to sex, while the new president—by his own account—once had a drinking problem.

In the real America, the toll is incalculable. Consider Areina Garcia, 34, mother of four children ages 1, 2, 4 and 7. She admits she was "selling my ass for drugs" and getting high in front of her kids. She didn't stop until her husband reported her to family court. Or Brian Kelly, 31, who started drinking at 8 while tailgating with his alcoholic parents at Notre Dame games. His crack habit landed him in a $14,000-a-month "country club" treatment program with a pool, tennis courts and nothing but what he calls "appeasement" of his problem. Now both Garcia and Kelly are midway through a no-nonsense, 12- to 15-month residential treatment program at Phoenix House, still at real risk of relapse, but with at least a fighting chance to salvage their lives.

The aggregate consequences of addiction are staggering. Consider that the number of inmates in American prisons more than tripled over the last 20 years to nearly 2 million, with 60 percent to 70 percent testing positive for substance abuse on arrest. These inmates are the parents of 2.4 million children, all of whom are disproportionately likely to follow their parents to jail. According to the exponential math of a Brown University study, if the prison population were to continue growing at the current rate, by 2053 the United States would actually have more people in prison than out.

Even greatly expanded prison capacity that consumes billions can't accommodate this flow. So over the next few years, as sentences from the high-crime 1980s are completed and reform of drugs laws accelerates, hundreds of thousands of offenders will be released or sentenced more leniently. Hard-core addicts in some jurisdictions are estimated to commit 100 petty crimes each per year. If their substance-abuse problems aren't addressed, the country will face another crime wave soon.

Even hard-liners in the war on drugs like to say that we can no longer incarcerate our way out of the problem

In an attempt to break the vicious cycle, drug addiction is increasingly being viewed more as a disease than a crime. (Drug trafficking is a different matter.) California approved Proposition 36 last fall, a landmark referendum that offers treatment options in place of jail for nonviolent offenders. New York is rewriting its draconian Rockefeller-era drug laws. The outgoing drug czar, retired Gen. Barry McCaffrey, says the phrase "drug war" should be retired in favor of "drug cancer." The straight-talking military man has little to say about interdiction. His No. 1 recommendation on leaving office last month was that insurance companies offer the same level of coverage for mental-health and drug disorders as they do for any other illness. This is unlikely (managed care has led to lower reimbursements for treatments). But even hard-liners are beginning to say that we can no longer incarcerate our way out of the problem.

OF COURSE OLD HABITS DIE HARD. WASHINGTON still directs two thirds of the federal drug budget (including $1.1 billion in military aid to Colombia) to law enforcement, while state legislatures—leery of seeming to coddle criminals—lag behind public opinion on funding treatment. So-called harm-reduction strategies like needle exchanges (common in Europe) have a tough time winning approval, despite many studies proving that they save lives. The new attorney general, John Ashcroft, has opposed not just needle exchanges, but a taxpayer-supported media campaign aimed at teens. The early signs are that the Bush team will essentially maintain the status quo on drug policy.

Even so, a "third way" consensus between liberals and conservatives is emerging, especially at the local level where the real money is spent. It combines flexible enforcement with mandatory treatment. The drug-court idea, which comes with strong backing from most prosecutors, is sometimes known as "coercive abstinence"—using the threat of jail to motivate substance abusers to get help. "The real, nut-cutting issue is motivation," says Joseph Califano, chairman of the National Center on Addiction and Substance Abuse. The research shows that those forced into treatment do at least as well as addicts who enroll voluntarily—often better, because they must stay in therapy longer or risk reincarceration. In all recovery programs, the best predictor of success is the length of treatment. While relapse is common, those who remain at least a year are more than twice as likely to stay clean.

So drug-treatment experts now often favor the "big foot" of law enforcement. "The legalizers don't understand the psychodynamics of addiction," says Dr. George De Leon, author of the National Institute on Drug Abuse's most thorough study of treatment. "The nature of the disorder is that the client is resistant to treatment." This suggests the need for intensive drug treatment not only in jail, where addicts are a captive audience, but after release, with sentences shortened in exchange for successful enrollment. Drug-court judges use carrots (gift certificates; the promise of fewer court dates) and sticks (return to jail) to change behavior.

Drug-policy reformers like Ethan Nadelman of the Lindesmith Center don't buy the approach: "Alcoholics don't have coerced treatment," Nadelman says. "So why should drug abusers?" But those who actually provide treatment say they have fewer empty beds when the courts are involved. They worry that California's Proposition 36 doesn't do enough to compel long-term treatment. Addicts will "get kind of a driver's-ed course in drugs that isn't going to force them to take a self-inventory and change themselves," says Dr. Mitchell Rosenthal, founder of Phoenix House, which operates residential-treatment centers in eight states.

Rosenthal says Phoenix House has relied on the criminal-justice system for its recent growth spurt. As in all treatment, the vast majority drop out before completing the program, but those who make it through the whole year have a surprisingly good prognosis. The research shows that about three quarters of those who graduate from 12-month residential programs are employed, drug-free and not in jail five years later. The results for in-prison programs and outpatient therapy are worse than for long-term residential care, but there, too, the key variable is length of treatment.

At the same time, all but the fanciest 28-day residential programs are less expensive than prison, and outpatient care is much cheaper. Even when you throw in the costs of the drug court, the total expense is less than half as much as jail, and the results are far more effective. Inmates assigned to drug courts in Los Angeles and Washington, D.C., were 30 percent less likely to be rearrested than those who went through conventional courts—a huge savings to society. In another survey, only about 10 percent of those under drug-court supervision tested positive for drugs; for those in regular probation, the "dirty urine" figures were one third.

Meanwhile, hundreds of laws remain on the books that make it hard to treat substance abuse as a public-health matter. Consider heroin addiction. In nine American cities, men 20 to 54 are more likely to die of a heroin overdose than in a car accident. But courts won't often authorize methadone treatment, and junkies routinely fail to report overdoses to the authorities for fear of being arrested. In "Traffic," the kids leave their overdosed friend at the hospital and run—a common response.

IN NEW MEXICO, WHERE GOP GOV. GARY JOHNSON is an outspoken drug reformer, the authorities are trying a new harm-reduction strategy to fight overdoses. Last month New Mexico doctors began giving addicts sy-

ringes full of Narcan, an easy-to-inject medication that counteracts the heroin, often saving lives. One test of the new public mood on drug-policy reform will be if other states follow suit.

New York is beginning to reassess its tough drug laws, which date from the 1970s. Last month Gov. George Pataki, once a major hard-liner, proposed cutting the minimum sentences for serious drug felons from 15 years to eight and giving judges more discretion. In reviewing the clemency process, Pataki says he found "dramatically unfair sentences—people sentenced to 15 years when their involvement was minimal." But at the federal level, so-called mandatory minimum sentencing requirements are in no danger of being repealed any time soon.

Spending priorities right now look pound foolish. The Center on Addiction and Substance Abuse released a study last week showing that states spend more than 13 percent of their total budgets just "shoveling up" the wreckage of addiction—as much as they appropriate for higher education and 100 times what they spend on prevention and treatment. Another study by Rand Corp. shows that every dollar spent on treatment saves seven dollars in services. That's because even if addicts eventually relapse, they are clean during their time in treatment, saving millions in acute health-care costs and law enforcement.

For all its promise, treatment remains a spit in the ocean of national substance abuse. Phoenix House, the nation's largest network of treatment centers, has only about 5,000 residents—out of more than a million people arrested every year on drug-related charges. California's Proposition 36 will fund 10,000 new treatment slots. But that's out of 160,000 inmates who need it. While drug courts are multiplying fast, they still make up a tiny percentage of all criminal courts. In other words, like treating addiction, changing national drug policy will take patience, commitment and time. All we know for sure is that we have no choice but to try.

With Michael Isikoff, Mark Hosenball
and Suzanne Smalley

UNIT 3

Groups and Roles in Transition

Unit Selections

Key Points to Consider

- Is the family in America in crisis? What indicators of family health have worsened, and what indicators have improved?

- What are the major contributions of father-child interactions in the development of children?

- What factors are influencing women's roles today? How are they changing women's lives?

- When marriages are working badly, should the couple stay together for the kids?

- Is the American male in crisis? If so, why?

- What factors create community? How can it be brought into being under today's conditions? What are the impediments to community? What are the consequences of weak communities? Does the Internet strengthen community?

 **Links: www.dushkin.com/online/**
These sites are annotated in the World Wide Web pages.

The Gallup Organization
http://www.gallup.com

Grass-Roots.org
http://www.iglou.com/why/ria.htm

The North-South Institute
http://www.nsi-ins.ca/ensi/index.html

PsychNet/American Psychological Association
http://www.apa.org/psychnet/

SocioSite: Feminism and Woman Issues
http://www.pscw.uva.nl/sociosite/TOPICS/Women.html

Primary groups are small, intimate, spontaneous, and personal. In contrast, secondary groups are large, formal, and impersonal. Primary groups include the family, couples, gangs, cliques, teams, and small tribes or rural villages. Primary groups are the main sources that the individual draws upon in developing values and an identity. Secondary groups include most of the organizations and bureaucracies in a modern society and carry out most of its instrumental functions. Often primary groups are formed within secondary groups such as a factory, school, or business.

Urbanization, geographic mobility, centralization, bureaucratization, and other aspects of modernization have had an impact on the nature of groups, the quality of the relationships between people, and individuals' feelings of belonging. The family, in particular, has undergone radical transformation. The greatly increased participation of women in the paid labor force and their increased careerism have led to severe conflicts for women between their work and family roles.

The first subsection of this unit deals with marriage and family in the context of dramatic changes in the culture and the economy. Everyone seems to agree that the family is in trouble, but Stephanie Coontz challenges this viewpoint in the first article in this subsection. She takes issue with the data presented for the decline of marriage thesis and offers evidence that marriage is strong today even though divorce is common. In fact, she argues that today's families are better than families a century ago in many ways. According to Coontz "the biggest problem facing most families… is not that our families have changed too much but that our institutions have changed too little." Another recent trend is for women not to rush into marriage. If this trend reduces the number of bad marriages, and therefore divorces, it is a very beneficial trend, according to Walter Kirn, who, in the next article, reviews the debate over whether a bad marriage or divorce is more harmful for the children. The evidence shows that both are bad for children.

The next subsection focuses on sexual behavior and gender roles. In "Now for the Truth About Americans and Sex," Philip Elmer-Dewitt reviews a recent national survey of American sexual behavior and corrects many common misimpressions. He points out, among other things, that Americans are more sexually faithful to their spouses than is commonly perceived. The next article in this subsection is Susan Faludi's sympathetic portrayal of the untenable situation of modern American men, which is that their condition contradicts their male role. Masculinity means being dominant and in control, but most men are neither. This contradiction is the clue to the mysterious crisis of the American male.

The last subsection of unit 3 looks at cities and communities. The first article in the unit deals with how cities are reviving after years of relative decline during which they had been gaining the poor and losing the rich. The traditional advantage of cities was their location benefits for manufacturing, but new technologies have greatly reduced these benefits. Now the main advantage of cities is their location benefits for services and for consumption. Many people think that certain cities are great places to live because they contain so many things to enjoy. The final article focuses on a new kind of community—the Internet. The decline of many kinds of community over the past few decades gives urgency to the question, "Does the Internet Strengthen Community?" William Galston argues that the Internet greatly expands choice and that one of the costs of the expansion of choice is that "the bonds linking us to others tend to weaken" and thereby "trigger an acute sense of loss, now expressed as a longing for community." Autonomy and bonding are somewhat incompatible. Galston also presents a sophisticated analysis of network communities and explains how they do not limit autonomy but also fail to achieve community.

THE AMERICAN FAMILY

New research about an old institution challenges the conventional wisdom that the family today is worse off than in the past. Essay by Stephanie Coontz

As the century comes to an end, many observers fear for the future of America's families. Our divorce rate is the highest in the world, and the percentage of unmarried women is significantly higher than in 1960. Educated women are having fewer babies, while immigrant children flood the schools, demanding to be taught in their native language. Harvard University reports that only 4 percent of its applicants can write a proper sentence.

Things were worse at the turn of the last century than they are today. Most workers labored 10 hours a day, six days a week, leaving little time for family life.

There's an epidemic of sexually transmitted diseases among men. Many streets in urban neighborhoods are littered with cocaine vials. Youths call heroin "happy dust." Even in small towns, people have easy access to addictive drugs, and drug abuse by middle-class wives is skyrocketing. Police see 16-year-old killers, 12-year-old prostitutes, and gang members as young as 11.

America at the end of the 1990s? No, America at the end of the 1890s.

The litany of complaints may sound familiar, but the truth is that many things were worse at the start of this century than they are today. Then, thousands of children worked full-time in mines, mills and sweatshops. Most

workers labored 10 hours a day, often six days a week, which left them little time or energy for family life. Race riots were more frequent and more deadly than those experienced by recent generations. Women couldn't vote, and their wages were so low that many turned to prostitution.

DAHLSTROM COLLECTION/TIME INC.

c. 1890 A couple and their six children sit for a family portrait. With smaller families today, mothers spend twice as much time with each kid.

In 1900 a white child had one chance in three of losing a brother or sister before age 15, and a black child had a fifty-fifty chance of seeing a sibling die. Children's-aid groups reported widespread abuse and neglect by parents. Men who deserted or divorced their wives rarely paid child support. And only 6 percent of the children graduated from high school, compared with 88 percent today.

LEWIS HINE/CULVER PICTURES

1915 An Italian immigrant family gathers around the dinner table in an apartment on the East Side of New York City. Today, most families still eat together—but often out.

Why do so many people think American families are facing worse problems now than in the past? Partly it's because we compare the complex and diverse families of the 1990s with the seemingly more standard-issue ones of the 1950s, a unique decade when every long-term trend of the 20th century was temporarily reversed. In the 1950s, for the first time in 100 years, the divorce rate fell while marriage and fertility rates soared, crating a boom in nuclear-family living. The percentage of foreign-born individuals in the country decreased. And the debates over social and cultural issues that had divided Americans for 150 years were silenced, suggesting a national consensus on family values and norms.

Some nostalgia for the 1950s is understandable: Life looked pretty good in comparison with the hardship of the Great Depression and World War II. The GI Bill gave a generation of young fathers a college education and a subsidized mortgage on a new house. For the first time, a majority of men could support a family and buy a home without pooling their earnings with those of other family members. Many Americans built a stable family life on these foundations.

But much nostalgia for the 1950s is a result of selective amnesia—the same process that makes childhood memories of summer vacations grow sunnier with each passing year. The superficial sameness of 1950s family life was achieved through censorship, coercion and discrimination. People with unconventional beliefs faced governmental investigation and arbitrary firings. African Americans and Mexican Americans were prevented from voting in some states by literacy tests that were not administered to whites. Individuals who didn't follow the rigid gender and sexual rules of the day were ostracized.

Leave It to Beaver did not reflect the real-life experience of most American families. While many moved into the middle class during the 1950s, poverty remained more widespread than in the worst of our last three recessions. More children went hungry, and poverty rates for the elderly were more than twice as high as today's.

Even in the white middle class, not every woman was as serenely happy with her lot as June Cleaver was on TV. Housewives of the 1950s may have been less rushed than today's working mothers, but they were more likely to suffer anxiety and depression. In many states, women couldn't serve on juries or get loans or credit cards in their own names.

And not every kid was as wholesome as Beaver Cleaver, whose mischievous antics could be handled by Dad at the dinner table. In 1955 alone, Congress discussed 200 bills aimed at curbing juvenile delinquency. Three years later, LIFE reported that urban teachers were being terrorized by their students. The drugs that were so freely available in 1900 had been outlawed, but many children grew up in families ravaged by alcohol and barbiturate abuse.

Rates of unwed childbearing tripled between 1940 and 1958, but most Americans didn't notice because unwed mothers generally left town, gave their babies up for adoption and returned home as if nothing had happened. Troubled youths were encouraged to drop out of high school. Mentally handicapped children were warehoused in institutions like the Home for Idiotic and Imbecilic Children in Kansas, where a woman whose sister had lived there for most of the 1950s once took me. Wives routinely told pollsters that being disparaged or ignored by their husbands was a normal part of a happier than-average marriage.

Many of our worries today reflect how much better we want to be, not how much better we used to be.

Denial extended to other areas of life as well. In the early 1900s, doctors refused to believe that the cases of gonorrhea and syphilis they saw in young girls could have been caused by sexual abuse. Instead, they reasoned, girls could get these diseases from toilet seats, a myth that terrified generations of mothers and daughters. In the 1950s, psychiatrists dismissed incest reports as Oedipal fantasies on the part of children.

Spousal rape was legal throughout the period and wife beating was not taken seriously by authorities. Much of what we now label child abuse was accepted as a normal part of parental discipline. Physicians saw no reason to question parents who claimed that their child's broken bones had been caused by a fall from a tree.

MARGARET BOURKE-WHITE

1937: The Hahn family sits in the living room of a working-class Muncie home, which rents for $10 a month. Class distinctions have eroded over 60 years.

American Mirror

Muncie, Ind. (pop. 67,476), calls itself America's Hometown. But to generations of sociologists it is better known as America's Middletown—the most studied place in the 20th century American landscape. "Muncie has nothing extraordinary about it," says University of Virginia professor Theodore Caplow, which is why, for the past 75 years, researchers have gone there to observe the typical American family. Muncie's averageness first drew sociologists Robert and Helen Lynd in 1924. They returned in 1935 (their follow-up study was featured in a LIFE photo essay by Margaret Bourke-White). And in 1976, armed with the Lynds' original questionnaires, Caplow launched yet another survey of the town's citizens.

Caplow discovered that family life in Muncie was much healthier in the 1970s than in the 1920s. No only were husbands and wives communicating more, but unlike married couples in the 1920s, they were also shopping, eating out, exercising and going to movies and concerts together. More than 90 percent of Muncie's couples characterized their marriages as "happy" or "very happy." In 1929 the Lynds had described partnerships of a drearier kind, "marked by sober accommodation of each partner to his share in the joint undertaking of children, paying off the mortgage and generally 'getting on.' "

Caplow's five-year study, which inspired a six-part PBS series, found that even though more moms were working outside the home, two thirds of them spent at least two hours a day with their children; in 1924 fewer than half did. In 1924 most children expected their mothers to be good cooks and housekeepers, and wanted their fathers to spend time with them and respect their opinions. Fifty years later, expectations of fathers were unchanged, but children wanted the same—time and respect—from their mothers.

This year, Caplow went back to survey the town again. The results (and another TV documentary) won't be released until December 2000.

—Sora Song

There are plenty of stresses in modern family life, but one reason they seem worse is that we no longer sweep them under the rug. Another is that we have higher expectations of parenting and marriage. That's a good thing. We're right to be concerned about inattentive parents, conflicted marriages, antisocial values, teen violence and child abuse. But we need to realize that many of our worries reflect how much better we *want* to be, not how much better we *used* to be.

Fathers in intact families are spending more time with their children than at any other point in the past 100 years. Although the number of hours the average woman spends at home with her children has declined since the early 1900s, there has been a decrease in the number of children per family and an increase in individual attention to each child. As a result, mothers today, including working moms, spend almost twice as much time with each child as mothers did in the 1920s. People who raised children in the 1940s and 1950s typically report that their own adult children and grandchildren communicate far better with their kids and spend more time helping with homework than they did—even as they complain that other parents today are doing a worse job than in the past.

Despite the rise in youth violence from the 1960s to the early 1990s, America's children are also safer now than they've ever been. An infant was four times more likely to die in the 1950s than today. A parent then was three times more likely than a modern one to preside at the funeral of a child under the age of 15, and 27 percent more likely to lose an older teen to death.

If we look back over the last millennium, we can see that families have always been diverse and in flux. In each period, families have solved one set of problems only to face a new array of challenges. What works for a family in one economic and cultural setting doesn't work for a family in another. What's helpful at one stage of a family's life may be destructive at the next stage. If there is one lesson to be drawn from the last millennium of family history, it's that families are always having to play catch-up with a changing world.

Take the issue of working mothers. Families in which mothers spend as much time earning a living as they do raising children are nothing new. They were the norm throughout most of the last two millennia. In the 19th century, married women in the United States began a withdrawal from the workforce, but for most families this was made possible only by sending their children out to work instead. When child labor was abolished, married women began reentering the workforce in ever large numbers.

For a few decades, the decline in child labor was greater than the growth of women's employment. The result was an aberration: the male-breadwinner family. In the 1920s, for the first time, a bare majority of American children grew up in families where the husband provided all the income, the wife stayed home full-time, and they and their siblings went to school instead of work. During the 1950s, almost two thirds of children grew up in such

MARK KAUFFMAN

1955 A family poses in Seattle. Husbands today are doing more housework.

increase from 1900 to 1950. Today, 40 percent of all marriages will end in divorce before a couple's 40th anniversary. Yet despite this high divorce rate, expanded life expectancies mean that more couples are reaching that anniversary than ever before.

Families and individuals in contemporary America have more life choices than in the past. That makes it easier for some to consider dangerous or unpopular options. But it also makes success easier for many families that never would have had a chance before—interracial, gay or lesbian, and single-mother families, for example. And it expands horizons for most families.

Women's new options are good not just for themselves but for their children. While some people say that women who choose to work are selfish, it turns out that maternal self-sacrifice is not good for children. Kids do better when their mothers are happy with their lives, whether their satisfaction comes from being a full-time homemaker or from having a job.

Largely because of women's new roles at work, men are doing more at home. Although most men still do less housework than their wives, the gap has been halved since the 1960s. Today, 49 percent of couples say they share childcare equally, compared with 25 percent of 1985.

Men's greater involvement at home is good for their relationships with their parents, and also good for their children. Hands-on fathers make better parents than men who let their wives do all the nurturing and childcare: They raise sons who are more expressive and daughters who are more likely to do well in school, especially in math and science.

The biggest problem is not that our families have changed too much but that our institutions have changed too little.

In 1900, life expectancy was 47 years, and only 4 percent of the population was 65 or older. Today, life expectancy is 76 years, and by 2025, about 20 percent of Americans will be 65 or older. For the first time, a generation of adults must plan for the needs of both their parents and their children. Most Americans are responding with remarkable grace. One in four households gives the equivalent of a full day a week or more in unpaid care to an aging relative, and more than half say they expect to do so in the next 10 years. Older people are less likely to be impoverished or incapacitated by illness than in the past, and they have more opportunity to develop a relationship with their grandchildren.

Even some of the choices that worry us the most are turning out to be manageable. Divorce rates are likely to remain high, but more non-custodial parents are staying

families, an all-time high. Yet that same decade saw an acceleration of workforce participation by wives and mothers that soon made the dual-earner family the norm, a trend not likely to be reversed in the next century.

What's new is not that women make half their families' living, but that for the first time they have substantial control over their own income, along with the social freedom to remain single or to leave an unsatisfactory marriage. Also new is the declining proportion of their lives that people devote to rearing children, both because they have fewer kids and because they are living longer. Until about 1940, the typical marriage was broken by the death of one partner within a few years after the last child left home. Today, couples can look forward to spending more than two decades together after the children leave.

The growing length of time partners spend with only each other for company has made many individuals less willing to put up with an unhappy marriage, while women's economic independence makes it less essential for them to do so. It is no wonder that divorce has risen steadily since 1900. Disregarding a spurt in 1946, a dip in the 1950s and another peak around 1980, the divorce rate is just where you'd expect to find it, based on the rate of in touch with their children. Child-support receipts are up. And a lower proportion of kids from divorced families are exhibiting problems than in earlier decades. Step-families are learning to maximize children's access to supportive adults rather than cutting them off from one side of the family.

Out-of-wedlock births are also high, however, and this will probably continue because the age of first marriage for women has risen to an all-time high of 25, almost five years above what it was in the 1950s. Women who marry at an older age are less likely to divorce, but they have more years when they are at risk—or at choice—for a nonmarital birth.

Nevertheless, births to teenagers have fallen from 50 percent of all nonmarital births in the late 1970s to just 30 percent today. A growing proportion of women who have a nonmarital birth are in their twenties and thirties and usually have more economic and educational resources than unwed mothers of the past. While two involved parents are generally better than one, a mother's personal maturity, along with her educational and economic status, is a better predictor of how well her child will turn out than her marital status. We should no longer assume that children raised by single parents face debilitating disadvantages.

As we begin to understand the range of sizes, shapes and colors that today's families come in, we find that the differences *within* family types are more important than the differences *between* them. No particular family form guarantees success, and no particular form is doomed to fail. How a family functions on the inside is more important than how it looks from the outside.

The biggest problem facing most families as this century draws to a close is not that our families have changed too much but that our institutions have changed too little. America's work policies are 50 years out of date, designed for a time when most moms weren't in the workforce and most dads didn't understand the joys of being involved in childcare. Our school schedules are 150 years out of date, designed for a time when kids needed to be home to help with the milking and haying. And many political leaders feel they have to decide whether to help parents stay home longer with their kids or invest in better childcare, preschool and afterschool programs, when most industrialized nations have long since learned it's possible to do both.

So America's social institutions have some Y2K bugs to iron out. But for the most part, our families are ready for the next millennium.

SHOULD YOU STAY TOGETHER FOR THE KIDS?

A controversial book argues that the damage from divorce is serious and lasting, but many argue that the remedy of parents staying hitched is worse than the ailment

By WALTER KIRN

ONE AFTERNOON WHEN JOANNE WAS nine years old she came home from school and noticed something missing. Her father's jewelry box had disappeared from its usual spot on her parents' bureau. Worse, her mother was still in bed. "Daddy's moved out," her mother told her. Joanne panicked. She began to sob. And even though Joanne is 40 now, a married Los Angeles homemaker with children of her own, she clearly remembers what she did next that day. Her vision blurred by tears, she searched through the house that was suddenly not a home for the jewelry box that wasn't there.

Time heals all wounds, they say. For children of divorce like Joanne, though, time has a way of baring old wounds too. For Joanne, the fears that her parents' split unleashed—of abandonment, of loss, of coming home one day and noticing something missing from the bedroom—deepened as the years went by. Bursts of bitterness, jealousy and doubt sent her into psychotherapy. "Before I met my husband," she remembers, "I sabotaged all my other relationships with men because I as-

sumed they would fail. There was always something in the back of my head. The only way I can describe it is a void, unfinished business that I couldn't get to."

For America's children of divorce—a million new ones every year—unfinished business is a way of life. For adults, divorce is a conclusion, but for children it's the beginning of uncertainty. Where will I live? Will I see my friends again? Will my mom's new boyfriend leave her too? Going back to the early '70s—the years that demographers mark as the beginning of a divorce boom that has receded only slightly despite three decades of hand wringing and worry—society has debated these children's predicament in much the same way that angry parents do: by arguing over the little ones' heads or quarreling out of earshot, behind closed doors. Whenever concerned adults talk seriously about what's best for the children of divorce, they seem to hold the discussion in a setting—a courtroom or legislature or university—where young folks aren't allowed.

That's changing. The children are grown now, and a number are speaking up,

telling stories of pain that didn't go away the moment they turned 18 or even 40. A cluster of new books is fueling a backlash, not against divorce itself but against the notion that kids somehow coast through it. Stephanie Staal's *The Love They Lost* (Delacorte Press), written by a child of divorce, is part memoir and part generational survey, a melancholy volume about the search for love by kids who remember the loss of love too vividly. *The Case for Marriage* by Linda Waite and Maggie Gallagher (Doubleday) emphasizes the positive, arguing that even rocky marriages nourish children emotionally and practically.

The most controversial book, comes from Judith Wallerstein, 78, a therapist and retired lecturer at the University of California, Berkeley. In *The Unexpected Legacy of Divorce* (Hyperion) she argues that the harm caused by divorce is graver and longer lasting than we suspected. Her work raises a question that some folks felt was settled back in the days of *Love, American Style*: Should parents stay together for the kids?

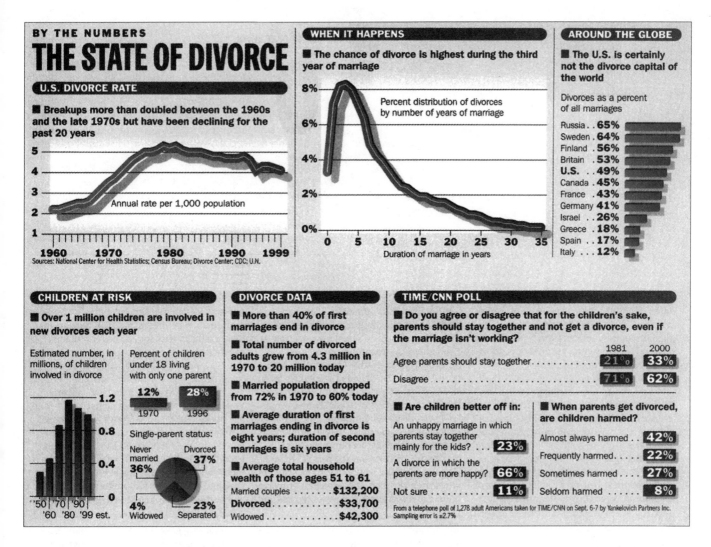

BY THE NUMBERS

THE STATE OF DIVORCE

U.S. DIVORCE RATE

■ Breakups more than doubled between the 1960s and the late 1970s but have been declining for the past 20 years

Annual rate per 1,000 population

1960 1970 1980 1990 1999

Sources: National Center for Health Statistics; Census Bureau; Divorce Center; CDC; U.N.

WHEN IT HAPPENS

■ The chance of divorce is highest during the third year of marriage

Percent distribution of divorces by number of years of marriage

Duration of marriage in years

AROUND THE GLOBE

■ The U.S. is certainly not the divorce capital of the world

Divorces as a percent of all marriages

Russia . . **65%**
Sweden . **64%**
Finland . **56%**
Britain . **53%**
U.S. . . **49%**
Canada . **45%**
France . **43%**
Germany **41%**
Israel . . **26%**
Greece . **18%**
Spain . . **17%**
Italy . . . **12%**

CHILDREN AT RISK

■ Over 1 million children are involved in new divorces each year

Estimated number, in millions, of children involved in divorce

'50 '70 '90
'60 '80 '99 est.

Percent of children under 18 living with only one parent

12% 1970   **28%** 1996

Single-parent status:

Never married **36%**   Divorced **37%**

4% Widowed   **23%** Separated

DIVORCE DATA

■ More than 40% of first marriages end in divorce

■ Total number of divorced adults grew from 4.3 million in 1970 to 20 million today

■ Married population dropped from 72% in 1970 to 60% today

■ Average duration of first marriages ending in divorce is eight years; duration of second marriages is six years

■ Average total household wealth of those ages 51 to 61

Married couples $132,200
Divorced $33,700
Widowed $42,300

TIME/CNN POLL

■ Do you agree or disagree that for the children's sake, parents should stay together and not get a divorce, even if the marriage isn't working?

	1981	2000
Agree parents should stay together	21%	33%
Disagree	71%	62%

■ Are children better off in:

An unhappy marriage in which parents stay together mainly for the kids? . . . **23%**

A divorce in which the parents are more happy? **66%**

Not sure **11%**

■ When parents get divorced, are children harmed?

Almost always harmed . . **42%**
Frequently harmed **22%**
Sometimes harmed **27%**
Seldom harmed **8%**

From a telephone poll of 1,278 adult Americans taken for TIME/CNN on Sept. 6-7 by Yankelovich Partners Inc. Sampling error is ±2.7%

Listening to children from broken families is Wallerstein's lifework. For nearly three decades, in her current book and two previous ones, she has compiled and reflected on the stories of 131 children of divorce. Based on lengthy, in-depth interviews, the stories are seldom happy. Some are tragic. Almost all of them are as moving as good fiction. There's the story of Paula, who as a girl told Wallerstein, "I'm going to find a new mommy," and as a young woman—too young, it turned out—impulsively married a man she hardly knew. There's Billy, born with a heart defect, whose parents parted coolly and amicably but failed to provide for his pressing medical needs.

It's the rare academic who can make a reader cry. Maybe that's why, with each new installment, Wallerstein's study has created shock waves, shaping public opinion and even the law. Her attention-getting style has proved divisive. For experts in the field of family studies (who tend to quarrel at least as bitterly as the dysfunc-

tional clans they analyze), she's a polarizing figure. To her admirers, this mother of three and grandmother of five, who has been married to the same man for 53 years, is a brave, compassionate voice in the wilderness. To her detractors, she's a melodramatic doomsayer, a crank.

What drew someone from such a stable background to the study of marital distress? At the end of the 1960s, Wallerstein, whose Ph.D. is in clinical psychology, moved from Topeka, Kans., in the ho-hum heartland, to swinging California. "Divorce was almost unheard of in the Midwest," she recalls. Not so on the Gold Coast, the state had just passed its pioneering no-fault divorce law. Wallerstein took a job consulting at a large community mental-health center in Marin County just as the social dam began to crack. "We started to get complaints," she says," from nursery school teachers and parents: 'Our children are having a very hard time. What should we do?'"

The prevailing view at the time, she says, was that divorce was no big deal for

kids. So much for the power of positive thinking. "We began to get all these questions," Wallerstein remembers. "The children were sleepless. The children in the nursery school were aggressive. They were out of control." When Wallerstein hit the library for answers, she discovered there were none. The research hardly existed, so she decided to do her own. She had a hunch about what she would learn. "I saw a lot of children very upset," she says, "but I fully expected that it would be fleeting."

Her hunch was wrong. Paradise for kids from ruptured families wasn't easily regained. Once cast out of the domestic garden, kids dreamed of getting back in. The result more often than not was frustration and anxiety. Children of divorce suffer depression, learning difficulties and other psychological problems more frequently than those of intact families. Some of Wallerstein's colleagues, not to mention countless divorced parents, felt they were being guilt-tripped by a square. They didn't want to hear this somber news.

DIVORCE/THE DEBATE

"We have to pay attention to what Judy Wallerstein says... It's another reason not to be sanguine about what happens to children following divorce and not to cling to this 1970s opinion that it's no big deal, they'll bounce back, just be happy yourself."
—BARBARA DAFOE WHITEHEAD, *author of* The Divorce Culture: Rethinking Our Commitments to Marriage and Family

"I think [Wallerstein] is wonderful at seeing the trees, but sometimes she misses the forest. For the most part, kids from divorced families are resilient. They bounce back from all the stresses. Some kids are at risk, but the majority are functioning well."
—ROBERT EMERY, *director of the University of Virginia's Center for Children, Families and the Law*

"[My parents] tried to stick it out for an extra year. That year was horrible... It's really devastating when your parents divorce. But it doesn't automatically mean that I wish my parents were still together. People who haven't gone through parental divorce don't really understand that."
—STEPHANIE STAAL, *author of* The Love They Lost: Living with the Legacy of Our Parents' Divorce

"I think the kids are better off if divorce is handled intelligently—that is, if both parents talk to the kids, explain what it is. Let's say each party remarries. The children get the benefit of now four adults in their life, instead of two. If everything works well, the kids benefit."
—LARRY KING, *five-times-divorced TV talk-show host*

Every marriage waxes and wanes... So thinking about getting divorced when things are awful is in some ways a short-sighted view. You're cutting off your foot because you have an ingrown toenail."
—LINDA WAITE, *co-author of* The Case for Marriage: Why Married People Are Happier, Healthier and Better Off Financially

"I'm not suggesting that divorce be outlawed. But people move too quickly without trying to work through their problems in the relationship."
—MARSHALL HERSKOVITZ, *co-creator of TV's* Once and Again

"What most of the large-scale scientific research shows is that although growing up in a divorced family elevates the risk for certain kinds of problems, it by no means dooms children to having a terrible life. The fact of the matter is that most kids from divorced families do manage to overcome their problems and do have good lives."
—PAUL AMATO, *professor of sociology, Penn State University*

Now, decades later, some still don't want to hear her. For parents, her book's chief finding, to be sure, is hardly upbeat or very reassuring; children take a long time to get over divorce. Indeed, its most harmful and profound effects tend to show up as the children reach maturity and struggle to form their own adult relationships. They're gun-shy. The slightest conflict sends them running. Expecting disaster, they create disaster. "They look for love in strange places," Wallerstein says. "They make terrible errors of judgment in whom they choose."

Marcie Schwalm, 26, a Bloomington, Ill, legal secretary whose parents split when she was four, illustrates Wallerstein's thesis well. As a young woman she couldn't seem to stick with the same boyfriend. "I thought guys were for dating and for breaking up with a few weeks later," she says. "I would go into a relationship wondering how it was going to end." Finally, Marcie says, a college beau told her she had a problem. She's married now, and her feelings about divorce have a hard-line, 1950s tone: "Divorce is not something I am going to go through. I would do whatever it takes to keep the marriage together."

Kristina Herrndobler, 17, isn't so sure that harmony can be willed. Now a high

school student in Benton, Ill., she too was four when her parents called it quits. She says she has no memories of the trauma, just an abiding skepticism about marriage and a resolve to settle for nothing less than the ideal man. "I don't want my kids to wind up in a single-parent situation," she says. "And I don't want to have kids with a man I don't want to be married to forever. I don't believe in the fairy tale. I hope it exists, but I really don't believe it does."

And therein lies another problem, according to Wallerstein: the belief, quite common in children of divorce, that marriage is either a fairy tale or nothing. These jittery, idealistic children tend to hold out for the perfect mate—only to find they have a very long wait. Worse, once they're convinced they've found him, they're often let down. High romantic expectations tend to give way, Wallerstein reports, to bitter disillusionments. Children from broken families tend to marry later, yet divorce more often than those from intact homes.

So divorce often screws up kids. In itself, this isn't news, though many experts feel Wallerstein overstates the case. That divorce may screw them up for a long, long time and put them at risk for everything from drug abuse to a loveless, solitary old

age is more disturbing—and even more debatable. Christy Buchanan, a professor of psychology at Wake Forest University and co-author of *Adolescents After Divorce* (Harvard), is typical of Wallerstein's detractors. "I think the main drawback of the sort of research she does is that you can't necessarily generalize it to a broad population," Buchanan says. "The other caution I would put forth is that she has a group of divorced families but no comparison group of nondivorced families. [Perhaps in response to this longstanding complaint, Wallerstein also interviewed children of intact marriages for her new book.] There's some good research suggesting that many of the problems that have been attributed to divorce in children were actually present prior to the divorce."

Not rigorous enough. Too gloomy. Those are the leading raps against Wallerstein. Paul Amato, a sociology professor at Penn state, has researched divorce and children for 20 years, casting the sort of wide statistical net that hardheaded academics favor and Wallerstein eschews as too impersonal. While Amato agrees with her about divorce's "sleeper effect" on children—the problems that crop up only after they're grown—he finds her work a bit of a bummer. "It's a dismal kind of pic-

VIEWPOINT

Is Divorce Getting a Bum Rap?

KATHA POLLITT

Are Americans a nation of frivolous divorcers who selfishly pursue the bluebird of happiness, oblivious to their children's needs? Divorce opponents like Judith Wallerstein seem to think most parents see divorce as a marvelous opportunity for the whole family. How immature do they think people are? All over America, unhappy spouses lie awake at night wondering if they and their kids can afford divorce—financially, socially, emotionally. Where will they live, how will they pay the bills, will the kids fall apart, will there be a custody battle, what will their families say? The very fact that so many people leave their marriage for a future with so many pitfalls proves that divorce is anything but a whim. Most people I know who split up (not to mention my ex and me) spend years working up to it.

SPLIT DECISIONS: "America doesn't need more 'good enough' marriages"

In her new book, Wallerstein argues that children don't care if their parents are happy—they just want the stability of a two-parent household, without which they would later flail through adulthood and have a hard time forming good relationships. This conclusion, like her other gloomy generalizations ("Parenting erodes almost inevitably at the breakup and does not get restored for years, if ever"), is based on a small, nonrepresentative sample of families who were going through divorce in 1971 in affluent Marin County, Calif. Wallerstein looks for evidence that divorce harms kids, and of course she finds it—now well into their mid-30s, her interviews still blame their parents' breakup for every rock on the path to fulfillment—but the very process of participating in a famous ongoing study about the effects of divorce encourages them to see their lives through that lens. What if she had spent as much time studying children whose parents had terrible marriages but stayed together for the kids? How many 35-year-old "children" would be blaming their problems on the nights they hid in their rooms while Mom and Dad screamed at each other in the kitchen? Wallerstein points out many children of divorce feel overly responsible for their parents' happiness. But what about the burden of knowing that one or both of your parents endured years of misery—for you?

As a matter of fact, we know the answer to that question. The baby boomers, who helped divorce become mainstream, were the products of exactly the kind of marriages the anti-divorcers approve of—the child-centered unions of the 1950s, when parents, especially Mom, sacrificed themselves on the altar of family values and the suburban respectability. To today's anti-divorcers those may seem like "good enough" marriages—husband and wife rubbing along for the sake of the children. The kids who lived with the silence and contempt said no thank you.

America doesn't need more "good enough" marriages full of depressed and bitter people. Nor does it need more pundits blaming women for destroying "the family" with what are, after all, reasonable demands for equality and self-development. We need to acknowledge that there are lots of different ways to raise competent and well-adjusted children, which—as according to virtually every family researcher who has worked with larger and more representative samples than Wallerstein's tiny handful—the vast majority of kids of divorce turn out to be. We've learned a lot about how to divorce since 1971. When Mom has enough money and Dad stays connected, when parents stay civil and don't bad-mouth each other, kids do all right. The "good enough" divorce—why isn't *that* ever the cover story?

Katha Pollitt is an author and a columnist for The Nation.

---

ture that she paints," he says. "What most of the large-scale, more scientific research shows is that although growing up in a divorced family elevates the risk for certain kinds of problems, it by no means dooms children to having a terrible life."

And what about children raised from the start by single moms? Last month, TIME ran a story about the challenges faced by single women having children of their own. But in all the coverage about how those women are coping, the impact on the kids is sometimes underplayed—and their issues are not that different from those of kids from divorced households. "Some studies have directly compared children who were raised by mothers who are continuously single with mothers who went through a divorce," says Amato. "In general, the outcomes for children seem to be pretty similar. It appears to increase the risk for some types of problems: in con-

duct, in school, in social relations. Neither one appears to be optimal for children."

Besides her conclusions on children's long-term prospects following divorce, Wallerstein makes another major point in her book—one that may result in talk-show fistfights. Here it is: children don't need their parents to like each other. They don't even need them to be especially civil. They need them to stay together, for better or worse. (Paging Dr. Laura!) This imperative comes with asterisks, of course, but fewer than one might think. Physical abuse, substance addiction and other severe pathologies cannot be tolerated in any home. Absent these, however, Wallerstein stands firm: a lousy marriage, at least where the children's welfare is concerned, beats a great divorce.

Them's fighting words.

The shouting has already started. Family historian Stephanie Coontz, author of

The Way We Never Were: American Families and the Nostalgia Trap (Basic) questions the value of papering over conflicts for the kids' sake. Sure, some parents can pull it off, but how many and for how long? For many couples," Coontz says, "things only get worse and fester, and eventually, five years down the road, they end up getting divorced anyway, after years of contempt for each other and outside affairs."

Coontz doesn't believe in social time travel. She doesn't think we can go back to *Leave It to Beaver* after we've seen *Once and Again*. Unlike Wallerstein, whose investigation is deep but rather narrow (the families in her original study were all white, affluent residents of the same Northern California county, including non-working wives for whom divorce meant a huge upheaval), Coontz takes a lofty, long view of divorce. "In the 1940s

BOOK EXCERPT

Fear of Falling

A sense that love is doomed often haunts the offspring of divorce as they grow up and try to build relationships of their own, says a controversial new book based on a 25-year study of 131 children. Here we follow a young woman's painful search for love that can last

BY JUDITH WALLERSTEIN, JULIA LEWIS AND SANDRA BLAKESLEE

WHEN MOST PEOPLE HEAR THE WORD DIVORCE, THEY THINK IT means one failed marriage. The child of divorce is thought to experience one huge loss of the intact family, after which stability and a second, happier marriage comes along. But this is not what happens to most children of divorce. They experience not one, not two, but many more losses as their parents go in search of new lovers or partners. Each of these throws the child's life into turmoil and brings back painful reminders of the first loss.

Children observe their parents' courtships with a mixture of excitement and anxiety. For adolescents, the erotic stimulation of seeing their parents with changing partners can be difficult to contain. Several young teenage girls in the study began their own sexual activity when they observed a parent's involvement in a passionate affair. Children watch their parents' lovers with everything from love to resentment, hoping for some clue about the future. They participate actively as helper, critic and audience. They are not afraid to intervene. One mother returning home from a date found her school-age children asleep in her bed. Since they'd told her earlier that they didn't like her boyfriend, she took the hint. Many new lovers are attentive to the children, regularly bringing little gifts. But even the most charming lovers can disappear overnight. Second marriages with children are much more likely to end in divorce than first marriages.

The experience of Karen, whose identity I have concealed here, is typical of many I have seen. Her father's second wife, who was nice to the children, left without warning three years into the marriage. After she was gone, her father had four more girlfriends who caused him a great deal of suffering when they also left. Karen's mother had three unhappy love affairs prior to her remarriage, which ended after five years. The childhood of Karen and her siblings were filled with a history of new attachments followed by losses and consequent distress for both parents. Karen's brother, at age 30, told me: "What is marriage? Only a piece of paper and a piece of metal. If you love someone, it breaks your heart." In this study, only 7 of the 131 children experienced stable second marriages in which they had good relationships on both sides of the divorced family. Can we be surprised that so many children of divorce conclude that love is fleeting?

When I turn to the notes of my interview with Karen 15 years after her parents' divorce, the image of a young woman crying inconsolably enters my mind. Karen was sitting on the sofa in my old office, with her chin in her hands and elbows on her knees, telling me about her live-in relationship with her boyfriend Nick. "I've made a terrible mistake," she said, twisting a damp tissue into the shape of a rope. "I can't believe I've gotten myself into this. It's what I grew up dreading most and look what happened."

Karen gripped her fingers tightly until her knuckles shone like moons. "What's wrong?" I asked, as gently as I could. "Everything," she moaned. "He drinks beer. He has no ambition, no life goals, no education, no regular job. When I come home after work,

he's just sitting there in front of the TV and that's where he's been all day." Then Karen's voice dropped. "But he loves me," she said in anguish. "He would be devastated if I ever left him." Even in her great distress and anger she was intensely cognizant of her boyfriend's suffering. I thought to myself, this epitomizes Karen—she's always aware of other people's hurts and suffering.

"But then why did you move in with him?"

"I'm not sure. I knew I didn't love him. But I was scared of marriage. I was scared of divorce, and I'm terrified of being alone. When Nick asked me to live with him, I was afraid that I'd get older and that I wouldn't have another chance. I kept thinking that I'd end up lonely like my dad. And Mom."

I looked at this beautiful young woman and shook my head in disbelief. Could she really think that this was all she could hope for? Karen must have read my mind because she quickly said, "I know. People have been telling me how pretty I am since I was a child. But I don't believe it. And I don't care."

"How did you meet Nick?"

She sighed as she answered, "Well, we hardly knew each other in high school. I think that he had a crush on me from afar. Then in my junior year I broke my ankle and during the six weeks that I was hobbling around, he was very kind to me, carrying my stuff and visiting me. He was the only one who took any care of me. He also comes from a divorced family with lots of troubles. When he dropped out of school, I felt very sorry for him."

"Then how did he come back into your life?"

"I was having a real bad time. My brother was getting into serious trouble with the law and my dad wouldn't do anything to help. I was frantic and beginning to realize that all my efforts to hold my family together were wasted. So when Nick asked me to move in with him, I said yes. Anything to get away, even though I knew from the outset he had no plans for the future. After the first day, I said to myself, 'Oh, my God, what did I do?' But at least I knew he won't betray me. At least I'm safe from that."

"Karen, this fear of betrayal is pretty central to you. You keep mentioning it."

"It's been central to my life," she agreed. "Both my parents played around. I saw it all around me. They felt that if you are not getting what you want, you just look elsewhere." (I've never heard anyone put the alternative morality of our divorce culture so succinctly.)

Like a good caregiver child, Karen reinstalled her troubled relationships with her mother and father into her early relationships with men. As rescuers, most young women like Karen are used to giving priority to the needs of others. Karen confessed that she had never in her life thought about what would make her happy. "That would be like asking for the moon," she said. "I was always too worried about my family to ask for me."

(continued)

Fear of Falling *(continued)*

What prompts so many children of divorce to rush into a cohabitation or early marriage with as much forethought as buying a new pair of shoes? Answers lie in the ghosts that rise to haunt them as they enter young adulthood. They live in fear that they will repeat their parents' history, hardly daring to hope that they can do better. Dating and courtship raise their hopes of being loved sky-high—but also their fears of being hurt and rejected. This amalgam of fear and loneliness can lead to multiple affairs, hasty marriages, early divorce, and—if no take-home lessons are gleaned from it all—a second and third round of the same.

Here's how it works: at the threshold of young adulthood, relationships move center stage. But for many that stage is barren of good memories of how an adult man and woman can life together in a loving relationship. The psychological scaffolding they need to construct a happy marriage has been badly damaged by the two people they depended on while growing up. Children learn all kinds of lessons at their parents' knees from the time they are born to the time they leave home. There is no more exciting image to the child than the frame that includes Mom and Dad kissing, fighting, conferring, frowning, crying, yelling or hugging. These thousand-and-one images are internalized, and they form the template for the child's view of how men and women treat each other, how parents and children communicate, how brothers and sisters get along.

Unlike children from intact families, children of divorce in our study spoke very little about their parents' interaction. Parents who divorce may think of their decision to end the marriage as wise, courageous and the best remedy for their unhappiness—indeed, it may be so—but for the child the divorce carries one meaning: the parents have failed at one of the central tasks of adulthood. Together and separately, they failed to maintain the marriage. This failure shapes the child's inner template of self and family. If they failed, I can fail too. And if, as happens so frequently, the child observes more failed relationships in the years after divorce, the conclusion is simple. *I have never seen a man and a woman together on the same beam. Failure is inevitable.*

When I talked with Karen again nine years later, at age 34, she told me on the phone that "I'm in a whole other place than our last meeting. It's all new." As she came through my front door, she looked radiant. I was suddenly aware that in all the years we've known each other, I had rarely seen her happy. She was dressed very simply in black wool slacks, white pullover and herringbone suit jacket. Her stunning blue eyes had a new twinkle that flashed as we greeted each other warmly.

I told her how lovely she looked and congratulated her on her forthcoming marriage. "Who's the lucky man?"

"We're both lucky," she said, settling on the sofa. "Gavin and I did everything differently compared to how I lived my life before." And she launched into her story. Within months of our last meeting, she had moved out of the apartment she shared with Nick and said goodbye. As she had anticipated, he was devastated, begged her to come back, and made her feel guiltier than ever.

"How were you able to leave?" I asked.

She answered slowly, her face pale. "I felt like I was dying. It has to be the hardest thing I've ever done and it took all my courage." She described how she would come home after work and find her partner lying on the couch, waiting for her to take charge. It was just like taking care of her mom. At that point, she realized she had to get out. Her escape took her to the East Coast, graduate school, and ultimately into a dream job—directing a regional public health program for handicapped children.

It was there that Karen met her fiancé, Gavin, an assistant professor of economics. As she told me about him, I smiled and said, "I remember when you thought you didn't have choices. It looks like you've made quite a few recently."

"I decided to take a chance, and I discovered what I want. And I finally figured out what I don't want. I don't want another edition of my relationships with my mom or dad. I don't want a man who is dependent on me."

"And you do want?"

"I want a lover and a husband. I'm no longer frantic to find just anybody because if I have to, I can live alone. I can stand on my own two feet. I'm no longer afraid." And then the sadness around her eyes returned. "But it's not really all behind me. Like I told you, part of me is always waiting for disaster to strike. It never really goes away, never."

In hearing story after story like Karen's, I realized that compared with children from intact families, children of divorce follow a different trajectory for growing up. *It takes them longer.* Their adolescence is protracted and their entry into adulthood is delayed. Children of divorce need more time to grow up because they have to accomplish more: they must simultaneously let go of the past and create mental models for where they are headed, carving their own way. Those who succeed deserve gold medals for integrity and perseverance. Having rejected their parents as role models, they have to invent who they want to be and what they want to achieve in adult life. This is far beyond what most adolescents are expected to achieve.

Children of divorce are held back from adulthood because the vision of it is so frightening. The fact that Karen and others were able to turn their lives around is very good news for all of us who have been worried about the long-term effects of divorce on children. It sometimes took many years and several failed relationships, but close to half of the women and over a third of the men in our study were finally able to create a new template with themselves in starring roles. They did it the hard way—by learning from their own experience. They got hurt, kept going, and tried again. Some had relatives, especially grandparents, who loved them and provided close-up role models. Some had childhood memories from before the divorce that gave them hope and self-confidence. Only a few had mentors, but when they came along they were greatly appreciated. One young man told me, "My boss has been like a father to me, the father that I always wanted and never had." Men and women alike were especially grateful to lovers who stood by them and insisted that they stick around for the long haul. Finally, a third of the men and women in our study sought professional help from therapists and found that they could establish a trusting relationship with another person and use it to get at the roots of their difficulties.

We now come to a final, critical question. What values does this generation hold regarding marriage and divorce? Their vote is clear. Despite their firsthand experience of seeing how marriages can fail, they sincerely want lasting, faithful relationships. No single adult in this study accepts the notion that marriage is going to wither away. They want stability and a different life for their children. They want to do things better than their parents.

What If They Tough It Out?

People tend to believe that if a husband and wife are unhappy with each other, their children will also be unhappy. What's left out of the equation are the many families like Gary's, where the parents stay together and try to keep the peace. Gary (whose identity I've concealed) described with gusto his happy memories of childhood play, but had not revealed what he meant by the "indoor version" of his family. "What was that all about?" I asked.

"There was this feeling of tension that you could cut with a knife," Gary replied. "As things got worse between them, there were fewer words and more and more tension. My brother and sister and I spent as much time out of the house as we could."

"Things got pretty bad when I was in junior high school," he said. "One morning, after I knew Dad hadn't been home the night before, I was feeling really low. I guess I was seriously worried that he wouldn't come back. Mom had been all teary-eyed and silent during breakfast. I got on my bike to ride to school but I just couldn't face going. So I rode down to Dad's store. I thought I'd just peek in to see if he was there. He saw me looking and must've sensed something was wrong because he just left off helping a customer and came straight out to me. I remember he looked tired but he also looked kind of alarmed. He asked if anything was wrong at home and looked relieved when I told him there wasn't.

"So we went back into his office and we talked. He said he didn't know why Mom was so angry and suspicious but that sometimes he had to leave because it got to him and made him angry. He pointed to the old leather couch in the office and told me that when he did leave, this was where he slept.

"That was when I asked him if they might divorce. I'll always remember this part. His face went all saggy like he was going to cry, and he reached out and hugged me hard. 'Let me tell you something, Sport. Marriage is like a roller coaster. It has real highs and real lows. The lows have been worse than I thought, and the highs have been better than I thought. The big picture is that I love your mother, and you kids are the high point of our marriage. The picture right now is your mother and I are in a slump, but we'll work our way out of it. I know we will because we love you kids so much. Our marriage has been challenging, but it's been a good ride, and I'm hanging on till the end.'"

Gary was choking up as he recalled his father's words and blinking back tears. Finally, he said, "That was one of the most important conversations of my whole life."

"For me it was definitely better that they stayed together," he said. "But that's because they were great parents. My brother, sister and I never doubted that they loved us. My mom was lonely and, as I look back, probably depressed, but she continued to be very interested in us and our schoolwork and our activities. In other words, our world was protected. But if they *had* split up, I'd lay you bets that my father would have been remarried in a flash. And maybe had a couple more kids. We would have definitely lost out."

"How?"

"He wouldn't have been around for me. I doubt that my mom would have remarried, although who knows? It was better for me and my brother and sister, even if our folks missed out on some goodies of life. I know that's selfish of me."

"Why do you say that?"

"Because I have no idea how unhappy my parents were. After all, there are a lot of other things in life besides kids. Now that I'm an adult, I feel terribly sorry for both of them."

the average marriage ended with the death of the spouse," Coontz says. "But life expectancy is greater today, and there is more potential for trouble in a marriage. We have to become comfortable with the complexity and ambiguity of every family situation and its own unique needs."

That's just a lot of fancy, high-flown talk to Wallerstein and her followers. Ambiguity doesn't put dinner on the table or drive the kids to soccer practice or save for their college education. Parents do. And parents tend to have trouble doing these things after they get divorced. In observing what goes wrong for kids when their folks decide to split, Wallerstein is nothing if not practical. It's not just the absence of positive role models that bothers her, it's the depleted bank accounts, the disrupted play-group schedules, the frozen dinners. Parents simply parent better, she's found, when there are two of them. Do kids want peace and harmony at home? Of course. Still, they'll settle for hot meals.

Wallerstein didn't always feel this way. Once upon a time, she too believed that a good divorce trumped a bad marriage where children were concerned. "The central paradigm now that is subscribed to throughout the country," says Wallerstein, "is if at the time of the breakup people will be civil with each other, if they can settle financial things fairly, and if the child is able to maintain contact with both parents, then the child is home free." Wallerstein helped build this mode, she says, but now she's out to tear it down. "I'm changing my opinion," she says flatly.

The family-values crowd is pleased as punch with Wallerstein's change of heart. Take David Blankenhorn, president of the Institute for American Values. "There was a sense in the '70s especially, and even into the '80s, that the impact of divorce on children was like catching a cold: they would suffer for a while and then bounce back," he says. "More than anyone else in the country, Judith Wallerstein has shown that

that's not what happens." Fine, but does this oblige couples to muddle through misery so that Johnny won't fire up a joint someday or dump his girlfriend out of insecurity? Blankenhorn answers with the sort of certainty one expects from a man with his imposing title. "If the question is, If unhappily married parents stay together for the sake of their kids, will that decision benefit their children?, the answer is yes."

We can guess how the moral stalwarts will answer such questions. What about ordinary earthlings? Virginia Gafford, 56, a pet-product saleswoman in Pawleys Island, S.C., first married when she was 19. The marriage lasted three years. She married again, had a second child, Denyse, and divorced again. Denyse was 14. She developed the classic symptoms. Boyfriends jilted her for being too needy. She longed for the perfect man, who was nowhere to be found. "I had really high expectations," says Denyse. "I wanted Superman, so they wouldn't do what Dad had done." Denyse is in college now and getting fine grades, but her mother still has certain regrets. "If I could go back and find any way to save that marriage, I'd do it," she says. "And I'd tell anyone else to do the same."

For Wallerstein and her supporters, personal growth is a poor excuse for dragging the little ones through a custody battle that just might divide their vulnerable souls into two neat, separate halves doomed to spend decades trying to reunite. Anne Watson is a family-law attorney in Bozeman, Mont., and has served as an administrative judge in divorce cases. She opposes tightening divorce laws out of fear that the truly miserable—battered wives, the spouses of alcoholics—will lose a crucial escape route. But restless couples who merely need their space, in her opinion, had better think twice and think hard. "If people are divorcing just because of choices they want to make, I think it's pretty tough on the kids," Watson says. "Just because you're going to feel better, will they?"

That, of course, is the million-dollar question. Wallerstein's answer is no, they'll feel worse. They'll feel worse for quite a while, in fact, and may not know why until they find themselves in court, deciding where their own kids will spend Christmas. It's no wonder Wallerstein's critics find her depressing.

Does Wallerstein's work offer any hope or guidance to parents who are already divorced? Quite a bit, actually. For such parents, Wallerstein offers the following advice; First, stay strong. The child should be assured that she is not suddenly responsible for her parents' emotional well-being. Two, provide continuity for the child, maintaining her usual schedule of activities. Try to keep her in the same playgroup, the same milieu, among familiar faces and accustomed scenes. Lastly, don't let your own search for new love preoccupy you at the child's expense.

Her chief message to married parents is clear: Suck it up if you possibly can, and stick it out. But even if you agree with Wallerstein, how realistic is such spartan advice? The experts disagree. Then again, her advice is not for experts. It's directed at people bickering in their kitchen and staring up at the ceiling of their bedroom. It's directed at parents who have already divorced and are sitting alone in front of the TV, contemplating a second try.

The truth and usefulness of Wallerstein's findings will be tested in houses and apartments, in parks and playgrounds, not in sterile think tanks. Someday, assuming we're in a mood to listen, millions of children will give us the results.

—Reported by Jeanne McDowell/Los Angeles, Timothy Padgett/Miami, Andrea Sachs/New York and David E. Thigpen/Chicago

Now for the Truth About Americans and
SEX

**The first comprehensive survey since Kinsey
smashes some of our most intimate myths**

PHILIP ELMER-DEWITT

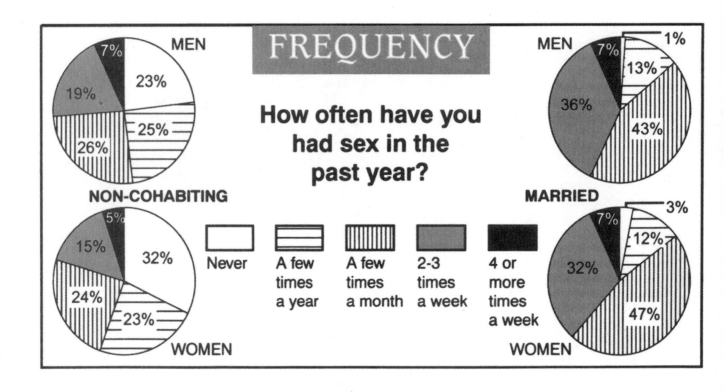

FREQUENCY

How often have you had sex in the past year?

MEN
7%
23%
19%
25%
26%

NON-COHABITING

5%
15%
32%
24%
23%

WOMEN

MEN
7%
1%
13%
36%
43%

MARRIED

7%
3%
12%
32%
47%

WOMEN

Never | A few times a year | A few times a month | 2-3 times a week | 4 or more times a week

IS THERE A LIVING, BREATHING ADULT WHO hasn't at times felt the nagging suspicion that in bedrooms across the country, on kitchen tables, in limos and other venues too scintillating to mention, other folks are having more sex, livelier sex, better sex? Maybe even that quiet couple right next door is having more fun in bed, and more often. Such thoughts spring, no doubt, from a primal anxiety deep within the human psyche. It has probably haunted men and women since the serpent pointed Eve toward the forbidden fruit and urged her to get with the program.

Still, it's hard to imagine a culture more conducive to feelings of sexual inadequacy than America in the 1990s. Tune in to the soaps. Flip through the magazines. Listen to Oprah. Lurk in the seamier corners of cyberspace. What do you see and hear? An endless succession of young, hard bodies preparing for, recovering from or engaging in constant, relentless copulation. Sex is every-

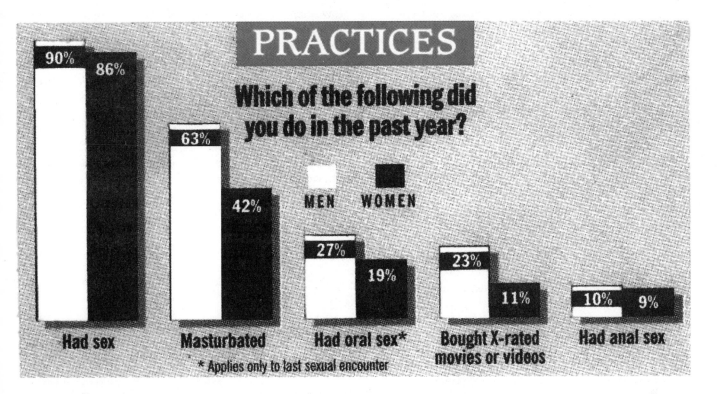

PRACTICES

Which of the following did you do in the past year?

90%   86%

63%   42%

MEN   WOMEN

27%   19%

23%   11%

10%   9%

Had sex   **Masturbated**   **Had oral sex***   **Bought X-rated movies or videos**   **Had anal sex**

* Applies only to last sexual encounter

where in America—and in the ads, films, TV shows and music videos it exports abroad. Although we know that not every ZIP code is a Beverly Hills, 90210, and not every small town a Peyton Place, the impression that is branded on our collective subconscious is that life in the twilight of the 20th century is a sexual banquet to which everyone else has been invited.

Just how good is America's sex life? Nobody knows for sure. Don't believe the magazine polls that have Americans mating energetically two or three times a week. Those surveys are inflated from the start by the people who fill them out: *Playboy* subscribers, for example, who brag about their sex lives in reader-survey cards. Even the famous Kinsey studies—which caused such a scandal in the late 1940s and early '50s by reporting that half of American men had extramarital affairs—were deeply flawed. Although Alfred Kinsey was a biologist by training (his expertise was the gall wasp), he compromised science and took his human subjects where he could find them: in boardinghouses, college fraternities, prisons and mental wards. For 14 years he collared hitchhikers who passed through town and quizzed them mercilessly. It was hardly a random cross section.

Now, more than 40 years after Kinsey, we finally have some answers. A team of researchers based at the University of Chicago has released the long-awaited results of what is probably the first truly scientific survey of who does what with whom in America and just how often they do it.

The findings—based on face-to-face interviews with a random sample of nearly 3,500 Americans, ages 18 to 59, selected using techniques honed through decades of po-

litical and consumer polling—will smash a lot of myths. "Whether the numbers are reassuring or alarming depends on where you sit," warns Edward Laumann, the University of Chicago sociologist who led the research team. While the scientists found that the spirit of the sexual revolution is alive and well in some quarters—they found that about 17% of American men and 3% of women have had sex with at least 21 partners—the overall impression is that the sex lives of most Americans are about as exciting as a peanut-butter-and-jelly sandwich.

Among the key findings:

- Americans fall into three groups. One-third have sex twice a week or more, one-third a few times a month, and one-third a few times a year or not at all.
- Americans are largely monogamous. The vast majority (83%) have one or zero sexual partners a year. Over a lifetime, a typical man has six partners; a woman, two.
- Married couples have the most sex and are the most likely to have orgasms when they do. Nearly 40% of married people say they have sex twice a week, compared with 25% for singles.
- Most Americans don't go in for the kinky stuff. Asked to rank their favorite sex acts, almost everybody (96%) found vaginal sex "very or somewhat appealing." Oral sex ranked a distant third, after an activity that many may not have realized was a sex act: "Watching partner undress."

- Adultery is the exception in America, not the rule. Nearly 75% of married men and 85% of married women say they have never been unfaithful.
- There are a lot fewer active homosexuals in America than the oft-repeated 1 in 10. Only 2.7% of men and 1.3% of women report that they had homosexual sex in the past year.

THE FULL RESULTS OF THE NEW SURVEY ARE SCHEDULED to be published next week as *The Social Organization of Sexuality* (University of Chicago; $49.95), a thick, scientific tome co-authored by Laumann, two Chicago colleagues—Robert Michael and Stuart Michaels—and John Gagnon, a sociologist from the State University of New York at Stony Brook. A thinner companion volume, Sex in America: A Definitive Survey (Little, Brown; $22.95), written with New York Times science reporter Gina Kolata, will be in bookstores this week.

54% of men think about sex daily. 19% of women do

But when the subject is sex, who wants to wait for the full results? Even before the news broke last week, critics and pundits were happy to put their spin on the study.

"It doesn't ring true," insisted Jackie Collins, author of *The Bitch, The Stud* and other potboilers. "Where are the deviants? Where are the flashers? Where are the sex maniacs I see on TV every day?"

"I'm delighted to hear that all this talk about rampant infidelity was wildly inflated," declared postfeminist writer Camille Paglia. "But if they're saying the sexual revolution never happened, that's ridiculous."

"Positively, outrageously stupid and unbelievable," growled *Penthouse* publisher Bob Guccione. "I would say five partners a year is the average for men."

"Totally predictable," deadpanned Erica Jong, author of the 1973 sex fantasy *Fear of Flying*. "Americans are more interested in money than sex."

"Our Puritan roots are deep," said *Playboy* founder Hugh Hefner, striking a philosophical note. "We're fascinated by sex and afraid of it."

"Two partners? I mean, come on!" sneered *Cosmopolitan* editor Helen Gurley Brown. "We advise our Cosmo girls that when people ask how many partners you've had, the correct answer is always three, though there may have been more."

Europeans seemed less surprised—one way or the other—by the results of the survey. The low numbers tend to confirm the Continental caricature of Americans as flashy and bold onscreen but prone to paralysis in bed. Besides, the findings were pretty much in line with recent studies conducted in England and France that also found low rates of homosexuality and high rates of marital fidelity. (The French will be gratified by what a comparison of these surveys shows: that the average Frenchman and -woman has sex about twice as often as Americans do.)

If the study is as accurate as it purports to be, the results will be in line with the experience of most Americans. For many, in fact, they will come as a relief. "A lot of people think something is wrong with them when they don't have sexual feelings," says Toby, a 32-year-old graduate student from Syracuse, New York, who, like 3% of adult Americans (according to the survey), has never had sex. "These findings may be liberating for a lot of people. They may say, 'Thank God, I'm not as weird as I thought.'"

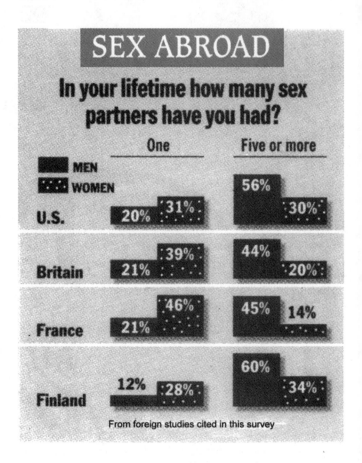

SEX ABROAD

In your lifetime how many sex partners have you had?

		One		Five or more	
■ MEN					
▓ WOMEN				56%	
U.S.		20%	31%		30%
Britain		21%	39%	44%	20%
France		21%	46%	45%	14%
Finland		12%	28%	60%	34%

From foreign studies cited in this survey

Scientists, on the whole, praise the study. "Any new research is welcome if it is well done," says Dr. William Masters, co-author of the landmark 1966 study Human Sexual Response. By all accounts, this one was very well done. But, like every statistical survey, it has its weaknesses. Researchers caution that the sample was too limited to reveal much about small subgroups of the population—gay Hispanics, for example. The omission of people over 59 is regrettable, says Shirley Zussman, past president of the American Association of Sex Educators, Counselors and Therapists: "The older population is more sexually active than a 19-year-old thinks, and it's good for both 19-year-olds and those over 59 to know that."

PARTNERS

How many sexual partners have you had since age 18?

MEN

3% 20% 21% 23% 16% 17%

WOMEN

3% 3% 6% 31% 36% 20%

HIGH SCHOOL GRADUATES (both sexes)

3% 30% 29% 20% 10% 7%

ALL COLLEGE GRADUATES (both sexes)

2% 24% 26% 24% 11% 13%

None 1 2-4 5-10 11-20 21 or more

The Chicago scientists admit to another possible defect: "There is no way to get around the fact some people might conceal information," says Stuart Michaels of the Chicago team, whose expertise is designing questions to get at those subjects people are most reluctant to discuss. The biggest hot button, he says, is homosexuality. "This is a stigmatized group. There is probably a lot more homosexual activity going on than we could get people to talk about."

The 2nd most appealing sex act: seeing partner undress

It was, in large part, to talk about homosexual activity that the study was originally proposed. The project was conceived in 1987 as a response to the AIDS crisis. To track the spread of the AIDS virus—and to mount an effective campaign against it—government researchers needed good data about how much risky sexual behavior (anal sex, for example) was really going on. But when they looked for scientific data about sex, they found little besides Kinsey and Masters and Johnson.

So the National Institutes of Health issued a formal request for a proposal, tactfully giving it the bland title "Social and Behavioral Aspects of Fertility Related Behavior" in an attempt to slip under the radar of right-wing politicians. But the euphemism fooled no one—least of all Jesse Helms. In the Reagan and Bush era, any government funding for sex research was suspect, and the Senator from North Carolina was soon lobbying to have the project killed. The Chicago team redesigned the study

several times to assuage conservative critics, dropping the questions about masturbation and agreeing to curtail the interview once it was clear that a subject was not at high risk of contracting AIDS. But to no avail. In September 1991 the Senate voted 66 to 34 to cut off funding.

The vote turned out to be the best thing that could have happened—at least from the point of view of the insatiably curious. The Chicago team quickly rounded up support from private sources, including the Robert Wood Johnson, Rockefeller and Ford foundations. And freed of political constraints, they were able to take the survey beyond behavior related to AIDS transmission to tackle the things inquiring minds really want to know: Who is having sex with whom? How often do they do it? And when they are behind closed doors, what exactly do they do?

The report confirms much of what is generally accepted as conventional wisdom. Kids *do* have sex earlier now: by 15, half of all black males have done it; by 17, the white kids have caught up to them. There *was* a lot of free sex in the '60s: the percentage of adults who have racked up 21 or more sex partners is significantly higher among the fortysomething boomers than among other Americans. And AIDS *has* put a crimp in some people's sex lives: 76% of those who have had five or more partners in the past year say they have changed their sexual behavior, by either slowing down, getting tested or using condoms faithfully.

But the report is also packed with delicious surprises. Take masturbation, for example. The myth is that folks are more likely to masturbate if they don't have a sex partner. According to the study, however, the people who masturbate the most are the ones who have the most sex. "If you're having sex a lot, you're thinking about sex a lot," says Gagnon. "It's more like Keynes (wealth begets wealth) and less like Adam Smith (if you spend it on this, you can't spend it on that)."

Or take oral sex. Not surprisingly, both men and women preferred receiving it to giving it. But who would have guessed that so many white, college-educated men would have done it (about 80%) and so few blacks (51%)? Skip Long, a 33-year-old African American from Raleigh, North Carolina, thinks his race's discomfort with oral sex may owe much to religious teaching and the legacy of slavery: according to local legend, it was something slaves were required to do for their masters. Camille Paglia is convinced that oral sex is a culturally acquired preference that a generation of college students picked up in the '70s from seeing Linda Lovelace do it in *Deep Throat*, one of the first—and last—X-rated movies that men and women went to see together. "They saw it demonstrated on the screen, and all of a sudden it was on the map," says Paglia. "Next thing you knew, it was in *Cosmo* with rules about how to do it."

More intriguing twists emerge when sexual behavior is charted by religious affiliation. Roman Catholics are the most likely to be virgins (4%) and Jews to have the most sex partners (34% have had 10 or more). The women most likely to achieve orgasm each and every time (32%) are, believe it or not, conservative Protestants. But Catholics edge out mainline Protestants in frequency of intercourse. Says Father Andrew Greeley, the sociologist-priest and writer of racy romances: "I think the church will be surprised at how often Catholics have sex and how much they enjoy it."

Among women 29% always had an orgasm during sex

But to concentrate on the raw numbers is to miss the study's most important contribution. Wherever possible, the authors put those figures in a social context, drawing on what they know about how people act out social scripts, how they are influenced by their social networks and how they make sexual bargains as if they were trading economic goods and services. "We were trying to make people think about sex in an entirely different way," says Kolata. "We all have this image, first presented by Freud, of sex as a riderless horse, galloping out of control. What we are saying here is that sex is just like any other social behavior: people behave the way they are rewarded for behaving."

Kolata and her co-authors use these theories to explain why most people marry people who resemble them in terms of age, education, race and social status, and why the pool of available partners seems so small—especially for professional women in their 30s and 40s. "You can still fall in love across a crowded room," says Gagnon. "It's just that society determines whom you're in the room with."

That insight, applied to AIDS, leads the Chicago team to a conclusion that is sure to get them into trouble. America's AIDS policy, they say, has been largely misdirected. Although AIDS spread quickly among intravenous drug users and homosexuals, the social circles these groups travel in are so rigidly circumscribed that it is unlikely to spread widely in the heterosexual population. Rather than pretend that AIDS affects everyone, they say, the government would be better advised to concentrate its efforts on those most at risk.

That's a conclusion that will not sit well with AIDS activists or with many health-policy makers. "Their message is shocking and flies against the whole history of this epidemic," says Dr. June Osborn, former chair of the National Commission on AIDS. "They're saying we don't have to worry if we're white, heterosexual adults. That gets the public off the hook and may keep parents from talking to their kids about sex. The fact is, teens are at enormous risk for experimentation."

Of married people, 94% were faithful in the past year

Other groups will find plenty here to make a fuss about. Interracial couples are likely to take offense at the author's characterization of mixed-race marriages as unlikely to succeed. And right-to-life activists who believe abortion is widely used as a cruel form of birth control are likely to be unconvinced by the finding that 72% of the women who have an abortion have only one.

Elsewhere in the study, the perceptual gulf between the sexes is reminiscent of the scene in *Annie Hall* where Woody Allen tells his psychiatrist that he and Annie have sex "hardly ever, maybe three times a week," and she tells hers that they do it "constantly; I'd say three times a week." In the Chicago study, 54% of the men say they think about sex every day or several times a day. By contrast, 67% of the women say they think about it only a few times a week or a few times a month. The disconnect is even greater when the subject turns to forced sex. According to the report, 22% of women say they have been forced to do sexual things they didn't want to, usually by someone they loved. But only 3% of men admit to ever forcing themselves on women. Apparently men and women have very different ideas about what constitutes voluntary sex.

But the basic message of *Sex in America* is that men and women have found a way to come to terms with each other's sexuality—and it is called marriage. "Our study," write the authors, "clearly shows that no matter how sexually active people are before and between marriages... marriage is such a powerful social institution that, essentially, married people are all alike—they are faithful to their partners as long as the marriage is intact."

Americans, it seems, have come full circle. It's easy to forget that as recently as 1948, Norman Mailer was still

HOMOSEXUALITY

MEN

Have you had sex with someone of your gender?

2.7%
In the past year

7.1%
Since puberty

1.3%   3.8%

Are you sexually attracted to people of the same gender?

6.2%

4.4%

WOMEN

using the word fug in his novels. There may have been a sexual revolution—at least for those college-educated whites who came of age with John Updike's swinging *Couples*, Philip Roth's priapic *Portnoy* and Jong's *Fear of Flying*—but the revolution turned out to have a beginning, a middle and an end. "From the time of the Pill to Rock Hudson's death, people had a sense of freedom," says Judith Krantz, author of *Scruples*. "That's gone."

It was the first survey—Kinsey's—that got prudish America to talk about sex, read about sex and eventually watch sex at the movies and even try a few things (at least once). Kinsey's methods may have been less than perfect,

but he had an eye for the quirky, the fringe, the bizarre. The new report, by contrast, is a remarkably conservative document. It puts the fringe on the fringe and concentrates on the heartland: where life, apparently, is ruled by marriage, monogamy and the missionary position. The irony is that the report Jesse Helms worked so hard to stop has arrived at a conclusion that should make him proud. And it may even make the rest of us a bit less anxious about what's going on in that bedroom next door.

—Reported by Wendy Cole/Chicago, John F. Dickerson/New York and Martha Smilgis/Los Angeles

The Betrayal Of The American Man

BOOK EXCERPT: Her groundbreaking 'Backlash' looked at the 'undeclared war on women.' Now in 'Stiffed,' the author explores the unseen war on men—the pressure to be masculine in a culture that no longer honors traditional codes of manhood.

By Susan Faludi

When I listen to the sons born after World War II, born to the fathers who won that war, I sometimes find myself in a reverie. I imagine a boy, in bed pretending to sleep, waiting for his father. The door opens, and the hall light streams in, casting a cutout shadow man across the bedroom floor. A minute later, the boy, wearing his coonskin cap and clutching his flashlight, races after his father along the shadowy upper hallway, down the stairs and out the screen door. The man and the boy kneel on the scratchy wool of the father's old navy peacoat, and the father snaps off the boy's flashlight. The father directs the boy's vision to a faraway glimmer. Its name is Echo. The boy looks up, knowing that the satellite his father is pointing out is more than just an object; it is a paternal gift rocketing him into his future, a miraculous inheritance encased in the transit of an artificial star, infinitesimally tiny, impossibly bright.

I knew this boy. Like everyone else who grew up in the late 1950s and early 1960s, I knew dozens of him. He was Bobby on the corner, who roamed the neighborhood with his cap gun and holster, terrorizing girls and household pets. He was Frankie, who blew off part of his pinkie while trying to ignite a miniature rocket in the schoolyard. Even if he wasn't brought out into the backyard and shown a satellite glinting in the sky, he was introduced to the same promise and the same vision, and by such a father. Many of these fathers were veterans of World War II or Korea, but their bloody paths to virility were not ones they sought to pass on, or usually even discuss. This was to be the era of manhood after victory, when the pilgrimage to masculinity would be guided not by the god of war Mars, but by the dream of a pioneering trip to the planet Mars. The satellite; here was a visible patrimony, a visual marker of vaulting technological power and progress to be claimed in the future by every baby-boom boy. The men of the fathers' generation had "won" the world and now they were giving it to their sons.

Four decades later, as the nation wobbled toward the millennium, its pulse-takers all seemed to agree that a domestic apocalypse was underway: American manhood was under siege. Newspaper editors, legislators, preachers, marketers, no matter where they perched on the political spectrum, had a contribution to make to the chronicles of the "masculinity crisis." Right-wing talk-radio hosts and left-wing men's-movement spokesmen found themselves uncomfortably on common ground. MEN ON TRIAL, the headlines cried, THE TROUBLE WITH BOYS. Journalists—myself included—raced to report on one young-male hot spot after another: Tailhook, the Citadel, the Spur Posse, South Central gangsters, militiamen blowing up federal buildings and abortion clinics, schoolyard shooters across the country.

CLOSING OF THE AMERICAN JOB

In the new economy, work moved from vital production
and job security to paper pushing and massive layoffs

The Broken Promise

On the surface, said Richard Foster, who came to McDonnell Douglas in the late '60s to work in the NASA space lab, life as an aerospace man seemed to offer the ultimate in masculine freedom. "It was idyllic," he told me. "All these little green lawns and houses all in a row. You could drive the freeways and plan your life out." But as time went on, he came to feel that it had all been planned without him, that he was expected to take the initiative in a game in which he was not even a player. "You began to feel so isolated," he said. Like the rest of the managers, he "belonged" to the company in only the most tenuous way. In the end, he would become a casualty of various corporate "cost-reduction" programs five times, his salary plunging from $80,000 to $28,000 to zero. Which was why he was sitting in a vinyl banquette in a chain restaurant in the shadow of McDonnell Douglas's blueglass tower in the middle of the afternoon, talking to me. "The next thing you know," he said, "you're standing outside, looking in. And you begin to ask, as a man, what is my role? What is it, really, that I do?"

About 11 miles up the road, a starkly different kind of leave-taking was unfolding at the Long Beach Naval Shipyard, one of the military bases slated for closure in 1995. If McDonnell Douglas had been the emblematic postwar corporation—full of functionaries whose jobs were unclear, even to themselves—the shipyard represented a particular vintage of American masculinity, monumental in its pooled effort, indefatigable in its industry and built on a sense of useful productivity. Ike Burr, one of the first black men to break into upper management, was a shipfitter who climbed steadily to project

superintendent. "Everything you ever dreamed of is here," Burr said. Unlike the McDonnell Douglas men, he wasn't referring to his dream house in the suburbs. He was talking about the work itself. "The shipyard is like a world within itself. Most items are one-of-a-type items, done once and not to be repeated. There's satisfaction in it, because you start and complete something. You *see* what you've created. The world of custom-made is finished—except here." After the shipyard's closing was announced, Burr postponed his official signing-out. He had found a temporary job at another military installation and was always "too busy" to get back to Long Beach to turn in his badge. But one morning he arrived to pay his last respects. He dressed sharply for the occasion: double-breasted gray suit, paisley tie and matching pocket hankie, even a hint of cologne. The morning management meeting was underway and he had been asked to stop by. He offered a few pointers, and then the shipyard commander gave an impromptu speech—about how Burr was the kind of guy "you could rely on to get the job done." Then he handed Burr a homemade plaque with a lengthy inscription.

Burr tucked it under his arm, embarrassed by the attention. "I better go get the signing-out business over," he said, his voice bumping over choppy seas. He headed out to make the rounds and get his termination physical. By late afternoon, Ike Burr had arrived at a small office, to sign a form surrendering the code word that gave him access to the yard. Though he burst out laughing as he signed, his words belied the laughter. "I have nothing in my possession," he said. "I have lost everything."

S.F.

In the meantime, the media's softer lifestyle outlets happily turned their attention to male-crisis lite: the retreat to cigar clubs and lap-dancing emporiums, the boom in male cosmetic surgery and the abuse of steroids, the brisk sales of Viagra. Social scientists pontificated on "endangered" young black men in the inner cities, Ritalin-addicted white "bad boys" in the suburbs, "deadbeat dads" everywhere and, less frequently, the anguish of downsized male workers. Social psychologists issued reports on a troubling rise in male-distress signals—from depressive disorders to suicides to certain criminal behaviors.

Pollsters investigated the electoral habits of a new voting bloc they called "the Angry White Male." Marketers hastened to turn the crisis into entertainment and profits from TV shows like "The Man Show" to T shirts that proclaimed DESTROY ALL GIRLS or WIFE BEATER. And by the hundreds of thousands, men without portfolio confirmed the male-crisis diagnosis, convening in

Washington for both the black Nation of Islam-led Million Man March and a largely white, evangelical-led Promise Keepers rally entitled, hopefully, "Stand in the Gap."

If so many concurred in the existence of a male crisis, consensus collapsed as soon as anyone asked the question Why. Everyone proposed a favorite whipping boy or, more often, whipping girl, and blame-seekers on all sides went after their selected culprits with righteous and bitter relish. Feminist mothers, indulgent liberals, videogame makers or testosterone itself all came under attack.

At Ground Zero of the Masculinity Crisis

THE SEARCH FOR AN ANSWER TO that question took me on a six-year odyssey, with stops along the way at a shuttered shipyard in Long Beach, a suburban living room where a Promise Keepers

group met, a Cleveland football stadium where fans grieved the loss of their team, a Florida horse farm where a Vietnam vet finally found peace, a grassy field in Waco where militiamen searched for an enemy and a slick magazine office where young male editors contended with a commodified manhood. But I began investigating this crisis where you might expect a feminist journalist to begin: at the weekly meetings of a domestic-violence group. Wednesday evenings in a beige stucco building a few blocks from the freeway in Long Beach, Calif., I attended a gathering of men under court order to repent the commission of an act that stands as the emblematic masculine sin of our age. What did I expect to divine about the broader male condition by monitoring a weekly counseling session for batterers? That men are by nature brutes? Or, more optimistically, that the efforts of such a group might point to methods of "curing" such beastliness?

GHETTO STAR

```
In a South-Central gang, Kody Scott finally felt useful as a man. But
the biggest part of the 'work' was promoting the gangster image.
```

Glamour in the 'Hood

My father's generation was the last responsible generation," said Sanyika Shakur (now Kody Scott's legally adopted name) as he welcomed me in August 1997 to his girlfriend's two-bedroom house in California's San Fernando Valley. Four years had passed since the publication of Shakur's best-selling memoir, "Monster: The Autobiography of an L.A. Gang Member," written while he was serving a four-year sentence for robbery at Pelican Bay State Prison. The book's cover photo of the pumped-up, bare-chested author clutching a semiautomatic MAC-10, combined with the much-advertised news of his six-figure advance, turned the former member of the Eight-Tray Gangsters (a Crips set in South-Central L.A.) into what he rightly called a "ghetto star."

Shakur had just been released from jail three days earlier, after a year's sentence for a parole violation, his second such since the publication of what was supposed to be his transformational autobiography. He had fled after his first violation, and the police eventually found him on a neighborhood porch, receiving a long line of autograph seekers. The dictates of a celebrity culture demanded a manhood forged by being glamorous, not responsible.

Getting a rep:
'If the media knows about you, damn, that's the top,' says Scott

---

As a young man, he had still hoped that he could demonstrate a workmanlike "usefulness" within his gang set. "You put in work and you feel needed in a gang. People would call on me because they needed me. You feel useful, and you're useful in your capacity as a man. You know, 'Don't send me no boys. Send me a man!'" But he was beginning to see his former life in a different light. What he once perceived as "work" now seemed more like PR. "What the work was," he said, "was anything you did in *promotion* for the gang." He found it amusing how the media viewed gangs as clannish and occult. "We're not a secret society. Our whole thing is writing on walls, tattoos on necks, maintaining visibility. Getting media coverage is the s—t! If the media knows about you, damn, that's the top. We don't recognize ourselves unless we're recognized on the news."

Kody Scott's image-enhancement strategies were not home-grown. "I got all these ideas from watching movies and watching television. I was really just out there acting from what I saw on TV." And he wasn't referring to "Superfly" or "Shaft." "Growing up, I didn't see one blaxploitation movie. Not one." His inspiration came from shows like "Mission: Impossible" and "Rat Patrol" and films like "The Godfather." "I would study the guys in those movies," he recalled, "how they moved, how they stood, the way they dressed, that whole winning way of dressing. Their tactics became my tactics. I went from watching "Rat Patrol" to being in it. His prime model was Arthur Penn's 1967 movie "Bonnie and Clyde." "I watched how in 'Bonnie and Clyde' they'd walk in and say their whole names. They were getting their reps. I took that and applied it to my situation." Cinematic gangsterism was his objective, and it didn't seem like much of a reach. "It's like there's a thin line in this country now between criminality and celebrity. Someone has to be the star of the 'hood. Someone has to do the advertising for the 'hood. And it's like agencies that pick a good-looking guy model. So it became, 'Monster Kody! Let's push him out there!'" He grinned as he said this, an aw-shucks smile that was, doubtless, part of his "campaign."

S.F.

Either way, I can see now that I was operating from an assumption both underexamined and dubious: that the male crisis in America was caused by something men were doing unrelated to something being done to them. I had my own favorite whipping boy, suspecting that the crisis of masculinity was caused by masculinity on the rampage. If male violence was the quintessential expression of masculinity run amok, then a domestic-violence therapy group must be at the very heart of this particular darkness.

I wasn't alone in such circular reasoning. I was besieged with suggestions along similar lines from journalists, feminists, antifeminists and other willing advisers. Women's rights advocates mailed me news clips about male office stalkers and computer harassers. That I was not ensconced in the courtroom for O. J. Simpson's murder trial struck many of my volunteer helpers as an appalling lapse of judgment. "The perfect case study of an American man who thinks he's entitled to just control everything and everybody," one of them suggested.

But then, I had already been attending the domestic-violence group for several months—the very group O. J. Simpson was, by coincidence, supposed to have attended but avoided with the promise that he would speak by phone to a psychiatrist—and it was already apparent to me that these men's crises did not stem from a preening sense of entitlement and control. Each new member in the group, called Alternatives to Violence, would be asked to describe what he had done to a woman, a request that was met invariably with the disclaimer "I was out of control." The counselors would then expend much energy showing him how he had, in fact, been in control the entire time. He had chosen his fists, not a knife; he had hit her in the stomach, not the face. No doubt the moment of physical contact for these men had grown out of a desire for supreme control fueled by a need to dominate. I cannot conceive of a circumstance that would exonerate such violence. By making the abusive spouse take responsibility for his actions, the counselors were pursuing a worthy goal. But the logic behind the violence still remained elusive.

A serviceman who had turned to nightclub-bouncer jobs and pastry catering after his military base shut down seemed to confirm the counselors' position one evening shortly before his "graduation" from the group. "I denied it before," he said of the night he pummeled his girlfriend. "I thought I'd blacked out. But looking back at that night, I didn't black out. I was feeling good. I was in power, I was strong, I was in control. I felt like a man." But what struck me most strongly was what he said next: that moment of control had been the only one in his recent life. "That feeling of power," he said, "didn't last long. Only until they put the cuffs on. Then I was feeling again like I was no man at all."

He was typical in this regard. The men I got to know in the group had, without exception, lost their compass in the world. They had lost or were losing jobs, homes, cars, families. They had been labeled outlaws but felt like castoffs. There was something almost absurd about these men struggling, week after week, to recognize themselves as dominators when they were so clearly dominated, done in by the world.

Underlying all the disagreement over what is confusing and unnerving to men runs a constant line of thinking that blinds us—whatever our political beliefs—to the nature of the male predicament. Ask feminists to diagnose men's problems and you will often get a very clear explanation: men are in crisis because women are properly challenging male dominance. Ask antifeminists and you will get a diagnosis that is, in one respect, similar. Men are troubled, many conservative pundits say, because women have gone far beyond their demands for equal treatment and now are trying to take power away from men.

The veterans of World War II were eager to embrace a manly ideal that revolved around providing rather than dominating. Ultimately, society double-crossed them.

Both the feminist and antifeminist views are rooted in a peculiarly modern American perception that to be a man means you are at the controls at all times. The popular feminist joke that men are to blame for everything is the flip side of the "family values" reactionary expectation that men should be in charge of everything.

The man controlling his environment is today the prevailing American image of masculinity. He is to be in the driver's seat, the king of the road, forever charging down the open highway, along that masculine Möbius strip that cycles endlessly through a numbing stream of movies, TV shows, novels, advertisements and pop tunes. He's a man because he won't be stopped. He'll fight attempts to tamp him down; if he has to, he'll use his gun. But we forget the true Daniel Boone frontiersmanship was only incidentally violent, and was based on creating, out of wilderness, a communal context to which a man could moor himself through work and family.

Modern debates about how men are exercising or abusing their control and power neglect to raise whether a lack of mooring, a lack of context, is causing men's anguish. If men are the masters of their fate, what do they do about the unspoken sense that they are being mastered, in the marketplace and at home, by forces that seem to be sweeping away the soil beneath their feet? If men are mythologized as the ones who make things happen, then how can they begin to analyze what is happening to them?

More than a quarter century ago, women began to free themselves from the box in which they were trapped by feeling their way along its contours, figuring out how it was shaped and how it shaped them. Women were able to take action, paradoxically, by understanding how they were acted upon. Men feel the contours of a box, too, but they are told that box is of their own manufacture, designed to their specifications. Who are they to complain? For men to say they feel boxed in is regarded not as laudable political protest but as childish whining. How dare the kings complain about their castles?

What happened to so disturb the sons of the World War II GIs? The prevailing narrative that the sons inherited—fashioned from the battlefronts of Europe and the Pacific, laid out in countless newspapers, newsreels and movies—was a tale of successful fatherhood and masculine transformation: boys whose Depression-era fathers could neither provide for them nor guide them into manhood were placed under the benevolent wing of a vast male-run orphanage called the army and sent into battle. There, firm but kindly senior officers acting as surrogate fathers watched over them as they were tempered into men in the heat of a heroic struggle against malevolent enemies. The boys, molded into men, would return to find wives, form their families and take their places as adults in the community of a nation taking its place as a grown-up power in the world.

This was the story America told itself in dozens of war movies in which tough but tenderhearted commanding officers prepared their appreciative "boys" to assume their responsibilities in male society. It was the theme behind the 1949 film "Sands of Iwo Jima," with John Wayne as Sergeant Stryker, a stern papa molding his wet-behind-the-ears charges into a capable fraternity. "Before I'm through with you, you're gonna move like one man and think like one man," he tells them. "If I can't teach you one way, I'll teach you another, but I'm gonna get the job done." And he gets the job done, fathering a whole squad of youngsters into communal adulthood.

The veterans of World War II were eager to embrace a masculine ideal that revolved around providing rather than dominating. Their most important experiences had centered on the support they had given one another in the war, and it was this that they wished to replicate. As artilleryman Win Stracke told oral historian Studs Terkel in "The Good War," he came home bearing this most cherished memory: "You had 15 guys who for the first time in their lives could help each other without cutting each other's throat or trying to put down somebody else through a boss or whatever. I had realized it was the absence of competition and all those phony standards that created the thing I loved about the army."

The fathers who would sire the babyboom generation would try to pass that experience of manhood on intact to their sons. The grunts who went overseas and liberated the world came home to the expectation that they would liberate the country by quiet industry and caretaking. The vets threw themselves into their federally funded educations, and later their defense-funded corporate and production-line jobs, and their domestic lives in Veterans Administration-financed tract homes. They hoped their dedication would be in the service of a higher national aim.

For their children, the period of soaring expectations that followed the war was truly the era of the boy. It was the culture of "Father Knows Best" and "Leave It to Beaver," of Pop Warner rituals and Westinghouse science scholarships, of BB guns and rocket clubs, of football practice and lettered jackets, of magazine ads where "Dad" seemed always to be beaming down at his scampy, cowboy-suited younger son or proudly handing his older son the keys to a brand-new convertible. It was a world where, regardless of the truth that lay behind each garden gate, popular culture led us to believe that fathers were spending every leisure moment in roughhouse play and model-air-plane construction with their beloved boys.

GONE TO SOLDIERS EVERY ONE

Michael Bernhardt went to Vietnam to honor his sense of justice. But the war destroyed his idea of manhood.

The Dogs of War

As far back as Michael Bernhardt could remember watching World War II movies, he could remember wanting to serve. The summers of his boyhood in the backyards of Long Island were one long idyll of war play on an imagined European front. "We had leaders," he said. "We attacked things with dirt bombs. We thought war was where we'd all go in together like D-Day and be part of this big coordinated army that would *do* something. And then you'd come back and have war stories to tell."

At his father's urging, Bernhardt headed off to college. But his mind was still on a military career. He joined not only Army ROTC but a special elite unit run by the Green Berets. Then in 1967, in the middle of his sophomore year, he dropped out and enlisted in the Army. He had only the haziest sense of what was going on in Vietnam: "It appeared to be about a small country that was having communism shoved down its throat, while we were trying, at least *ostensibly*, to give people a chance to do what they wanted to do. If I didn't go, somebody'd have to go in my place, which went against everything I'd grown up with."

Bernhardt ended up in Vietnam with Charlie Company, on the ground as a horrified witness to the My Lai massacre. He was the first soldier to break the silence and talk in public about what had happened in the face of the Army's cover-up. That decision caused great tension with the father he loved. "He believed that dissent and opposition to the government were uncalled for," said Bernhardt. "He never doubted authority. Nor did I. Up until Vietnam, it never occurred to me that I'd be opposed to the authorities, not in a million years."

After Bernhardt left the Army, he found himself sinking into another quagmire, the collapsing American economy of the 1970s. He bounced around Florida, working on a land surveyor's crew, then at a sign shop that made billboards for Sheraton and Kmart. He lived in a trailer, parked in a vacationer's lot on the Gulf of Mexico. But it wasn't really the recession that threw his peacetime life into disarray. Vietnam had changed forever his idea of a code of masculinity. "For years, I had been asking myself, did I do the right stuff? And I had thought that you just added it all up and you could say, This is my manliness score. You get points for going through the service, and bonus points for extra military stuff, and points for a job and a marriage and kids. But it didn't add up. There were all these people walking around with a high score who weren't much of a man in my estimation." Finally, he stopped keeping score, went back to college and got a degree in biology. He married and bought 10 acres of land in the Florida panhandle where he and his wife keep horses and a dozen stray dogs and cats. "In Charlie Company, cowardice and courage was all turned around. If you showed any sign of caring, it was seen as a sign of weakness. If you were the least bit concerned about the civilians, you were considered pathetic, definitely not a man." Now he's turned that experience around once more. "If you can define your manhood in terms of caring," he said, "then maybe we can come back from all that."

S.F.

In the aspiring middle-class suburb where I came of age, there was no mistaking the belief in the boy's pre-eminence; it was evident in the solicitous attentions of parents and schoolteachers, in the centrality of Cub Scouts and Little League, in the community life that revolved around boys' championships and boys' scores—as if these outposts of tract-home America had been built mainly as exhibition rings for junior-male achievement, which perhaps they had.

The "New Frontier" of space turned out to be a void no man could conquer, let alone colonize. The astronaut was no Daniel Boone, just a flattened image for TV viewers to watch.

The speech that inaugurated the shiny new era of the 1960s was the youthful John F. Kennedy's address to the Democratic National Convention, a month before the launch of Echo. The words would become, along with his Inaugural oration, a haunting refrain in adolescent male consciousness. What Kennedy implicitly presented was a new rite of passage for an untested male generation. "The New Frontier of which I speak is not a set of promises," he told them. "It is a set of challenges." Kennedy understood that it was not enough for the fathers to win the world for their sons; the sons had to feel they had won it for themselves. If the fathers had their Nazis and "Nips," then Kennedy would see to it that the sons had an enemy, too. He promised as much on Inauguration Day in 1961, when he spoke vaguely but unremittingly of communism's threat, of a country that would be defined by its readiness to "pay any price" and "oppose any foe." The fight was the thing, the only thing, if America was to retain its masculinity.

The drumrolls promised a dawning era of superpower manhood to the boy born on the New Frontier, a masculine honor and pride in exchange for his loyalty. Ultimately, the boy was double-crossed. The fix was in from the start: corporate and cold-war America's promise to continue the World War II GI's wartime experience of belonging, of meaningful engagement in a mission, was never authentic. "The New Frontier" of space turned out to be a void that no man could conquer, let along colonize. The astronaut was no Daniel Boone; he was just a flattened image for TV viewers to watch—and eventually, to be bored by. Instead of sending its sons to Normandy, the government dispatched them to Vietnam, where the enemy was unclear and the mission remained a tragic mystery. The massive managerial bureaucracies of postwar "white collar" employment, especially the defense contractors fat on government largesse, produced "organization men" who often didn't even know what they were managing—and who suspected they weren't really needed at all. What these corporations offered was a secure job, not a vital role—and not even that secure. The postwar fathers' submission to the national-security state would, after a prosperous period of historically brief duration, be rewarded with pink slips, with massive downsizing, union-breaking and outsourcing. The boy who had been told he was going to be the master of the universe and all that was in it found himself master of nothing.

As early as 1957, the boy's diminished future was foreshadowed in a classic sci-fi film. In "The Incredible Shrinking Man," Scott Carey has a good job, a suburban home, a pleasure boat, a pretty wife. And yet, after he passes through a mist of atomic radiation while on a boating vacation in the Pacific, something happens. As he tells his wife in horror, "I'm getting smaller, Lou, every day."

As Carey quite literally shrinks, the promises made to him are broken one by one. The employer who was to give him lifetime economic security fires him. He is left with only feminine defenses, to hide in a doll house, to fight a giant spider with a sewing pin. And it turns out that the very source of his diminishment is implicitly an atomic test by his own government. His only hope is to turn himself into a celebrated freak and sell his story to the media. "I'm a big man!" Carey says with bitter sarcasm. "I'm famous! One more joke for the world to laugh at."

The more Carey shrinks, the more he strikes out at those around him. "Every day I became more tyrannical," he comments, "more monstrous in my domination of my wife." It's a line that would ring a bell for any visitor to the Alternatives to Violence group and for any observer of the current male scene. As the male role has diminished amid a sea of betrayed promises, many men have been driven to more domineering and some even "monstrous" displays in their frantic quest for a meaningful showdown.

The Ornamental Culture

IF FEW MEN WOULD DO WHAT Shawn Nelson did one evening in the spring of 1995, many could relate. A former serviceman whose career in an army tank unit had gone nowhere, a plumber who had lost his job, a former husband whose wife had left him, the 35-year-old Nelson broke into the National Guard armory, commandeered an M-60 army tank and drove it through the streets of San Diego, flattening fire hy-

drants, crushing 40 cars, downing enough utility poles to cut off electricity to 5,000 people. He was at war with the domestic world that he once thought he was meant to build and defend. He was going to drive that tank he had been meant to command if it killed him. And it did. The police shot Shawn Nelson to death through the turret hatch.

If a man could not get the infrastructure to work for him, he could at least tear it down. If the nation would not provide an enemy to fight, he could go to war at home. If there was to be no brotherhood, he would take his stand alone. A handful of men would attempt to gun down enemies they imagined they saw in family court, employee parking lots, McDonald's restaurants, a Colorado schoolhouse and, most notoriously, a federal office building in Oklahoma. A far greater number would move their destruction of the elusive enemy to the fantasy realm to a clear-cut and controllable world of action movies and video combat, televised athletic tournaments and pay-per-view ultimate-fighting bouts.

But none of it would satisfy, because the world and the fight had changed.

What is left out of the nostalgia of baby-boom men for their heroic World War II fathers is how devastatingly unfathered and unprepared for manhood some of those sons were

---

A few glamorous men understood intuitively that in the coming media and entertainment age the team of men at work would be replaced by the individual man on display. Elevated onto the new pedestal of mass media and entertainment, they were unreachable. Like the astronauts who were their forebears, the new celebrated men—media stars, moussed models, telegenic baby moguls—existed in a realm from which all lines to their brothers had been cut. Where we once lived in a society in which men participated by being useful in public life, we now are surrounded by a culture that encourages people to play almost no functional public roles, only decorative or consumer ones.

Ornamental culture has proved the ultimate expression of the century, sweeping away institutions in which men felt some

sense of belonging and replacing them with visual spectacles that they can only watch and that benefit global commercial forces they cannot fathom. Celebrity culture's effects on men go far beyond the obvious showcasing of action heroes and rock musicians. The ordinary man is no fool: he knows he can't be Arnold Schwarzenegger. Nonetheless, the culture re-shapes his most basic sense of manhood by telling him that masculinity is something to drape over the body, not draw from inner resources; that it is personal, not societal; that manhood is displayed, not demonstrated. The internal qualities once said to embody manhood—surefootedness, inner strength, confidence of purpose—are merchandised to men to enhance their manliness. What passes for the essence of masculinity is being extracted and bottled and sold back to men. Literally, in the case of Viagra.

The culture that '90s men are stranded in was birthed by their fathers' generation—by men who, weary of Depression and wartime deprivation, embraced the new commercialized American dream. What gets left out of the contemporary nostalgia of baby-boom men for their World War II fathers—evidenced in the huge appetite for the film "Saving Private Ryan" and books like Tom Brokaw's "The Greatest Generation"—is what those fathers did after the war. When "Dateline NBC" produced a documentary based on Brokaw's book, celebrating the World War II "tougher than tough" heroes, especially relative to their pampered sons, the troubling subtext was how devastatingly unfathered those sons were, how inadequately they'd been prepared for manhood by their "heroic" fathers.

The men I came to know in the course of researching this book talked about their father's failures in the most private and personal terms, pointing inevitably to the small daily letdowns: "My father didn't teach me how to throw a ball" or "My father was always at work." That their fathers had emotionally or even literally abandoned the family circle was painful enough. But these men suspected, in some way hard to grasp, that their fathers had deserted them in the public realm, too. "My father never taught me how to be a man" was the refrain I heard over and over again. Down the generations, the father wasn't simply a good sport who bought his son a car for graduation. He was a human bridge connecting the boy to an adult life of public engagement and responsibility.

WHAT'S TROUBLING TROUBLED BOYS

As old measures of masculinity faded, the swaggering boys of the Spur Posse made a game of sexual conquest

Who's Keeping Score

The Spur Posse burst out of the orderly suburb of Lakewood, Calif., as America's dreaded nightmare—teenage boys run amok, a microcosm of a misogynistic and violent male culture. In March 1993 police arrested nine Spurs, ages 15 to 19, on suspicion of nearly 20 counts of sexual crimes. In the end, prosecutors concluded that the sex was consensual and all but one count were dropped. But for a time that spring, it was difficult to flip the channels without running into one Spur or another, strutting and bragging their way through the TV talk shows. "You gotta get your image out there," explained Billy Shehan, then 19, a Spur who was not among those arrested but who, despite honor grades and a promising future, felt compelled to hit the media circuit. "It all about building that image on a worldwide basis." Tirelessly, the Spurs repeated the details of their sex-for-points intramural contest, in which each time you had sex with a girl you racked up a point. And for four years running, the winner was Billy Shehan—with a final score of 67.

The media-paid trip that Billy took to New York City with two fellow Spurs started out with many promises. "First they said to us, 'New York! For free!'" Billy recalled. "'We'll give you $1,000, and you'll have limos every day, and elegant meals, and elegant this and elegant that.'" On the ride from the airport to the hotel, Billy felt like a long-exiled prince come to claim his kingdom. "Here I was in this limo in this giant-ass city, and it was like I owned the taxis and the cars, I owned the buildings and all the girls in the windows in the buildings. I felt like I could do whatever I wanted. I had instant exposure."

For the next week and a half, the shows vied for the Spurs' attention. "For 11 days, these guys were our best friends," Billy said

of the TV producers. "They showered admiration on us." One night, Billy said, a senior staffer from "Night Talk With Jane Whitney" took them in a limo to a strip bar, a club in Queens called Goldfingers. "The Maury Povich Show" wooed the boys by sending them our for the evening with four young women from the program's staff. Afterward, the Spurs took a cab to Times Square. "Everything was a fantasy," Billy recalled, "like I was in Mauryland. Like the whole city was a talk show." Billy had his tape recorder out, and he was talking into it as he walked. Suddenly, two hands reached out from the darkness and yanked him between two buildings. "He was holding something against me that felt like a gun," Billy said. The man ripped the tape recorder out of his hands, extracted his wallet and fled. Billy lay in his hotel room all night listening to his heart pound. The next morning he phoned the staff of "The Maury Povich Show" and demanded that they reimburse him for the robbery. When they declined, he refused to go on the program. "I felt they owed me something."

Billy did, however, make an appearance on "Night Talk With Jane Whitney," where he would be much vilified for his boast about scoring his 67th point that week with a girl he lured back to his hotel room. And then he'd return home, poorer and without taped memories. "For a while when I got back," Billy said, "everybody recognized me because of the shows. But now…" His voice trailed off. "Uh, you know something sort of funny?" he said. "I didn't get that [final sex] point. The producer said, 'Act like you got a point on the show.' So I did." He gave a short, bitter laugh. "I even wrote a song about it later. 'Everyone thought I was a 67, when I was just a 66.'"

S.F.

The guiding standards of the fathers, the approving paternal eye, has nearly vanished in this barren new landscape, to be replaced by the market-share standards of a commercial culture, the ogling, ever-restless eye of the camera. By the end of the century, every outlet of the consumer world—magazines, ads, movies, sports, music videos—would deliver the message that manhood had become a performance game to be won in the marketplace, not the workplace, and that male anger was now part of the show. An ornamental culture encouraged young men to see surliness, hostility and violence as expressions of glamour. Whether in Maxim magazine or in Brut's new "Neanderthal" ads, boorishness became a way for men to showcase themselves without being feminized before a potentially girlish mirror. But if celebrity masculinity enshrined the pose of the "bad boy," his rebellion was largely

cosmetic. There was nowhere for him to take a grievance because there was no society to take it to. In a celebrity culture, earnestness about social and political change was replaced by a pose of "irony" that was really just a sullen and helpless paralysis.

In a culture of ornament, manhood is defined by appearance, by youth and attractiveness, by money and aggression, by posture and swagger and "props," by the curled lip and flexed biceps, by the glamour of the cover boy and by the market-bartered "individuality" that sets one astronaut or athlete or gangster above another. These are the same traits that have long been designated as the essence of feminine vanity—the objectification and mirror-gazing that women have denounced as trivializing and humiliating qualities imposed on them by a misogynist culture. No wonder men are in such agony. At the

close of the century, men find themselves in an unfamiliar world where male worth is measured only by participation in a celebrity-driven consumer culture and awarded by lady luck.

The more I consider what men have lost—a useful role in public life, a way of earning a decent living, respectful treatment in the culture—the more it seems that men are falling into a status oddly similar to that of women at midcentury. The '50s housewife, stripped of her connections to a wider world and invited to fill the void with shopping and the ornamental display of her ultrafemininity, could be said to have morphed into the '90s man, stripped of his connections to a wider world and invited to fill the void with consumption and a gym-bred display of his ultramasculinity. The empty compensations of a "feminine mystique" are transforming into the empty compensations of a masculine mystique, with a gentlemen's cigar club no more satisfying than a ladies' bake-off.

But women have rebelled against this mystique. Of all the bedeviling questions my travels and research raised, none struck me more than this: why don't contemporary men rise up in protest against their betrayal? If they have experienced so many of the same injuries as women, the same humiliations, why don't they challenge the culture as women did? Why can't men seem to act?

The stock answers don't suffice. Men aren't simply refusing to "give up the reins of power," as some feminists have argued. The reins have already slipped from most of their hands. Nor are men merely chary of expressing pain and neediness, particularly in an era where emoting is the coin of the commercial realm. While the pressures on men to imagine themselves in control of their emotions are impediments to male revolt, a more fundamental obstacle overshadows them. If men have feared to tread where women have rushed in, then maybe women have had it easier in one very simple regard: women could frame their struggle as a battle against men.

For the many women who embraced feminism in one way or another in the 1970s, that consumer culture was not some intangible force; they saw it as a cudgel wielded by men against women. The mass culture's portfolio of sexist images was propaganda to prop up the myth of male superiority, the argument went. Men, not the marketplace, many women believed, were the root problem and so, as one feminist activist put it in 1969, "the task of the women's liberation movement is to collectively combat male domination in the home, in bed, on the job." And indeed, there were virulent, sexist attitudes to confront. But the 1970s model of confrontation could get feminism only halfway to its goal.

The women who engaged in the feminist campaigns of the '70s were able to take advantage of a ready-made model for revolt. Ironically, it was a male strategy. Feminists had a clearly defined oppressive enemy: the "patriarchy." They had a real frontier to conquer: all those patriarchal institutions, both the old ones that still rebuffed women, like the U.S. Congress or U.S. Steel, and the new ones that tried to remold women, like Madison Avenue or the glamour and media-pimp kingdoms of Bert Parks and Hugh Hefner. Feminists also had their own army of "brothers": sisterhood. Each GI Jane who participated in this struggle felt useful. Whether she was

working in a women's-health clinic or tossing her bottles of Clairol in a "freedom trash can," she was part of a greater glory, the advancement of her entire sex. Many women whose lives were touched by feminism felt in some way that they had reclaimed an essential usefulness; together, they had charged the barricades that kept each of them from a fruitful, thriving life.

The male paradigm of confrontation, in which an enemy could be identified, contested and defeated, proved useful to activists in the civil-rights movement, the antiwar movement, the gay-rights movement. It was, in fact, the fundamental organizing principle of virtually every concerted countercultural campaign of the last half century. Yet it could launch no "men's movement." Herein lies the critical paradox, and the source of male inaction: the model women have used to revolt is the exact one men not only can't use but are trapped in.

Men have no clearly defined enemy who is oppressing them. How can men be oppressed when the culture has already identified them as the oppressors, and when even they see themselves that way? As one man wrote plaintively to Promise Keepers, "I'm like a kite with a broken string, but I'm also holding the tail." Men have invented antagonists to make their problems visible, but with the passage of time, these culprits—scheming feminists, affirmative-action proponents, job-grabbing illegal aliens—have come to seem increasingly unconvincing as explanations for their situation. Nor do men have a clear frontier on which to challenge their intangible enemies. What new realms should they be gaining—the media, entertainment and image-making institutions of corporate America? But these are institutions already run by men; how can men invade their own territory? Is technological progress the frontier? Why then does it seem to be pushing men into obsolescence, socially and occupationally? And if the American man crushes the machine, whose machine has he vanquished?

The male paradigm of confrontation has proved worthless to men. Yet maybe that's not so unfortunate. The usefulness of that model has reached a point of exhaustion anyway. The women's movement and the other social movements have discovered its limits. Their most obvious enemies have been sent into retreat, yet the problems persist. While women are still outnumbered in the executive suites, many have risen in the ranks and some have

achieved authoritative positions often only to perpetuate the same transgressions as their male predecessors. Women in power in the media, advertising and Hollywood have for the most part continued to generate the same sorts of demeaning images as their male counterparts. Blaming a cabal of men has taken feminism about as far as it can go. That's why women have a great deal at stake in the liberation of the one population uniquely poised to discover and employ a new paradigm—men.

Beyond the Politics of Confrontation

THERE ARE SIGNS THAT MEN ARE seeking such a breakthrough. When the Million Man March and Promise Keepers attracted record numbers of men, pundits scratched their heads—why would so many men want to attend events that offered no battle plan, no culprit to confront? No wonder critics who were having trouble placing the gatherings in the usual frame of political conflict found it easier to focus their attentions on the reactionary and hate-mongering attitudes of the "leaders" of these movements, concluding that the real "agenda" must be the anti-Semitism of the Nation of Islam's Louis Farrakhan or the homophobia and sexism of Promise Keepers founder Bill McCartney. But maybe the men who attended these mass gatherings weren't looking for answers that involved an enemy. As Farrakhan's speech, chock-full of conspiracy theories and numerological codes, dragged on, men in droves hastened for the exits. "What was really fantastic about the day was just being together with all these men, and thinking about what I might do differently," George Henderson, a 48-year-old social worker, told me as he headed out early. The amassing of huge numbers of men was a summoning of courage for the unmapped journey ahead.

American men have generally responded well as caretakers in times of crisis, whether that be in wars, depressions or natural disasters. The pre-eminent contemporary example of such a male mobilization also comes on the heels of a crisis: gay men's response to AIDS. Virtually overnight, just as the Depression-era Civilian Conservation Corps built dams and parks and salvaged farmland, so have gay men built a network of clinics, legal and psychological services, fund-raising and political-action brigades, meals on wheels, even laundry assistance. The courage of these caregivers has generated, even in this homophobic nation, a wellspring of admiration and respect. They had a job to do and they did it.

Social responsibility is not the special province of masculinity; it's the lifelong work of all citizens in a community where people are knit together by meaningful and mutual concerns. But if husbanding a society is not the exclusive calling of "husbands," all the better for men's future. Because as men struggle to free themselves from their crisis, their task is not, in the end, to figure out how to be masculine—rather, their masculinity lies in figuring out how to be human. The men who worked at the Long Beach Naval Shipyard, where I spent many months, didn't go there and learn their crafts as riggers, welders and boilermakers to be masculine; they were seeking something worthwhile to do. Their sense of their own manhood flowed out of their utility in a society, not the other way around.

And so with the mystery of men's non-rebellion comes the glimmer of an opening, a chance for men to forge a rebellion commensurate with women's and, in the course of it, to create a new paradigm for human progress that will open doors for both sexes. That was, and continues to be, feminism's dream, to create a freer, more humane world. It will remain a dream without the strength and courage of men who are today faced with a historic opportunity: to learn to wage a battle against no enemy, to own a frontier of human liberty, to act in the service of a brotherhood that includes us all.

Reprinted from *Newsweek*, September 13, 1999, pp. 48-58. Excerpted from *Stiffed: The Betrayal of the American Man*, © 1999 by Susan Faludi. Reprinted by permission of William Morrow/HarperCollins Publishers, Inc.

DEMAND FOR DENSITY?

The Functions of the City in the 21st Century

by Edward L. Glaeser

Is the city becoming obsolete? Many social observers believe that it is. In their view, improved information and transportation technology has deprived urban density of its raison d'etre. They also argue that many cities have caused themselves irreparable damage by pursuing policies that have attracted the poor and repelled the rich. The combination of foolish policies and technological change, they say, has doomed the city.

Ongoing technological developments do indeed have massive implications for urban form. It is also true that many cities have followed policies that, in hindsight, appear unwise. Without question some cities are in deep decline. Some may not recover. But the turn of the new millennium does not presage the end of a ten-thousand-year pattern of increasing urbanization.

In the cities of America's South and West, where new construction is unfettered, urban population growth continues apace. Edge cities—so called after Joel Garreau's 1991 book by that name—may not look exactly like the older, denser cities of the Northeast, but they confirm the ongoing importance of urban agglomerations. Continued demand for urban proximity is also evident from the path of real estate prices in traditional urban areas. In many older cities, where construction is sharply constricted by the costs of building up and, often, by zoning regulations, increased demand shows up not in population growth, but in higher housing prices. For example, real housing prices grew more than 4.5 percent a year in Boston and San Francisco between 1983 and 1998, though both cities' populations barely budged. And the real estate booms in cities such as New York and Chicago confirm that demand for many of the older urban areas remains strong.

Are cities here to stay? Envisioning their future requires understanding their functions. Ultimately, it's true that the future of cities depends on the demand for urban density. And the demand for density depends on what density does.

Cities: A Moving Experience

Density has important benefits for both production and consumption, primarily because it lowers transport costs. In production, cities traditionally lower the cost of moving goods, people, and ideas. In consumption, they provide access to large public goods and to specialized services. Cities can also provide a desirable (or undesirable) social milieu for consumers, which may be extremely important to the future of cities.

I begin the risky project of crystal ball gazing by noting two trends expected to continue into the foreseeable future. The first is rising incomes, accompanied by increased demand for luxury goods and, especially important for commuting, a higher opportunity cost of time. The second trend, improving technology for transporting objects and ideas, may eliminate some of the productive functions of cities, but may make cities more valuable in other ways.

Today one venerable urban edge—in the cost of transporting goods—has disappeared. As a result, manufacturing has already left the cities, and large-scale wholesale trade is about to follow. But the urban advantage in moving people is still enormously important, both in the service sector, which requires interpersonal contact, and in the labor market, which allows people to switch jobs without switching homes. Cities also remain key in moving ideas.

As important as the production side is, the future of most cities depends on their being desirable places for consumers to live. As consumers become richer and firms become mobile, location choices are based as much on their advantages for workers as on their advantages for firms. Some cities, such as San Francisco, seem to appeal strongly to consumers. Other cities do not. The ones that are attractive have thrived in both property values and population.

Production in the City: Transporting Goods

Businesses have long located in cities to minimize transport costs of all kinds, especially the cost of moving goods. America's familiar port cities—Boston, New York, and San Francisco—grew up because firms wanted to save money receiving raw materials and shipping finished products. Soon the impetus toward growth in such cities transcended the port function, as new firms were attracted less by the port and more by the area's firms and growing population base.

By the last few decades of the 20th century, transport costs for goods had declined so much that it was no longer essential for manufacturing plants to be close to customers and suppliers. Indeed, declining transport costs have driven a de-urbanization of manufacturing almost as striking as manufacturing's overall decline. In 1950, seven out of the eight largest U.S. cities had more manufacturing (as a share of employment) than did the nation as a whole. In 1990, six out of the eight largest cities had less manufacturing (as a share) than did the United States as a whole. And following on the heels of manufacturing in leaving the city is the land-intensive wholesale trade.

But cities' decreasing ability to provide cheap transport for goods may turn out to have a silver lining. As Matthew Kahn has pointed out, for example, improvements in Pittsburgh's environmental quality subsequent to the departure of the manufacturing industry there appear to have attracted the better-educated residents who have spurred the city's rebirth. Census data abundantly document the reluctance of richer people to live close to manufacturing. Not only is it futile for big cities to struggle to hold on to shipyards and big manufacturing plants, it may be counterproductive because heavy industry repels high human capital urban residents.

Moving People: Urban Labor Markets

Although cities have lost their edge in the cost of moving goods, they retain it in the cost of moving people, which is critically important in many service industries. As the economy becomes more service oriented, that advantage may well rise in importance.

Dense urban labor markets are attractive to both firms and workers in the service industry. As J. Kolko has noted, service industry firms tend to locate near each other because they all use the same types of workers. Silicon Valley's continued ability to attract new firms, for example, appears to stem in large part from its labor force of skilled specialists. In turn, the agglomeration of firms provides workers with a form of labor market insurance. In single-company towns—witness Detroit—the entire work force suffers if the main employer falters. In a multi-industry town, by contrast, workers can respond to a downturn in demand simply by switching firms. The key point is that cities allow workers to switch jobs without moving residences.

The urban labor market gives workers greater flexibility in other ways. Unlike their peers in small towns, young workers in a big city can switch from job to job as they figure out what to do with their lives. Likewise, competitive demand for skills in dense cities enables workers to invest in education and training, confident of reaping large returns.

Despite constant improvements in transport technology for people (better cars, airline deregulation), it is not obvious whether the costs of moving people are rising or falling. What is clear is that incomes are rising—and with them the opportunity cost of lost time. The ability of cities to save on transport costs for people thus becomes all the more important.

Extreme density is not essential to cities' labor market advantages (Silicon Valley is the classic example of a moderately dense urban area that functions well as a labor market). But increasing proximity is continually valuable for business services. The strengths of downtown Manhattan, for example, come in part from the vast supply of nearby business services. And the same goes for consumer services. The more density, the better when it comes to the supply of restaurants or stores. Analysts who think that cities' chief function is to provide services will value high-density urban areas. Those who believe that their function is to provide large urban labor markets will put their money on edge cities.

The Idea-Based City

Cities are also productive because they move ideas. Patent citations, for example, are remarkable for their geographic localization—inventors appear especially susceptible to the influence of other inventors who are close at hand. As several studies have confirmed, large urban areas are often particularly exciting centers of ferment and product innovation.

The swift movement of ideas in the city spurs production in several ways. People and firms who want to be innovators will come to the city to reap the benefits of the creative milieu. The advantages to being the first innovator in most industries, especially those such as information technology and fashion, appear to be rising. As knowledge becomes an increasingly dominant part of production, the edge from being in a city seems likely to grow.

Even firms that are not seeking to be innovators themselves will be drawn to urban areas to get access to the latest technologies. As the spread of ideas quickens, however, and as the differences in knowledge across space lessen, this effect of the idea-based city will presumably decline.

Finally, idea flows in cities increase the accumulation of skills on the individual level. The rich presence of role models and mentors in bigger cities hastens the accumulation of skills, as does the wider range of experiences available. Compare, for example, the medical problems encountered by an intern in a small-town hospital and those faced by an intern in an urban hospital. And because cities facilitate specialization—Adam Smith observed more than two centuries ago that people in rural areas tend to be generalists, while city residents are inclined to be specialists—the same time spent learning in a city may lead to more expertise in one's particular area.

Whether cities will retain their edge in moving ideas depends on whether information technology will eliminate the need for face-to-face interactions. Here, the evidence is mixed. Although many people thought a century ago that telephones were going to eliminate the advantages of cities, telephone use today is highest among people who live close to one another. And although faxes and e-mail were supposed to eliminate the need to meet face-to-face, business travel has been booming over the past 15 years. One can certainly build a case that face-to-face contact and electronic contact are complements rather than substitutes. As such, electronic technologies are unlikely to eliminate the informational advantages of cities any time soon.

The Consumer's City

Evidence increasingly suggests that cities that thrive will have to be attractive places for people to live. As incomes rise, the demand for a pleasant local environment will surely continue to increase. The cities that succeed in the next century will be those that can remake themselves as consumer cities. The success of New York over the past eight years comes in part from the success of Wall Street. But New York's reinvigoration also comes from its ability to reduce crime and sell itself on the basis of its many advantages as an exciting place to live.

Perhaps the most striking evidence for the importance of consumer cities is the rise of reverse commuting. Traditionally, people lived in suburbs and worked in cities. Today, patterns are often reversed. Clearly, the desire of large numbers of consumers to live far from their jobs in urban areas implies the desirability of cities as places to live.

One way to see the relative attractiveness of a place is the gap between housing costs and wages. Between 1980 and 1990 increases in a metropolitan area's size pushed wages up marginally, but pushed housing costs up much more. (For the statistically minded, the elasticity of wages with respect to metropolitan area size went from .051 to .082, while the elasticity of housing costs with respect to metropolitan area size rose from .114 to .225.) The substantial increase in housing relative to wages reflects the possibility that the value of the amenities of the largest metropolitan areas has risen steeply.

But have central cities themselves done well? Within cities, both rents and incomes rose steeply closest to the city center during 1980–90. A strengthening of the trend through the 1990s suggests that these neighborhoods are indeed becoming more appealing, especially to the rich. Much of this growth probably comes from rising wages and the rising opportunity cost of time. But the important fact is that some types of consumers who once would have moved to the suburbs are choosing cities.

As with production, cities' consumption advantages stem from lower transport costs. In the market sector, the advantages are greater access to, and greater variety of, services. The wealth of restaurants and stores and the dizzying array of goods available from them surely make cities attractive to consumers. And despite the advent of Internet shopping, stores will continue to attract customers, particularly for the most expensive commodities. The large market size of cities also makes it possible to support big art museums, symphonies, and professional sports teams. Smaller areas cannot provide all these public goods, and their value favors the largest cities.

Although analysts are just beginning to understand the importance of consumer preferences in driving the success of different places, it seems clear that if cities are to succeed, one of their functions must be to please consumers. A rich variety of services, a thriving social environment, and access to public amenities can make big cities consumer havens.

Policy Implications

Given cities' comparative advantage in moving people and ideas and in being pleasant places to live, what are the policy implications for both city and national leaders? In any policy discussion, it is crucial to distinguish between the obligations of these two types of leaders. City leaders have an obligation to build their cities. National leaders should focus on the well-being of their nation as a whole and not favor any particular region.

The most reliable predictor of urban growth—aside from the weather—is the human capital level of a city's work force. The median years of education of a city's work force, in particular, goes far to predict the growth of its population, income, and housing. Two key ways for city leaders to build human capital are by emphasizing quality education and by avoiding an emphasis on redistributive spending, such as welfare, public health, and public housing. This latter recommendation goes against the admirable impulses of most city leaders, who wish to alleviate the pain in the lives of their city's poorest residents. But for cities to undertake large-scale redistribution is counterproductive: they only damage themselves (and their residents) in the process. Redistribution at the city level causes wealthy and skilled citizens to avoid the city, badly erodes the tax base, and leaves the poor isolated.

The obligation of national and state leaders is to fashion public policies that are spatially neutral across areas. These government leaders must eliminate the pieces of spatial non-neutrality that now exist, particularly those that artificially attract the poor to, and repel the wealthy from, big cities. Some spatially neutral national and state policies can benefit cities in important ways. If, for example, the state and national governments were to assume the full burden of redistribution, they would help keep big cities from being poverty centers. And if state governments were to move to a system of statewide education vouchers, they would both increase the quality of schooling available to poor children in cities and provide a major incentive for the wealthy to live in cities. Cities, being large markets, will benefit much more than low-density suburbs from the competition introduced by a voucher system. Indeed, evidence from the Chilean voucher program shows the tendency of the program to favor the larger cities. And if suburbs lost their edge in education, cities would become much more attractive to many families with children.

Looking Ahead

The future of the city depends on the continued advantages of density. The high density levels of traditional downtowns will continue to be valuable if center cities maintain a productive edge in their ability to speed the flow of ideas and if they keep and develop any advantages they may have as centers for consumption. Traditional cities that rely on manufacturing face an extremely uncertain future, because poverty makes them unattractive as consumer havens. They will continue to exist as long as their housing stock remains, but their populations will continue to shrink. The dominant urban form of the future, almost unquestionably, will be the edge city with its moderate density levels.

Edward L. Glaeser is professor of economics at Harvard University and a research associate at the National Bureau of Economic Research.

Does the Internet Strengthen Community?

William A. Galston

Suppose that in the summer of 1952, someone had organized a conference on the social consequences of television. The participants would have faced two crucial problems. First, social reality was moving faster than empirical scholarship. Television was diffusing at an explosive rate, from a relative rarity in the late 1940s to near-ubiquity only a decade later. Scholars in 1952 studying the social effects of television might have noted how neighbors crowded into a living room to watch the only set on the block, and they might have drawn conclusions about the medium's community-reinforcing tendencies that would have seemed antique only a few years later.

The second problem would have been even more daunting. Reasoning by analogy from, for example, the automobile's effects on sexual morality in the 1920s, the participants might have suspected that television's unintended consequences would turn out to be at least as significant as its directly contemplated purposes. But they would have been hard-pressed to move much beyond this general insight. The emergence of a new communications technology within a complex social system was bound to reconfigure everything from intimate relations to the distribution of public power. But how, exactly?

According to Alan Ehrenhalt, the front stoop was one of the centers of social life in Chicago's blue-collar neighborhoods of the early 1950s. But during that decade, the introduction of television into nearly every home affected not only the dissemination of news and entertainment, but also patterns of social interaction. Families spent more time clustered around the television set, and less talking with their neighbors on the street. In turn, the increased atomization of social life had important ripple effects. Spontaneous neighborhood oversight and discipline of children became harder to maintain, and less densely populated streets opened the door for increased criminal activity.

I don't mean to suggest (nor does Ehrenhalt) that television was solely responsible for these changes; the advent of air conditioning also helped depopulate streets by making the indoors far more habitable during summer's dog days, and important cultural changes reduced the influence of various forms of authority that helped hold neighborhoods and communities together. I do want to suggest, however, that today it is as if it were 1952 for the Internet, and the methodological problems I have just sketched are the ones we must confront in assessing the impact of this new medium.

As individual choice expands, the bonds linking us to others tend to weaken.

In the face of such challenges, it is natural, perhaps inevitable, that our thought will prove less flexible and our imagination less capacious than the future we seek to capture. In our mind's eye, we may hold constant what will prove to be most mutable. One of my favorite examples of this principle in the past (there are many) comes from an article published in the *St. Louis Globe-Democrat* in 1888:

> The time is not far distant when we will have wagons driving around with casks and jars of stored electricity, just as we have milk and bread wagons at present.... The arrangements will be of such a character that houses can be supplied with enough stored electricity to last twenty-four hours. All that the man with the cask will have to do will be to drive up to the back door, detach the cask left the day before, replace it with a new one, and then go to the next house and do likewise.

As Carolyn Marvin points out, this vision of the future reflects the assumption of, and hope for, the continuation of the economically and morally self-sufficient household, not beholden to outside forces, and going about its own business—a way of life undermined by the very patterns of distribution and concentration that electrical power helped foster.

I draw two lessons from this cautionary example. First, in speculating about the effects of the Internet on community life, we should be sensitive to the often surprising ways in which market forces can shape emerging technologies to upset entrenched social patterns. (This maxim is particularly important for an era such as ours, in which the market is practically and ideologically ascendant.) Second, we should be as self-conscious as possible about the cultural assumptions and trends that will shape our use of, and response to, new technologies such as the Internet. Contemporary American society, I would argue, is structured by two principal cultural forces: the high value attached to individual choice, and the longing for community.

Choice and Community

During the past generation, scholars in a range of disciplines have traced the rise of choice as a core value. Daniel Yankelovich suggests that what he calls the "affluence effect"—the psychology of prosperity that emerged as memories of the Depression faded—weakened traditional restraints:

> People came to feel that questions of how to live and with whom to live were a matter of individual choice not to be governed by restrictive norms. As a nation, we came to experience the bonds to marriage, family, children, job, community, and country as constraints that were no longer necessary.

In Ehrenhalt's analysis, the new centrality of choice is a key explanation for the transformation of Chicago's neighborhoods since the 1950s. Lawrence Friedman argues that individual choice is the central norm around which the modern American legal system has been restructured. Alan Wolfe sees individual choice at the heart of the nonjudgmental tolerance that characterizes middle-class morality in contemporary America.

The problem (emphasized by all these authors) is that as individual choice expands, the bonds linking us to others tend to weaken. To the extent that the desire for satisfying human connections is a permanent feature of the human condition, the expansion of choice was bound to trigger an acute sense of loss, now expressed as a longing for community. (The remarkable public response to Robert Putnam's "Bowling Alone" can in part be attributed to this sentiment.) But few Americans are willing to surrender the expansive individual liberty they now enjoy, even in the name of stronger marriages, neighborhoods, or citizenship. This tension constitutes what many Americans

experience as the central dilemma of our age: as Wolfe puts it, "how to be an autonomous person and tied together with others at the same time."

I do not believe that this problem can ever be fully solved; to some extent, strong ties are bound to require compromises of autonomy, and vice versa. (This exemplifies Isaiah Berlin's pluralist account of our moral condition: the genuine goods of life are diverse and in tension with one another, so that no single good can be given pride of place without sacrificing others.) Still, there is an obvious motivation for reducing this tension as far as possible—that is, for finding ways of living that combine individual autonomy and strong social bonds.

Anecdotal evidence suggests that online groups fill a range of significant needs for their participants.

This desire gives rise to a concept that I will call "voluntary community." This conception of social ties compatible with autonomy has three defining conditions: low barriers to entry, low barriers to exit, and interpersonal relations shaped by mutual adjustment rather than hierarchical authority or coercion. Part of the excitement surrounding the Internet is what some see as the possibility it offers of facilitating the formation of voluntary communities, so understood. Others doubt that the kinds of social ties likely to develop on the Internet can be adequate substitutes—practically or emotionally—for the traditional ties they purport to replace.

Are Online Groups "Communities"?

In a prophetic account written thirty years ago, Licklider and Taylor suggested that "life will be happier for the on-line individual because the people with whom one interacts most strongly will be selected more by commonality of interests and goals than by accidents of proximity." Whether Internet users are in fact happier and, if so, because they are users, remains to be seen and may never be known (the problems of research design for that issue boggle the mind). The underlying hypothesis—that "accidents of proximity" are on balance a source of unhappiness—seems incomplete at best. But Licklider and Taylor were certainly right to predict that online communication would facilitate the growth of groups with shared interests. Indeed, participation in such groups is now the second most frequent interactive activity (behind email) among Internet users.

Anecdotal evidence suggests that these groups fill a range of significant needs for their participants. For some, the exchange of information and opinions about shared enthusiasms—e.g., rock groups, sports teams—is satisfying as an end in itself. For others, this exchange serves important personal or professional goals. Those suffering from specific diseases can share information about promising doctors, therapies, and treatment centers more widely and rapidly than ever before. A friend of mine who works as the lone archivist in a city library system tells me that participating in the online group of archivists from around the country mitigates her otherwise intense sense of personal and professional isolation. In this regard, computer-mediated communication can be understood as raising to a higher power the kinds of non-place-based relationships and associations that have existed for centuries in industrialized societies.

But are these shared activities "communities"? What is at stake in this question? J. Snyder, a commentator skeptical of the claims of technocommunitarian enthusiasts, argues as follows:

> A community is more than a bunch of people distributed in all 24 time zones, sitting in their dens and pounding away on keyboards about the latest news in alt.music.indigo-girls. That's not a community; it's a fan club. Newsgroups, mailing lists, chat rooms—call them what you will—the Internet's virtual communities are not communities in almost any sense of the word. A community is people who have greater things in common than a fascination with a narrowly defined topic.

Note that this objection revolves around the substance of what members of groups have in common, not the nature of the communication among them. By this standard, stamp clubs meeting face to face would not qualify as communities. Conversely, Jews in the diaspora would constitute a community, even if the majority never meet one another face to face, because what they have in common is a sacred text as an authoritative guide to the totality of temporal and spiritual existence.

While many kinds of groups can undergo rapid changes of membership, they may respond differently.

To assess these claims, we may begin with Thomas Bender's classic definition of community:

> A community involves a limited number of people in a somewhat restricted social space or network held together by shared understandings and a sense of obligation. Relationships are close, often intimate, and usually face to face. Individuals are bound together by affective or emotional ties rather than by a perception of individual self-interest. There is a "we-ness" in a community; one is a *member*.

Upper-middle-class American professionals tend to dismiss this picture of community as the idealization of a past that never was. But Bender insists that it offers a tolerably accurate picture of town life in America prior to the twentieth century:

> The town was the most important container for the social lives of men and women, and community was found within it.... The geographic place seems to have provided a supportive human surround that can be visualized in the image of concentric circles.... The innermost ring encompassed kin, while the second represented friends who were treated as kin. Here was the core experience of community. Beyond these rings were two others: those with whom one dealt regularly and thus knew, and, finally, those people who were recognized as members of the town but who were not necessarily known.

A recent personal experience has convinced me that community, so understood, is not simply part of a vanished past. On a recent trip to Portugal, my family stopped for the night at the small town of Condeixa, about ten miles south of the medieval university of Coimbra. After dinner I went to the village square, where I spent one of the most remarkable evenings of my life. Children frolicked on playground equipment set up in the square. Parents occupied some of the benches positioned under symmetrical rows of trees; on others, old men sat and talked animatedly. At one point a group of middle-aged men, some carrying portfolios of papers, converged on the square and discussed what seemed to be some business or local matter. The square was ringed by modest cafés and restaurants, some catering to teenagers and young adults, others to parents and families. From time to time a squabble would break out among the children playing in the square; a parent would leave a café table, smooth over the conflict, and return to the adult conversation. As I was walking around the perimeter of the square, I heard some singing. Following the sound, I peered into the small Catholic church on the corner and discovered a young people's choir rehearsing for what a poster on the next block informed me was a forthcoming town festival in honor of St. Peter.

Many aspects of this experience struck me forcibly, particularly the sense of order, tranquility, and human connection based on years of mutual familiarity, stable social patterns, and shared experience. I was not surprised to learn subsequently that about half of all young people born in Portuguese small towns choose to remain there throughout their adult lives—a far higher percentage than for small-town youth in any other nation of western Europe.

Bender's examples of community (and my own) are place-based. But it is important not to build place, or face-to-face relationships, into the definition of community. To do this would be to resolve by fiat, in the negative, the relationship between community and the Internet. Instead, I suggest that we focus on the four key structural features of community implied by Bender's account—limited membership, shared norms, affective ties, and a sense of mutual obligation—and investigate, as empirical questions, their relationship to computer-mediated communication.

Limited Membership

While technical restrictions do exist and are sometimes employed, a typical feature of online groups is weak control over the admission of new participants. Anecdotal evidence suggests that many founding members of online groups experience the rapid influx of newer members as a loss of intimacy and dilution of the qualities that initially made their corner of cyberspace attractive. Some break away and start new groups in an effort to recapture the original experience.

It is unlikely that online groups will serve as significant training grounds for the exercise of voice—a traditional function of Tocquevillean associations.

Weak control over membership is not confined to electronic groups, of course. Up to the early 1840s, for example, Boston was conspicuous among American cities for the relative stability and homogeneity of its population, which contributed to what outside observers saw as the communitarian intimacy and solidarity of Boston society. And then, in the single year of 1847, more than 37,000 immigrants arrived in a city of less than 115,000. By the mid-1850s, more than one third of its population was Irish. Boston was riven, and the consequences persisted for more than a century.

While many kinds of groups can undergo rapid changes of membership, they may respond differently. In a famous discussion, Albert Hirschman distinguishes between two kinds of responses—exit and voice—to discontent within organizations. "Exit" is the act of shifting membership to new organizations that better meet needs, while "voice" is the effort to alter the character of existing

organizations. Exit is, broadly speaking, market-like behavior, while voice is political.

An hypothesis: when barriers to leaving old groups and joining new ones are relatively low, exit will tend to be the preferred option; as these costs rise, the exercise of voice becomes more likely. Because it is a structural feature of most online groups that border-crossings are cheap, exit will be the predominant response to dissatisfaction. If so, it is unlikely that online groups will serve as significant training grounds for the exercise of voice—a traditional function of Tocquevillean associations. In Boston, by contrast, because the perceived cost of exit was high, the Brahmins stayed, struggled, and ultimately worked out a modus vivendi with their Irish neighbors—a process that took over a hundred years. The mutual accommodation of the two groups helped develop one of this country's richest political traditions.

In a diverse democratic society, politics requires the ability to deliberate, and compromise, with individuals unlike oneself. When we find ourselves living cheek by jowl with neighbors with whom we differ but whose propinquity we cannot easily escape, we have powerful incentives to develop modes of accommodation. On the other hand, the ready availability of exit tends to produce internally homogeneous groups that may not communicate with other groups and lack incentives to develop shared understandings across their differences. One of the great problems of contemporary American society and politics is the proliferation of narrow groups and the weakening of structures that create incentives for accommodation. It is hard to see how the multiplication of online groups will improve this situation.

Shared Norms

A different picture emerges when we turn our attention from intergroup communication to the internal life of online groups. Some case studies suggest that online groups can develop complex systems of internalized norms. These norms arise in response to three kinds of imperatives: promoting shared purposes; safeguarding the quality of group discussion; and managing scarce resources in what can be conceptualized as a virtual commons.

As Elinor Ostrom has argued, the problem of regulating a commons for collective advantage can be solved through a wide range of institutional arrangements other than private property rights or coercive central authority. Internet groups rely to an unusual degree on norms that evolve through iteration over time and are enforced through moral suasion and group disapproval of conspicuous violators. This suggests that despite the anarcho-libertarianism frequently attributed to Internet users, the medium is capable of promoting a kind of socialization and moral learning through mutual adjustment.

I know of no systematic research exploring these moral effects of group online activities and their consequences (if any) for offline social and political behavior. One obvious hypothesis is that to the extent that young online users come to regard the internal structure of their groups as models for offline social and political groups, they will be drawn to (or demand) more participatory organizations whose norms are enforced consensually and informally. If so, it would be important to determine the extent to which this structure reflects the special imperatives of organizations where barriers to entrance and exit are low. The ideal of voluntary community reinforced by the Internet is likely to run up against the coercive requisites of majoritarian politics.

Affective Ties

Proponents of computer-mediated communication as the source of new communities focus on the development of affective ties among online group members. Thus, Howard Rheingold, while acknowledging concerns that people interacting online "lack the genuine personal commitments to one another that form the bedrock of genuine community," insists that cyberculture can overcome this limitation. He defines "virtual communities" as "social aggregations that emerge from the Net when enough people carry on… public discussions long enough, with sufficient human feeling, to form webs of personal relationships."

Internet enthusiasts have deconstructed the ideal of face-to-face communications.

Here, the crucial empirical question is the relationship between face-to-face communication (or its absence) and the development of affective ties. How important are visual and tonal cues? How important is it to have some way of comparing words and deeds? Here's one hypothesis: it is impossible to create ties of depth and significance between A and B without each being able to assess the purposes and dispositions that underlie the other's verbal communications. Is the interlocutor sincere or duplicitous? Does he really care about me, or is he merely manipulating my desire for connection to achieve (unstated) purposes of his own? Is the overall persona an interlocutor presents to me genuine or constructed? We all rely on a range of nonverbal evidence to reduce (if never quite eliminate) our qualms about others' motivations and identities.

Internet enthusiasts respond to these questions by deconstructing the ideal of face-to-face communication. They point out (correctly) that duplicity and manipula-

tion have been enduring facts of human history and that the advent of computer-mediated communication raises at most questions of degree rather than kind. I must confess that I come away unconvinced. Considerable evidence suggests that the Internet facilitates the invention of online personalities at odds with offline realities and that the ability to simulate identities is one of its most attractive features for many users (gender-bending is said to be especially popular). But the playful exercise of the imagination, whatever its intrinsic merits and charms, is not readily compatible with the development of meaningful affective ties. (Devotees of what might be called postmodern psychology, with its emphasis on social construction and *bricolage* and rejection of the distinction between surface and depth, might want to quarrel with this. So be it. I see no way of discussing affective ties without invoking some distinction between genuine and spurious emotions and identities.)

Community requires some heightened identification with other members that engenders a willingness to sacrifice on their behalf.

Another hotly debated issue is the relationship between computer-mediated communication and the tendency to express strong sentiments in antisocial ways. Some researchers have argued that because the absence of visual and tonal cues makes it more difficult to see the pain words can inflict, the Internet reduces restraints on verbal behavior and invites individuals to communicate in impulsive ways. (An analogy would be the asserted desensitizing effects of high-altitude bombing.) Other researchers argue that it is precisely the absence of traditional cues that promotes the formation of social norms for Internet speech and that there is no evidence that this speech is more antisocial on average than is face-to-face communication. Given the fragmentary evidence, I see no way of resolving this debate right now.

Mutual Obligation

The final dimension of community to be considered here is the development of a sense of mutual obligation among members. Recall John Winthrop's famous depiction of the communal ideal aboard the *Arbella*:

> We must entertain each other in brotherly affection, we must be willing to abridge ourselves of our superfluities, for the supply of others' necessities…. We must delight in each other, make

others' conditions our own, rejoice together, mourn together, labor and suffer together.

While this may seem too demanding, at the very least community requires some heightened identification with other members that engenders a willingness to sacrifice on their behalf.

The technology critic Neil Postman argues that whatever may be the case with norms and emotions, there's no evidence that participants in online groups develop a meaningful sense of reciprocal responsibility or mutual obligation. Groups formed out of common interests need not develop obligations because by definition the interest of each individual is served by participating in the group. (If that ceases to be the case, it is almost costless to leave the group.) The problem is that bonds created by "interests" (in either sense of the term) provide no basis for the surrender of interests—that is, for sacrifice.

I find it intriguing that many defenders of online groups concede Postman's factual premise but deny its normative relevance. Nessim Watson, for example, argues that communities characterized by a strong sense of mutual obligation have virtually disappeared in contemporary America; to single out online groups for criticism on this score is both unfair and an exercise in nostalgia. Efforts to resuscitate the obsolescent idea of mutual obligation are likely to prove counterproductive:

> Those who champion Postman's noble metaphor of community as common obligation are most often faced with the task of dragging other community members kicking and screaming into their part of the obligation. Attempts to construct community usually result in the increased frustration of organizers and the increased cynicism of participants toward the entire idea of community.

In late twentieth-century America, Watson concludes, there is no alternative to voluntary community based on perceptions of individual interest; we will have to get along as best we can without antique norms and practices of sacrifice and mutual obligation.

The idea of voluntary community reinforced by the Internet is likely to run up against the coercive requisites of majoritarian politics.

I very much doubt that our society—or any society—can indefinitely do without these civic virtues. The question of whether emerging forms of group activity help foster these virtues or reinforce their absence is likely to prove significant for the future.

Conclusion

I conclude by restating what appears to me to be the central question. Many Americans today are looking for ways of reconciling powerful but often conflicting desires for autonomy and connection. The idea of voluntary community draws its appeal from that quest: if we are linked to others by choice rather than accident, if our interaction with them is shaped by mutual adjustment rather than hierarchical authority, and if we can set aside these bonds whenever they clash with our individual interests, then the lamb of connection can lie down with the lion of autonomy. Online groups are paradigmatic examples of voluntary community—whence the enthusiasm they have aroused in many quarters.

It is far too early to know what kinds of effects such groups will have over time on the relations between individuals and communities in America. But three kinds of structural doubts can be raised about the civic consequences of voluntary communities. Because they emphasize exit as a response to discontent and dissatisfaction, they do not promote the development of voice; because they emphasize personal choice, they do not acknowledge the need for authority; because they are brought together and held together by converging individual interests, they neither foster mutual obligation nor lay the basis for sacrifice.

In today's cultural climate, the response to these doubts is obvious: anything less than voluntary community will trap individuals in webs of oppressive relations. And what could be worse than that? My answer: learning to make the best of circumstances one has not chosen is part of what it means to be a good citizen and mature human being. We should not organize our lives around the fantasy that entrance and exit can always be cost-free. Online groups can fulfill important emotional and utilitarian needs. But they must not be taken as comprehensive models of a future society.

—**William A. Galston**

This essay has been excerpted from *democracy.com? Governance in a Networked World*, edited by Elaine Ciulla Kamarck and Joseph S. Nye, Jr. Copyright ©1999 by Hollis Publishing Company; reprinted with permission. Sources: Alan Ehrenhalt, *The Lost City: Discovering the Forgotten Virtues of Community in the Chicago of the 1950s* (Basic Books, 1995); Carolyn Marvin, *When Old Technologies Were New: Thinking about Communications in the Late Nineteenth Century* (Oxford University Press, 1988); Daniel Yankelovich, "How Changes in the Economy Are Reshaping American Values," in *Values and Public Policy*, edited by Thomas E. Mann and Timothy Taylor (Brookings

Institution Press, 1994); Lawrence Friedman, *The Republic of Choice: Law, Authority, and Culture* (Harvard University Press, 1990); Alan Wolfe, *One Nation After All* (Viking, 1998); Robert D. Putnam, "Bowling Alone: America's Declining Social Capital," *Journal of Democracy*, vol. 6, no. 1 (January 1995); Steven G. Jones, ed., *Virtual Culture: Identity and Communication in Cybersociety* (Sage, 1977) (contains quotations from Licklider and Taylor, and from Howard Rheingold); "Technology and Online Use Survey," The Pew Center for the People and the Press (1996) (this survey measures frequency of participation in online groups; cited in Pippa Norris, "Who Surfs? New Technology, Old Voters, and Virtual Democracy in America," in *democracy.com? Governance in a Networked World*); J. Snyder, "Get Real," *Internet World*, vol. 7, no. 2 (1996); Thomas Bender, *Community and Social Change in America* (Johns Hopkins University Press, 1982); Doris Kearns Goodwin, *The Fitzgeralds and the Kennedys: An American Saga* (St. Martin's Press, 1987) (on the Brahmins and the Irish in Boston); Margaret McLaughlin, Kerry K. Osborne, and Christine B. Smith, "Standards of Conduct on Usenet," and Nancy K. Baym, "The Emergence of Community in Computer-Mediated Communication," both in *Cybersociety: Computer-Mediated Communication and Community*, edited by Steven G. Jones (Sage, 1995); Nessim Watson, "Why We Argue about Virtual Community: A Case Study of the Phish.Net Fan Community," in *Virtual Culture: Identity and Communication in Cybersociety* (see full citation above); Elinor Ostrom, *Governing the Commons: The Evolution of Institutions for Collective Action* (Cambridge University Press, 1990); Guiseppe Mantovani, *New Communication Environments: From Everyday to Virtual* (Taylor & Francis, 1996) (on the absence of traditional visual and tonal cues in online communications); Neil Postman, *Technopoly: The Surrender of Culture to Technology* (Vintage, 1993).

This article originally appeared in the *Report from the Institute for Philosophy and Public Policy*, Volume 19, Number 4, Fall 1999. © 1999. Reprinted by permission.

UNIT 4

Stratification and Social Inequalities

Unit Selections

Key Points to Consider

- Explain why you believe that technology could either reduce or increase social inequalities.

- What inequalities do you find unacceptable, and what inequalities do you find acceptable?

- Why is stratification such an important theme in sociology?

- Which social groups are likely to rise in the stratification system in the next decade? Which groups will fall? Why?

- How does stratification along income lines differ from stratification along racial or gender lines?

 **Links: www.dushkin.com/online/**
These sites are annotated in the World Wide Web pages.

American Scientist
http://www.amsci.org/amsci/amsci.html

Joint Center for Poverty Research
http://www.jcpr.org

Patterns of Variability: The Concept of Race
http://www.as.ua.edu/ant/bindon/ant101/lectures/race/race1.htm

The Urban Institute
http://www.urban.org/welfare/overview.htm

People are ranked in many different ways by physical strength, education, wealth, or other characteristics. Those who are rated highly often have power over others, special status, and prestige. The differences among people constitute their life chances, the probability that an individual or group will be able to obtain the valued and desired goods in a society. These differences are referred to as stratification, the system of structured inequalities in social relationships.

In most industrialized societies, income is one of the most important divisions among people. Karl Marx described stratification in terms of class rather than income. For him social class referred mainly to two distinct groups: those who control the means of production and those who do not. This section examines the life chances of the rich and the poor and of various disadvantaged groups, which best demonstrates the crucial features of the stratification system in the United States.

The first subsection of this unit deals with the differences between classes and income levels. Inequality of income has increased, but so has equality of opportunity. Cait Murphy's article examines this trend more closely. "Are the Rich Cleaning Up?" describes the growth in income inequality since 1973 and the different viewpoints concerning the consequences of these changes on American society and values. It attributes the growing income gap to the increasing premium of a college education in the demand for labor, the changing family structure (single parent families among the poor and two-worker families among the rich), the relative decline in the minimum wage, the decline in unions, and immigration. Cait Murphy also discusses solutions but finds little merit in many popular proposals. Isabel Sawhill, in her article "Still the Land of Opportunity?" presents an up-to-date picture of inequality in America with special emphasis on the degree of equality of opportunity. The changes in the past decade are mixed.

The American welfare system is addressed in the second subsection of unit 4. The first article describes the generous welfare system for the rich, and the next describes the stingy and disappearing welfare system for the poor. Donald Barlett and James Steele explain how corporations milk federal, state, and local governments of billions of dollars. It comes as no surprise to a student of society that the political economy is set up to benefit the upper class and the powerful but the extent of that bias, when pointed out, can shock us anyway. The article on welfare reviews the research analyzing the results of the 1996 welfare reform. Caseloads have declined over 50 percent, and 60 percent of those leaving the system are working, but much of this change may be due to the economy. Isabel Sawhill concludes that the reform has had positive impacts in moving welfare mothers to the labor force, but she also reviews many concerns about its impacts in the current recession.

The most poignant inequality in America is the gap between blacks and whites. Recently there has been considerable good news that the gap has been closing and many indicators that quality of life has improved for blacks. Ed Marciniak begins by acknowledging that blacks have made wonderful progress since the mid-sixties, but that racism continues and will not be eliminated by the perpetuation of gripes between blacks and whites. A cooperative spirit is needed. The next article, "Where Bias Begins: The Truth About Stereotypes," by Annie Murphy Paul provides some guidance for the next stage in black/white relations. She reports on the recent findings on biases and stereotypes. The truth about the inevitability of bias is disturbing because it means that solving prejudice is very difficult.

The last subsection of unit 4 deals with sex inequalities. In the first article of the section, Judy Olian documents the many forms of sex inequality. She also explains why the inequality persists. Beside discrimination she blames quite different formative experiences for boys and girls and the different attitudes that result from them, as well as several factors that operate in adult life. In the next article, Toni Nelson describes the worldwide oppression of women and the frequent violence done to them. Some of these injustices result from pure greed and exploitation. Female genital mutilation (FGM) is one aspect of unequal rights for women that has come to the attention of the American public, because some women have sought political asylum in the United States to escape this practice.

The articles in this unit portray tremendous differences in wealth and life chances among people. Systems of inequality affect what a person does and how he or she does it. An important purpose of this unit is to help you become more aware of how stratification operates in social life.

Still the land of opportunity?

ISABEL V. SAWHILL

This article is based, in part, on *Getting Ahead: Economic and Social Mobility in America*, by Daniel P. McMurrer and Isabel V. Sawhill, Urban Institute Press, Washington, D.C., 1998.

AMERICA is known as "the land of opportunity." But whether it deserves this reputation has received too little attention. Instead, we seem mesmerized by data on the distribution of incomes which show that incomes are less evenly distributed than they were 20 or 30 years ago. In 1973, the richest 5 percent of all families had 11 times as much income as the poorest one-fifth. By 1996, they had almost 20 times as much. But it is not only the distribution of income that should concern us. It is also the system that produces that distribution.

Indeed, I would argue that one cannot judge the fairness of any particular distribution without knowing something about the rules of the game that gave rise to it. Imagine a society in which incomes were as unequal as they are in the United States but where everyone had an equal chance of receiving any particular income—that is, in which the game was a completely unbiased lottery. Although some, especially those who are risk adverse, might blanch at the prospect of losing, and might wish for a more equal set of outcomes a priori (as most fatuously argued by John Rawls), others might welcome the chance to do exceedingly well. But—and this is the important point—no one could complain that they hadn't had an equal shot at achieving a good outcome. So the perceived fairness of the process is critical, and the rules governing who wins and who loses matter as much as the outcomes they produce.

In talking about this issue, we often invoke the phrase "equal opportunity," but we seldom reflect on what we really mean by "opportunity," how much of it we really have, and what we should do if it's in short supply. Instead, we have an increasingly sterile debate over income equality. One side argues for a redistribution of existing incomes, through higher taxes on the wealthy and more income support for the poor. The other side argues that inequality reflects differences in individual talent and effort, and as such is a spur to higher economic growth, as well as just compensation for unequal effort and skill. If there is any common ground between these two views, it probably revolves around the idea of opportunity and the measures needed to insure that it exists.

Opportunity first

The American public has always cared more about equal opportunity than about equal results. The commitment to provide everyone with a fair chance to develop their own talents to the fullest is a central tenet of the American creed. This belief has deep roots in American culture and American history and is part of what distinguishes our public philosophy from that of Europe. Socialism has never taken root in American soil.

Public opinion is only one reason to refocus the debate. Another is that the current emphasis on income inequality begs the question of how much inequality is too much. Virtually no one favors a completely equal distribution of income. Inequality in rewards encourages individual effort and contributes to economic growth. Many would argue that current inequalities far exceed those needed to encourage work, saving, and risk taking, and further that we need not worry about the optimal degree of inequality in a society that has clearly gone beyond that point. But the argument is hard to prove and will not satisfy those who believe that inequality is the price we pay for a dynamic economy and the right of each individual to retain the benefits from his or her own labor. In light of these debates, if any public consensus is to be found, it is more likely to revolve around the issue of opportunity than around the issue of equality.

A final reason why opportunity merits our attention is that it gets at the underlying processes that produce inequality. It addresses not just the symptoms but the causes of inequality. And a deeper understanding of these causes can inform not only one's sense of what needs to be done but also one's sense of whether the existing distribution of income is or is not a fair one.

Three societies

Consider three hypothetical societies, all of which have identical distributions of income as conventionally measured. The first society is a meritocracy. It provides the most income to those who work the hardest and have the greatest talent, regardless of class, gender, race, or other characteristics. The second one, I will call a "fortune-cookie society." In this society, where one ends up is less a matter of talent or energy than pure luck. The third society is class-stratified. Family background in this society is all important, and thus you need to pick your parents well. The children in this society largely end up where they started, so social mobility is small to nonexistent.

The United States and most other advanced countries are a mixture of these three ideal types. Given a choice between the three, most people would probably choose to live in a meritocracy. Not only do the rules determining success in a meritocracy produce greater social efficiency but, in addition, most people consider them inherently more just. Success is dependent on individual action. In principle, by making the right choices, anyone can succeed, whereas in a class-stratified or fortune-cookie society, people are buffeted by forces outside their control. So, even if the distribution of income in each case were identical, most of us would judge them quite differently. We might even prefer to live in a meritocracy with a less equal distribution of income than in a class-stratified or fortune-cookie society with a more equal distribution. Indeed, social historians have found this to be the case. The American public accepts rather large disparities in income and wealth because they believe that such disparities are produced by a meritocratic process. Even those at the bottom of the distribution believe that their children will do better than they have. It is this prospect, and the sense of fairness that accompanies it, that has convinced the American body politic to reject a social-welfare state.

For the last 25 years, the top one-fifth of the population has been improving their prospects while the other 80 percent has lagged behind. Yet no one has rebelled. The many have not imposed higher taxes on the few. (Small steps in this direction were taken in 1993, but the Democratic president who proposed them later apologized to a group of wealthy donors for doing so.) Even welfare recipients tell survey researchers that they consider the new rules requiring them to work at whatever job they can get fair. They plan on "bettering themselves." Such optimism flies in the face of studies suggesting that women on welfare (and those similar to them) will earn poverty-level wages for most of their lives. But it is an optimism that is characteristically, if in this case poignantly, American.

Several points need to be made about our purported meritocracy. The first is that even a pure meritocracy leaves less room for individual agency than is commonly believed. Some of us are blessed with good genes and good parents while others are not. The second is that the United States, while sharing these inherent flaws with other meritocracies, remains a remarkably dynamic and fluid society. Although it is not a pure meritocracy, it has moved closer to that ideal than at any time in its past. The third point is that, in the past, a rapid rate of economic growth provided each new generation with enhanced opportunities. It was this fact, in large part, that contributed to our image as the land of opportunity. But a mature economy cannot count on this source of upward mobility to leaven existing disparities; it needs instead to repair its other two opportunity-enhancing institutions: families and schools. The remainder of this essay elaborates on each of these points.

The inherent limits of a meritocracy

In a meritocracy, one would expect to find considerable social and economic fluidity. In such a system, the abler and more ambitious members of society would continually compete to occupy the top rungs. Family or class background, per se, should matter little in the competition while education should matter a lot.

The social-science literature contains a surprising amount of information on this topic. Based on my own reading of this literature, I would argue that social origins or family background matter a good deal. Not everyone begins the race at the same starting line. The kind of family into which a child is born has as much or more influence on that child's adult success than anything else we can measure. Yes, education is important too, but when we ask who gets a good education, it turns out to be disproportionately those from more advantaged backgrounds. Well-placed parents are much more likely to send their children to good schools and to encourage them to succeed academically. In short, although not as evident as in a class-stratified society, even in a meritocracy one had better pick one's parents well.

Why do families matter so much? There are at least three possibilities. The first is that well-placed parents can pass on advantages to their children without even trying: They have good genes. The second is that they have higher incomes, enabling them to provide better environments for their children. The third is that they are simply better parents, providing their children an appropriate mix of warmth and discipline, emotional security and intellectual stimulation, and preparation for the wider world.

It has proved difficult to discover which of these factors is most important. However, as Susan Mayer demonstrates in her recent book, *What Money Can't Buy*, the role of material resources has probably been exaggerated.

Most studies have failed to adjust for the fact that parents who are successful in the labor market have competencies that make them good parents as well. It is these competencies, rather than the parents' income, that help their children succeed. I don't want to leave the impression that income doesn't matter at all. It enables families to move to better neighborhoods; it relieves the stresses of daily living that often produce inadequate parenting; and, most obviously, it enables parents to purchase necessities. Still, additional income assistance, although possibly desirable on other grounds, is not likely to produce major changes in children's life prospects.

Genes clearly matter. We know this from studies of twins or siblings who have been raised apart. However, IQ or other measures of ability are at least somewhat malleable, and differences in intelligence only partially explain who ends up where on the ladder of success. Good parenting and an appropriate home environment are much harder to measure, but studies suggest that they may explain a substantial portion of the relationship between family background and later success in school or in the labor market. In addition, children with two parents fare much better than those with only one, in part because they have higher incomes but also because the presence of a second parent appears, according to all of the evidence, to be beneficial in and of itself.

So, for whatever reason, families matter. Unless we are willing to take children away from their families, the deck is stacked from the beginning. And even if one could remove children from their homes, there would still be the pesky little matter of differences in genetic endowments. Since a meritocracy has no good way of dealing with these two fundamental sources of inequality, it is a pipe dream to think that it can provide everyone with an equal chance. If we want a society in which there is less poverty and more equality, we will have to work harder and more creatively to compensate for at least some of these initial advantages and disadvantages.

How much social mobility?

Whatever its flaws, a meritocracy is clearly better than some of the alternatives. Although economic and social mobility may be inherently limited, it exists. But just how much of it do we actually have in the United States? Do families matter so much that children can rarely escape their origins? Do people move up and down the economic ladder a little or a lot? Before attempting to answer these questions, let us consider a simple example of a society consisting of only three individuals: Minnie, Mickey, and Mighty.

Assume that Minnie, Mickey, and Mighty start with incomes (or other valued goods) of $20,000, $30,000, and $40,000 respectively. Now imagine that Minnie's children do extremely well, moving from an income of $20,000 to one of $40,000. Mighty's children, by contrast, fall in status or well-being from $40,000 to $20,000. Mickey's situation doesn't change. This is the sort of social mobility we would expect to find in a meritocracy. It is a story of rags to riches (or the reverse) in a generation. *Note that the distribution of income, as conventionally measured, has not changed at all.* As Joseph Schumpeter once put it, the distribution of income is like the rooms in a hotel—always full but not necessarily with the same people.

This same rags-to-riches story can occur over a lifetime as well as between generations. Those at the bottom of the income scale often move up as they accumulate skills and experience, add more earners to the family, or find better jobs. Those at the top may move down as the result of a layoff, a divorce, or a business failure. Thus any snapshot of the distribution of incomes in a single year is unlikely to capture the distribution of incomes over a lifetime. For example, in a society in which everyone was poor at age 25 but rich at age 55, the distribution of annual incomes for the population as a whole would be quite unequal, but everyone would have the same lifetime incomes!

Now note that it is theoretically possible for the distribution of income to become more unequal at the same time that the Minnies of the world are improving their status. Is this what happened over the last few decades in the United States? The answer is yes and no. On the one hand, we know that there is a lot of income mobility within the population. Every year, about 25 percent or 30 percent of all adults move between income quintiles (say, from being in the bottom one-fifth of the income distribution to being in the second lowest fifth.) This rate increases with time, approaching 60 percent over a 10-year period. So there is considerable upward and downward movement. A lot of the Minnies in our society move up, and a lot of the Mightys move down. A few of the Minnies may even trade places with the Mightys of the world, as in our example. On the other hand, most people don't move very far; many remain stuck at the bottom for long periods; and some apparent moves are income reporting errors. (These are particularly large among the very poor and the very wealthy whose incomes tend to come from unearned sources that are difficult to track and that they may be reluctant to reveal.) Most importantly, from the data we have, there is no suggestion of more mobility now than there was 20 or 30 years ago. So one can't dismiss complaints about growing income inequality with the argument that it has been accompanied by *more* opportunity than in the past for everyone to share in the new wealth.

But what about Minnie's and Mighty's children? Suppose we look at mobility across generations instead of looking at it across their own life cycles? Here, the news is much more positive. Social mobility in America appears to have increased, at least since 1960, and probably going back to the middle of the last century (though the data for measuring such things is much better for the more recent period). This conclusion is based on studies done by Michael Hout, David Grusky, Robert Hauser,

David Featherman, and others—studies that show less association between some measure of family background and eventual adult career success now than in the past. This association has declined by as much as 50 percent since the early 1960s, according to Hout.

What has produced this increase in social mobility? The major suspects are a massive broadening of educational opportunities, the increased importance of formal education to economic success, and more meritocratic procedures for assigning workers to jobs (based on "what you know rather than who you know"). In addition, the extension of opportunities to some previously excluded groups—most notably women and blacks—has produced greater diversity in the higher, as well as the lower, ranks.

How much economic mobility?

Now return to our three-person society and consider a second scenario. In this one, the economy booms, and Minnie, Mickey, and Mighty all double their initial incomes from $20,000, $30,000, and $40,000 to $40,000, $60,000, and $80,000. Clearly, everyone is better off, although the relative position of each (as well as the distribution of income) is exactly the same as before. It is this sort of economic mobility, rather than social mobility per se, that has primarily been responsible for America's reputation as the land of opportunity. In other words, the growth of the economy has been the most important source of upward mobility in the United States; it is the reason that children tend to be better off than their parents. In a dynamic economy, a farmer's son can become a skilled machinist, and the machinist's son a computer programmer. Each generation is better off than the last one even if there is no social mobility. (Class-based differentials in fertility aside, social mobility—as distinct from economic mobility—is, by definition, a zero-sum game.)

But, as important as it was historically, economic mobility has been declining over the past few decades for the simple reason that the rate of economic growth has slowed. Young men born after about 1960, for example, are earning less (in inflation-adjusted terms) than their fathers' generation did at the same age. It would be nice to assume that a higher rate of growth is in the offing as we enter a new century. Certainly, new technologies and new markets abroad make many observers optimistic. But whatever the force of these developments, they haven't yet improved the fortunes of the youngest generation.

In sum, both these factors—the increase in social mobility and the decline in economic mobility—have affected prospects for the youngest generation. The good news is that individuals are increasingly free to move beyond their origins. The bad news is that fewer destina-

tions represent an improvement over where they began. For those concerned about the material well-being of the youngest generation, this is not a welcome message. But for those concerned about the fairness of the process, the news is unambiguously good.

Class stratification

Not only has economic growth slowed but its benefits now accrue almost entirely to those with the most education. Simply being a loyal, hard-working employee no longer guarantees that one will achieve the American dream. Whatever progress has been made in extending educational opportunities, it has not kept pace with the demand. Men with a high-school education or less have been particularly hard hit. The combination of slower growth and a distribution of wage gains that have favored women over men and the college educated over the high-school educated since the early 1970s has hurt poorly educated men. Their real incomes are less than one-half what they otherwise would have been in 1995. Education is, to put it simply, the new stratifying variable in American life. This, of course, is what one would hope for in a meritocracy, but only if everyone has a shot at a good education.

It is said that Americans would rather talk about sex than money. But they would rather talk about money than class, and some would rather not talk about the underclass at all. Many people consider the label pejorative, but research completed in the past decade suggests that such a group may indeed exist. Its hallmark is its lack of mobility. This group is not just poor but persistently poor, often over several generations. It is concentrated in urban neighborhoods characterized by high rates of welfare dependency, joblessness, single parenthood, and dropping out of school. It is disproportionately made up of racial and ethnic minorities. Although still relatively small (a little under three million people in 1990, according to an Urban Institute analysis of Census data), it appears to be growing. Anyone who doubts the existence of such a group need only read the detailed first-hand portrayals of ghetto life in Alex Kotlovitz's *There are No Children Here*, Leon Dash's *Rosa Lee*, or Ron Suskind's *A Hope in the Unseen*. These accounts suggest that dysfunctional families, poor schools, and isolation from mainstream institutions are depriving a significant segment of our youth of any prospect of one day joining the middle class.

All of this is by way of a caution: Whatever the broader trends in economic and social mobility, there may be enclaves that get left behind. Moreover, one can argue that it is this subgroup—and their lack of mobility—that should be our main concern. The very existence of such a group threatens our sense of social cohesion and imposes large costs on society. Its nexus with race is particularly disturbing.

What to do?

If families and education matter so much, we had best look to them as sources of upward mobility for all Americans—and especially for those stuck at the bottom of the economic ladder. Imagine a world in which everyone graduated from high school with the basic competencies needed by most employers—a world in which no one had a child before they were married and all had a reasonably decent job. Even if these parents held low-wage jobs, and one of them worked less than full-time, they would have an income sufficient to move them above the official poverty line (about $12,000 for a family of three in 1995). The entry-level wage for a male high-school graduate in 1995 was $15,766. If his wife took a half-time job at the minimum wage, they could earn another $5,000 a year. No one should pretend that it is easy to live on $20,000 a year, especially in an urban area. Rent, utilities, and work-related expenses alone can quickly gobble up most of this amount. It would make enormous sense, in my view, to supplement the incomes of such families with an earned income tax credit, subsidized health care, and subsidized child care.

What does not make sense is to insist that the public continue to subsidize families started by young unwed mothers. As of 1990, 45 percent of all first births were to women who were either teenagers, unmarried, or lacking a high-school degree. Add in all those with high-school diplomas that are worthless in the job market, and the picture is even grimmer. *There is no public-policy substitute for raising a child in a home with two parents who are adequately educated.*

Of course, poorly educated parents are nothing new. In fact, the proportion of mothers who are high-school graduates is higher now than it has ever been. But bear in mind that in the past mothers were not expected to work (in part because far more of them were married), that the economy didn't require people of either sex to have nearly as much education, and that the proportion of children in single-parent families was a fraction of what it is today. Because of increases in divorce and especially out-of-wedlock childbearing, we now have a situation in which three-fifths of all children will spend time in a fatherless family. Almost one-third of all children are born out of wedlock in the United States, and the proportion exceeds one-half in such cities as New York, Chicago, Philadelphia, Detroit, and Washington, D.C. One needn't be an advocate of more traditional family values to be worried about the economic consequences of such social statistics. In fact, the growth of never-married mothers can account for almost all of the growth in the child poverty rate since 1970.

Where does the cycle stop? Urban schools that half a century ago may have provided the children of the poor a way into the middle class are now more likely to lock them into poverty. More than half of fourth and eighth graders in urban public schools fail to meet even minimal standards in reading, math, or science, and more than half of students in big cities will fail to graduate from high school. How can America continue to be the land of opportunity under these circumstances? If families and schools are critical to upward mobility, these children have little chance of success. We have no choice but to address both of these issues if we want to provide opportunities for the next generation.

Strengthening families

Despite all the talk about the deterioration of the family, no one knows quite what to do about the problem. Welfare reform, which has not only eliminated AFDC as a permanent source of income for young mothers but also made young fathers more liable to pay child support, may well deter some out-of-wedlock childbearing. The next step should be to make the Earned Income Tax Credit (EITC) more marriage friendly. Today, as a result of the credit, a working single parent with two children can qualify for almost $4,000 a year. But if she marries another low-wage earner, she stands to lose most or all of these benefits. Congress should consider basing the credit on individual, rather than family, earnings. (A requirement that couples split their total earnings before the credit rate was applied would prevent benefits from going to low-wage spouses in middle-income families.) Such a revised EITC would greatly enhance the incentive to marry.

Equally important, we should find top-quality child care for those children whose mothers are required to work under the new welfare law. Indeed, such care might provide them with the positive experiences that they often fail to get within the home. Such intervention, if properly structured to accomplish this goal, can pay rich dividends in terms of later educational attainment and other social outcomes. The research on this point is, by now, clear. Although early gains in IQ may fade, rigorous studies have documented that disadvantaged children who receive a strong preschool experience are more likely to perform well in school.

Some argue that out-of-wedlock childbearing is the result of a lack of jobs for unskilled men. Although I don't think the evidence backs this view, it may have some merit. If so, we should offer jobs to such men in a few communities and see what happens. But we should tie the offer of a job to parental responsibility or give preference to men who are married.

Finally, I am convinced that messages matter. Many liberals argue that young women are having babies out of wedlock because they or their potential spouses are poor and face bleak futures. It is said that such women have no choice but to become unwed mothers. As an after-the-fact explanation, this may be partly true, but it is often accompanied by too ready an acceptance of early, out-of-wedlock childbearing by all concerned. Such fatalistic expectations have a way of becoming self-fulfilling. Just as it is wrong to presume that poor children can't excel in school, so too it is wrong to suggest to young women from disadvantaged backgrounds that early, out-of-wedlock childbearing is their only option. The fact remains that education and deferred childbearing, preferably within marriage, are an almost certain route out of poverty. Perhaps if more people were willing to deliver this message more forcefully, it would begin to influence behavior. Though the question needs to be studied more closely, it would appear that the decline in welfare caseloads since 1993 was triggered, in part, by a new message. Moreover, the new emphasis on conservative values may have contributed to the decrease in teen pregnancy and early childbearing since 1991. These new values can explain as much as two-thirds of the decline in sexual activity among males between 1988 and 1995, according to an Urban Institute study.

Fixing urban schools

We must stem the tide of early, out-of-wedlock births for one simple reason: Even good teachers cannot cope with large numbers of children from poor or dysfunctional homes. And equally important, children who are not doing well in school are more likely to become the next generation of teenage mothers. This is a two-front war in which success on one front can pay rich dividends on the other. Lose the battle on one front, and the other is likely to be lost as well.

That many schools, especially those in urban poor neighborhoods, are failing to educate their students is, I think, no longer in dispute. What is contested is how to respond. Some say that the solution lies in providing vouchers to low-income parents, enabling them to send their children to the school of their choice. Others argue that school choice will deprive public schools of good students and adequate resources. They favor putting more money into the public schools. But choice programs have the potential to provide a needed wake up call to these same schools. Too many people are still defending a system that has shortchanged the children of the poor. Public schools are not about to disappear, and no one should believe that choice programs alone are a sufficient response to the education crisis. We should be equally attentive to the new choice programs and to serious efforts to reform the public schools.

In Chicago, for example, a new leadership team took over the school system in 1995–96 and instituted strong accountability measures with real consequences for schools, students, and teachers. Failure to perform can place a school on probation, lead to the removal of a principal, or necessitate that a student repeat a grade. New supports, such as preschool programs, home visiting, after-school and summer programs, and professional development of teachers, are also emphasized. Early indications are that these efforts are working to improve Chicago's public schools.

A more equal chance

I began with a plea that we focus our attention less on the distribution of income and more on the opportunity each of us has to achieve a measure of success, recognizing that there will always be winners and losers but that the process needs to be as fair and open as possible. It can be argued that the process is, to one degree or another, inherently unfair. Children do not have much opportunity. They do not get to pick their parents—or, for that matter, their genetic endowments. It is these deepest of inequalities that have frustrated attempts to provide a greater measure of opportunity. Education is supposed to be the great leveler in our society, but it can just as easily reinforce these initial inequalities.

Thus any attempt to give every child the same chance to succeed must come to terms with the diversity of both early family environments and genetic endowments. In policy terms, this requires favoring the most disadvantaged. Numerous programs from Head Start to extra funding for children in low-income schools have attempted to level the playing field. But even where such efforts have been effective, they have been grossly inadequate to the task of compensating for differences in early environment. Assuming we are not willing to contemplate such radical solutions as removing children from their homes or cloning human beings, we are stuck with a certain amount of unfairness and inequality.

The traditional liberal response to this dilemma has been to redistribute income after the fact. It is technically easy to do but likely to run afoul of public sentiment in this country, including the hopes and dreams of the disadvantaged themselves. They need income; but they also want self-respect. In my view, we must find ways to strengthen families and schools in ways that give children a more equal chance to compete for society's prizes. To do otherwise runs counter to America's deepest and most cherished values.

ISABEL V. SAWHILL is a senior fellow at the Brookings Institution and author (with Daniel P. McMurrer) of *Getting Ahead: Economic and Social Mobility in America* (Urban Institute Press).

Are the Rich Cleaning Up?

Blue-collar workers make less than they did a generation ago,
while the earnings of professionals have soared.
How do we fix that? Do we even need to?

By Cait Murphy

The average price of a Manhattan apartment south of Harlem has hit more than $850,000—at a time when two-fifths of New York City's residents make $20,000 or less a year. In Silicon Valley teachers struggle with the rent while dot-com-rich parents wonder how to cope with "affluenza"—the perils of new and great wealth. (Hint: Just don't buy that helicopter.) In leafy suburbs nurses and cops commute from 50 miles away: They cannot afford to live near their work.

This dichotomy—between new wealth and the not-so-wealthy—has lately become something of an academic and political obsession. Economists and social scientists have turned the study of income inequality into a thriving cottage industry. And while the rich-poor gap has not cropped up explicitly in the presidential campaign, it is the subtext for a number of front-burner issues like tax cuts, educational reform, and the "digital divide." When a politician uses the word "fairness" in an economic debate, that's often shorthand for "inequality."

Why the concern about inequality? Basically, because there's more of it. From 1977 on, the cash earnings of the poorest fifth of the U.S. population fell about 9%, estimates the Center on Budget and Policy Priorities; middle-class earnings rose 8%; and upper-income earnings, 43%. The exact numbers are hotly contested, but it is clear that the distance between the top and the bottom tiers of the income distribution has grown strikingly since the 1970s. By some measures, Americans' earnings are more unequal today than at any time in the past 60 years; at best, even after the past several years, when income has grown

throughout the income distribution, the gap has plateaued at or near record levels.

Of course, no serious person would argue that everyone should get the same-sized piece of the economic pie. That would be unfair to those who work hard, as opposed to those who watch reruns of *Gilligan's Island* all day. And if spectators want to pay more to watch a baseball game than, say, a badminton match, there is no reason both sets of athletes must be paid alike. At the same time, no serious person would deny that inequality can hit such levels (think medieval societies) that it comprises both an ethical problem and a threat to social peace (the peasants revolt). Finally, there is little disagreement about whether inequality has increased. It has. But there is also massive mud-wrestling about how much it has grown, why, and what it all means.

FORTUNE will spare you the arcane details—for now, anyway. But the fundamental argument about inequality is simple. The pessimists contend that income distribution has grown so lopsided that all society is worse off. Richard Freeman of Harvard speculates that there is a link between inequality and crime. He notes that high school dropouts fill the nation's jails—and that these men have lost the most ground economically. Edward Wolff of New York University contends that if young men had a better shot at earning a stable living they might be more willing to marry and stop having children on a freelance basis. Robert Greenstein of the Center on Budget and Policy Priorities argues that earnings disparities are one of the reasons that almost one in five children lives in poverty.

America's lowest-paid workers make less, as a percentage of the median wage (the point at which 50% are above and 50% below), than their counterparts in any other country (38%, compared with 46% in Britain and Japan and more than 50% in France and Germany). This means that many low-skilled parents just cannot earn enough to escape poverty. "If there were somewhat less inequality," Greenstein concludes, "more would have a better standard of living."

There is also considerable (but contentious) literature that more-equal societies are healthier. And there is the inchoate but deeply felt belief that inequality at current levels is simply un-American. It gives the rich too loud a voice. It makes it too hard for those at the bottom to rise to prosperity. And it allows the wealthy to separate themselves from society through private clubs, private schools, and gated communities.

The optimists respond to that critique with a polite yawn. Or perhaps a rude word along the lines of "Rubbish!" Sure, inequality has grown, but so what? As long as people at the bottom have not become absolutely worse off, goes this set of arguments, it doesn't matter that the rich got richer faster. And no, the poor are not worse off. Though men's earnings seem to have fallen since 1973 (and maybe they haven't), women's have clearly risen. That trend and smaller households mean that family income and income per head have increased all along the income distribution. Housing quality and access to medical care have improved markedly for the poor since 1973. Besides, people don't necessarily stay in the same position. They move up and down the income ladder: Horatio Alger was not just making stuff up. Today's income distribution is the result of long-standing economic forces and social trends. Nothing is broke, so don't fix it.

Those are the broad outlines of a debate in which the devil is most definitely in the details. What follows is a primer of the arguments, followed by a suggestion about how to get out of this thicket.

What are people so concerned about? Students of inequality use several tools in their trade. One is the Gini coefficient; a 0 coefficient is perfect equality (everyone has exactly the same share of the economic pie). A coefficient of 1 is perfect inequality (Bill Gates gets it all). In America the coefficient has risen from 0.323 in 1974 to 0.375 in 1997, according to the Luxembourg Income Study, higher than in any other rich country. Britain's is 0.346, Germany's 0.300, Canada's 0.286, and Sweden's 0.222.

Matters naturally are not quite that straightforward. Alan Greenspan has pointed out that while the Gini coefficient is comparatively high for income, when applied to consumption it is about 25% lower. In other words, poorer people are spending more like the rich; they are, for example, almost as likely to own such things as dryers and microwave ovens. So the economic distance between the top and the bottom may be narrower than the income numbers suggest. And Europe's greater equality may simply reflect the widely accepted premise that while America has adapted to economic change by allowing inequality to rise, Europe has adjusted by allowing higher unemployment. Which is better?

'50s-era Pennsylvania steelworkers could support their families on one income. Today they probably couldn't: Wages for blue-collar men have plunged since 1973.

Another favored analytical tool for measuring inequality is to divide the population into fifths, or quintiles, and see what share of the nation's earnings each fifth took home. According to the Census Bureau, in 1998 the bottom 20% earned only 3.6% of total income (4.2% in 1973), compared with more than 49% for the top 20% (44% in 1973).

But wait a minute. The Heritage Foundation points out that the Census defines quintiles in terms of households—and households in the bottom quintile are much smaller than those at the top. Therefore, while there are 64 million people in the richest quintile, there are fewer than 40 million in the poorest one. Adjust for population, and the share of the bottom fifth grows. Also, many Americans have income that is not in the form of wages or cash transfers—food stamps and housing subsidies for the poor, realized capital gains for the better-off. Adjust for that, and the distribution narrows again, as it does after accounting for taxes. Should the adjustment include Medicaid and Medicare? If so (and that is debatable), the gap shrinks further still; put it all together, and Heritage figures that the bottom quintile takes in 9.4% of national income, and the top 39.6%.

There is, then, no consensus on how to measure inequality. There is, however, broad agreement that it has indeed grown. Since the early 1970s the cash incomes of the rich have indeed risen faster than those of the poor, with the middle class hanging in there; the higher up the income ladder, the faster the growth. That may help explain why the poverty rate, now 12.7%, has still not dipped to 1973 levels (11.1%). Median household income (the point at which 50% are above and 50% below) has grown grudgingly, rising about 9% in real terms from 1973 to 1998 and passing its 1989 peak only in 1998.

Men have had a particularly dismal time. The median income of men is significantly lower than in 1973 ($27,394 then vs. $25,212 in 1997, in 1997 dollars). Men under 45 are making less now, in real terms, than they did in 1967, and blue-collar workers have taken the biggest hit. Blacks and women, however, have seen their earnings rise.

Inequality by the Numbers

Since the 1970s, a rising share of the national income has gone to the richest Americans.
In the growing disparity, women and blacks have gained more than white men, and married couples
have remained far less likely than female-headed households to live below the poverty level.

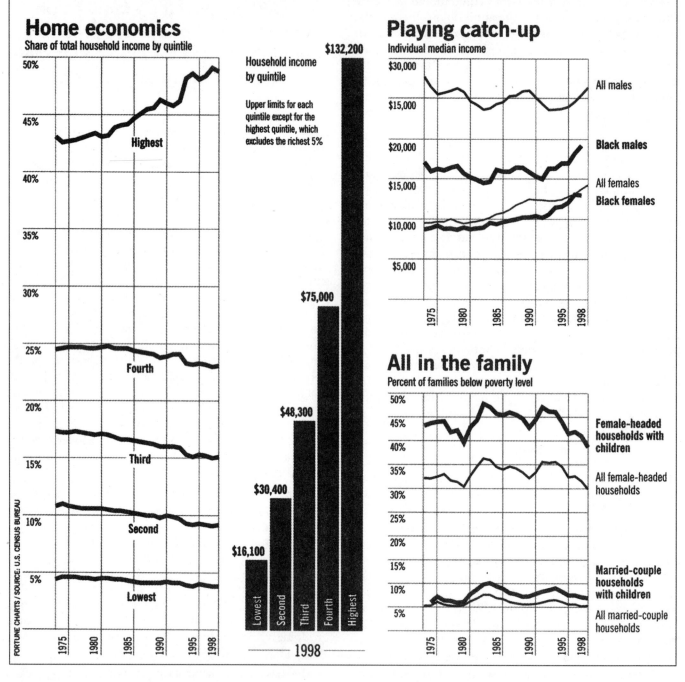

Home economics
Share of total household income by quintile

Highest
Fourth
Third
Second
Lowest

FORTUNE CHARTS / SOURCE: U.S. CENSUS BUREAU

Household income by quintile

Upper limits for each quintile except for the highest quintile, which excludes the richest 5%

$132,200
$75,000
$48,300
$30,400
$16,100

Lowest | Second | Third | Fourth | Highest

— 1998 —

Playing catch-up
Individual median income

All males
Black males
All females
Black females

All in the family
Percent of families below poverty level

Female-headed households with children
All female-headed households
Married-couple households with children
All married-couple households

Why is inequality increasing? Income inequality is increasing because wage inequality is. The U.S. economy has evolved to reward highly educated people even more than in the past—a trend that social scientists, in a flight of whimsy, call "skill-biased technological change." This means that demand for labor has shifted toward the skilled and away from the unskilled. Brains beat brawn—hands down.

Marriage is good economics. Married couples with children have a median income above $52,000—more than twice that of single-parent households.

That explains the rise in the college premium—the extra income college graduates can expect to earn compared with those who finish only high school. The premium rose much faster in the U.S. than in Europe because the supply of graduates in the U.S. did not rise as fast in the 1980s and 1990s as the demand for them; Europe came closer to matching demand and supply. It sounds like a tautology, and perhaps it is: Income shifted toward the more highly skilled because employers would pay more for their services. But it really is that simple.

Of course, that by itself doesn't explain the income gap. Another significant factor has been family structure. Weighing on the downscale side of income distribution has been the burgeoning number of single-parent families, particularly those headed by never-married mothers; overall, single-parent families earn about half as much as two-parent households. On the upscale side, there has been an increase in families in which both spouses make lots of money. To put it another way, there are almost 2 ½ times as many people working in the richest fifth of households as in the poorest fifth. Less than a third of the people in the bottom quintile live in households headed by a married couple; the rest are single (55%) or in single-parent families. In the top quintile some 90% live in married-couple families.

Changes in family structure account for more than a third of the increase in income inequality since 1979, figures Gary Burtless of the Brookings Institution, making it a slightly more important factor than the widening wage gap. Lynn Karoly of the Rand Institute in California calculates that the wage gap is a bigger deal, but no matter: No one disputes that both factors are crucial.

Other suspects in the inequality lineup are the declining minimum wage (lower in real terms than in 1973), declining unionization among men (accounting for as much as 20% of the gap, estimates Freeman), deregulation (protected industries kept wages high), immigration (which can depress wages), and trade (that giant sucking sound). Higher levels of entrepreneurship may also be associated with higher inequality.

All those things probably count, but to a minor degree compared with the changes in earnings patterns and family structure. Immigrants, for example, can drive down wages in local labor markets, particularly among the low-skilled, but that effect is muted across the country as a whole. When it comes to trade, the effect is even more difficult to identify. While some companies have certainly shipped jobs to cheaper climes, most U.S. trade is with other rich countries, and most low-paid jobs are domestic,

such as cleaning or food service. Remember, too, that to critique immigration and trade strictly in terms of their impact on inequality is to look through a cracked mirror: Doing so ignores the contributions immigrants make to America and the opportunities wrought by freer trade.

What is more important than any of these individual factors, Karoly notes, is how all of them have reinforced one another. At the same time, there have been few countervailing forces. The U.S. could have tried to slow these trends, as Europe has done, through high minimum wages or centralized wage bargaining or protective trade barriers or high taxes. It chose not to.

What can be done?   The primary rule of economic policy should be like that of medicine: First, do no harm. And the problem with many of the knee-jerk policy responses to inequality is that they cannot pass that test. Looking at the list of culprits responsible for the run-up in inequality, for instance, one could argue for less technological change, less trade, more regulation, and less entrepreneurship. Would America really be better off with such an economic blueprint? To ask the question is to answer it.

Immigrants work disproportionately at the bottom end of the labor market. Where they cluster in large numbers, they can drive down wages among the low-skilled.

Even the more plausible approaches carry side effects worth thinking about. Take unions. Unions are an essential part of a free society, and they do an excellent job of raising wages for members. But they can also be associated with not-so-good things, such as protecting their workers at the expense of those trying to get into the labor market—an important factor in the high level of European unemployment. In July, Alan Greenspan contended that it was America's greater labor-market flexibility that had allowed it to take advantage of information technologies faster and more fully than Europe; tech-led productivity has been the bedrock of America's recent wage and productivity surge. In this context, the case for actively encouraging more unionization begins to weaken.

What about raising the minimum wage? That's plausible too, and the increased minimum wage probably played a role in steadying inequality in the past few years. Moreover, countries like France, which has a high minimum wage, have seen inequality grow much less. America may be robust enough to swallow the proposed minimum-wage increase to $6.15. But there is clearly a point where a minimum wage can become burdensome, killing job opportunities, as has happened in Europe. And raising the minimum wage is an awkward way to lessen inequality. Most minimum-wage workers do not live in low-income households (think of suburban teens), and many poor households have no workers at all. So most of the gain from a higher minimum wage goes to families that are not poor. Worse, the Organization for Economic Cooperation and Development has documented a connection between the minimum wage and youth unemployment: the higher the wage, the more idle youngsters. That has to be a large part of the reason a quarter of France's under-25-year-olds are out of work.

Is all this simply an argument for complacency? Not quite. It is really an argument for looking at the issue from a different perspective. Let's face it: Normal Americans do not fret about rising Gini coefficients or quintile displacements. They do, however, worry if hard-working people, even professionals, cannot find a home of their own that fits their means. They don't want children suffering, even if their parents made bad choices. They believe that opportunity is available to all and that government should not hinder people's ability to take care of themselves. Americans, in short, are hapless at class warfare (perhaps because they are so absorbed in racial and ethnic issues). If they were better at it, they would be howling, say, at the proposed death of the death tax, which applies to only a tiny share of estates. Instead, most people want it killed. The attitude seems to be, "Hey, that might be my estate someday."

Given such attitudes, a plausible list of goals for government might go something like this:

- Enhance the prospects of poor children.
- Improve living conditions.
- Reward work.
- Bolster family responsibility.
- Keep taxes from impoverishing people.
- Ensure mobility.

And surprise, surprise: American social policy in the 1980s and '90s has done almost precisely that. The Reagan Administration can take credit for the 1986 tax reform, which released many lower-income Americans from federal income-tax liability. The earned-income-tax credit (EITC), also a Reagan-era initiative, supplements the pay of low-wage workers with children through a refundable tax credit of up to 40% of earnings. The Bush and Clinton Administrations expanded the EITC (the latter in the teeth of strong Republican opposition). Both also expanded the provision of support services for poor children outside the home—child care, foster care, Head Start, and so on. Child-support enforcement expanded under all three (with, it has to be said, spotty results), and health insurance and child-care subsidies for poor children expanded under Bush and Clinton. The welfare reform of 1996 (in the teeth of strong Democratic opposition) explicitly connected working to the receipt of benefits. Overall, these policies make up a broadly consistent approach that Americans are in tune with—and that has delivered real improvements.

Perhaps, then, the way to remedy inequality is not so much to try to lessen the Gini coefficient—through redistributive taxation, for example—but to ameliorate the problems of those snagged at the bottom. One such problem is clearly housing. There is a gap between the growing numbers of low-income renters (10.5 million in 1995) and the shrinking numbers of low-cost rental units (6.1 million). A record 5.4 million households spend more than half of their income on rent or live in substandard housing. The feds can and should do more in this regard by boosting the number of housing vouchers. (Congress eliminated new housing vouchers for four years in the 1990s; the 2000 budget envisions expansion.)

College graduates have always made more money than their less educated peers. And even as the number of college students has risen, so has the income premium conferred by a degree.

But inequality begins at home. It is not coincidental that two cities with massive affordability problems—New York and San Francisco—may also have the most tortured housing markets in the country. Byzantine regulations suppress new construction and raise its cost. Insiders—those who have scored a price-controlled apartment—benefit at the expense of outsiders, who pay prices exaggerated by the artificially induced constraint in supply. So while rent decontrol rarely makes the egalitarian to-do list, it deserves to be on it. And Silicon Valley and other wealthy communities should take a hard look at regulations—two-acre zoning and the like—that put up a KEEP OUT sign for the unrich.

Expanding the EITC further—by increasing the credit (particularly to families with three or more children) and extending it to childless full-time workers—would also help. The EITC is first-rate social policy. Essentially it promises parents that if they work, their income will exceed the poverty line. In 1998, EITC supplements lifted almost five million people out of poverty, and that money has proved an important carrot to get former welfare recipients into the job market. A further expansion would put more dollars in low earners' pockets and reduce the ranks of the working poor, without the scattershot effect of the minimum wage. It also makes perfect equity sense in the context of the tax cuts both parties are fiddling with. Don't believe the fluff: Tax cuts would benefit the better-off most, for the very good reason that they pay the lion's share of taxes. The top 1% of earners, for example, pays almost a fifth of all individual federal income taxes, according to the Congressional Budget Office, and the top fifth almost 60%. The bottom two quintiles contribute 8%.

An expanded EITC, in combination with tax cuts, would spread tax largesse all the way up and down the income distribution. Along the same lines, states that are considering cutting taxes would do well to cut sales taxes, which hit the poor hardest, rather than income taxes. Or they could start or expand their own versions of the EITC, as more than a dozen states have already done.

Third, surely a country as rich and talented as America can figure out some way to ensure reasonable, regular health care at a level of access that, say, Ireland provided in the 1960s. There has been expansion of guaranteed medical provision for poor children, but about 15% still slip between the cracks. A system with fewer gaps could also promote mobility; it is scary for low-income people in a job with health coverage to try to improve their position by moving to a new job without it.

Fourth, let's remember that not every problem comes with a ready solution, from government or anywhere else. For example, it would be an unambiguously good thing for America as a whole if families formed more readily and stayed together more reliably. This would also narrow wage inequality and boost family income. It's just far from obvious how to get there from here.

Social policy is not a field of dreams; miracles are rare. Across the rich world, estimates Ignazio Visco of the OECD, the long-term poor are some 2% to 4% of the population. But at any given time, these families make up half of the population living in poverty—everyone else moves up and out. The major problem in such homes is not lack of money but disorganization, illness, lack of social skills, and general cluelessness. In her book *What Money Can't Buy*, Susan Mayer of the University of Chicago argues that after basic needs are met, additional income has little effect on children's prospects. Using a form of regression analysis that only a social scientist could love (or indeed understand), Mayer estimates that doubling the income of the poor would reduce high school dropout rates by one percentage point, increase education by a few months, have no effect on teen pregnancy, and possibly worsen male idleness. "Any realistic redistribution strategy," she concludes, "is likely to have a relatively small impact on the overall incidence of social problems." Enhancing living standards to provide dignity and reasonable comfort is a social good in itself.

But humility is warranted in terms of the long-range benefits of doing so.

In the long run, because so much of inequality is connected with the higher returns on skills, it is crucial that Americans learn the things they need to know in order to succeed. Which brings us to education, the most important component of the mobility that is the bedrock of the American dream. Poor people in poor communities are educationally shortchanged, and the problems begin early. That Americans of almost any intellectual level can find a college to accept them does not excuse the lack of basic skills too many high school graduates demonstrate. Money may be part of the answer, but only part. Cash can be spent wisely or stupidly; there is, at best, an ambiguous correlation between spending and achievement. But evidence indicates that increased attention to education in early childhood brings enduring and positive results. It's clear that there has to be more emphasis on accountability and outcomes—what children actually learn—as opposed to how much is being spent. That's beginning to happen. And it's hard to believe that competition—vouchers, charter schools, and the like—would not be a goad to improvement.

Finally, let's remember that nothing good is going to happen if the economy goes into the tank. Tight labor markets have done more to make welfare reform work than any aspect of its design; productivity has driven up wages since 1993 faster than any transfer program could have done. Remedies to inequality that hurt the economy as a whole will hurt the poor first and worst.

Laura D'Andrea Tyson, former head of the Council of Economic Advisors under President Clinton, offered a striking way of looking at these issues at a Federal Reserve conference in 1998. Imagine the income distribution, she suggested, as an apartment building in which the penthouse is more and more luxurious, and the basement, in which a number of dwellers (and their children) are stuck year after year, is rat infested. What to do? Well, some social critics, offended by the presence of wealth amid such distress, would like to pillage the penthouse. Tyson simply notes, "We need to do something about that rat-infested basement." Taking care of the rats and making sure people can climb out of the cellar: That seems about right.

CORPORATE WELFARE

A TIME investigation uncovers how hundreds of companies get on the dole—and why it costs every working American the equivalent of two weeks' pay every year

By Donald L. Barlett and James B. Steele

HOW WOULD YOU LIKE TO PAY ONLY A QUARTER OF THE REAL ESTATE TAXES you owe on your home? And buy everything for the next 10 years without spending a single penny in sales tax? Keep a chunk of your paycheck free of income taxes? Have the city in which you live lend you money at rates cheaper than any bank charges? Then have the same city install free water and sewer lines to your house, offer you a perpetual discount on utility bills—and top it all off by landscaping your front yard at no charge?

Fat chance. You can't get any of that, of course. But if you live almost anywhere in America, all around you are taxpayers getting deals like this. These taxpayers are called corporations, and their deals are usually trumpeted as "economic development" or "public-private partnerships." But a better name is corporate welfare. It's a game in which governments large and small subsidize corporations large and small, usually at the expense of another state or town and almost always at the expense of individual and other corporate taxpayers.

Two years after Congress reduced welfare for individuals and families, this other kind of welfare continues to expand, penetrating every corner of the American economy. It has turned politicians into bribery specialists, and smart business people into con artists. And most surprising of all, it has rarely created any new jobs.

While corporate welfare has attracted critics from both the left and the right, there is no uniform definition. By TIME's definition, it is this: any action by local, state or federal government that gives a corporation or an entire industry a benefit not offered to others. It can be an outright subsidy, a grant, real estate, a low-interest loan or a government service. It can also be a tax break—a credit, exemption, deferral or deduction, or a tax rate lower than the one others pay.

The rationale to curtail traditional welfare programs, such as Aid to Families with Dependent Children and food stamps, and to impose a lifetime limit on the amount of aid received, was compelling: the old system didn't work. It was unfair, destroyed incentive, perpetuated dependence and distorted the economy. An 18-month TIME investigation has found that the same indictment, almost to the word, applies to corporate welfare. In some ways, it represents pork-barrel legislation of the worst order. The difference, of course, is that instead of rewarding the poor, it rewards the powerful.

And it rewards them handsomely. The Federal Government alone shells out $125 billion a year in corporate welfare, this in the midst of one of the more robust economic periods in the nation's history. Indeed, thus far in the 1990s, corporate profits have totaled $4.5 trillion—a sum equal to the cumulative paychecks of 50 million working Americans who earned less than $25,000 a year, for those eight years.

During one of the most robust economic periods in our nation's history, the Federal Government has shelled out $125 billion in corporate welfare, equivalent to all the income tax paid by 60 million individuals and families.

That makes the Federal Government America's biggest sugar daddy, dispensing a range of giveaways from tax abatements to price supports for sugar itself. Companies get government money to advertise their products; to help build new plants, offices and stores; and to train their workers. They sell their goods to foreign buyers that make the acquisitions with tax dollars supplied by the U.S. government; engage in foreign transactions that are insured by the government; and are excused from paying a portion of their income tax if they sell products overseas. They pocket lucrative government contracts to carry out ordinary business operations, and government grants to conduct research that will improve their profit margins. They are extended partial tax immunity if they locate in certain geographical areas, and they may write off as business expenses some of the perks enjoyed by their top executives.

The justification for much of this welfare is that the U.S. government is creating jobs. Over the past six years, Congress appropriated $5 billion to run the Export-Import Bank of the United States, which subsidizes companies that sell goods abroad. James A. Harmon, president and chairman, puts it this way: "American workers... have higher-quality, better-paying jobs, thanks to Eximbank's financing." But the numbers at the bank's five biggest beneficiaries—AT&T, Bechtel, Boeing, General Electric and McDonnell Douglas (now a part of Boeing)—tell another story. At these companies, which have accounted for about 40% of all loans, grants and long-term guarantees in this decade, overall employment has fallen 38%, as more than a third of a million jobs have disappeared.

The picture is much the same at the state and local level, where a different kind of feeding frenzy is taking place. Politicians stumble over one another in the rush to arrange special deals for select corporations, fueling a growing economic war among the states. The result is that states keep throwing money at companies that in many cases are not serious about moving anyway. The companies are certainly not reluctant to take the money, though, which is available if they simply utter the word relocation. And why not? Corporate executives, after all, have a fiduciary duty to squeeze every dollar they can from every locality waving blandishments in their face.

State and local governments now give corporations money to move from one city to another—even from one building to another—and tax credits for hiring new employees. They supply funds to train workers or pay part of their wages while they are in training, and provide scientific and engineering assistance to solve workplace technical problems. They repave existing roads and build new ones. They lend money at bargain-basement interest rates to erect plants or buy equipment. They excuse corporations from paying sales and property taxes and relieve them from taxes on investment income.

There are no reasonably accurate estimates on the amount of money states shovel out. That's because few want you to know. Some say they maintain no records. Some say they don't know where the files are. Some say the information is not public. All that's certain is that the figure is in the many billions of dollars each year—and it is growing, when measured against the subsidy per job.

In 1989 Illinois gave $240 million in economic incentives to Sears, Roebuck & Co. to keep its corporate headquarters and 5,400 workers in the state by moving from Chicago to suburban Hoffman Estates. That amounted to a subsidy of $44,000 for each job.

In 1991 Indiana gave $451 million in economic incentives to United Airlines to build an aircraft-maintenance facility that would employ as many as 6,300 people. Subsidy: $72,000 for each job.

In 1993 Alabama gave $253 million in economic incentives to Mercedes-Benz to build an automobile-assembly plant near Tuscaloosa and employ 1,500 workers. Subsidy: $169,000 for each job.

And in 1997 Pennsylvania gave $307 million in economic incentives to Kvaerner ASA, a Norwegian global engineering and construction company, to open a shipyard at the former Philadelphia Naval Shipyard and employ 950 people. Subsidy: $323,000 for each job.

This kind of arithmetic seldom adds up. Let's say the Philadelphia job pays $50,000. And each new worker pays $6,700 in local and state taxes. That means it will take nearly a half-century of tax collections from each individual to earn back the money granted to create his or her job. And that assumes all 950 workers will be recruited from outside Philadelphia and will relocate in the city, rather than move from existing jobs within the city, where they are already paying taxes.

All this is in service of a system that may produce jobs in one city or state, thus fostering the illusion of an uptick in employment. But it does not create more jobs in the nation as a whole. Market forces do that, and that's why 10 million jobs have been created since 1990. But most of those jobs have been created by small- and medium-size companies, from high-tech start-ups to franchised cleaning services. FORTUNE 500 companies, on the other

hand, have erased more jobs than they have created this past decade, and yet they are the biggest beneficiaries of corporate welfare.

To be sure, some economic incentives are handed out for a seemingly worthwhile public purpose. The tax breaks that companies receive to locate in inner cities come to mind. Without them, companies might not invest in those neighborhoods. However well intended, these subsidies rarely produce lasting results. They may provide short-term jobs but not long-term employment. And in the end, the costs outweigh any benefits.

And what are those costs? The equivalent of nearly two weekly paychecks from every working man and woman in America—extra money that would stay in their pockets if it didn't go to support some business venture or another.

If corporate welfare is an unproductive end game, why does it keep growing in a period of intensive government cost cutting? For starters, it has good p.r. and an army of bureaucrats working to expand it. A corporate-welfare bureaucracy of an estimated 11,000 organizations and agencies has grown up, with access to city halls, statehouses, the Capitol and the White House. They conduct seminars, conferences and training sessions. They have their own trade associations. They publish their own journals and newsletters. They create attractive websites on the Internet. And they never call it "welfare." They call it "economic incentives" or "empowerment zones" or "enterprise zones."

Whatever the name, the result is the same. Some companies receive public services at reduced rates, while all others pay the full cost. Some companies are excused from paying all or a portion of their taxes due, while all others must pay the full amount imposed by law. Some companies receive grants, low-interest loans and other subsidies, while all others must fend for themselves.

In the end, that's corporate welfare's greatest flaw. It's unfair. One role of government is to help ensure a level playing field for people and businesses. Corporate welfare does just the opposite. It tilts the playing field in favor of the largest or the most politically influential or most aggressive businesses....

From Welfare to Work

Making Welfare a Way Station, Not a Way of Life

BY ISABEL SAWHILL

In 1996 Congress reformed a welfare system that was deeply unpopular with the American public. Although Republicans pushed hard for reform, many Democrats—led by former President Bill Clinton—went along, and in the end both parties took credit for the new law. The system was transformed from one that handed out cash to one that required work and penalized with a loss of benefits those who failed to comply with the requirement. What had been called Aid to Families with Dependent Children (AFDC) became Temporary Assistance for Needy Families (TANF). The use of the word "temporary" was noteworthy. Welfare was to be a way station, not a way of life.

Although most politicians supported these changes, many scholars and advocates for the poor complained that the new law was a voyage into uncharted waters—an experiment with the lives of some of the nation's most vulnerable citizens and their children. Noncitizens who were legal residents of the United States were dealt an even bigger blow, as they and their children lost many benefits previously available to them. In this special issue of the *Brookings Review*, our contributors assess the results of the experiment to date and reflect on next steps, including what modifications may be needed when Congress reau-

thorizes the law in 2002 and what directions all this suggests for antipoverty policy in the United States. This introductory essay builds on their insights but contains my own assessment as well.

Is Welfare Reform Working?

Not surprisingly, the answer to the question of whether welfare reform is working depends on whom you ask. That said, even the law's critics point to at least some successes while its supporters acknowledge some limitations.

All our contributors agree that caseloads have declined far more than expected (from 5 million families in 1994 to 2.2 million in June 2000), that about 60 percent of those who have left welfare are working, that employment rates among single mothers have increased dramatically, and that child poverty has declined. They also agree that a substantial minority of mothers who have left the rolls are not working and that many of those who remain on the rolls may have difficulty finding or keeping jobs because of poor schooling, substance abuse, depression, or other barriers to employment. Finally, those who are working tend to earn low wages (about $7.00 an hour on average) making it hard for them to support their families.

Another concern, noted by Wendell Primus, Mark Greenberg, and Tom Downey in particular, is that the poverty rate has not fallen as much as the caseload. Fewer poor children are receiving assistance. In addition, the incomes of the poorest one-fifth of single-parent families have continued to fall, many families remain in deep poverty, and according to some reports, requests for emergency assistance have grown. Overall, 700,000 families were significantly worse off in 1999 than their counterparts in 1995.

Because welfare reform was implemented during an unprecedented economic expansion, questions also must be raised about how much of the good news should be attributed to the 1996 law and how much to a strong economy or to the growth of other programs such as the earned income tax credit (EITC) over this same period. Research on this question doesn't permit firm answers, but almost everyone agrees that all three have been important. In his essay, Ron Haskins compares the 1990s with the 1980s, when employment also expanded strongly but without comparable declines in caseloads. The data he cites suggest that welfare reform played an important, and probably a critical, role.

Still, many people remain uneasy about what will happen should the economy sink into a prolonged recession. An economic downturn would not only swell the caseload, according to this view, but strain state budgets, perhaps forcing some states to cut benefits. At a minimum, states would likely reduce spending on an array of supportive services for those making the transition from welfare to work and for other low-income families.

Mickey Kaus considers the longer-term implications of welfare reform. He notes that reform was at least partially motivated by a view that the old system of no-strings entitlements had encouraged the growth of an urban underclass, characterized by idleness and out-of-wedlock childbearing. For many, dismantling this system is the key to reconnecting an isolated and stigmatized group of the poor to work and marriage. Even if the short-term result were to make this group worse off, Kaus argues, these longer-term goals should be pursued. The major purpose of the 1996 law, after all, was not to end poverty or improve material well-being, but to end dependency and encourage the formation of stable two-parent, married families. Although the family formation goals have not yet been achieved, some signs are encouraging. Teen pregnancy and birth rates have plummeted, and the proportion of children born outside marriage has leveled off. Lack of more definitive progress in family formation should not be surprising, for such cultural changes are deep-seated and likely to be decades in the making. In the meantime, the dramatic increase in employment among never-married mothers has had one unintended consequence: by creating greater sympathy for their lives, it has made new supports for this group politically feasible and thereby transformed the debate about poverty. No longer is the debate primarily about how much cash assistance and support services to

provide to mothers who stay home with their children; it is about how much assistance to give them once they are working to support these same children.

One important feature of the new law was the enormous discretion it gave the states. Several contributors (Richard Nathan and Tom Gais, Mark Greenberg, and Bruce Katz and Katherine Allen) address the question of devolution and how welfare reform has played out differently in various parts of the country. Most states have embraced the goal of getting recipients into jobs as quickly as possible, a strategy that appears more cost-effective than providing substantial up-front education and training. But it is also a strategy dictated in large measure by federal rules that require states to place an increasing fraction of their caseloads in jobs and that reward them for doing so by freeing up funds for other, related purposes. Many states also supplement the limited earnings of those moving into jobs by allowing them to keep a portion of their welfare check. And as Gordon Berlin notes, these efforts to make work pay, although more costly than mandating work alone, can produce more positive effects not only on employment and earnings but also on some measures of child well-being. A key issue for the future will be whether welfare reform is about improving the lives of families and children or about ending dependency and saving money for taxpayers. Thus far, different states have adopted different approaches, with Minnesota, for example, emphasizing making work pay while Texas and Wisconsin have put more emphasis on ending dependency. And whatever formal policy choices states may make, local practices vary substantially not only from one state to another but even from one county to another within a state.

For these and other reasons, caseloads have declined unevenly. On average nationwide they have dropped by more than half, but that average reflects sharp variations—from 90 percent in Wyoming and 79 percent in Wisconsin to 46 percent in California and 26 percent in Hawaii between January of 1994 and June of 2000. And as Katz and Allen note, declines have been slower in the cities than outside of them, so that more and more of the caseload is concentrated in urban counties.

Not surprisingly, states are happy with their new role and are likely to want a simple extension of the law when it is reauthorized in 2002. But the wide latitude given states by the law must be balanced against the need for accountability. Today policymakers lack good information about what states are doing, where federal funds are being spent, who is receiving what services, and what happens to families after they leave welfare. Data on such matters have never been adequate, but as Nathan and Gais, as well as Greenberg, note, devolution has entailed real losses in information.

Does the Law Need to Be Changed?
Vin Weber observes that neither of the political parties in Washington is advocating major changes in welfare law.

Both are more likely to fine-tune or modify it in ways that build on, rather than reverse, its current thrust. From a local perspective as well, some stability could be useful; too much change at the federal level makes life difficult for those with day-to-day responsibility for implementing the law.

Nonetheless, debates will undoubtedly arise about funding as well as other matters. Conservatives may argue that states no longer need so much money in the face of falling caseloads while liberals will want to expand funding to serve both those who remain on the rolls and a broader group of low-income working families. Currently, states receive $16.5 billion a year from Washington to assist needy families with children. States are required to maintain their own spending at 75–80 percent of what they spent during the early 1990s, or around $11 billion a year. Because caseloads have declined sharply, states have reaped a windfall and now have much more to spend per family on welfare than they did before 1996. But if caseloads should rise again in response to a recession, states are likely to need more than the small contingency fund now available for this purpose. Because the allocation of federal funds among states is based on commitments that historically favored high-benefit states, another issue is the fairness of providing more than twice as much federal money for a poor child in a wealthy state as for one in a poorer state.

One of the new law's most contentious issues has always been its five-year limit on the time families may receive federally funded benefits. Because the time limit will not begin to kick in until this coming fall, its full effects have not yet been felt. Should states start implementing it in the midst of a recession, the resulting harm to families could produce an outcry that might well change the debate. But states have other options. They may use their own funds to keep families on the rolls longer or may put families into community service jobs. Federal rules already allow states to exempt 20 percent of their caseload from the limit, and states may ask Washington to liberalize those rules.

The issues of funding and time limits will almost surely be linked to a broader debate about the purposes of the law. Once the goal of welfare reform is broadened beyond providing cash assistance to needy families to include encouraging marriage, making work pay, and helping families with problems ranging from substance abuse to mental health, the adequacy of any particular level of resources is unclear. Indeed, one danger is that funding will be set based on historical experience while the objectives expand in new directions. In particular, several contributors argue that the law should give much more attention to reducing poverty and finding strategies and performance measures that relate to this larger goal.

Beyond Welfare: The Unfinished Agenda

Certainly, the new welfare law, and any modifications to it in 2002, will not end the debate about poverty in the United States. That debate is ongoing and will always involve disputes about the balance between individual and social responsibility. In 2002 the reauthorization of TANF and related legislation, such as food stamps and the child care block grant, will provide an opportunity to reengage that debate.

I would argue that the three most important aspects of that broader debate are what society owes to those who work but remain poor; what, if anything, can be done to reduce childbearing outside of marriage; and how to break the cycle of poverty for children growing up in low-income communities.

Supports for the working poor have expanded over the past two decades, especially since 1990. The earned income tax credit is now the nation's largest antipoverty program by far. Future debates are likely to center on whether it can be further expanded to encourage work and marriage while minimizing error and fraud. Other support strategies likely to be discussed are subsidized child care or health insurance for low-income adults, a higher minimum wage, refundable tax credits for children in families that work, or cash supplements paid through the welfare system for those in low-paid jobs. Concerns about whether the least skilled will be able to find work in a less robust economy may also be addressed. Although few states have chosen to back up the work requirement in the new welfare law with community service jobs for those unable to find jobs in the private sector, linking the two has broad appeal. Liberals have always liked the idea of guaranteeing a job to those unable to find work and conservatives have come to understand that last-resort jobs in the public sector make a tough work requirement more politically acceptable as well as easier to enforce.

The key challenges now are to provide greater supports for low-wage work, reduce childbearing outside of marriage, and ensure that more children have a good start in life.

Reducing childbearing outside of marriage is a more daunting challenge. Not only is there less consensus about this as a goal, but also there are far fewer workable remedies. Nonetheless, reducing out-of-wedlock childbearing was a key goal of the 1996 legislation and for good reason. The growth of single-parent families, driven almost entirely by out-of-wedlock childbearing in recent years, has substantially worsened child poverty. Wade Horn suggests that public policy might encourage marriage by reducing the marriage penalty in the EITC, by helping fathers earn enough to support their children, and by funding programs that enhance the marital and parenting skills of high-risk families. But he admits that such strategies may not change people's behavior. The fact that many women in these communities begin childbearing at a very early age—typically in their teens—suggests the need to prevent early sex and pregnancy. The 1996 law provided funding for abstinence education programs whose efficacy remains unproven. Bearing in mind that the typical teenager spends about 7 hours a day watching television, surfing the Internet, and reading popular magazines, reaching them through these popular media may be far more cost-effective than school or community-based programs regardless of whether the message is abstinence or safer sex. In short, emphasis needs to be placed as much on changing cultural norms through creative use of the media as on offering more sex education programs. And with so many mothers now working, and some evidence that this has created problems for their adolescent children, more after-school programs may be needed as well.

Breaking the cycle of child poverty is a high priority for many but often gets lost in discussions of the welfare system. To the extent it is discussed, it is usually in the context of providing child care for mothers leaving welfare for work. Most observers recognize that the children of these mothers will need some sort of care, but they cannot agree whether the available care is adequate and whether improving it could be one way to break the cycle of poverty. Thus far, there is little evidence that requiring mothers to work has harmed their children. But the goal of leaving no child behind goes beyond doing no harm. In fact, many believe that if every young child of a mother leaving welfare had access to Head Start or another high-quality early education program, more children would reach school age ready to learn and, with appropriate follow-up in the elementary grades, go on to greater success as adults.

Looking Ahead

Welfare reform has been far more successful than most people anticipated. Caseloads are down, employment among single mothers is up, and poverty rates have fallen. In the absence of a major recession that reverses all this good news, it is unlikely that the direction of current policy will be reversed or that major features of the 1996 law will be modified. That doesn't mean there won't be some changes and that reauthorization won't or shouldn't catalyze a broader debate about antipoverty policy in the United States. The most important challenges in this regard are to provide greater supports for low-wage work, to reduce childbearing outside of marriage, and to ensure that more children have a good start in life.

Isabel Sawhill is a senior fellow in the Brookings Economic Studies program and a co-director of the Brookings Welfare Reform & Beyond Initiative.

From *Brookings Review,* Summer 2001, pp. 4-7. © 2001 by The Brookings Review.

RACISM ISN'T WHAT IT USED TO BE

But not everyone has noticed

Ed Marciniak

A new vocabulary is surfacing to assess the state of race relations in the United States. The operative words and approaches signal remarkable changes.

In the 1960s our racial language was dominated by "civil rights," "integration," "desegregation," "prejudice," "discrimination," "colored," and "Negroes." Nowadays, the comparable words and ideas have become: "racism," "diversity," "hate crimes," "racial profiling," "redlining," "reparations," "blacks," and "African Americans."

We are in transition, striving to find a racial vocabulary appropriate to today's society and culture. This is a touchy, controversial endeavor.

The 1960s, furthermore, emphasized equality of treatment—in employment, voting, housing, and government services. In the new millennium the stress has shifted to equality of results. Now the assumption of some is that ethnic and racial groups should be proportionately represented in occupations, incomes, wealth, college graduations, achievements, and failures. On the other hand, black athletes now dominate the nation's sports, such as track, basketball, football, and baseball (almost). Inequality is not the same as inequity.

The variations in language reflect the notable developments in race relations since 1963 when Martin Luther King Jr. gave his "I Have a Dream" speech to two hundred thousand people, culminating the March on Washington. Or since 1964 when Congress enacted the U.S. Civil Rights Act. Consider only a few of the changes:

In 1966, 42 percent of American blacks had incomes below the official poverty line. Recently, the U.S. Census Bureau reported that 24 percent of the nation's blacks were under that poverty line. At the same time, the poverty rate for whites was 8 percent.

Nationwide, the count of black elected officials zoomed from some 100 in the 1960s to 9,000 in the new millennium. In political jurisdictions where the voting majority is of one race, candidates of another continue to gain office.

We now have a national holiday in January honoring a black minister who preached and practiced nonviolence. And it can no longer be claimed that 11 A.M. on Sunday is the nation's most segregated hour of the week.

Affirmative-action programs originally intended for blacks now embrace Hispanics, Asians, women, and/or gays. Some university affirmative-action programs give priority to students in poverty.

The reading public has come to realize that Toni Morrison is black and a writer. But she is not a black writer.

Hispanics will soon overtake blacks as the largest "minority." Meanwhile, efforts to create ongoing coalitions among blacks, Hispanics, and Asians have not been successful.

A growing number of blacks who have "made it" want to be seen as having arrived there by their own ability rather than affirmative action. In California, Florida, Michigan, and Texas, for example, affirmative-action programs based on race in college admissions have been challenged by whites, and also by some blacks.

These racial changes since the 1960s—and others too numerous to highlight—have encouraged a new generation of black leaders to recommend that priority also be given to those social problems that only tortuously can be linked solely to racism. They point, for example, to the prevalence of black-on-black crime, absentee fathers, the disproportion of AIDS among blacks compared to whites, the large number of single-parent black households in public-housing projects, and the poorly performing public schools in those neighborhoods. The victims of black crime are predominantly black.

That is why in Chicago last year, U.S. Representative Bobby Rush (D-Ill.) convened a summit on black-on-black crime and asked the attendees to "find alternatives to the culture of gun violence. It is critical we teach by example the true method of conflict resolution… " At about the same time, James T. Meeks, vice president of Jesse Jackson's Rainbow/Push coalition, appealed to fellow blacks: "Let's stop blaming everybody else for the problems of black men and start doing something for ourselves. Yes, white folks have treated us wrong. Yes, there is an injustice, but we're doing a whole lot of stuff to ourselves. To black America, if you want to help, we've got to start in our own house."

Several years ago, the need for such self-scrutiny was dramatically summarized in the *Economist* (March 7, 1998):

> Black unemployment in desperate ghettos is not obviously the result of racism. Most of the worst-stricken cities are run by black mayors, after all; and social services that might once have ignored the plight of blacks are also run by blacks. Black entrepreneurs as well as white ones have fled the inner cites for the suburbs.… A bigger cause of black poverty is that 70 percent of all black children are born out of wedlock.… During the Depression, poverty was acute but families were more cohesive.

In spite of an era of high prosperity, the persistence of child poverty among blacks (and whites), can be attributed, in the main, to the decline in marriage and to the tide of single-parent households. Statistics for 1999 from the U.S. Census Bureau confirmed this conclusion: 50 percent of black children under six in families without a father lived in poverty, while only 9 percent of those in a two-parent family were poor.

While the new black leaders may echo the *Economist*'s devastating overview, they do not deny that racism exists. For them, however, racism as *the* reason for the durability of black poverty has become more difficult to substantiate. Consequently, they search for new ways to eradicate disparities in income, seeking additional means of uprooting black poverty. They struggle to have their voices heard and their proposals implemented. In doing so, they play down white guilt and black helplessness.

On the other hand, the racial gains since the 1960s, the disturbing social conditions within some black communities, and the calls for self-help initiatives have put traditional civil-rights leaders on the defensive. Disinclined to air "dirty linen" in public, they continue viewing the world through the prism of race. As a result, the civil-rights establishment now strives even harder to keep racism high on the nation's agenda and conscience. How? By shunning the more favorable data about black achievement. They publicize instead anecdotal data about racism's presence to garner support for their contention that the nation's 34 million blacks are still the victims and that racism is omnipresent.

In their eagerness, hyperbole often suffuses their arguments. Alabama's Southern Poverty Law Center recently claimed in a fund-raising letter: "I'm sure that you are well aware that our schools are racked with racial strife and intolerance against those who are different. Some call it a national crisis. Our communities are seething with racial violence. African Americans, Hispanics, and Asian Americans are assaulting each other."

In their tug of war with the venerable civil-rights establishment, new—and increasingly influential—black leaders no longer seek to divide (victimizers vs. victims). Instead, they hope to unite blacks and whites so that together they will address the serious social problems that beset inner-city neighborhoods. Their first priority goes to reducing urban poverty. In the new millennium, a new civil-rights agenda is being fashioned to promote two-parent families, curb street violence, improve public schools, reduce dependency on drugs, and uproot poverty. These objectives may prove to be more difficult to achieve than the equal-opportunity goals of the civil-rights movement in the 1960s, but they are no less worthy of pursuit.

Ed Marciniak is president of the Institute of Urban Life at Loyola University, Chicago.

Don Wycliff

Ed Marciniak is absolutely right when he says we are struggling for a new way to talk intelligently and usefully about race. But what inhibits such conversation, I think, is less the lack of a new vocabulary than the persistence of an old one: the vocabulary of racial guilt and innocence. Our whole racial "dialogue" has become a contest to establish or escape guilt, and, as a result, is shot through with dishonesty.

Most white people—or what appears to me to be most—seem intent mainly on establishing their personal innocence: innocence of racial bias, of discrimination, of any connection to or benefit from slavery. Not only is this beside the point, it's also impossible. One cannot escape the personal implications of membership in a society, no matter how personally blameless one may be. Where race in America is concerned, there are no innocents.

For their part, black people—or at least black leaders—seem more intent than ever on pressing the issue of white personal guilt: for slavery, for segregation, for lingering discrimination, for whatever deficits African Americans still suffer. More than three decades into the nation's effort to pay off that promissory note Martin Luther King Jr.

spoke of in his "I Have a Dream" speech, black leaders seem intent on denying that anything at all has changed, determined not to "let the white man off the hook." As a black man, a Christian, and a person who has required the forgiveness and forbearance of others more than once in his life, I am deeply troubled by this particular gambit. The notion of acting as moral prosecutor and judge of a fellow human being strikes me as odious. I take seriously the scriptural admonition against judging others, "for the measure by which you measure is the measure by which you will be measured." There is nothing more foolish and unbecoming, it seems to me, than to go about peering into the eyes of others in search of motes.

(I am reminded in this connection of an e-mail sent me by a black friend of about my age, fifty-four, after the recent deadly school shooting in San Diego. It was a newspaper column in which the writer, a white man, urged other whites to face up to the fact that this kind of behavior was a white kid's malady. My friend underscored that point in his accompanying note. I didn't reply to him, but if I had I would have told him you could bet that, before this terrible phenomenon runs its course, there'll be a black kid somewhere who will do the same thing. There is no racial immunity to the sort of demons that possess children and propel them to such murderous lunacy. To think such immunity exists is to succumb to the pride that goes before a fall—and an embarrassment.)

Not only is such moral prosecution foolish and unbecoming, it's ineffective. Increasingly over the last two decades, white people have given evidence that they have hardened to this sort of thing, that they're through feeling racial guilt—whether they ought to be or not. Obviously, not all take this attitude, but a growing number that now seem to be a majority do. This refusal of guilt first manifested itself in the election of Ronald Reagan and has continued ever since—even through the two Clinton administrations. Paralleling this change has been another: the loss by blacks of the moral high ground that goes along with victim status. Frankly, given the very real and dramatic progress African Americans have made over the last three and one-half decades, it is hard to sustain the argument that we remain, as a group, victims of a relentless and unyielding societal racism. To be sure, racism persists and continues to distort lives. Probably in no area is its effect greater than in law enforcement and criminal justice. The ruinous rates of black unwed motherhood to which Marciniak refers are not unrelated to the depressing rates of arrest and incarceration of black men, so many of whom are thereby rendered "unmarriageable."

But to contend, as some black spokesmen do, that racism remains the defining fact of black life in this country, that "a black man just can't get ahead," is simply, demonstrably false. There are too many exceptions, too many success stories, for that to be true. Such exceptions are now, arguably, the rule. But it wasn't just a general perception of steadily increasing black progress that eroded the notion of blacks as victims and changed the moral equation on race. Had that been the case, I don't think there would be the raw edginess to race relations that is so much in evidence now. No, there was one very specific and singular event that, I believe, sealed the change. That event was the trial of O.J. Simpson and the reaction of black people to it.

It appeared to many whites—and I hear this every time a hot racial issue is aired in the newspaper—that a black man got away with murder in this high-profile case by portraying himself as a victim of police racism. Not only did blacks on the Simpson jury let him get away, but the black community at large applauded it, demonstrating thereby that racial solidarity was more important than justice. Or so the thinking goes. I don't think it was fully appreciated at the time what a watershed in race relations the Simpson verdict was. Indeed, grotesque as the idea may seem, the Simpson case is emblematic of what many white and black conservative critics consider the grievous defect of affirmative action and other programs of racial redress: a black man escaped responsibility for the killing of two white persons so that society could make redress for his supposed victimization by a social institution, the police. Take away the homicidal element and these critics see the same principle at work in, for example, the University of Michigan affirmative-action cases: In an attempt to redress historical social wrongs, less-deserving minority applicants are favored over more-deserving white ones. It's an argument that, it appears, the Supreme Court is ready to buy.

So if there is unfinished business in the area of racial equality and the old vocabulary of racial guilt and innocence have become impediments, what's to be done? We could do far worse, I think, than go back to Martin Luther King Jr. for instruction and example. King and his "dream" are invoked so frequently and wantonly nowadays that I have almost grown tired of them. I know that's heresy, but there is a treacly quality to so much of the talk about King and his dream that it is like an overdose of candy. However, the fact is that King preached hard truths and he was not a man to take the easy road. He entered by the narrow gate—the gate of nonviolent direct action. You almost never hear anyone talk about that anymore. The genius of his approach was manifold. It involved direct action, an active challenge to injustice. But it was nonviolent, a refusal to use what he considered immoral means to achieve a moral end. It put the onus on those maintaining the system of injustice to respond—and to live with themselves afterward. It forced them to confront their consciences, not to listen to moral harangues.

That last fact is critical, especially in our over-the-top, in-your-face, finger-wagging age, when nobody feels any compunction about calling attention to the faults and failures of others. King had the grace and the good sense not to go about acting as moral prosecutor of his fellow humans—even if he may privately have considered them monsters. That may have been a tactical decision—like leaving room in a diplomatic negotiation for one's rival to gracefully back down, to save face. I like to think his belief in nonviolence was an expression of real grace, the result of King's having received forgiveness for his sins and thereby being inclined to forgive others. But whether King's attitude was tactical or something more—or something else entirely—I don't see any contemporary black leader who behaves that way. And that's a real loss because King's approach is the only way whites can be rendered receptive again to the need to exert themselves to rectify what remains of racism in American society.

We in the United States have made an amazing racial revolution over the last three and one-half decades. There may be another nation that has done as much, but if there is, I don't know of it. We must tell our people—black,

white, brown, red, yellow—all about that revolution. We need to give ourselves a big round of applause. Then we must challenge ourselves—without condemning—to finish the job. And we must do it in terms that will cause people to nod "yes" instead of turning away in disgust. I personally am fond of those words from the preamble to the Constitution, the ones about creating "a more perfect union." Where is the Martin Luther King of our age, or the Abraham Lincoln, or the Lyndon Johnson, or the Cesar Chavez, who can speak those words in a way that will move us to the next stage of the struggle for American union?

Don Wycliff *is public editor of the* Chicago Tribune.

From *Commonweal*, June 1, 2001, pp. 12-14. © 2001 by Commonweal Foundation. Reprinted by permission. For subscriptions, call toll-free: 1-888-495-6755.

WHERE BIAS BEGINS:
THE TRUTH ABOUT
STEREOTYPES

**Psychologists once believed that only bigoted people used stereotypes.
Now the study of unconscious bias is revealing the unsettling truth:
We all use stereotypes, all the time, without knowing it.
We have met the enemy of equality, and the enemy is us.**

By Annie Murphy Paul

Mahzarin Banaji doesn't fit anybody's idea of a racist. A psychology professor at Yale University, she studies stereotypes for a living. And as a woman and a member of a minority ethnic group, she has felt first-hand the sting of discrimination. Yet when she took one of her own tests of unconscious bias, "I showed very strong prejudices," she says. "It was truly a disconcerting experience." And an illuminating one. When Banaji was in graduate school in the early 1980s, theories about stereotypes were concerned only with their explicit expression: outright and unabashed racism, sexism, anti-Semitism. But in the years since, a new approach to stereotypes has shattered that simple notion. The bias Banaji and her colleagues are studying is something far more subtle, and more insidious: what's known as automatic or implicit stereotyping, which, they find, we do all the time without knowing it. Though out-and-out bigotry may be on

the decline, says Banaji, "if anything, stereotyping is a bigger problem than we ever imagined."

Previously researchers who studied stereotyping had simply asked people to record their feelings about minority groups and had used their answers as an index of their attitudes. Psychologists now understand that these conscious replies are only half the story. How progressive a person seems to be on the surface bears little or no relation to how prejudiced he or she is on an unconscious level—so that a bleeding-heart liberal might harbor just as many biases as a neo-Nazi skinhead.

As surprising as these findings are, they confirmed the hunches of many students of human behavior. "Twenty years ago, we hypothesized that there were people who said they were not prejudiced but who really did have unconscious negative stereotypes and beliefs," says psychologist Jack

Dovidio, Ph.D., of Colgate University. "It was like theorizing about the existence of a virus, and then one day seeing it under a microscope."

The test that exposed Banaji's hidden biases—and that this writer took as well, with equally dismaying results—is typical of the ones used by automatic stereotype researchers. It presents the subject with a series of positive or negative adjectives, each paired with a characteristically "white" or "black" name. As the name and word appear together on a computer screen, the person taking the test presses a key, indicating whether the word is good or bad. Meanwhile, the computer records the speed of each response.

A glance at subjects' response times reveals a startling phenomenon: Most people who participate in the experiment—even some African-Americans—respond more quickly when a positive word is paired with a white name or a negative word with a black name. Because our minds are more accustomed to making these associations, says Banaji, they process them more rapidly. Though the words and names aren't subliminal, they are presented so quickly that a subject's ability to make deliberate choices is diminished—allowing his or her underlying assumptions to show through. The same technique can be used to measure stereotypes about many different social groups, such as homosexuals, women, and the elderly.

THE UNCONSCIOUS COMES INTO FOCUS

From these tiny differences in reaction speed—a matter of a few hundred milliseconds—the study of automatic stereotyping was born. Its immediate ancestor was the cognitive revolution of the 1970s, an explosion of psychological research into the way people think. After decades dominated by the study of observable behavior, scientists wanted a closer look at the more mysterious operation of the human brain. And the development of computers—which enabled scientists to display information very quickly and to measure minute discrepancies in reaction time—permitted a peek into the unconscious.

LIKE THE CULTURE, OUR MINDS ARE SPLIT ON THE SUBJECTS OF RACE, GENDER, SEXUAL ORIENTATION.

At the same time, the study of cognition was also illuminating the nature of stereotypes themselves. Research done after World War II—mostly by European émigrés struggling to understand how the Holocaust had happened—concluded that stereotypes were used only by a particular type of person: rigid, repressed, authoritarian. Borrowing from the psychoanalytic perspective then in vogue, these theorists suggested that biased behavior emerged out of internal conflicts caused by inadequate parenting.

The cognitive approach refused to let the rest of us off the hook. It made the simple but profound point that we all use categories—of people, places, things—to make sense of the world around us. "Our ability to categorize and evaluate is an important part of human intelligence," says Banaji. "Without it, we couldn't survive." But stereotypes are too much of a good thing. In the course of stereotyping, a useful category—say women—becomes freighted with additional associations, usually negative. "Stereotypes are categories that have gone too far," says John Bargh, Ph.D., of New York University. "When we use stereotypes, we take in the gender, the age, the color of the skin of the person before us, and our minds respond with messages that say hostile, stupid, slow, weak. Those qualities aren't out there in the environment. They don't reflect reality."

Bargh thinks that stereotypes may emerge from what social psychologists call in-group/out-group dynamics. Humans, like other species, need to feel that they are part of a group, and as villages, clans, and other traditional groupings have broken down, our identities have attached themselves to more ambiguous classifications, such as race and class. We want to feel good about the group we belong to—and one way of doing so is to denigrate all those who aren't in it. And while we tend to see members of our own group as individuals, we view those in out-groups as an undifferentiated—stereotyped—mass. The categories we use have changed, but it seems that stereotyping itself is bred in the bone.

Though a small minority of scientists argues that stereotypes are usually accurate and can be relied upon without reservations, most disagree—and vehemently. "Even if there is a kernel of truth in the stereotype, you're still applying a generalization about a group to an individual, which is always incorrect," says Bargh. Accuracy aside, some believe that the use of stereotypes is simply unjust. "In a democratic society people should be judged as individuals and not as members of a group," Banaji argues. "Stereotyping flies in the face of that ideal."

PREDISPOSED TO PREJUDICE

The problem, as Banaji's own research shows, is that people can't seem to help it. A recent experiment provides a good illustration. Banaji and her colleague, Anthony Greenwald, Ph.D., showed people a list of names—some famous, some not. The next day the subjects returned to the lab and were shown a second list, which mixed names from the first list with new ones. Asked to identify which were famous, they picked out the Margaret Meads and the Miles Davises—but they also chose some of the names on the first list, which retained a lingering familiarity that they mistook for fame. (Psychologists call this the "famous overnight-effect.") By a margin of two-to-one, these suddenly "famous" people were male.

Participants weren't aware that they were preferring male names to female names, Banaji stresses. They were simply drawing on an unconscious stereotype of men as more important and influential than women. Something similar happened when she showed subjects a list of people who might be criminals: without knowing they were doing so, participants picked out an overwhelming number of African-American names. Banaji calls this kind of stereotyping *implicit*, because people know they are making a judgment—but just aren't aware of the basis upon which they are making it.

Even further below awareness is something that psychologists call automatic processing, in which stereotypes are triggered by the slightest interaction or encounter. An experiment conducted by Bargh required a group of white participants to perform a tedious computer task. While performing the task, some of the participants were subliminally exposed to pictures of African-Americans with neutral expressions. When the subjects were then asked to do the task over again, the ones who had been exposed to the faces reacted with more hostility to the request—because, Bargh believes, they were responding in kind to the hostility which is part of the African-American stereotype. Bargh calls this the "immediate hostile reaction," which he believes can have a real effect on race relations. When African-Americans accurately perceive the hostile expressions that their white counterparts are unaware of, they may respond with hostility of their own—thereby perpetuating the stereotype.

Of course, we aren't completely under the sway of our unconscious. Scientists think that the automatic activation of a stereotype is immediately followed by a conscious check on unacceptable thoughts—at least in people who think that they are not prejudiced. This internal censor successfully restrains overtly biased responses. But there's still the danger of leakage, which often shows up in non-verbal behavior: our expressions, our stance, how far away we stand, how much eye contact we make.

THE CATEGORIES WE USE HAVE CHANGED, BUT STEREOTYPING ITSELF SEEMS TO BE BRED IN THE BONE.

The gap between what we say and what we do can lead African-Americans and whites to come away with very different impressions of the same encounter, says Jack Dovidio. "If I'm a white person talking to an African-American, I'm probably monitoring my conscious beliefs very carefully and making sure everything I say agrees with all the positive things I want to express," he says. "And I usually believe I'm pretty successful because I hear the right words coming out of my mouth." The listener who is paying attention to non-verbal behavior, however, may be getting quite the opposite message. An African-American student of Dovidio's recently told him that when she was growing up, her mother had taught her to observe how white people moved to gauge their true feelings toward blacks. "Her mother was a very astute amateur psychologist—and about 20 years ahead of me," he remarks.

WHERE DOES BIAS BEGIN?

So where exactly do these stealth stereotypes come from? Though automatic-stereotype researchers often refer to the unconscious, they don't mean the Freudian notion of a seething mass of thoughts and desires, only some of which are deemed presentable enough to be admitted to the conscious mind. In fact, the cognitive model holds that information flows in exactly the opposite direction: connections made often enough in the conscious mind eventually become unconscious. Says Bargh: "If conscious choice and decision making are not needed, they go away. Ideas recede from consciousness into the unconscious over time."

Much of what enters our consciousness, of course, comes from the culture around us. And like the culture, it seems that our minds are split on the subjects of race, gen-

der, class, sexual orientation. "We not only mirror the ambivalence we see in society, but also mirror it in precisely the same way," says Dovidio. Our society talks out loud about justice, equality, and egalitarianism, and most Americans accept these values as their own. At the same time, such equality exists only as an ideal, and that fact is not lost on our unconscious. Images of women as sex objects, footage of African-American criminals on the six o'clock news,—"this is knowledge we cannot escape," explains Banaji. "We didn't choose to know it, but it still affects our behavior."

WE HAVE TO CHANGE HOW WE THINK WE CAN INFLUENCE PEOPLE'S BEHAVIORS. IT WOULD BE NAIVE TO THINK THAT EXHORTATION IS ENOUGH.

We learn the subtext of our culture's messages early. By five years of age, says Margo Monteith, Ph.D., many children have definite and entrenched stereotypes about blacks, women, and other social groups. Adds Monteith, professor of psychology at the University of Kentucky: "Children don't have a choice about accepting or rejecting these conceptions, since they're acquired well before they have the cognitive abilities or experiences to form their own beliefs." And no matter how progressive the parents, they must compete with all the forces that would promote and perpetuate these stereotypes: peer pressure, mass media, the actual balance of power in society. In fact, prejudice may be as much a result as a cause of this imbalance. We create stereotypes—African-Americans are lazy, women are emotional—to explain why things are the way they are. As Dovidio notes, "Stereotypes don't have to be true to serve a purpose."

WHY CAN'T WE ALL GET ALONG?

The idea of unconscious bias does clear up some nettlesome contradictions. "It accounts for a lot of people's ambivalence toward others who are different, a lot of their

inconsistencies in behavior," says Dovidio. "It helps explain how good people can do bad things." But it also prompts some uncomfortable realizations. Because our conscious and unconscious beliefs may be very different—and because behavior often follows the lead of the latter—"good intentions aren't enough," as John Bargh puts it. In fact, he believes that they count for very little. "I don't think free will exists," he says, bluntly—because what feels like the exercise of free will may be only the application of unconscious assumptions.

Not only may we be unable to control our biased responses, we may not even be aware that we have them. "We have to rely on our memories and our awareness of what we're doing to have a connection to reality," says Bargh. "But when it comes to automatic processing, those cues can be deceptive." Likewise, we can't always be sure how biased others are. "We all have this belief that the important thing about prejudice is the external expression of it," says Banaji. "That's going to be hard to give up."

One thing is certain: We can't claim that we've eradicated prejudice just because its outright expression has waned. What's more, the strategies that were so effective in reducing that sort of bias won't work on unconscious beliefs. "What this research is saying is that we are going to have to change dramatically the way we think we can influence people's behaviors," says Banaji. "It would be naive to think that exhortation is enough." Exhortation, education, political protest—all of these hammer away at our conscious beliefs while leaving the bedrock below untouched. Banaji notes, however, that one traditional remedy for discrimination—affirmative action—may still be effective since it bypasses our unconsciously compromised judgment.

But some stereotype researchers think that the solution to automatic stereotyping lies in the process itself. Through practice, they say people can weaken the mental links that connect minorities to negative stereotypes and strengthen the ones that connect them to positive conscious beliefs. Margo Monteith explains how it might work. "Suppose you're at a party and someone tells a racist joke—and you laugh," she says. "Then you realize that you shouldn't have laughed at the joke. You feel guilty and become focused on your thought processes. Also, all sorts of cues become associated with laughing at the racist joke: the person who told the joke, the act of telling jokes, being at a party drinking." The next time you encounter these cues, "a warning signal of sorts should go off—'wait, didn't you mess up in this situation before?'—and your responses will be slowed and executed with greater restraint."

That slight pause in the processing of a stereotype gives conscious, unprejudiced beliefs a chance to take over. With time, the tendency to prevent automatic stereotyping may itself become automatic. Monteith's research suggests that, given enough motivation, people may be able to teach themselves to inhibit prejudice so well that even their tests of implicit bias come clean.

The success of this process of "de-automatization" comes with a few caveats, however. First, even its proponents concede that it works only for people disturbed by the discrepancy between their conscious and unconscious beliefs, since unapologetic racists or sexists have no motivation to change. Second, some studies have shown that attempts to suppress stereotypes may actually cause them to return later, stronger than ever. And finally, the results that Monteith and other researchers have achieved in the laboratory may not stick in the real world, where people must struggle to maintain their commitment to equality under less-than-ideal conditions.

Challenging though that task might be, it is not as daunting as the alternative researchers suggest: changing society itself. Bargh, who likens de-automatization to closing the barn door once the horses have escaped, says that "it's clear that the way to get rid of stereotypes is by the roots, by where they come from in the first place." The study of culture may someday tell us where the seeds of prejudice originated; for now the study of the unconscious shows us just how deeply they're planted.

Reprinted with permission from *Psychology Today*, May/June 1998, pp. 52-55, 82. © 1998 by Sussex Publishers, Inc.

The Past and Prologue

FEMALE EXECUTIVES AND PROFESSIONALS

Address by JUDY OLIAN, *Dean of Penn State's Smeal College of Business Administration*
Delivered to the Penn State Professional Women's Network, New York city, New York, February 7, 2001

Thanks so much for this warm invitation to this terrific group of women. It's not a topic I talk much about. I usually contemplate the future of business, networked organizations, or the Smeal College, and I haven't taken much time to collect the information or to introspect about women's professional or executive careers. If I were to do that, I probably would have been tempted to reflect on female professional experiences by extrapolating from my own, and from my friends' and acquaintances' personal work histories. And, if I were to generalize from the power concentrated in this room, all is well among female professional America! There are many extraordinarily successful women here tonight whose expertise and professionalism have propelled them to the senior ranks of public and private organizations. Is that the whole story? I'm not sure.

This invitation prompted me to dig a little, so if you'll forgive me, I'll present a lot of numbers, I'll probably flood you with numbers and survey results as ingredients in shaping this story. Each of us will stir this pot of ingredients and see probably a slightly different picture or taste a slightly different dish, to use the metaphor. I'd be especially interested in hearing these differences in perception as we open the floor up for discussion. Let me start with a few factoids about the state of women in business in the year 2000.

In the year 2000:

46.5% of the workforce is female

29.5% of the managerial and professional specialty positions are held by women

12.5% of corporate officers are women among Fortune 500

11.7% of Fortune 500 members of the Board of Directors are women

That's 419 of the Fortune 500 who have female Board members, slightly down from the prior year

6.2% of the highest titled in the Fortune 500 are women

4.1% of the top earners are women, and I remind you that as a baseline, 46.5% of the workforce is female

2 of the Fortune 500 CEOs are women, 1 less than in the prior year

The only indicator that seems to go up consistently in the Fortune 500 is the number of companies with more than 3 female directors (it's now 45, up from 34 companies the prior year). I'll talk later about tokenism issues, and whether there's a minimum threshold, a small critical mass of people before one can break a dominant pattern. Interestingly, there seem to be more successes among the Fortune 500 than among the Fortune 501–1,000, perhaps because of the concerted public efforts and visibility of the Fortune 500.

If I compare the Fortune 500 to the Fortune 501–1000:

11.7% of the Fortune 500 versus 8.5% of the Fortune 501–1000 Board seats are held by women

16% of the Fortune 500 versus 38% of the Fortune 501 to 1000 companies have zero women on the Board, that is, the Fortune 500 are more than twice as likely to have female board members

84% of the Fortune 500 have at least one woman on the Board, compared to 62% among Fortune 501–1000. So, the numbers are far less attractive in the Fortune 501 to 1000.

Those are just the raw numbers on the "state of the world"—for professional women in the U.S. What accounts for this story in the year 2001—37 years after passage of Title VII of the Civil Rights Act of 1964 which assured equal opportunity for both men and women? My hypothesis, is that three areas account for the critical path differences between men and women:

Formative experiences
Career take-off experiences

Career experiences

1. Let's start with formative experiences. What happens pre-entry into business school careers is not equal between the genders:

Looking at pre-career experiences, boys choose computer sciences or computer engineering 5 times more frequently than girls, even though both agree on the importance of computer skills. That's from an Arthur Anderson survey of 650, 15–18 year olds, [C] 2000.

Boys are twice as likely to want to be CEO of tech company, versus girls aspiring to a career in health services, to be CEO of a clothing company, teacher, or small business owner (Anderson survey).

92% of girls report the need for female role models, but don't see enough of them (Anderson survey).

Today, overall, 48% of business students are women at the undergraduate level, and at the MBA level in top Business Schools that declines to 30% who are women.

From a Catalyst survey of 888 women and 796 males who are MBA alumni of top Business Schools (© 2000), the biggest reported reason for the relative scarcity of women in MBA programs is the absence of female role models. We saw that in the statistics presented earlier among business corporations, boards and CEO's. That is true also for Business Schools—22% of faculty across all B Schools are women, 7% of deans across all B Schools are women and certainly fewer among the major business schools.

Female MBAs report lower confidence in their math abilities.

Male freshmen report double the confidence in their computer skills than women, even though there is virtually identical computer use (from a UCLA survey of 400,000 incoming freshmen in 2000).

Women are less likely to be in feeder careers for MBAs—25% of males getting MBAs have engineering backgrounds vs. 9% of female MBAs; conversely, 23% of females getting MBAs are from the arts and humanities compared to 14% of males.

Both males and females see business careers as incompatible with work and life balance. But, women MBAs rate free time and relaxation as very important, more so than do men (60% women vs. 47% men who rate this as very important).

Few women view wealth accumulation as very important to them, 15% women vs. 22% men (GMAC).

These pre-business differences in self-confidence factors, aspirations, and feeder entry points into MBA programs account for some differences in the likelihood of getting an MBA, and the expectations about pay-offs from a business career. Undoubtedly that affects the extent to which women pursue MBAs, and what they aspire to do afterwards.

My second hypothesis is that the difference in the population of male and female professional demographics is attributable to early career take-off experiences.

When women accept jobs post-business education, they are more likely to be affected by location preferences (50% of women versus 35% of men indicate location as key), perhaps because women have more mobility constraints.

Women's choices after their business education are much more likely to be affected by their perception of jobs' contribution to society (14% of women say that's very important vs. 7% for men—GMAC).

Women are much more likely to be affected by the availability of family friendly benefits in their first job (8% vs. 2% for men—GMAC survey).

Among B School graduates, men are much more likely to start in management positions (36% vs. 27% of women—GMAC survey).

More men are in line positions post MBA (45% vs. 37% among women); more women are in staff positions post MBA (40% women vs. 30% men).

Men are more likely to work in Finance and General management; women are more likely to work in consulting.

Men are generally more satisfied with their career advancement.

Even when women take global assignments which is critical for their subsequent career progression, they appear to make their decision with more constraints. They are more likely to be single than are men, and if they are married, they are twice as likely than men to have a fully employed working spouse. So, there is a greater likelihood of making this choice because they are single rather than married, or if they are married they are more constrained than men because of a less movable spouse.

The third conjecture for why the world looks different for professional women is that they experience different career outcomes, and make different career decisions based on their career experiences.

When men change employers during the course of their career, their average salary increase is $25,000 compared to an average salary increase for women of $10,000. This figure controls for job tenure and any other job differences between the men and women. Why? The authors of this study just recently published by the Academy of Management suggest it has to do with more extensive social net works that men have, and pure discrimination.

Women report significantly more time out of their careers over the course of their first ten years post-MBA—an average of 22 months out of the workforce versus 10 months for men. The reasons for women are much more likely to be family related—birth/adoption, childcare, versus for men it's attributed to company mergers, company dissolutions, or reorganizations.

Women MBA graduates are much more likely to work part-time than male MBA graduates (27% vs. 5%), mainly again for childcare and birth/adoption reasons.

Among graduates of MBA programs, women are more likely than men to cite flexibility, lifestyle issues as reasons to start their own business, compared to male entrepreneurs who cite market, financial, and personality reasons such as independence to start their own businesses.

Women entrepreneurs are more likely to own small businesses (71% of female entrepreneurs have businesses of less than $250,000 in revenues a year, compared to 22% of male entrepreneurs); however bigger entrepreneurs with more than $1M in revenues a year are much more likely to be men (62% vs. 17% among women).

Men are much more likely to work continuously post MBAs (61% vs. 29% among women), and the differences are more extreme among MBA grads with children, where women are more likely to disrupt their career.

Interestingly, men and women are dissatisfied with their work/life balance (25% of men and 33% of women). The dissatisfaction with work/life balance goes up linearly, the more hours the person works.

Males and females use flex-time and telecommuting similarly, but again, women are much more likely to resort to part-time work, leave, or compressed work weeks in response to these difficulties.

Among MBA graduates from the Catalyst survey, the top three reasons cited by female executives as barriers to their advancement at work are:

Stereotyping and preconceptions (partially a function of whom they report to, and who reports to them)

Exclusion from informal networks—whether it's golf, sports, spectator events or late night drinking

Inhospitable corporate environments. In fact, just last week, in the Chronicle of Higher Education, I was looking at a statement coming out of the top eight universities in the country. The statement acknowledged mistreatment of female faculty in the sciences and engineering and described various steps that they are going to take to remedy that mistreatment—a public acknowledgement of the in-hospitality of those corporate environments.

Based on this factual "dump" of survey and demographic data, what overarching conclusions can we reach regarding women professionals as a group? Any generalized conclusions, of course, overlook huge individual differences, as is evident in this room.

There are similarities between male and female career experiences.

There are very few differences between men and women regarding their satisfaction with career and job opportunities post MBA.

There are few differences between men and women regarding risk preferences and personal investment decisions.

More women than men are "CEOs at home"—62% of women vs. 38% of men manage their home checking account, 53% women vs. 38% men create the family budget, 46% of women vs. 42% of men make the family's savings and investment decisions (WingspanBank.com survey)

Both are dissatisfied with work/home imbalances

But there are also some real differences:

The cultures of our upbringing, preparatory experiences and self concepts create differences in confidence factors that are critical to choice of business careers especially true of men and women's self concepts true of their math and computer skills and aspirations.

Women make, or are channeled into, initial career choices that are not natural feeders into graduate business education or business careers.

Once into a career women choose, or are assigned, non-line positions or functional areas which are not as visible or natural springboards for promotion.

If in global positions, they're either single, or have less flexibility because of the complexity of a working spouse.

Women appear to respond (by choice or situation) in different ways than men to the extreme stresses associated with work/home imbalances. They respond by reducing or withdrawing entirely from their work involvement.

As entrepreneurs, they go for more modest ventures than men.

The low numbers in female enrollment in MBA Programs (and actually that's a modest decline relative to more recent years), is not due to their entrepreneurial ventures. It's more due to perceived lack of role models, lack of hospitality of the work environment, and balance challenges.

Knowing what we know about female executive styles, how do women fit with the changing workplace, merged global markets and the transformation to a technology based economy? In a nutshell, today's and tomorrow's organizations are going to be global, churning and changing, flat, relying very heavily on networked technologies that empower through knowledge sharing and through various options for work arrangements. Tomorrow's organizations offer opportunities for entrepreneurship in yet to be founded industries, with rewards for creativity and risk taking.

Is that good news or bad news for women? I think it's both.

The bad news is that organizations without boundaries, that are so porous between work and non-work, pose huge challenges for personal balance. The absence of boundaries between work and non-work means that people are tethered all the time, and if they're tethered, that exacerbates the challenges of balance between work and personal lives. Women may suffer even more given their unequal burden regarding family care, at least to date.

Women are also more prone to make choices to avoid competition and conflict. That's based on the work of Deborah Tannen and Judy Rosener and various developmental psychologists. Fighting for scarce resources in competitive situations creates conflict, often inevitable in leadership positions. Women have to make those choices, and sometimes play those roles, despite their disposition against such behaviors (again, ignoring individual differences).

We know, also from developmental psychologists, that women are less likely to be self-promoting and are more deferential, not a recipe for leadership and visibility enhancement. Women may not network as well, especially when they're in predominantly male corporations and functions. Churning organizations that repeatedly change configurations through mergers, acquisitions, and reorganizations place an even greater premium on networking, and whom you know.

Women may not be as good as men at creating a network around them that supports their leadership, that is, others who handle conflict and deliver the bad news on their behalf, and therefore protect their leadership position.

And, women still cite as barriers the stereotypes and attributions made by others—colleagues, superiors and subordinates—that reflect others' discomfort with their power and leadership, which may lead to disadvantage. This may not be intentional discrimination, but merely discomfort with their role as leaders, resulting in exactly the same kind of disadvantage in promotion or placement.

The good news, and I think it's very good news, is that knowledge organizations do place a premium on functioning without a formal power base. Women do that better, according again to developmental psychologists, Deborah Tannen, Judy Rosener and others. Women tend to be more interactive and transformational leaders, and tend not to lead through command, control, reward, and punishment. Women tend to derive their power from their personal charisma, from their work record and accomplishments, and from personal relationships, not from hierarchy, title, and position. In today's flat, organizations that really fits well.

Women tend also to be more comfortable with sharing power and inviting participation, perfect for today's flat, knowledge-based organization. And they tend to recognize and enhance the self-worth of others, again suited to today's flat, knowledge-based organization.

The fiber optically networked workplace does create more options on how to work—when, where, how much—so that it may, over time, reduce the disadvantaged choices that women are making. Over time, virtual workplace structures may alleviate the juggling played between work and non-work and the difficulties both men and women confront because of the balance challenges. But women will especially benefit because, at this point, the data demonstrate that they assume the disproportionate burden.

The other piece of good news is that once women become more than a token, and the threshold of "the first one" is crossed, it seems to get a little easier (e.g., Boards of Directors with 3 or more women).

In sum, this is a mixed view and a set of conjectures that I propose to you. I presented a mind boggling set of numbers and survey data and I'm interested in your reactions on the basis of experience, or your insights into survey data. Thank you for your patience. I genuinely appreciated the opportunity to introspect, through you, more than you can imagine.

From *Vital Speeches of the Day,* April 15, 2001, pp. 398-401. © 2001 by City News Publishing Company, Inc.

VIOLENCE AGAINST WOMEN

It may be the biggest human rights issue in the world—and it is certainly one of the least discussed. Yet increasingly, women are finding ways to fight the mutilation, rape, beating, and murder that have been their lot.

Toni Nelson

A GIRL IS MUTILATED IN EGYPT

It is not a ritual that many people would expect—much less want—to witness. Yet in the fall of 1994, the television network CNN brought the practice of female genital mutilation (FGM) into living rooms around the world, by broadcasting the amputation of a young Egyptian girl's clitoris. Coinciding with the United Nations International Conference on Population and Development in Cairo, the broadcast was one of several recent events that have galvanized efforts to combat the various forms of violence that threaten women and girls throughout the world. The experience suffered by 10-year-old Nagla Hamza focused international attention on the plight of the more than 100 million women and girls in Africa victimized by FGM. In doing so, it helped spur conference delegates into formulating an official "Programme of Action" that condemned FGM and outlined measures to eliminate the practice.

Euphemistically referred to as female circumcision, FGM encompasses a variety of practices ranging from excision, the partial or total removal of the clitoris and labia minora, to infibulation, in which all the external genitals are cut away and the area is restitched, leaving only a small opening for the passage of urine and menstrual blood. Nagla's mutilation, performed by a local barber without anesthesia or sanitary precautions, was typical. Although the physical and psychological consequences of FGM are severe and often life-threatening, the practice persists due to beliefs that emerged from ancient tribal customs but which have now come to be associated with certain major religions. In Israel, for instance, FGM is practiced by Jewish migrants from the Ethiopian Falasha community; elsewhere in Africa, it is found among Christian and Islamic populations. But FGM has no inherent association with any of these religions. Although some Islamic scholars consider it an important part of that religion, FGM actually predates Islam, and neither the Qur'an, the primary source for Islamic law, nor the Hadith, collections of the Prophet Mohammed's lessons, explicitly require the practice.

Justifications for FGM vary among the societies where it occurs (FGM is practiced in 28 African nations, as well as in scattered tribal communities in the Arabian Peninsula and various parts of South Asia). But most explanations relate in some way to male interest in controlling women's emotions and sexual behavior. One of the most common explanations is the need to lessen desire so women will preserve their virginity until marriage. The late Gad-Alhaq Ali Gad-Alhaq, Sheik of Cairo's al-Azhar Islamic University at the time of the CNN broadcast, explained it this way: the purpose of FGM is "to moderate sexual desire while saving womanly pleasures in order that women may enjoy their husbands." For Mimi Ramsey, an anti-FGM activist in the United States who was mutilated in her native Ethiopia at age six, FGM is meant to reinforce the power men have over women: "the reason for my mutilation is for a man to be able to control me, to make me a good wife." Today, migrants are bringing FGM out of its traditional societies and into Europe, North America, and Australia. Approximately 2 million girls are at risk each year.

As in other countries where the practice is commonplace, Egypt's official policy on FGM has been ambiguous. Although a Ministry of Health decree in 1959 prohibited health professionals and public hospitals from performing the procedure, and national law makes it a crime to permanently mutilate anyone, clitoridectomies and other forms of FGM are not explicitly prohibited. An estimated 80 percent of Egyptian women and girls, or more than 18 million people, have undergone some form of FGM, which is often carried out by barbers in street booths on main squares of both small towns and large cities.

Before the CNN broadcast, Egyptian public opinion seemed to be turning against the practice. In early 1994, activists founded the Egyptian Task Force Against Female Genital Mutilation. Later that year, during the population conference, Population and Family Welfare Minister Maher Mahran vowed to delegates that "Egypt is going to work on the elimination of female genital mutilation." Plans were even laid for legislation that would outlaw FGM. But some members of Egypt's religious community saw the broadcast as a form of Western imperialism and used it to challenge both the secular government of Hosni Mubarak and the conference itself.

In October 1994, Sheik Gad-Alhaq ruled that FGM is a religious obligation for Muslims. The same month, Minister of Health Dr. Ali Abdel Fattah issued a decree permitting the practice in selected government hospitals. The Minister's directive came just 10 days after a committee of experts convened by him condemned FGM and denied that it had any religious justification. Fattah affirmed his personal opposition, but insisted that the decree was necessary to "save those victimized girls from being 'slaughtered' by unprofessionals."

In the wake of the Minister's decision, plans for the bill outlawing FGM were postponed. Contending that Fattah had effectively legalized the procedure, national and international nongovernmental organizations sought to reverse the decision through petition drives, public education initiatives, and lawsuits. And on October 17, 1995, Fattah reversed his decision, and the Ministry of Health once again banned FGM in public hospitals. The anti-FGM legislation, however, remains on hold.

VIOLENCE IS A UNIVERSAL THREAT

Egypt's confused and ambivalent response to FGM mirrors in many ways the intensifying international debate on all forms of violence against women. And even though FGM itself may seem just a grotesque anomaly to people brought up in cultures where it isn't practiced, FGM is grounded in attitudes and assumptions that are, unfortunately, all too common. Throughout the world, women's inferior social status makes them vulnerable to abuse and denies them the financial and legal means necessary to improve their situations. Over the past decade, women's groups around the world have succeeded in showing how prevalent this problem is and how much violence it is causing—a major accomplishment, given the fact that the issue was not even mentioned during the

first UN Women's Conference in 1975 or in the 1979 UN Convention on All Forms of Discrimination Against Women. But as the situation in Egypt demonstrates, effective policy responses remain elusive.

Violence stalks women throughout their lives, "from cradle to grave"—in the judgment of *Human Development Report 1995*, the UN's annual assessment of social and economic progress around the world. Gender-specific violence is almost a cultural constant, both emerging from and reinforcing the social relationships that give men power over women. This is most obvious in the implicit acceptance, across cultures, of domestic violence—of a man's prerogative to beat his wife. Large-scale surveys in 10 countries, including Colombia, Canada, and the United States, estimate that as many as one-third of women have been physically assaulted by an intimate male partner. More limited studies report that rates of physical abuse among some groups in Latin America, Asia, and Africa may reach 60 percent or more.

Belying the oft-cried cliché about "family values," studies have shown that the biggest threat to women is domestic violence. In 1992, the *Journal of the American Medical Association* published a study that found that women in the United States are more likely to be assaulted, injured, raped, or murdered by a current or former male partner than by all other types of attackers combined. In Canada, a 1987 study showed that 62 percent of the women murdered in that year were killed by an intimate male partner. And in India, the husband or in-laws of a newly married woman may think it justified to murder her if they consider her dowry inadequate, so that a more lucrative match can be made. One popular method is to pour kerosene on the woman and set her on fire—hence the term "bride burning." One in four deaths among women aged 16 to 24 in the urban areas of Maharashtra state (including Bombay) is attributed to "accidental burns." About 5,000 "dowry deaths" occur in India every year, according to government estimates, and some observers think the number is actually much higher. Subhadra Chaturvedi, one of India's leading attorneys, puts the death toll at a minimum of 12,000 a year.

The preference for sons, common in many cultures, can lead to violence against female infants—and even against female fetuses. In India, for example, a 1990 study of amniocentesis in a large Bombay hospital found that 95.5 percent of fetuses iden-

tified as female were aborted, compared with only a small percentage of male fetuses. (Amniocentesis involves the removal of a sample of amniotic fluid from the womb; this can be used to determine the baby's sex and the presence of certain inherited diseases.) Female infanticide is still practiced in rural areas of India; a 1992 study by Cornell University demographer Sabu George found that 58 percent of female infant deaths (19 of 33) within a 12-village region of Tamil Nadu state were due to infanticide. The problem is especially pronounced in China, where the imposition of the one-child-per-family rule has led to a precipitous decline in the number of girls: studies in 1987 and 1994 found a half-million fewer female infants in each of those years than would be expected, given the typical biological ratio of male to female births.

Women are also the primary victims of sexual crimes, which include sexual abuse, rape, and forced prostitution. Girls are the overwhelming target of child sexual assaults; in the United States, 78 percent of substantiated child sexual abuse cases involve girls. According to a 1994 World Bank study, *Violence Against Women: The Hidden Health Burden*, national surveys suggest that up to one-third of women in Norway, the United States, Canada, New Zealand, Barbados, and the Netherlands are sexually abused during childhood. Often very young children are the victims: a national study in the United States and studies in several Latin American cities indicate that 13 to 32 percent of abused girls are age 10 and under.

Rape haunts women throughout their lives, exposing them to unwanted pregnancy, disease, social stigma, and psychological trauma. In the United States, which has some of the best data on the problem, a 1993 review of rape studies suggests that between 14 and 20 percent of women will be victims of completed rapes during their lifetimes. In some cultures, a woman who has been raped is perceived as having violated the family honor, and she may be forced to marry her attacker or even killed. One study of female homicide in Alexandria, Egypt, for example, found that 47 percent of women murdered were killed by a family member following a rape.

In war, rape is often used as both a physical and psychological weapon. An investigation of recent conflicts in the former Yugoslavia, Peru, Kashmir, and Somalia by the international human rights group, Human Rights Watch, found that "rape of women civilians has been deployed as a tactical weapon to terrorize civilian communities or to achieve 'ethnic cleansing.'" Studies suggest that tens of thousands of Muslim and Serbian women in Bosnia have been raped during the conflict there.

A growing number of women and girls, particularly in developing countries, are being forced into prostitution. Typically, girls from poor, remote villages are purchased outright from their families or lured away with promises of jobs or false marriage proposals. They are then taken to brothels, often in other countries, and forced to work there until they pay off their "debts"—a task that becomes almost impossible as the brothel owner charges them for clothes, food, medicine, and often even their own purchase price. According to Human Rights Watch, an estimated 20,000 to 30,000 Burmese girls and women currently work in brothels in Thailand; their ranks are now expanding by as many as 10,000 new recruits each year. Some 20,000 to 50,000 Nepalese girls are working in Indian brothels. As the fear of AIDS intensifies, customers are demanding ever younger prostitutes, and the age at which girls are being forced into prostitution is dropping; the average age of the Nepalese recruits, for example, declined from 14–16 years in the 1980s, to 10–14 years by 1994.

THE HIDDEN COSTS OF VIOLENCE

Whether it takes the form of enforced prostitution, rape, genital mutilation, or domestic abuse, gender-based violence is doing enormous damage—both to the women who experience it, and to societies as a whole. Yet activists, health officials, and development agencies have only recently begun to quantify the problem's full costs. Currently, they are focusing on two particularly burdensome aspects of the violence: the health care costs, and the effects on economic productivity.

The most visible effects of violence are those associated with physical injuries that require medical care. FGM, for example, often causes severe health problems. Typically performed in unsterile environments by untrained midwives or barbers working without anesthesia, the procedure causes intense pain and can result in infection or death. Long-term effects include chronic pain, urine retention, abscesses, lack of sexual sensitivity, and depression. For the approximately 15 percent of mutilated women who have been infibulated, the health-related consequences are even

worse. Not only must these women be cut and stitched repeatedly, on their wedding night and again with each childbirth, but sexual dysfunction and pain during intercourse are common. Infibulated women are also much more likely to have difficulties giving birth. Their labor often results, for instance, in vesico-vaginal fistulas— holes in the vaginal and rectal areas that cause continuous leakage of urine and feces. An estimated 1.5 to 2 million African women have fistulas, with some 50,000 to 100,000 new cases occurring annually. Infibulation also greatly increases the danger to the child during labor. A study of 33 infibulated women in delivery at Somalia's Benadir Hospital found that five of their babies died and 21 suffered oxygen deprivation.

Other forms of violence are taking a heavy toll as well. A 1994 national survey in Canada, for example, found that broken bones occurred in 12 percent of spousal assaults, and internal injuries and miscarriages in 10 percent. Long-term effects may be less obvious but they are often just as serious. In the United States, battered women are four to five times more likely than non-battered women to require psychiatric treatment and five times more likely to attempt suicide. And even these effects are just one part of a much broader legacy of misery. A large body of psychological literature has documented the erosion of self-esteem, of social abilities, and of mental health in general, that often follows in the wake of violence. And the problem is compounded because violence tends to be cyclical: people who are abused tend to become abusers themselves. Whether it's through such direct abuse or indirectly, through the destruction of family life, violence against women tends to spill over into the next generation as violence against children.

Only a few studies have attempted to assign an actual dollar value to gender-based violence, but their findings suggest that the problem constitutes a substantial health care burden. In the United States, a 1991 study at a major health maintenance organization (a type of group medical practice) found that women who had been raped or beaten at any point in their lifetimes had medical costs two-and-a-half times higher during that year than women who had not been victimized. In the state of Pennsylvania, a health insurer study estimated that violence against women cost the health care system approximately $326.6 million in 1992. And in Canada, a 1995 study of violence against women,

which examined not only medical costs, but also the value of community support services and lost work, put the annual cost to the country at Cdn $1.5 billion (US $1.1 billion).

One important consequence of violence is its effect on women's productivity. In its *World Development Report 1993*, the World Bank estimated that in advanced market economies, 19 percent of the total disease burden of women aged 15 to 44— nearly one out of every five healthy days of life lost—can be linked to domestic violence or rape. (Violence against women is just as pervasive in developing countries, but because the incidence of disease is higher in those regions, it represents only 5 percent of their total disease burden.) Similarly, a 1993 study in the United States showed a correlation between violence and lower earnings. After controlling for other factors that affect income, the study found that women who have been abused earn 3 to 20 percent less each year than women who have not been abused, with the discrepancy depending on the type of sexual abuse experienced and the number of perpetrators.

Violence can also prevent women from participating in public life—a form of oppression that can cripple Third World development projects. Fear may keep women at home; for example, health workers in India have identified fear of rape as an impediment to their outreach efforts in rural sites. The general problem was acknowledged plainly in a UN report published in 1992, *Battered Dreams: Violence Against Women as an Obstacle to Development*: "Where violence keeps a woman from participating in a development project, force is used to deprive her of earnings, or fear of sexual assault prevents her from taking a job or attending a public function, development does not occur." Development efforts aimed at reducing fertility levels may also be affected, since gender-based violence, or the threat of it, may limit women's use of contraception. According to the 1994 World Bank study, a woman's contraceptive use often depends in large part on her partner's approval.

A recurrent motive in much of this violence is an interest in preventing women from gaining autonomy outside the home. Husbands may physically prevent their wives from attending development meetings, or they may intimidate them into not seeking employment or accepting promotions at work. The World Bank study relates a chilling example of the way in which violence can be used to control women's behavior: "In a particularly gruesome example of male backlash, a female leader of the highly successful government sponsored Women's Development Programme in Rajasthan, India, was recently gang raped [in her home in front of her husband] by male community members because they disapproved of her organizing efforts against child marriage." The men succeeded in disrupting the project by instilling fear in the local organizers.

WOMEN BREAK THE SILENCE

"These women are holding back a silent scream so strong it could shake the earth." That is how Dr. Nahid Toubia, Executive Director of the U.S.-based anti-FGM organization RAINBO, described FGM victims when she testified at the 1993 Global Tribunal on Violations of Women's Human Rights. Yet her statement would apply just as well to the millions of women all over the world who have been victims of other forms of violence. Until recently, the problem of gender-based violence has remained largely invisible. Because the stigma attached to many forms of violence makes them difficult to discuss openly, and because violence typically occurs inside the home, accurate information on the magnitude of the problem has been extremely scarce. Governments, by claiming jurisdiction only over human rights abuses perpetrated in the public sphere by agents of the state, have reinforced this invisibility. Even human rights work has traditionally confined itself to the public sphere and largely ignored many of the abuses to which women are most vulnerable.

But today, the victims of violence are beginning to find their voices. Women's groups have won a place for "private sphere" violence on human rights agendas, and they are achieving important changes in both national laws and international conventions. The first major reform came in June 1993, at the UN Second World Conference on Human Rights in Vienna. In a drive leading up to the conference, activists collected almost half a million signatures from 124 countries on a petition insisting that the conference address gen-

der violence. The result: for the first time, violence against women was recognized as an abuse of women's human rights, and nine paragraphs on "The equal status and human rights of women" were incorporated into the Vienna Declaration and Programme of Action.

More recently, 18 members of the Organization of American States have ratified the Inter-American Convention on the Prevention, Punishment and Eradication of Violence Against Women. Many activists consider this convention, which went into effect on March 5, 1995, the strongest existing piece of international legislation in the field. And the Pan American Health Organization (PAHO) has become the first development agency to make a significant financial commitment to the issue. PAHO has received $4 million from Sweden, Norway, and the Netherlands, with the possibility of an additional $2.5 million from the Inter-American Development Bank, to conduct research on violence and establish support services for women in Latin America.

National governments are also drawing up legislation to combat various forms of gender violence. A growing number of countries, including South Africa, Israel, Argentina, the Bahamas, Australia, and the United States have all passed special domestic violence laws. Typically, these clarify the definition of domestic violence and strengthen protections available to the victims. In September 1994, India passed its "Pre-natal Diagnostic Techniques (Regulation and Prevention of Misuse) Act," which outlaws the use of prenatal testing for sex-selection. India is also developing a program to eradicate female infanticide. FGM is being banned in a growing number of countries, too. At least nine European countries now prohibit the practice, as does Australia. In the United States, a bill criminalizing FGM was passed by the Senate in May, but had yet to become law. More significant, perhaps, is the African legislation: FGM is now illegal in both Ghana and Kenya.

It is true, of course, that laws don't necessarily translate into real-life changes. But it is possible that the movement to stop FGM will yield the first solid success in the struggle to make human rights a reality for women. Over the past decade, the Inter-

African Committee on Traditional Practices Affecting the Health of Women and Children, an NGO dedicated to abolishing FGM, has set up committees in 25 African countries. And in March 1995, Ghana used its anti-FGM statute to arrest the parents and circumciser of an eight-year-old girl who was rushed to the hospital with excessive bleeding. In Burkina Faso, some circumcising midwives have been convicted under more general legislation. These are modest steps, perhaps, but legal precedent can be a powerful tool for reform.

In the United States, an important precedent is currently being set by a 19-year-old woman from the nation of Togo, in west Africa. Fleeing an arranged marriage and the ritual FGM that would accompany it, Fauziya Kasinga arrived in the United States seeking asylum in December 1994. She has spent much of the time since then in prison, and her request for asylum, denied by a lower court, is at the time of writing under appeal. People are eligible for asylum in the United States if they are judged to have a reasonable fear of persecution due to their race, religion, nationality, political opinions, or membership in a social group. However, U.S. asylum law makes no explicit provision for gender-based violence. In 1993, Canada became the world's first country to make the threat of FGM grounds for granting refugee status.

Whichever way the decision on Kasinga's case goes, it will be adopted as a binding general precedent in U.S. immigration cases (barring the passage of federal legislation that reverses it). But even while her fate remains in doubt, Kasinga has already won an important moral victory. Her insistence on her right *not* to be mutilated—and on the moral obligation of others to shield her from violence if they can—has made the threat she faces a matter of conscience, of politics, and of policy. Given the accumulating evidence of how deeply gender-based violence infects our societies, in both the developing and the industrialized countries, we have little choice but to recognize it as the fundamental moral and economic challenge that it is.

Toni Nelson is a staff researcher at the Worldwatch Institute.

From *World Watch*, July/August 1996, pp. 33–38. © 1996 by the Worldwatch Institute. Reprinted by permission.

UNIT 5

Social Institutions: Issues, Crises, and Changes

Unit Selections

Key Points to Consider

- Discuss whether or not it is important to preserve some continuity in institutions.

- How can institutions outlive their usefulness?

- Why are institutions so difficult to change? Cite examples where changes are instituted from the top down and others where they are instituted from the bottom up. Do you see a similar pattern of development for these types of changes?

- Is it possible to reform the political system to greatly reduce the corrupting role of money in politics? Why, or why not?

- What basic changes in the economic system are evident in the things that you observe daily?

- How should issues like abortion and gay rights be decided?

 **Links: www.dushkin.com/online/**
These sites are annotated in the World Wide Web pages.

International Labour Organization (ILO)
http://www.ilo.org
IRIS Center
http://www.iris.umd.edu
Marketplace of Political Ideas/University of Houston Library
http://info.lib.uh.edu/politics/markind.htm
National Center for Policy Analysis
http://www.ncpa.org
National Institutes of Health (NIH)
http://www.nih.gov

Social institutions are the building blocks of social structure. They accomplish the important tasks of society—for example, regulation of reproduction, socialization of children, production and distribution of economic goods, law enforcement and social control, and organization of religion and other value systems.

Social institutions are not rigid arrangements; they reflect changing social conditions. Institutions generally change slowly. At the present time, however, many of the social institutions in the United States and many other parts of the world are in crisis and are undergoing rapid change. Eastern European countries are literally transforming their political and economic institutions. Economic institutions, such as stock markets, are becoming truly international, and when a major country experiences a recession, many other countries feel the effects. In the United States, major reform movements are active in political, economic, family, medical, and educational institutions.

The first subsection of unit 5 examines American political institutions. In the first article, G. William Domhoff examines the power structure of the American political system and finds it dominated by the corporate community. But how does his view account for democracy and the power that it gives the average person? What about the evident influence of workers, liberals, environmentalists, and challenge groups? Domhoff argues that these forces may get media coverage, but they cannot prevent the corporate community from controlling the federal government on basic issues of income, wealth, and economic power. Moreover, he shows how this community exercises its power.

A major means used by the economic elite to control the government is through campaign contributions. The public has been scandalized by the role of campaign financing in influencing the actions of lawmakers, and rightly so. This is the topic of the next article, which looks at this method of influence over political leaders by the corporate community. Everyone knows that the big corporations use campaign contributions and other means to obtain special favors or privileges. The authors, however, tell some stories that give deeper insights into the way that the lobby game works and how it harms the average American. In contrast, the next article is one of those uncommon accounts of successful government actions that serve the public good. Several policies dealing with the environment, health, and safety have greatly benefited American citizens.

The next subsection deals with the economy. Its articles analyze problems of production and the excessive demands of work. The major change in the realm of production is globalization. Tony Clarke describes the increasing power of the multinational corporations, which "now hold the reins of power more firmly than do many of the world's governments." Unfortunately, the mechanisms are weak for making the global economy that is produced by these corporations sufficiently accountable to governments and institutions that can protect the interests of the people.

The next article examines how and why work "is taking over our lives—invading our homes, haunting our holidays, showing up for dinner." An important theme that Mark Hunter develops is that "the distinction between work and leisure no longer exists."

The social sphere is also in turmoil, as illustrated by the articles in the last subsection. A key issue for many parents and

children is the quality of education, and the public's perception is rather negative. James Comer reviews many suggested solutions to the failure of American schools and finds them deficient because they are not based on sound principles of child development. The real solution requires powerful positive social interactions between students and teachers. Another prominent and highly contested social issue is abortion, and in the next report, Frederica Mathewes-Green tries to find areas of agreement and compromise in this field of battle. She finds that no one thinks that abortion is a positive event; for some people, however, it is better than the alternatives. Why not improve the alternatives and make abortion unnecessary, she asks.

The next article is full of pain and death, for it deals with the worldwide epidemic of AIDS, with its focus on sub-Saharan Africa where 70 percent of those infected with HIV/AIDS reside. Of course, we would expect the various governments to do everything in their power to stop the epidemic and help the victims. And we would expect the friends and relatives of the victims to have compassion toward them. Unfortunately the true story is quite ugly. The shocking failure of many societies in the AIDS crisis reveals the fragility of these societies. The unbelievable cruelty of the treatment of the AIDS victims by relatives and others reveals the depths of the evil that many people are capable of when they are afraid. In the final article, Andrew Greeley shows that the predicted decline of religion with the advance of science never happened. Indeed, he shows that religion is strong and vibrant in America and has a bright future. He also describes many interesting changes in religious and moral beliefs and attitudes in the United States.

Who Rules America?

G. William Domhoff

Power and Class in the United States

Power and *class* are terms that make Americans a little uneasy, and concepts like *power elite* and *dominant class* immediately put people on guard. The idea that a relatively fixed group of privileged people might shape the economy and government for their own benefit goes against the American grain. Nevertheless,... the owners and top-level managers in large income-producing properties are far and away the dominant power figures in the United States. Their corporations, banks, and agri-businesses come together as a *corporate community* that dominates the federal government in Washington. Their real estate, construction, and land development companies form *growth coalitions* that dominate most local governments. Granted, there is competition within both the corporate community and the local growth coalitions for profits and investment opportunities, and there are sometimes tensions between national corporations and local growth coalitions, but both are cohesive on policy issues affecting their general welfare, and in the face of demands by organized workers, liberals, environmentalists, and neighborhoods.

As a result of their ability to organize and defend their interests, the owners and managers of large income-producing properties have a very great share of all income and wealth in the United States, greater than in any other industrial democracy. Making up at best 1 percent of the total population, by the early 1990s they earned 15.7 percent of the nation's yearly income and owned 37.2 percent of all privately held wealth, including 49.6 percent of all corporate stocks and 62.4 percent of all bonds. Due to their wealth and the lifestyle it makes possible, these owners and managers draw closer as a common social group. They belong to the same exclusive social clubs, frequent the same summer and winter resorts, and send their children to a relative handful of private schools. Members of the corporate community thereby become a *corporate rich* who create a nationwide *social upper class* through their social interaction.... Members of the growth coalitions, on the other hand, are *place entrepreneurs,* people who sell locations and buildings. They come together as local upper classes in their respective cities and sometimes mingle with the corporate rich in educational or resort settings.

The corporate rich and the growth entrepreneurs supplement their small numbers by developing and directing a wide variety of nonprofit organizations, the most important of which are a set of tax-free charitable foundations, think tanks, and policy-discussion groups. These specialized nonprofit groups constitute a *policy-formation network* at the national level. Chambers of commerce and policy groups affiliated with them form similar policy-formation networks at the local level, aided by a few national-level city development organizations that are available for local consulting.

Those corporate owners who have the interest and ability to take part in general governance join with top-level executives in the corporate community and the policy-formation network to form the *power elite,* which is the leadership group for the corporate rich as a whole. The concept of a power elite makes clear that not all members of the upper class are involved in governance; some of them simply enjoy the lifestyle that their great wealth affords them. At the same time, the focus on a leadership group allows for the fact that not all those in the power elite are members of the upper class; many of them are high-level employees in profit and nonprofit organizations controlled by the corporate rich....

The power elite is not united on all issues because it includes both moderate conservatives and ultraconservatives. Although both factions favor minimal reliance on government on all domestic issues, the moderate conservatives sometimes agree to legislation advocated by liberal elements of the society, especially in times of social upheaval like the Great Depression of the 1930s and the Civil Rights Movement of the early 1960s. Except on defense spending, ultraconservatives are characterized by a complete distaste for any kind of government programs under any circumstances—even to the point of opposing government support for corporations on some issues. Moderate conservatives often favor foreign aid, working through the United Nations, and making attempts to win over foreign enemies through patient diplomacy, treaties, and trade agreements. Historically, ultraconservatives have opposed most forms of foreign involvement, although they have become more tolerant of foreign trade agreements over the past thirty or forty years. At the same time, their hostility to the United Nations continues unabated.

Members of the power elite enter into the electoral arena as the leaders within a *corporate-conservative coalition,* where they are aided by a wide variety of patriotic, antitax, and other single-issue organizations. These conservative advocacy organizations are funded in varying degrees by the corporate rich, direct-mail appeals, and middle-class conservatives. This coalition has played a large role in both political parties at the presidential level and usually succeeds in electing a conservative majority to both houses of Congress. Historically, the conservative majority in Congress was made up of most Northern Republicans and most Southern Democrats, but that arrangement has been changing gradually since the 1960s as the conservative Democrats of the South are replaced by even more conservative Southern Republicans. The corporate-conservative coalition also has access to the federal government in Washington through lobbying and the appointment of its members to top positions in the executive branch....

Despite their preponderant power within the federal government and the many useful policies it carries out for them, members of the power elite are constantly critical of government as an alleged enemy of freedom and economic growth. Although their wariness toward government is expressed in terms of a dislike for taxes and government regulations, I believe their underlying concern is that government could change the power relations in the private sphere by aiding average Americans through a number of different avenues: (1) creating government jobs for the unemployed; (2) making health, unemployment, and welfare benefits more generous; (3) helping employees gain greater workplace rights and protections; and (4) helping workers organize unions. All of these initiatives are opposed by members of the power elite because they would increase wages and taxes, but the deepest opposition is toward any government support for unions because unions are a potential organizational base for advocating the whole range of issues opposed by the corporate rich....

Where Does Democracy Fit In?

...[T]o claim that the corporate rich have enough power to be considered a dominant class does not imply that lower social classes are totally powerless. *Domination* means the power to set the terms under which other groups and classes must operate, not total control. Highly trained professionals with an interest in environmental and consumer issues have been able to couple their technical information and their understanding of the legislative and judicial processes with well-timed publicity, lobbying, and lawsuits to win governmental restrictions on some corporate practices. Wage and salary employees, when they are organized into unions and have the right to strike, have been able to gain pay increases, shorter hours, better working conditions, and social benefits such as health insurance. Even the most powerless of people—the very poor and those discrim-

inated against—sometimes develop the capacity to influence the power structure through sit-ins, demonstrations, social movements, and other forms of social disruption, and there is evidence that such activities do bring about some redress of grievances, at least for a short time.

More generally, the various challengers to the power elite sometimes work together on policy issues as a *liberal-labor coalition* that is based in unions, local environmental organizations, some minority group communities, university and arts communities, liberal churches, and small newspapers and magazines. Despite a decline in membership over the past twenty years, unions are the largest and best-financed part of the coalition, and the largest organized social force in the country (aside from churches). They also cut across racial and ethnic lines more than any other institutionalized sector of American society....

The policy conflicts between the corporate-conservative and liberal-labor coalitions are best described as *class conflicts* because they primarily concern the distribution of profits and wages, the rate and progressivity of taxation, the usefulness of labor unions, and the degree to which business should be regulated by government. The liberal-labor coalition wants corporations to pay higher wages to employees and higher taxes to government. It wants government to regulate a wide range of business practices, including many that are related to the environment, and help employees to organize unions. The corporate-conservative coalition resists all these policy objectives to a greater or lesser degree, claiming they endanger the freedom of individuals and the efficient workings of the economic marketplace. The conflicts these disagreements generate can manifest themselves in many different ways: workplace protests, industrywide boycotts, massive demonstrations in cities, pressure on Congress, and the outcome of elections.

Neither the corporate-conservative nor the liberal-labor coalition includes a very large percentage of the American population, although each has the regular support of about 25–30 percent of the voters. Both coalitions are made up primarily of financial donors, policy experts, political consultants, and party activists....

Pluralism. The main alternative theory [I] address.... claims that power is more widely dispersed among groups and classes than a class-dominance theory allows. This general perspective is usually called *pluralism,* meaning there is no one dominant power group. It is the theory most favored by social scientists. In its strongest version, pluralism holds that power is held by the general public through the pressure that public opinion and voting put on elected officials. According to this version, citizens form voluntary groups and pressure groups that shape public opinion, lobby elected officials, and back sympathetic political candidates in the electoral process....

The second version of pluralism sees power as rooted in a wide range of well-organized "interest groups" that are often based in economic interests (e.g., industrialists, bankers, labor unions), but also in other interests as well (e.g., environmental, consumer, and civil rights groups). These interest groups join together in different coalitions depending on the specific issues. Proponents of this version of pluralism sometimes concede that public opinion and voting have only a minimal or indirect influence, but they see business groups as too fragmented and antagonistic to form a cohesive dominant class. They also claim that some business interest groups occasionally join coalitions with liberal or labor groups on specific issues, and that business-dominated coalitions sometimes lose. Furthermore, some proponents of this version of pluralism believe that the Democratic Party is responsive to the wishes of liberal and labor interest groups.

In contrast, I argue that the business interest groups are part of a tightly knit corporate community that is able to develop classwide cohesion on the issues of greatest concern to it: opposition to unions, high taxes, and government regulation. When a business group loses on a specific issue, it is often because other business groups have been opposed; in other words, there are arguments within the corporate community, and these arguments are usually settled within the governmental arena. I also claim that liberal and labor groups are rarely part of coalitions with business groups and that for most of its history the Democratic Party has been dominated by corporate and agribusiness interests in the Southern states, in partnership with the growth coalitions in large urban areas outside the South. Finally, I show that business interests rarely lose on labor and regulatory issues except in times of extreme social disruption like the 1930s and 1960s, when differences of opinion between Northern and Southern corporate leaders made victories for the liberal-labor coalition possible....

How the Power Elite Dominates Government

This [section] shows how the power elite builds on the ideas developed in the policy-formation process and its success in the electoral arena to dominate the federal government. Lobbyists from corporations, law firms, and trade associations play a key role in shaping government on narrow issues of concern to specific corporations or business sectors, but their importance should not be overestimated because a majority of those elected to Congress are predisposed to agree with them. The corporate community and the policy-formation network supply top-level governmental appointees and new policy directions on major issues.

Once again, as seen in the battles for public opinion and electoral success, the power elite faces opposition from a minority of elected officials and their supporters in labor unions and liberal advocacy groups. These opponents are sometimes successful in blocking ultra-conservative initiatives, but most of the victories for the liberal-labor coalition are the result of support from moderate conservatives....

Appointees to Government

The first way to test a class-dominance view of the federal government is to study the social and occupational backgrounds of the people who are appointed to manage the major departments of the executive branch, such as state, treasury, defense,

and justice. If pluralists are correct, these appointees should come from a wide range of interest groups. If the state autonomy theorists are correct, they should be disproportionately former elected officials or longtime government employees. If the class-dominance view is correct, they should come disproportionately from the upper class, the corporate community, and the policy-formation network.

There have been numerous studies over the years of major governmental appointees under both Republican and Democratic administrations, usually focusing on the top appointees in the departments that are represented in the president's cabinet. These studies are unanimous in their conclusion that most top appointees in both Republican and Democratic administrations are corporate executives and corporate lawyers—and hence members of the power elite....

Conclusion

This [section] has demonstrated the power elite's wide-ranging access to government through the interest-group and policy-formation processes, as well as through its ability to influence appointments to major government positions. When coupled with the several different kinds of power discussed in earlier [sections] this access and involvement add up to power elite domination of the federal government.

By *domination,* as stated in the first [section], social scientists mean the ability of a class or group to set the terms under which other classes or groups within a social system must operate. By this definition, domination does not mean control on each and every issue, and it does not rest solely on involvement in government. Influence over government is only the final and most visible aspect of power elite domination, which has its roots in the class structure, the corporate control of the investment function, and the operation of the policy-formation network. If government officials did not have to wait for corporate leaders to decide where and when they will invest, and if government officials were not further limited by the general public's acceptance of policy recommendations from the policy-formation network, then power elite involvement in elections and government would count for a lot less than they do under present conditions.

Domination by the power elite does not negate the reality of continuing conflict over government policies, but few conflicts, it has been shown, involve challenges to the rules that create privileges for the upper class and domination by the power elite. Most of the numerous battles within the interest-group process, for example, are only over specific spoils and favors; they often involve disagreements among competing business interests.

Similarly, conflicts within the policy-making process of government often involve differences between the moderate conservative and ultraconservative segments of the dominant class. At other times they involve issues in which the needs of the corporate community as a whole come into conflict with the needs of specific industries, which is what happens to some extent on tariff policies and also on some environmental legislation. In neither case does the nature of the conflict call into question the domination of government by the power elite.

...Contrary to what pluralists claim, there is not a single case study on any issue of any significance that shows a liberal-labor victory over a united corporate-conservative coalition, which is strong evidence for a class-domination theory on the "Who wins?" power indicator. The classic case studies frequently cited by pluralists have been shown to be gravely deficient as evidence for their views. Most of these studies reveal either conflicts among rival groups within the power elite or situations in which the moderate conservatives have decided for their own reasons to side with the liberal-labor coalition....

More generally, it now can be concluded that all four indicators of power introduced in [the first section] point to the corporate rich and their power elite as the dominant organizational structure in American society. First, the wealth and income distributions are skewed in their favor more than in any other industrialized democracy. They are clearly the most powerful group in American society in terms of "Who benefits?" Second, the appointees to government come overwhelmingly from the corporate community and its associated policy-formation network. Thus, the power elite is clearly the most powerful in terms of "Who sits?"

Third, the power elite wins far more often than it loses on policy issues resolved in the federal government. Thus, it is the most powerful in terms of "Who wins?" Finally, as shown in reputational studies in the 1950s and 1970s,... corporate leaders are the most powerful group in terms of "Who shines?" By the usual rules of evidence in a social science investigation using multiple indicators, the owners and managers of large income-producing properties are the dominant class in the United States.

Still, as noted at the end of the first [section], power structures are not immutable. Societies change and power structures evolve or crumble from time to unpredictable time, especially in the face of challenge. When it is added that the liberal-labor coalition persists in the face of its numerous defeats, and that free speech and free elections are not at risk, there remains the possibility that class domination could be replaced by a greater sharing of power in the future.

HOW THE LITTLE GUY GETS CRUNCHED

When powerful interests shower Washington with millions in campaign contributions, they often get what they want. But it's ordinary citizens and firms that pay the price—and most of them never see it coming

By Donald L. Barlett and James B. Steele

I̲T̲ W̲A̲S̲ J̲U̲S̲T̲ Y̲O̲U̲R̲ T̲Y̲P̲I̲C̲A̲L̲ P̲I̲E̲C̲E̲ O̲F̲ congressional dirty work. As 1999 wound down, the House and Senate passed the District of Columbia Appropriations Act. You might think that would be a boring piece of legislation. You would be wrong. For buried in the endless clauses authorizing such spending items as $867 million for education and $5 million to promote the adoption of foster children was Section 6001: Superfund Recycling Equity. It had nothing to do with the District of Columbia, nor appropriations, nor "equity" as it is commonly defined.

Instead Section 6001 was inserted in the appropriations bill by Senator Trent Lott of Mississippi, the Senate majority leader, to take the nation's scrap-metal dealers off the hook for millions of dollars in potential Superfund liabilities at toxic-waste sites. In doing so, Lott had the support of colleagues in both parties.

This early Christmas present to the scrap-metal dealers—who contributed more than $300,000 to political candidates and committees during the 1990s—made them very happy. Others in the recycling chain were not so happy. All of a sudden, they were potentially responsible for millions of dollars in damages the junkmen might otherwise have had to pay.

While clever in its obscurity, Section 6001 is not an especially big giveaway by Capitol Hill standards. Rather, it is typical among the growing litany of examples of how Washington extends favorable treatment to one set of citizens at the expense of another. It's a process that frequently causes serious, sometimes fatal economic harm to unwary individuals and businesses that are in the way.

How do you get that favorable treatment? If you know the right people in Congress and in the White House, you can often get anything you want. And there are two surefire ways to get close to those people:

- Contribute to their political campaigns.
- Spend generously on lobbying.

If you do both of these things, success will maul you like groupies at a rock concert. If you do neither—and this is the case with about 200 million individuals of voting age and several million corporations— those people in Washington will treat you accordingly. In essence, campaign spending in America has divided all of us into two groups: first- and second-class citi-

zens. This is what happens if you are in the latter group:

You pick up a disproportionate share of America's tax bill.

You pay higher prices for a broad range of products, from peanuts to prescription drugs.

You pay taxes that others in a similar situation have been excused from paying.

You are compelled to abide by laws while others are granted immunity from them.

You must pay debts that you incur while others do not.

You are barred from writing off on your tax return some of the money spent on necessities while others deduct the cost of their entertainment.

You must run your business by one set of rules while the government creates another set for your competitors.

In contrast, first-class citizens—the fortunate few who contribute to the right politicians and hire the right lobbyists—enjoy all the benefits of their special status. Among them:

If they make a bad business decision, the government bails them out.

If they want to hire workers at below-market wage rates, the government provides the means to do so.

If they want more time to pay their debts, the government gives them an extension.

If they want immunity from certain laws, the government gives it.

If they want to ignore rules their competitors must comply with, the government gives its approval.

If they want to kill legislation that is intended for the public good, it gets killed.

Call it government for the few at the expense of the many. Looked at another way, almost any time a citizen or a business gets what it wants through campaign contributions and lobbying, someone else pays the price for it. Sometimes it's a few people, sometimes millions. Sometimes it's one business, sometimes many. In short, through a process often obscured from public view, Washington anoints winners and creates losers. Among the recent winners and the wannabes, who collectively have contributed millions of dollars to candidates and their parties and spent generously on lobbying:

• **TAX-FREE PROFITS** Last December, President Clinton signed into law the Ticket to Work and Work Incentives Improvement Act, hailing the legislation as providing "the most significant advancement for people with disabilities since the Americans with Disabilities Act almost a decade ago." He called it "a genuinely American bill."

Indeed so. For it also provided something quite unrelated to disabilities: a lucrative tax break for banks, insurers and financial-service companies. A provision woven into the legislation allowed the foreign subsidiaries of these businesses to extend the income-tax-free status of foreign earnings from the sale of securities, annuities and other financial holdings. Among the big winners: American International Group Inc., an insurance giant, as well as the recently formed Citigroup. Overall, the tax break will cost the U.S. Treasury $1.5 billion in the next two years, just as it did

in the past two years. The amount is equivalent to all the income taxes paid over four years by 300,000 individuals and families that earn between $25,000 and $30,000 a year.

• **THE GREAT S&L GIVEBACK** Owners of savings and loan associations, many of whom are suing the Federal Government for clamping down on them during the S&L crisis in the 1980s, will benefit from a one-paragraph clause that was slipped into legislation that will hold the U.S. government liable for billions of dollars in damage claims because federal regulators nixed certain accounting practices. As is typical with special-interest measures, there were no hearings or estimates of the cost before the clause mysteriously showed up in the Omnibus Consolidated and Emergency Supplemental Appropriations Act of 1998. Among the potential beneficiaries: billionaires Ron Perelman and the Pritzker and Bass families. The losers: all other taxpayers, who will have to pick up the tab.

THE FUTURE PROMISES MUCH MORE OF THE same. In this presidential election year, companies and industries that hope for special treatment in the new decade are busy making their political contributions and their connections. Examples:

• **A LONGER LIFE FOR GOLDEN DRUGS** Major pharmaceutical companies will seek legislation to extend the patent life on their most valuable drugs. In the past, such giveaways were often inserted into unrelated legislation and covered a single drug or two. But this year, watch for heavy lobbying for the granddaddy of all patent extenders. It would protect pharmaceutical company sales of $3 billion annually and add years to the profitable life of at least seven expensive drugs, such as Schering-Plough's Claritin for allergies and Eulexin for prostate cancer, SmithKline Beecham's Relafen for arthritis and G.D. Searle's Daypro for arthritis. The big losers: patients, especially senior citizens on fixed incomes, who must buy expensive prescription drugs instead of cheaper generic versions. Estimates of the added cost run from $1 billion to $11 billion over the next decade.

• **CARS WITH A CHECKERED PAST** The National Automobile Dealers Association is pushing for a federal law regulating the sale of rebuilt wrecked cars. Like a lot of special-interest legislation, the Na-

tional Salvage Motor Vehicle Consumer Protection Act, as it's called, sounds good. No one is likely to argue with its call for federal standards to govern the sale of "nonrepairable and rebuilt vehicles." But look closely. The fine print actually provides minimal standards, gives states the option of ignoring these, applies to only half the cars on the road and keeps secret the history of near totaled vehicles. Sponsored by majority leader Lott, the bill has cleared the Senate Commerce Committee, whose chairman, presidential candidate John McCain, is a co-sponsor. Losers: consumers who unknowingly buy rebuilt wrecks at inflated prices.

Over and over, Washington extends favored treatment to those who pay up—at the expense of those who don't

---

BOTH THE RECIPIENTS OF CAMPAIGN CONtributions and the givers insist that no public official is for sale, that no favors are granted in exchange for cash. Few people believe that; U.S. Supreme Court Justice David Souter summed up the prevailing public attitude during arguments in a case that led the Justices last week to uphold the current $1,000 limit on individual campaign contributions. (Donations to parties are still unlimited.) Said Souter:

"I think most people assume—I do, certainly—that someone making an extraordinarily large contribution is going to get some kind of an extraordinary return for it. I think that is a pervasive assumption. And… there is certainly an appearance of, call it an attenuated corruption, if you will, that large contributors are simply going to get better service, whatever that service may be, from a politician than the average contributor, let alone no contributor."

Campaign-finance reform has emerged as an issue during the budding presidential race. Three of the four leading candidates are for it; one is against. McCain has made limiting campaign contributions his defining issue, although the Arizona Republican has accepted contributions from corporations seeking favors from his Commerce committee. Bill Bradley has also spoken out for reform, calling for public financing of elections. Vice President Gore, although involved in the Clinton Administration's 1996 fund-raising scandals, also advocates publicly funded campaigns. Only Texas Governor George W. Bush favors the status quo.

Just how obsessed with raking in cash are the 535 members of Congress?

A veteran Washington lawyer who once served an apprenticeship with a prominent U.S. Senator relates a telling experience. The lawyer, who represents an agency of a state government, visited the home office of a Congressman in that state to discuss a national issue affecting the agency and, indirectly, the Congressman's constituents. After an effusive greeting, the Congressman's next words were brief and to the point:

"How much money can you contribute?"

The stunned lawyer explained that he represented a state agency and that state governments do not contribute to political candidates. As if in response to hearing some programmed words that altered his brain circuitry, the Congressman changed his tone and demeanor instantly. Suddenly, he had more pressing obligations. He would be unable to meet with the lawyer. Rather, he said, an aide would listen to whatever it was the lawyer had to say.

Of course, those who give money to political candidates or their parties don't necessarily get everything they seek. Often the reason is that their opponents are just as well connected. But they do get access—to the Representative or Senator, the White House aide or Executive Branch official—to make their case.

Try it yourself. You won't get it.

Bits and pieces of the story of those who give the money and what they get in return have been told, here and elsewhere. But who gets hurt—the citizens and businesses that do not play the game—remains an untold story.

Over the next nine months, continuing until the presidential election in November, TIME will publish periodic reports examining the anonymous victims of big money and politics.

Editor's note: In early 2002, Congress considered the Shays-Meehan campaign finance reform bill. It passed in the House, but it was delayed in the Senate.

Where the Public Good prevailed

Lessons from Success Stories in Health

BY STEPHEN L. ISSACS AND STEVEN A SCHROEDER

Many Americans know, all too well, what is wrong with health care. Ask the single mother who waits half a day in a crowded clinic for a five-minute visit with a harried physician, or the unemployed worker who has been downsized out of his job and his health insurance. Their experience tells a devastating tale about our system's shortcomings.

But there is another, equally important story that concerns the problems we don't see anymore—at least not in the numbers of the past young victims of polio, mumps, and measles; preschoolers with neurological problems caused by lead poisoning; people in the prime of life dying prematurely from tuberculosis and influenza; hordes of patients with rotting teeth. While we need to address persistent inequities, we also need to understand the basis of victories in public health—not just to keep up our hopes, but to learn how research, advocacy, public discussion, and policy fit together in successful campaigns for change.

GETTING THE LEAD OUT

Children in America today carry far less lead in their blood than they did just 20 years ago. The origins of that change go back nearly a century to 1904, when Australian pediatrician J. Lockhart Gibson found that lead paint caused lead poisoning of children in Queensland. A decade later, reports linking neurological damage in American children to lead began to appear. Mounting evidence of the metal's harmful effects led to sporadic local efforts to prevent poisoning caused by lead paint.

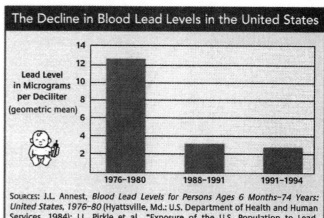

The Decline in Blood Lead Levels in the United States

SOURCES: J.L. Annest, *Blood Lead Levels for Persons Ages 6 Months–74 Years: United States, 1976–80* (Hyattsville, Md.: U.S. Department of Health and Human Services, 1984); J.L. Pirkle et al., "Exposure of the U.S. Population to Lead, 1991–1994," *Environmental Health Perspectives* 106, no. 11 (1998): 745–750.

The single greatest source of lead, however, came from automobile engines. Leaded gasoline was introduced in the American market in 1923, less than a year after Thomas Midgely and his co-workers at the General Motors Research Corporation in Dayton, Ohio, discovered that adding tetraethyl lead to gasoline as an antiknock agent gave cars more zip and allowed them to go farther on a tank of gas. The potential health effects of tetraethyl lead became known shortly after its discovery. In 1924 a fire in Standard Oil's lead processing plant in Bayway, New Jersey, led to five deaths and caused severe tremors, psychosis, hallucinations, and other symptoms of serious lead poisoning in 35 injured workers.

The next year, the U.S. surgeon general convened a conference on the safety of lead in gasoline. Although public-health advocates testified in opposition to the release of a poison—lead—into the air, the lead, automotive, and chemical industries dominated the conference. Representing Standard Oil of New Jersey, Frank Howard said, "We have an apparent gift of God—tetraethyl lead" and accused opponents of standing in the way of progress. The surgeon general concluded that there were no good grounds for prohibiting the use of leaded gasoline as a motor fuel.

So matters stood until the 1960s, when a new generation of scientists began challenging the assertion that lead was harmless. Dr. Herbert Needleman, who became an advocate for efforts to lower lead levels, revealed that extremely low amounts could damage a child's nervous system. At hearings on air pollution chaired by Senator Edmund Muskie in 1966, Clair Patterson, a highly respected California Institute of Technology geochemist, testified that the amount of lead in the air was 100 times what it had been in the 1930s. The Muskie hearings led, ultimately, to passage of the Clean Air Act of 1970, which required automakers to reduce hazardous emissions drastically.

In fulfilling the mandate of the Clean Air Act, the newly formed Environmental Protection Agency began issuing standards for the maximum level of lead in gasoline. These regulations were consistently challenged by the lead and petroleum-refining industries. For example, in 1973 the EPA issued its initial lead standard—one that was to be phased in over five years beginning in 1975. The Ethyl Corporation promptly went to court. The lawsuit, ultimately resolved in the EPA's favor by the U.S. Court of Appeals, delayed implementation of the standard for two years.

Next-came a challenge from another direction. In the anti-regulation climate of the 1980s, Vice President George Bush's Task Force on Regulatory Relief pressured the EPA to roll back its lead standard. Activists from the Natural Resources Defense Council, the Environmental Defense Fund, Consumers Union, and other organizations fought back, and the press jumped on the story. "Incredibly, the Reagan administration appears willing to risk the health of hundreds of thousands of anonymous preschoolers, just so the oil companies can make a few bucks" wrote influential columnist Jack Anderson. At congressional hearings, witnesses presented new evidence demonstrating the effects of even very low levels of lead on the nervous systems of children.

At about this time, the U.S. Centers for Disease Control analyzed the results of the second National Health and Nutrition Examination Survey (NHANES). The survey showed that levels of lead in Americans' blood had dropped 37 percent between 1976 and 1980, largely because of reduced lead in gasoline. In the face of these data, plus all the negative publicity it was receiving, the EPA backed down. Instead of weakening the lead standard, it toughened it.

By the early 1990s, Congress was again involved. The 1990 amendments to the Clean Air Act banned the manufacture, sale, or introduction after 1992 of any engine requiring leaded gasoline. Congress also prohibited the use of all leaded gasoline for highway use after 1995. Since 1996, an outright ban on leaded gasoline has been in effect. These actions complemented laws that ban lead in paint, food containers, and solder joints. While lead-based paint continues to be a serious health hazard in inner-city buildings, legal restrictions have eliminated most new sources of lead poisoning. The results have been impressive. The third NHANES found that the average blood lead level in the United States had dropped by 78 percent between 1976 and 1994, largely because lead had virtually disappeared from gasoline—and because researchers and policy makers had overcome entrenched industry opposition in order to improve the public's health.

GETTING THE FLUORIDE IN

Sometimes the obstacle to better health isn't an economic interest but public hysteria. Fluoridation has proved to be one of the cheapest, most effective public-health measures of the past century. Yet during the Red Scare of the 1950s, it faced strenuous opposition from groups who feared that it was part of a communist plot to poison Americans.

The origins of fluoridation also go back a century, to 1901, when Frederick McKay opened a dental practice in Colorado Springs, Colorado, and noticed that many of his patients had chocolate-like stains on their teeth. Even stranger, few of these patients had cavities. Dr. McKay spent the next 40 years investigating why some people developed what came to be known as Colorado Brown Stain. By 1931 scientists had established a link between fluorine and mottled teeth, and attention turned to whether fluorine protected against tooth decay.

Enter the U.S. government. H. Trendley Dean, director of dental research at the National Institutes of Health, collected water samples and examined children's teeth throughout the country; and in 1943, he concluded that children exposed to minuscule amounts of fluorine in water developed few or no cavities and avoided brown teeth. The next step for the Public Health Service was to test this conclusion. In January 1945, Grand Rapids, Michigan, became the first community to add fluoride, a compound of the element fluorine, to its drinking water, while residents of neighboring Muskegon, who continued to drink unfluoridated water, served as the comparison group. Three other communities began testing fluoride in the water shortly thereafter. The results were dramatic. In the four demonstration communities, cavities fell by 40 percent to 60 percent. Even as results were coming in, activists were campaigning to have fluoride added to the water supply. Wisconsin was the hotbed of dental activism; 50 communities in the state fluoridated their water by 1950. That year, under intense pressure from pro-fluoridation advocates, the Public Health Service and the American Dental Association endorsed fluoridation.

Then came Joe McCarthy and the backlash. In 1949, Stevens Point, Wisconsin, became the first community to

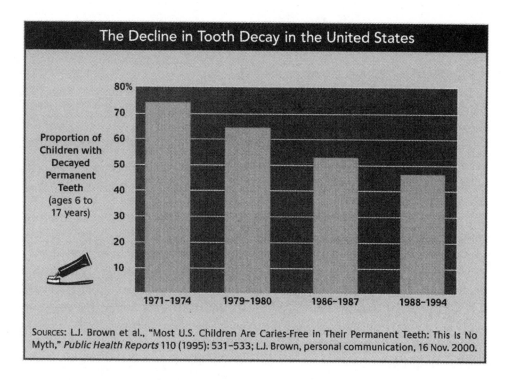

The Decline in Tooth Decay in the United States

Proportion of Children with Decayed Permanent Teeth (ages 6 to 17 years)

1971-1974   1979-1980   1986-1987   1988-1994

SOURCES: L.J. Brown et al., "Most U.S. Children Are Caries-Free in Their Permanent Teeth: This Is No Myth," *Public Health Reports* 110 (1995): 531–533; L.J. Brown, personal communication, 16 Nov. 2000.

reject fluoridation of the community's water supply. Opposition in other communities followed. At the height of the Cold War, opponents linked fluoridation to a perceived communist threat and spread tales of dead fish washing up on the shores of fluoridated reservoirs.

Those in favor of fluoridation struck back. The endorsements of major dental and medical organizations, supported by ongoing research, provided persuasive support for the safety of water fluoridation. When opponents went to court, they invariably lost as judges upheld local decisions to fluoridate water as a legitimate exercise of governmental authority. Of the 50 largest cities in the United States, 43 presently have fluoridated water systems. Some 62 percent of Americans live in communities with fluoridated water supplies. Cavities in children have dropped significantly (although the oral health of poor children is worse than that of well-to-do children). In the years 1971–1974, 74 percent of children six to 17 years old had one or more cavities in their permanent teeth. By the period 1988–1994, the percentage had dropped to 46 percent.

THE AUTO-SAFETY CRUSADE

Public-health progress has often had to overcome the belief that nothing can be done about a problem until individuals improve their behavior. From the time of the nation's first automobile fatality, conventional wisdom had it that traffic accidents were the fault of bad drivers, not of the automobile itself. This viewpoint was articulated pithily by Harry Barr, Chevrolet's chief engineer: "We feel our cars are quite safe and reliable…. If drivers did everything they should, there wouldn't be any accidents."

By the 1950s, however, a respectable body of thought began to challenge the conventional wisdom. The medical profession—most particularly physicians who treated crash victims—weighed in early. By the mid-1950s, both the American Medical Association and the American College of Surgeons were recommending that automobile manufacturers design their cars for better passenger safety and equip them with safety belts. Triggered by concerns about the mounting toll of highway deaths, Senator Abraham Ribicoff of New York convened hearings that began in 1965 and continued into 1966. A 32-year-old lawyer named Ralph Nader was the star witness. Nader's book *Unsafe at Any Speed*, published in 1965, lambasted the automobile industry for its lack of concern about safety, singling out General Motors for selling the Chevrolet Corvair, an automobile produced with a defective and dangerous gas tank. The rest is the stuff of legend: GM hired private detectives to tail Nader and come up with dirt about his personal life, which they failed to do. When the attempted smear campaign came to light in March 1966, Nader became an instant national hero and used his new celebrity as a platform to promote auto safety.

The publicity galvanized public opinion and provided the impetus for Congress to pass the National Traffic and Motor Vehicle Safety Act and the Highway Safety Act in 1966. These laws established the National Highway Safety Bureau, the precursor of today's National Highway Traffic Safety Administration, and gave it the authority to set automobile safety standards.

As in the case of lead, new legislation precipitated legal and regulatory battles about how the law should be interpreted and carried out. Proposed federal regulations required that cars come equipped with padded instrument

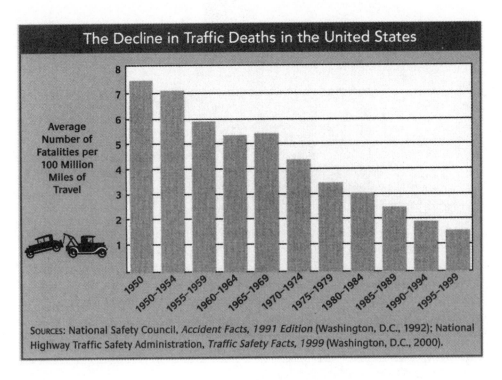

The Decline in Traffic Deaths in the United States

Average Number of Fatalities per 100 Million Miles of Travel

SOURCES: National Safety Council, *Accident Facts, 1991 Edition* (Washington, D.C., 1992); National Highway Traffic Safety Administration, *Traffic Safety Facts, 1999* (Washington, D.C., 2000).

panels and seat belts, among other safety features. These rules were challenged by automobile manufacturers as unrealistic and by consumer safety advocates as weak and ineffectual. The battle over seat belts and, later, air bags lasted nearly a decade. Now, of course, they are both standard equipment.

During the late 1970s and early 1980s, an extraordinary grass-roots movement took shape across the nation. Doris Aiken founded Remove Intoxicated Drivers (RID) in 1978 after a drunk driver ran over and killed a teenager in her hometown of Schenectady, New York. Candy Lightner organized Mothers Against Drunk Driving (MADD) in 1980 after her daughter was run over and killed by a man who had been drinking. Aiken and Lightner cultivated the media, who responded by regularly featuring the speeches and activities of the anti-drunk-driving activists, particularly those of the charismatic Lightner. Hundreds of newspapers and magazine articles reported on the victims of drunk driving and their families. Drunk driving was the subject of television specials and dramatizations. Activists formed chapters of RID, MADD, and SADD (Students Against Driving Drunk) in communities around the country and began telling their stories though the media, providing victims' services, lobbying government officials, and monitoring the courts.

The effect of this grass-roots movement on public policy was stunning. Between 1981 and 1985 alone, state legislatures passed 478 laws to deter drunk driving. In 1982 Congress passed the Alcohol Traffic Safety Act, which provided extra funds to states that enacted stricter drunk-driving laws. To be eligible, a state had to require that a blood alcohol level of .10 percent was conclusive evidence of drunkenness. (The permissible alcohol level was lowered to .08 in 2000.) Two years later, in 1984, Congress stepped

in again and passed a law requiring states to enact a minimum drinking age of 21 or lose some of their federal highway funds. All states eventually complied.

Since the 1970s, public attitudes have changed remarkably. Drunk driving is no longer tolerated in a way it once was; even the liquor and beer industry recommends that drinkers give their car keys to a "designated driver" (a term that would not have been understood two decades ago). Behavior has changed, too. Between 1982 and 1999, deaths from alcohol-related crashes dropped by 37 percent. Safer cars, improved highways, better emergency medical services, and a decline in drunk driving have sent the nation's traffic fatality rate tumbling. On average in 1950, 7.6 individuals were killed for every 100 million vehicle miles traveled. By 1999 that statistic had plummeted to 1.6 persons—a decrease of more than 75 percent.

AN UNFINISHED CRUSADE

Not very long ago, a movie star drawing slowly on a cigarette was considered the height of sophistication; medical-society meetings took place in rooms clouded with tobacco smoke; R.J. Reynolds and Philip Morris were considered so powerful that few dared to challenge them.

How things have changed! Planes are now smoke-free, as are many restaurants and offices; Joe Camel has been put out to pasture; and the $246-billion settlement between the tobacco companies and the states made front-page headlines. Americans have given up smoking in record numbers, and many of those who continue are trying to kick the habit. The percentage of adult male smokers in the United States dropped from a high of more than 50 percent in 1965 to about 26 percent in 1998. The percentage of adult fe-

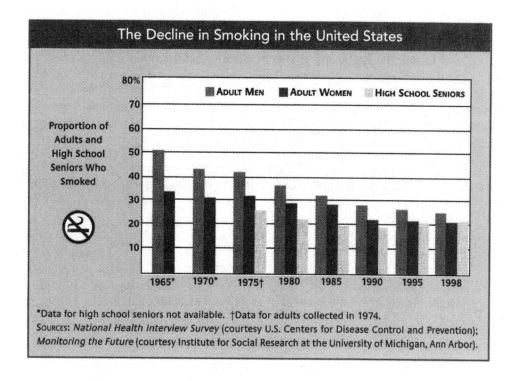

The Decline in Smoking in the United States

Proportion of Adults and High School Seniors Who Smoked

■ ADULT MEN ■ ADULT WOMEN □ HIGH SCHOOL SENIORS

1965* 1970* 1975† 1980 1985 1990 1995 1998

*Data for high school seniors not available. †Data for adults collected in 1974.
SOURCES: *National Health Interview Survey* (courtesy U.S. Centers for Disease Control and Prevention); *Monitoring the Future* (courtesy Institute for Social Research at the University of Michigan, Ann Arbor).

male smokers fell from its high of 34 percent in 1965 to 22 percent in 1998. Teenagers present more of a mixed picture. Although the percentage of American high school seniors who smoke daily decreased from a high of 29 percent in 1976 to a low of 17 percent in 1990, it then rose to 22 percent in 1998, before dropping slightly, to 21 percent, in 2000. Research, advocacy, media coverage, public education, politics, and government contributed to this unexpected transformation.

While the dangers of tobacco have long been recognized (in 1604 King James I branded the tobacco habit as "a loathsome custom to the Eye, Harmfull to the Braine, and dangerous to the lungs"), the scientific community ignored smoking until the last half of the twentieth century. As late as 1948, the *Journal of the American Medical Association (JAMA)* wrote, "More can be said on behalf of smoking as a form of escape from tension than against it."

Only two years later, in May 1950, *JAMA* published two articles linking smoking and lung cancer. In one of them, Ernst Wynder (who remained an anti-tobacco activist until his death in 1999) and Evarts Graham reported that of the more than 600 lung cancer patients they interviewed, 97 percent were moderately heavy to very heavy smokers. From there, the evidence mushroomed. By the late 1980s, some 60,000 studies had made it abundantly clear that tobacco causes cancers, stroke, and heart disease.

From published research to public awareness, however, there is often a long journey. In the case of smoking, the federal government played a critical role in narrowing the distance. In 1964 Surgeon General Luther Terry's widely publicized report woke up the nation to the dangers of tobacco. And in 1986, C. Everett Koop, surgeon general during the Reagan administration, reported that secondhand smoke caused cancers and other life-threatening illnesses—a finding that legitimized local, state, and federal efforts to limit smoking in public places.

Public-health advocates challenged the tobacco industry and kept the issues alive. Among the leaders were John Banzhaf, a Georgetown University law professor, whose organization ASH (Action on Smoking and Health) brought lawsuits and petitioned regulatory agencies, and Stanton Glantz, a University of California professor, whose advocacy groups Californians for Nonsmokers' Rights and, later, Americans for Nonsmokers' Rights, fought for the enactment of local and state anti-tobacco measures. Long-established organizations also joined the fray. The American Cancer Society, the American Lung Association, and the American Heart Association were relatively early participants. In 1982 these three organizations formed the Coalition on Smoking and Health, directed by Matt Myers, another longtime antismoking activist. The American Medical Association was the last to come to the table. Long ambivalent about smoking, the AMA ultimately proved to be an influential ally through its *Journal* articles and its work to organize antismoking coalitions.

Although some media organizations were slow to publicize the dangers of smoking (tobacco ads are a significant source of advertising revenues), others played an important early role. In December of 1952, *Reader's Digest* ran an article entitled "Cancer by the Carton." In it the most widely read magazine of its day reported, in plain English, the link between smoking and lung cancer and accused the tobacco industry of a cover-up. From then on, despite the best efforts of the tobacco industry, the danger of tobacco has become increasingly well known.

Laws and regulations have long been the backbone of antismoking efforts. A week after the release of the surgeon general's report in 1964, the Federal Trade Commission proposed that cigarette packages and advertising carry a strong warning label. In response the tobacco industry cried foul and tried to sabotage the legislation, a scenario that was to be replayed many times in the succeeding years. Ultimately, in 1965, over the fierce opposition of the tobacco industry, Congress passed a law requiring that cigarette packs and ads carry a watered-down warning. This was the first of many federal laws and regulations aimed at reducing smoking. Equally if not more important were local ordinances and state laws banning smoking in public places and making the sale of cigarettes to minors illegal. As Victor Crawford, a former Tobacco Institute lobbyist who became an anti-tobacco advocate after developing lung cancer, recalled, "We [the tobacco lobby] could never win at the local level. The reason is that all the health advocates are local activists who run the little political organizations. On the local level, I couldn't compete with them."

While Americans' attitudes toward smoking have changed, the tobacco industry remains a formidable force. Cigarettes and spit tobacco are still attractive to young people, and the commitment of the Bush administration to tobacco-control measures is, at best, uncertain. While the victories won so far in the national effort against tobacco are a cause for cheering, it is too early to celebrate them as permanent.

INGREDIENTS OF SUCCESS

Cavities, lead poisoning, traffic fatalities, smoking—although serious health concerns remain, each of these examples involves a success story. These experiences are not triumphs of medical technology; rather—and this may explain why they are unappreciated—they are the result of social and behavioral change. Four elements shared by these quiet victories offer lessons for shaping public policy.

1. Highly credible scientific evidence can persuade policy makers and withstand attack from those whose interests are threatened. Tobacco is the clearest example. The evidence linking smoking with cancer and other deadly illnesses was so strong and so consistent that—over the legal and scientific objections of the tobacco companies—it provided a scientific basis for legislation, regulations, and judicial decisions; ultimately, it was persuasive enough to move public opinion. Similarly, well-structured comparative trials provided convincing evidence that moderate amounts of fluoride added to the water supply reduced tooth decay. The federal government's National Health and Nutrition Examination Surveys gave the EPA the foundation on which to base regulations—strongly challenged by the gasoline and lead lobbies—that eventually eliminated lead from the nation's gasoline supply.

2. Public-health campaigns need advocates who are passionately committed to their cause, who have the inner resources to withstand the tremendous pressure applied by the industries whose practices they are criticizing, and who continue to fight even at the risk of their professional reputations. Ralph Nader, Candy Lightnet, Herbert Needleman, and other crusaders have had a tremendous effect on social policy. But advocacy from outside the system is rarely enough. When government agencies and their leaders speak out, new ideas about public health become more acceptable to the mainstream media and the populace. Similarly, campaigns for change gain legitimacy from the backing of authoritative groups outside government, notably professional societies—such as the American Medical Association on seat belts, the American Dental Association on fluoridated water, and the American Cancer Society on tobacco.

3. Public awareness and discussion depend on a partnership with the media. Advocates need the media to reach the public, and the media, looking for good stories, also need the advocates. "Behind virtually every public-health-and-safety measure enacted in this half-century has been a media advocacy campaign to dramatize both the risks and the public-policy solution" says the Advocacy Institute's Michael Pertschuk. As a result of the media, few now doubt that smoking is bad for health, that drinking and driving is a lethal combination, that seat belts save lives, and that fluoridated water prevents cavities.

> For all our country's achievements, the United States still ranks 24th in measures of national health, according to the World Health Organization

4. Law and regulation, often at the federal level, have been critical elements in focusing Americans' attention on health concerns, providing policy direction, and setting standards that have led to improvement in the public's health. Despite all the criticism they have received, federal laws and regulations have vastly improved people's health. They have been—and continue to be—the underpinning that protects the health of the American public.

Because of the Clean Air Act, the Lead-Based Paint Act, and federal regulations that reduced or eliminated other sources of lead contamination, lead poisoning has been significantly reduced as a health concern. Because of highway safety laws and federal regulations mandating the use of seat belts and other safety features, drivers and their passengers are now much safer. Because of congressionally mandated warning labels on cigarette packs, bans on cigarette advertising, and similar legislation, plus lawsuits by state attorneys general and local ordinances banning smoking in public places, the nation is moving toward kicking the nicotine habit. Even at a time when many people are disillusioned with government, its role in protecting the health of the public cannot be underestimated.

As impressive as these victories appear, the United States still has a long way to go even to catch up with the rest of the developed world. For all our achievements, we still rank 24th in measures of national health, according to the World Health Organization. Imagine what we could do if we had social movements against homicide, HIV infection, unhealthy foods, and physical inactivity that could match what public-health initiatives have achieved in such areas as lead and tobacco. Without the energy of such social movements, the United States will be doomed to suffer from inferior health, no matter how much we invest in basic biomedical research or cutting-edge medical technologies. Yet if we put that research to positive use in the public arena, combine it with committed advocacy, and follow up with intelligent policy-making, we can do much to improve America's health—not with miracles but with just hard work.

For more on success stories in public health, see the links to this article at www.prospect.prg.

STEPHEN L. ISAACS is the president of Health Policy Associates in San Francisco. STEVEN A. SCHROEDER is the president of the Robert Wood Johnson Foundation.

Twilight of the Corporation

In the last decade or so, the transnational corporation has virtually supplanted the nation state as the central institution dominating the lives of people in most parts of the world. By creating a global market system that now spans the four corners of the planet, the transnational corporation has moved into the very centre of our history as a dynamic colonial force reshaping the destiny of peoples and nations. Larger and more powerful than anything before, these corporations now hold the reins of power more firmly than do many of the world's governments.

By Tony Clarke

There is nothing really new about naming corporations as agents of colonialism. After all, the original forms of what we call today transnational corporations (TNCs), were huge exploration enterprises like the East India and the Hudson Bay companies which were granted royal charters by European states to expand their empires by conquering new lands and markets in Africa, Asia and the Americas during the 16th and 17th centuries. What is new today, however, is that transnational corporations now wield more economic and political clout than the vast majority of nation states, not only in the so-called developing countries of the South but in the industrialized West as well.

In less than 20 years, the number of globe-spanning corporations has jumped from seven to over 45,000, a 650 percent increase. Today, 52 of the top 100 economies around the world are transnational corporations rather than nation states. Mitsubishi is bigger than Indonesia (the Earth's fourth most populous country), General Motors is larger than either Denmark of Norway, Daimler-Chrysler now outstrips South Africa and Saudi Arabia, and Siemens' yearly income is greater than Ireland's or Chile's. Indeed, the combined annual revenues of the biggest 200 corporations is greater than those of 182 nation states which, in turn, are responsible for the livelihood of over four-fifths of humanity on this planet.

Today, 52 of the top 100 economies around the world are transnational corporations rather than nation states. Mitsubishi is bigger than Indonesia (the Earth's fourth most populous country), General Motors is larger than either Denmark or Norway, Daimler-Chrysler now outstrips South Africa and Saudi Arabia, and Siemens' yearly income is greater than Ireland's or Chile's.

Yet, what is perhaps most striking about the global corporation today is not just its vast economic clout but the way it penetrates and controls the social, cultural and political lives of peoples and nation states. Since the collapse of the Berlin Wall ten years ago, symbolizing the triumph of capitalism over communism, the transnational corporation has essentially supplanted the nation state as the central institution dominating the lives of people in most parts of the world. By creating a global market system that now spans the four corners of the planet, the transnational corporation has moved into the very centre of our history as a dynamic colonial force re-shaping the destiny of peoples and nations.

Colonial Machines

As Edward Goldsmith demonstrated… , colonial forms of development are alive and well today. According to the 1998 United Nations Human Development Report, the income disparity between the top 20 percent and the bottom 20 percent of the world's population is now 150 to 1, double what it was 30 years ago. The 225 richest individuals on this planet, most of whom are the heads of powerful transnational enterprises, have a combined wealth equal to the annual income of half of humanity. As the *Guardian* put it in response to a question about the difference between Zambia and Goldman Sachs: "One is an African country that makes 2.2 billion a year and shares it among 25 million people. The other is an investment bank that makes 2.6 billion and shares it among 161 people."

In the South today, transnational corporations continue to operate as colonial machines by producing and re-producing inequality and dependency. Foreign direct investment through TNCs has replaced the World Bank, the International Monetary Fund and foreign aid by governments as the main source of capital for economic development. Structural adjustment programmes imposed by the World Bank since the 1980s in exchange for debt relief has made it easier for TNCs to manufacture products for export, extract valuable natural resources, obtain generous investment incentives, take advantage of cheap labour conditions, redirect local production priorities, and endlessly repatriate profits, unfettered by government intervention or regulation.

Now, the prime role of governments is to provide a secure place and climate for profitable transnational investment and competition. In other words, security for investors, but not for citizens.

In an age of economic globalisation, however, transnational corporations function as colonial machines in the West as well as in the South. The fact that TNCs can move their operations from one country to another at a moment's notice for more profitable investment opportunities has taken its toll in terms of lowering real wages, environmental safeguards, corporate tax revenues, local development priorities and social security in most northern industrialized countries. For the most part, foreign-based corporations are no longer obligated to meet performance standards (for example, local job creation quotas, quotas on natural resources) while domestic corporations which have gone global have largely abandoned their national/local responsibilities in favour of larger markets and lower production costs elsewhere (including over 800 free-trade zones around the world

where no requirements to meet labour, social, and environmental standards exist).

At the same time, TNCs are exercising increasing control over the social and ecological lives of peoples in the West. After two decades of deregulation and privatisation, corporations are now moving in to take over social priorities on a for-profit basis that used to be the public responsibility of the state in many countries, such as health care, education, social security, and criminal justice. "Growing-up corporate" as Ralph Nader calls it, is becoming a way of life. Bio-technology corporations are radically altering the food chain with genetically engineered products while chemical industries continue to poison the atmosphere with toxic wastes, big timber companies clear-cut the planet's remaining forests, deep sea trawlers scrape the ocean floor depleting fish stocks, and corporations make plans for profitable investments in bulk water exports.

But, perhaps the most significant colonial development has been the corporate takeover of democratic life in the West. In the capital cities of Europe, Japan and North America, TNCs have become sophisticated political machines. Armed with a battery of policy research institutes, big business lobbying machinery, legal and public relations firms, and political advertising apparatus (not to mention lucrative donations to political parties as an insurance policy), corporations are able to determine, if not dictate, government legislation and policy making on a wide range of economic, social, and environmental issues. Through this process, basic citizens' rights have been hijacked by vested corporate interests while growing numbers of people and their associations have become politically disenfranchised.

Corporate Rule

Yet, this is only part of the picture. As neo-colonial machines, TNCs have, to an increasing degree, been invested with the authority to govern and rule. From their outset, corporations have been given the sanction to operate by the Crown or the State. The first TNCs commissioned to find valuable resources in the New World were initially given royal charters by the monarchies of England, France, Spain, Portugal and the Netherlands. Following in this tradition, governments continued to give corporations the legal permission to operate by granting charters and licences of authority. Without a charter or licence, essentially no corporation has the legal right to own property, borrow money, sign contracts, hire or fire, accumulate assets or debts.

At the same time, this corporate authority has been further consolidated by changes in legal doctrine through the courts. Under both national and international law, corporations achieved legal status as "persons" and "citizens" with political rights. Moreover, this was a first-class citizenship which gave corporations more protection over property rights, declaring that corporate contracts and the rate of return on investment were property that could not be meddled with by citizens or by their elected representatives. Not only do corporations have legal rights and protection when it comes to market transactions such as the buying and selling of property or their products, but also free speech in the form of political advertising as well as the right to sue for injuries, slander or libel. In the US, corporations were also granted "eminent domain" under the law, with the result that jury trials were eliminated for determining whether corporate practices cause harm or injury and, if so, what damages should be assessed.

Without the state, however, corporations would neither have sufficient authority nor the legitimacy required to govern or rule, especially in democratic societies. To obtain this authority, global corporations in the West began to focus their energies on restructuring the role of governments to more directly serve the interests of transnational investment and competition. As far as big business was concerned, the Keynesian social welfare state, which had been built up in the industrialized West and parts of the South since World War II, had become the main obstacle. After all, the Keynesian model of government (named after the British economist, John Maynard Keynes) was designed to intervene in the market-place to ensure that it operated on behalf of the common good or the public interest.

Any country that decides, for example, to ban the export of raw logs as a means of conserving its forests, or ban the use of carcinogenic pesticides, can be charged under the WTO by member states on behalf of their corporations for obstructing the free flow of trade and investment.

Starting with the Trilateral Commission 25 years ago—whereby David Rockefeller brought together 325 Chief Executive Officers (CEOs), presidents, prime ministers, and senior government officials from Europe, Japan and North America—a strategy was put in place to dismantle and replace the Keynesian state. Subsequently, big business coalitions like the European Round Table of Industrialists and the US Business Round Table were formed primarily to reorganise the role and functions of governments to respond to the interests of transnational capital and the new global market discipline. With the Thatcher and Reagan governments of the early 1980s, the social welfare state was gradually dismantled and has since been replaced by the 'security state'. Now, the prime role of governments is to provide a secure place and climate for profitable transnational investment and competition. In other words, *security* for investors, but not for citizens.

Imperial Order

By the same token, it was equally imperative for the CEOs of the world's leading TNCs to consolidate their authority and power in relation to the major institutions of global governance. In the early 1980s, the UN Centre for Transnational Corporations, which had been established to monitor the operations of TNCs and develop an international code of conduct, was effectively dismantled in response to mounting pressure by the corporate elite in the US and other major industrialized countries. During this period, the so-called Washington Consensus calling for the liberalisation of trade, investment and finance was vigorously promoted through the Bretton Woods institutions, namely, the GATT, the IMF and the World Bank.

An Economic Constitution for the Planet

When the Canada-US Free Trade Agreement was concluded, President Reagan described it as the "economic constitution of North America". Recently the director general of the World Trade Organisation (WTO), Renato Ruggiero, used similar language to describe the WTO. Like constitutions, trade agreements set out the fundamental rights of their constituents. But these "economic constitutions" have been negotiated behind closed doors with little if any input from any sector other than business. It isn't surprising then, that under the WTO only corporations are the beneficiaries of the rights it creates, and the interest of others in society are nowhere to be found.
—*Steven Shrybman, the World Trade Organisation: A Guide for Environmentalists*

The turning point, however, came with the creation of the World Trade Organisation (WTO) in 1994. Crafted behind closed doors by trade bureaucrats and corporate lobbyists, the WTO was designed to become eventually a global governing institution regarding trade, investment and finance. To carry out its mandate, the WTO was given not only judicial powers to adjudicate trade disputes, but also legislative powers. Under the WTO, a group of unelected trade officials would, in effect, have the power to override economic, social and environmental policy decisions of nation states and democratic legislatures around the world.

"We are writing the constitution of a single global economy… the question is where—not whether—work or trade and investment would take place"—Renato Ruggiero

Any country that decides, for example, to ban the export of raw logs as a means of conserving its forests, or ban the use of carcinogenic pesticides, can be charged under the WTO by member states on behalf of their corporations for obstructing the free flow of trade and investment. A secret tribunal of trade officials would then decide whether these laws were "trade restrictive" under the WTO rules and should therefore be struck down. Once the secret tribunal issues its edict, no appeal is possible. The country convicted is obligated to change its laws or face the prospect of perpetual trade sanctions.

Although the WTO was initially organised to focus on trade, its centrepiece was to be a global investment treaty. In December 1996, the now outgoing director general of the WTO, Renato Ruggiero, declared that the establishment of a global investment treaty in the WTO was the same as developing a constitution for the global economy. But it was the Organisation for Economic Co-operation and Development (OECD), the "rich nations club" of the 29 top industrialized countries, that began negotiating a Multilateral Agreement on Investment (MAI), which was to have been brought back to the WTO and imposed on the developing countries of the South.

Building from a blueprint drafted by the International Chamber of Commerce, the MAI was originally designed to grant sovereign powers to TNCs that were equal to, if not greater than, nation states in the global economy. Not only was the MAI crafted as a "corporate bill of rights" with a body of rules and disciplines to protect foreign investors and their investments, but it gave corporations themselves the power tools to enforce these rules. Under the investor-state mechanism of the MAI, foreign-based corporations would have the power to sue governments directly for alleged violations of the investment rules, thereby ratcheting down any unwanted laws, policies or programmes.

Global Casino

By officially suspending negotiations on the MAI in December 1998, however, the OECD effectively handed back to the WTO the task of establishing a global investment treaty. While this dramatic turn of events was due, in part, to widespread public opposition against the MAI mounted by civil society groups in many OECD countries, the financial meltdown in Asia was also a major causal factor. The sudden collapse of south-east Asian currencies in late 1997 created the worst economic chaos of the past quarter-century as millions lost their jobs,

prices skyrocketed, bankruptcies soared and real wages were slashed.

As the financial crisis spread to Russia and then on to Brazil, governments involved in negotiating the MAI became increasingly nervous about the further erosion of their economic sovereignty. After all, the Asian financial meltdown had been primarily triggered by speculators engaged in fly-by-night investments and the inability of governments to regulate sudden movements of capital flows in and out of their countries. The MAI would have put a set of handcuffs on governments, prohibiting them from regulating capital flows in order to mitigate against the destabilising effects of speculative investments on their economies.

Indeed, the global economy today is largely fuelled by a financial casino in which most investors have become speculators or gamblers. Instead of buying long-term shares in companies for the production of goods and services, investors now put most of their money in mutual funds where they can speculate or gamble on fluctuations in prices or the value of currencies. Speculative investment, in other words, has supplanted productive investment as the engine of the global economy.

With one keystroke, currency traders can move vast sums of money around the world instantaneously, speculating on price fluctuations in money markets on a 24-hour basis. The power of these speculators was dramatically illustrated in 1992 when financier George Soros, following a bet with then UK Prime Minister John Major, sold $10 billion worth of British pounds on international money markets for a $1 billion profit and, in doing so, single-handedly managed to force a devaluation of the pound and scuttle a new proposal for an exchange rate system in the European Union at the same time.

As writer David Korten, a former World Bank official, describes it: "The world is now ruled by a global financial casino staffed by faceless bankers and hedge-fund speculators who operate with a herd mentality in the shadowy world of global finance." "Each day," says Korten, "they move more than two trillion dollars around the world in search of quick profits and safe havens, sending exchange rates and stock markets into wild gyrations wholly unrelated to any underlying economic reality. With abandon they make and break national economies, buy and sell corporations and hold politicians hostage to their interests."

CORPORATESPEAK

"Since there are over 14,000 McDonalds world-wide, we figure there will be at least one thing in the US to make the rest of the world feel at home."
—McDonalds, 1993

In turn, this global casino is largely responsible for the recent wave of corporate merger mania. In 1998, corporate mergers skyrocketed to record levels of $1.2 trillion, including nine of the top ten of all time (for example the Exxon-Mobil merger in the energy sector). With every new merger and acquisition, stock prices climb, thereby giving corporations more cash to buy up competitors. A vicious cycle of continuous mergers and acquisitions is generated. In the long term, however, most mergers do not result in productive gains and stock prices tend to be overvalued, thereby creating an "asset bubble". When shareholders, particularly speculative investors, fail to see the gains, the bubble is likely to burst with profoundly negative economic consequences.

As we move into the 21st century, the time has come for citizen movements to focus their energies on this new corporate colonialism. Only by tackling the corporate power that is the driving force behind both the nation state and economic globalisation today, will we be able to build a truly common struggle, North and South, for democratic social change.

Tony Clarke is director of the Polaris Institute in Canada and chair of the Committee on Corporations of the International Forum on Globalisation. He is the author of several best-selling books: *Silent Coup: The Big Business Takeover of Canada* and (with Maude Barlow) *MAI: The Multilateral Agreement on Investment and the Threat to Canadian Sovereignty.*

Work Work Work **Work!**

It's taking over our lives—invading our homes, haunting our holidays, showing up for dinner. **Should we care?**

by Mark Hunter

YOU'VE HEARD THE JOKE BY NOW, BUT IT RINGS so true that it bears retelling: A guy reads a headline saying "Clinton creates 8 million jobs", and he cracks wearily, "Yeah, and I got three of 'em."

That gag may be the epitaph of the 1990s. In a very real sense, all of us—not just the 13 percent of us working two or three part-time jobs to survive—have three jobs. There's the work we do for a living, the work we do for ourselves (in many cases, to make sure we still can make a living tomorrow), plus the combination of housework and caregiving. Researchers differ on how much time we put into each of these categories, but most agree on one crucial point: The total keeps growing. As my brother Richard, a vice president of the Gartner Group, a high-tech advisory company, puts it: "It's like trying to fit a size 12 into a size eight shoe."

By far the biggest chunk of our time still goes to the work we do for a living. A survey of some 3,000 employees nationwide by the Families and Work Institute (FWI), a New York nonprofit organization that addresses work and family issues, discovered that over the past two decades, the average time spent at a full-time job has risen from 43.6 to 47.1 hours per week. Over a year, that comes to about four extra weeks—the same figure that Juliet B. Schor arrived at in her controversial 1991 study, *The Overworked American*, one of the first books to document what she called "the decline of leisure."

This fact hit home for me when I returned to the U.S. in 1996 after a decade abroad. I began to notice that not one of the other seven people in my office left their desks at lunchtime, the way folks used to. Throw in that traditional half-hour lunch break, and that's another two-and-a-half hours every week that many people give to work—or about three more weeks per year. Likewise, the Bureau of Labor Statistics reports that since 1985 paid vacation time has declined, and so has the average time that workers take off sick. Not surprisingly, more than one third of

the people in the FWI survey said that they "often or very often feel used up at the end of the workday." It's true that some researchers, like John Robinson, a sociology professor at the University of Maryland, argue that it's mainly the well-off among us who are working more, as a matter of choice, and that on average our leisure time has increased. But that's not what I see all around me.

Simultaneously, the old line between work life and private life is vanishing. In trying to understand why employees often refused to take advantage of maternity leave and flex-time, sociologist Arlie Hochschild, author of *The Time Bind*, discovered, to her amazement, that work has become a form of 'home' and home has become 'work.' "She reports that many people now see their jobs as a more appreciative, personal sort of social world" compared with their homes, where in the age of divorce and double careers, "the emotional demands have become more baffling and complex." When I interviewed 40 men about their work-life tradeoffs, every one of them said that it was easier to be a success on the job than in his personal relationships. Is it just a coincidence that hit TV shows like *Taxi* or *Murphy Brown* substituted the workplace "family" for the domestic setting of *The Brady Bunch*?

Work has penetrated the home in another potent way, notes market researcher Judith Langer, who has interviewed several hundred people on this subject over the past ten years: "People feel that what they're required to do at work has spilled over into the rest of their lives—reading, keeping up with trends in their fields, keeping up with e-mail and voice mail. We had a guy come into a focus group carrying all the publications that had hit his desk that day and complain, 'Monday weighs 20 pounds.'"

Personal technology has turned what once were hobbies into jobs: When my brother goes home from the office, he fires up his PC and checks the online orders for his self-produced harmonica records. And when the one third of Americans with managerial or professional jobs leave home, work follows them on a cell phone, pager, or modem. This past winter I received numerous business-related e-mail messages from an executive who was on a hiking trip deep in the mountains of Utah. (Emergency rescue crews have reported finding stranded hikers in the wilderness who had filled their backpacks with a portable computer, but forgotten to bring enough food and water.) The next time a cell phone rings in a restaurant at dinner-time, notice how many people automatically reach for theirs, because it might be a business call. In the 1960s and 1970s, stress experts called this kind of thing multiphasic behavior, otherwise known as doing several tasks at once. Nowadays we call it efficiency.

The distinction between work and leisure no longer exists

Ironically, the Baby Boomers, who came of age shout-ing their contempt for the man in the gray flannel suit, have done more than any other generation to erase the line between work and private life. Among the first to spot this paradox was Alvin Toffler in his 1980 futurist manifesto, *The Third Wave*. While most observers took those in the hippie movement for a bunch of unwashed, lazy bums, Toffler realized that they were really the pro-totype of a new kind of worker, the "prosumer"—people who, like frontier farmers, produce a share of what they consume, from home medicine to clothing (my fiancee creates a wardrobe every two years) to home-baked bread, instead of buying it all in the marketplace. "Once we recognize that much of our so-called leisure time is in fact spent producing goods and services for our own use," he noted, "then the old distinction between work and leisure falls apart."

Just as they turned the home into a workplace, Boomers redefined the ideal workplace as a playground. At the end of the 1970s, pollster Daniel Yankelovich found that this "New Breed" of Americans believed that work should be first and foremost a means to self-fulfill-ment—unlike their parents, who were taught by the Depression that any job that pays a secure wage was worth keeping. When Catalyst, a New York nonprofit or-ganization that seeks to advance women in business, sur-veyed more than 800 members of two-career couples about what mattered most to them on the job, at the top of the list were emotional benefits such as supportive management, being able to work on their own, and hav-ing control over their product.

Our careers now start earlier and end later, reversing a trend that reached its peak after World War II, when child labor virtually disappeared and retirement became a right. These days, so many teenagers have jobs—and as a result are cutting back on sleep, meals, and homework—that the National Research Council has called for strict new limits on the hours they're allowed to work. At the same time, the number of people 55 and older who still are in the labor force has increased by 6 million since 1950, and most of that increase is women. The Department of Labor projects that this number is going to grow by an-other 6 million by the year 2006.

None of this was supposed to happen. Only a genera-tion ago, the conventional wisdom among economists was that America was turning into an "affluent society", in which ever more efficient technology would produce an abundance of wealth that we could enjoy with less and less labor. Science-fiction novelists like Kurt Vonnegut imag-ined a society in which a tiny elite ran the show, while ev-eryone else sat around bored. In their vision, work would no longer be a burden, but a privilege for the happy few.

There are a lot of reasons why things didn't turn out quite that way. One is the Vietnam War, which heated the American economy to the boiling point just as the oil shocks of the 1970s arrived—a combination that led to double-digit inflation and sapped the value of wages. Then successive waves of recession, mergers, and down-sizing crashed through the American economy during the '80s. With few exceptions, one of the surest ways to raise a company's stock price—and along with it the value of its executives' stock options—was to fire a piece of its workforce. (Fortunately, downsizing appears to be losing steam, as Wall Street begins to suspect it as a des-perate attempt to make a company's bottom line look good in the short term.) Gradually, overtime pay replaced wage increases as the main way to stay ahead of the bills.

The Baby Boom played a role here, too. With so many Boomers competing for jobs, they became cheap for em-ployers: "For the first time in recent American history," marvels Landon Y. Jones in *Great Expectations: America and the Baby Boom Generation*, "the relative earnings of col-lege graduates *declined*." In order to maintain or, in many cases to surpass, the lifestyles of their parents—more Baby Boomers now own homes and, on average, bigger homes than Americans did in the 1950s—they have gone deeply into debt. About one fourth of the average fam-ily's income now goes to pay various creditors, more than in any previous generation.

Just as the feminist revolution was urging women to do something with their lives besides raise kids and clean house, it became difficult for the average family to make ends meet without two incomes. Today, in nearly four out of five couples—compared with one out of five in 1950—both partners are in the labor force, with women working nearly as many hours for pay as men. One posi-tive result is that since the late 1970s men have taken over a steadily growing (though still smaller) share of the childcare and household chores—nearly two hours' worth per day that used to be considered women's work.

Yet even visionary feminists like Dorothy Dinnerstein, who predicted this shift in her landmark 1976 book, *The Mermaid and the Minotaur*, did not foresee that it would also have a negative impact on our intimate lives. The Internet site BabyCenter recently polled roughly 2,000 of its new-mother visitors on whether they did or would return to work after their child was born. Two out of three survey participants said that they would go back to work within six months, but only one out of six said that she found the move "satisfying"; twice as many called it "wrenching." Men are also feeling the pinch." I have absolutely no time for myself or my friends," a married male executive and father complained to a Catalyst researcher. "Not enough time for us as a couple, and even the extended family say they don't see us enough."

Work is focusing us to constantly learn new ways of working

In previous decades, surveys showed that the biggest source of problems for married couples was money; now, when both partners are asked what is the biggest challenge they face, the majority of two-career couples answer "too little time." Not surprisingly, a growing number of leading-edge companies now offer working couples flexible schedules, expanded parental leave, and other benefits that allow their employees to reconcile their jobs with their personal lives.

Paradoxically, the same technology that was supposed to make us all wealthy loafers has contributed to the work-life squeeze. Computers and the changes they wrought have eliminated entire categories of jobs—when was the last time, for example, you talked to a human operator, instead of an automated phone tree, when you called a big company? In his book *The End of Work*, Jeremy Rifkin warned that this trend would end by puffing nearly all of us out of a job—a neat Doomsday inversion of the old "affluent society" prophecy. But many economists argue that new jobs will be created by new technology, just as they always have been. Perhaps, but the pressures to adapt to these rapid technological changes are greater than ever.

Computers have even changed the rhythm of our work, giving us more of a say in how the job is done because technology-savvy frontline personnel become responsible for decisions that managers used to make, as they constantly feed information up and down the line. The same applies to managers, whose desktop PCs, equipped with software that does everything from keeping appointments to formatting business letters and writing contracts, have largely replaced personal secretaries. We get more control—which happens to be one of the key measures of job satisfaction—but in return we end up giving more of ourselves to the job.

Beyond requiring us to put in longer hours for fear of losing our jobs, work is changing us in positive ways. In particular, it is literally forcing us to expand beyond the limits of what we previously thought we could accom-

plish, to constantly learn new ways of working. A lifelong career now means lifelong retraining. As the Radcliffe Public Policy Institute in Cambridge, Massachusetts, reports, "The qualities that once nearly guaranteed lifelong employment—hard work, reliability, loyalty, mastery of a discrete set of skills—are often no longer enough." That message has come through loud and clear. About one out of 12 Americans moonlights from his or her principal job in order to learn new skills or weave a "safety net" in case that job is lost. And American universities, starved for students only a few years ago as the Baby Boom grew up and out of the classrooms, have found a burgeoning new market in older workers. Census data show that by 1996 an incredible 468,000 college students were age 50 and older—an increase of 43 percent since 1990.

I don't have to look far to see that trend at work. My brother's wife earned her degree as a geriatric nurse in her late 40s, and it's now her part-time career. My mother, who runs her own public-relations agency, is working toward a degree as an English-language teacher, which will become her post-"retirement" career. And I'm riding that same train. This year I began teaching myself to write code for the Internet, just like my friend Randy, a former magazine editor who spent years of evenings learning to make Web pages in order to support his family. Why? Because by the year 2006 there will be fewer jobs for journalists, according to the Department of Labor. Like everyone else, I've got a choice between moving up—or out.

And there's real excitement in acquiring fresh skills—including the joy of proving wrong the adage that old dogs can't learn new tricks. But many older workers are not getting a chance to share in that excitement: They are being shunted aside from the retraining they will need to stay in the labor market at a moment when they are the fastest-growing share of the labor force. And the point at which a worker on the rise becomes a worker who's consigned to history is coming earlier in people's careers, usually around age 44, according to the Bureau of Labor Statistics. This situation persists at a time when a 77-year-old astronaut named John Glenn just went back into space—and while the minimum age for receiving Social Security benefits is rising.

Perhaps more managers should look at the hard science on this question. In a survey of the available research, Paula Rayman, director of the Radcliffe Public Policy Institute notes that there are "at least 20 studies showing that vocabulary, general information, and judgment either rise or never fall before age 60." Despite these results, they found that managers "consistently made different hiring, promotion, training, and discipline decisions based *solely* [my emphasis] on the age of the workers."

A recent survey of 405 human-resources professionals found that only 29 percent of them make an active effort to attract and/or retain older workers. Among those employers who have made such efforts, establishing opportunities for advancement, skills training, and part-time

six survival tips

THE RULES OF THE GAME MAY HAVE CHANGED, BUT midcareer and older workers still hold a number of aces—among them experience, wisdom, and adaptability. Here's some expert advice on how to play your cards and strengthen your hand for the future, gleaned from John Thompson, head of IMCOR, an interim executive placement firm in Stamford, Connecticut; Peter Cappelli, professor of management at The Wharton School in Philadelphia and author of *The New Deal at Work* (Harvard Business School Press 1999); and management gurus N. Fredric Crandall and Marc J. Wallace, authors of *Work and Rewards in the Virtual Workplace* (AMACOM, 1998)

LEARN WHILE YOU EARN If your company will pay for you to attend college-level courses to up-grade your skills, great. If not, take them anyway. Anything computer-related is a good bet. Microsoft offers training programs via organizations such as AARP.

FLEX YOUR MUSCLES By offering to work hours that younger workers may shun because of family and other commitments, you set yourself apart, especially in the eyes of employers in service industries who need 24-hour or seven-a-day week staffing. Employers such as the Home Shopping Network now rely on mature workers to fill a variety of positions.

CAST A WIDE NET The World Wide Web has radically changed the employment scene. A growing selection of jobs are being posted there, and so are résumés. Take a look at the Working Options section on AARP's Web site at www.aarp.org/working_options/home.html for career guidance and links to resources, including America's Job Bank.

BECOME AN MVP Do something to make yourself invaluable. For example, consider becoming a mentor to a young, up-and-coming manager who may need just the kind of guidance an experienced hand can offer. Another option: Seek out projects that matter to your boss and allow you to showcase your talents.

TEST THE WATERS Temporary workers are the fastest-growing segment of the labor force, for good reason. Companies faced with budget-cutting pressures are loathe to add full-time, permanent workers who drive up salary and benefit costs. It gives you an opportunity to try out an alternate career to see if it really fits. And temporary work often is the pathway to a permanent gig.

BE A COMEBACK KID Even if you're planning to retire or cut back from full-time work, don't forget job possibilities with your current employer. GE's information unit in Rockville, Maryland, offers a Golden Opportunity program that lets retirees work up to 1,000 hours a year, and many firms in Southern California use retirees to help with special engineering projects.

—*Tim Smart*

work arrangements are the most common. Overall, older employees are rated highly for loyalty and dedication, commitment to doing quality work, reliability in a crisis, solid work performance, and experience. This has given rise to a new phenomenon, in which downsized older workers are coming back to the workplace as consultants, temps. or contingent workers hired to work on specific projects.

Many who possess skills that are high in demand, like computer experts or financial advisers are finding fresh opportunities: Brokerage firms, for example, have discovered that their clients enjoy having investment counselors whose life experience is written on their faces.

Other countries are grappling with this issue as well. The Danish government, for example now offers salaried one-year training programs to unemployed workers over age 50. The German government has made it more costly for companies to downsize. And the French government is experimenting with ways to reduce the hours people spend on the job, to spread the work around. For Americans, however, the likely solution will depend on the ability of older workers to take control of their careers as never before, to think of themselves as independent contractors—units of one, so to speak—and, to do whatever they can to enhance their value. At a time when work has become, all-encompassing for many of us, it remains an eminently desirable endeavor. And although much is uncertain about the future, one thing is clear: Work will be part of it.

Mark Hunter is the author of five books, including The Passions of Men: Work and Love in the Age of Stress *(Putnam, 1988). He lives in Paris.*

Schools That Develop Children

BY JAMES P. COMER

American schools are said to be failing. Like nineteenth-century medicine men, everybody is promoting everything, whether there is any evidence that it works or not. Over here we have vouchers, charters, privatization, longer school days, summer school, and merit pay. Over there we have the frequent testing of students, the testing of teachers, smaller class size, report cards on schools, and high-stakes accountability. And over here, a very special offer: student uniforms, flag-raising ceremonies every morning, the posting of the Ten Commandments on schoolhouse walls, and sophisticated diagnostic instruments to identify children at risk for acting violently—when many administrators and teachers can't even identify children who need glasses.

Most of these "cures"—traditional and reform—can't work or, at best, will have limited effectiveness. They all are based on flawed models. We will be able to create a successful system of education nationwide only when we base everything we do on what is known about how children and youths develop and learn. And this knowledge must be applied throughout the enterprise of education—in child rearing before school age, in schools and school districts, in schools of education, in state education departments, in legislatures, and everywhere else that personnel preparation takes place and school policy is made.

Given the purpose of education—to prepare students to become successful workers, family members, and citizens in a democratic society—even many "good" traditional schools, as measured by high test scores, are not doing their job adequately. But test scores alone are too narrow a measure. A good education should help students to solve problems encountered at work and in personal relationships, to take on the responsibility of caring for themselves and their families, to get along well in a variety of life settings, and to be motivated, contributing members of a democratic society. Such learning requires conditions that promote positive child-and-youth development.

Children begin to develop and learn through their first interactions with their consistent caretakers. And the eventual learning of basic academic skills—reading, writing,

mathematics—and development are inextricably linked. Indeed, learning is an aspect of development and simultaneously facilitates it. Basic academic skills grow out of the fertile soil of overall development; they provide the platform for higher-order learning.

Through the early interactions, a bond is established that enables the child to imitate, identify with, and internalize the attitudes, values, and ways of their caretakers, and then those of other people around them. These people become important because they mediate (help make sense of and manage) a child's experiences and protect the child and help him or her to grow along the important developmental pathways—physical, social-interactive, psycho-emotional, ethical, linguistic, intellectual-cognitive, and eventually academic. The more mature thus help the less mature to channel potentially harmful aggressive energy into the energy of constructive learning, work, and play. But good early development is not a kind of inoculation that will protect a child for life. Future good development builds on the past and is mediated continuously by more mature people, step by step.

Understanding this process is no longer a matter of conjecture or the whining of "fuzzy-headed" social scientists or, as in my case, psychiatrists. Hard science—brain research—has confirmed the nature and critical importance of this interactive process. Without it children can lose the "sense"—the intelligence potential—they were born with. Children who have had positive developmental experiences before starting school acquire a set of beliefs, attitudes, and values—as well as social, verbal, and problem-solving skills, connections, and power—that they can use to succeed in school. They are the ones best able to elicit a positive response from people at school and to bond with them.

People at school can then influence children's development in ways similar to competent parents. To be successful, schools must create the conditions that make good development and learning possible: positive and powerful social and academic interactions between students and staff. When this happens, students gain social and academic competence, confidence, and comfort. Also, when parents and their social networks value school success and school experiences are positive and powerful, students are likely to acquire an internal desire to be successful in school and in life, and to gain and express the skills and behavior necessary to do so.

Vouchers do not address the challenge of child development. They simply change mechanisms of infrastructure, curriculum, and service delivery.

In order to realize the full potential of schools and students, we must create—and adequately support—a wide and deep pool of teachers and administrators who, in addition to having thorough knowledge of their disciplines, know how children develop generally and academically and how to support that development. They must be able to engage the families of students and the institutions and people in communities in a way that benefits student growth in school and society.

Vouchers and similar reforms currently being touted do not address these standards. They are simply changes in infrastructure, curriculum, and service delivery. They do not offer the potential for a nationwide transformation that a developmental focus does. And vouchers can reduce funds needed to improve the schools that must educate the majority of American children.

THE CHALLENGE OF CHANGE

The function of promoting good child-and-youth development and achievement was once served in our society through families and their social networks and through community life in small towns and rural areas. If students did not do well in school, they could leave, earn a living, still take care of themselves and their families, and become positive, contributing members of their communities. Despite massive and rapid scientific, technological, and social change, children have the same needs they always did: They must be protected and their development must be guided and supported by the people around them. They cannot rear themselves.

High mobility and modern communication created by technological change have undermined supports for child-and-youth development. Children experience many stimulating models of potentially troublesome behaviors—often in the absence of emotionally meaningful, influential adults. As a result, too many young people receive too little help in learning to manage feelings and act appropriately on the increased and more stimulating information they re-

ceive. This makes adequate social, psychological, and ethical development difficult.

Meanwhile, the new economy has made a high level of development and education a necessity for 90 percent of the population instead of the 20 percent we got by with half a century ago. Yet the rise of technology has led to an overvaluation of measured intelligence rather than an appreciation of overall development and the kind of intellectual growth that promotes strong problem-solving capacities.

Many successful people are inclined to attribute their situations to their own ability and effort—making them, in their minds, more deserving than less successful people. They ignore the support they received from families, networks of friends and kin, schools, and powerful others. They see no need for improved support of youth development. These misperceptions influence many education policies and practices.

Adequate support for development must be restored. And school is the first place this can happen. It is the common pathway for all children—the only place where a significant number of adults are working with young people in a way that enables them to call on family and community resources to support growth systematically and continually. And school is one of the few places where students, staff, and community can create environments in which to help young people achieve the necessary levels of maturity.

In the early 1980s, James Coleman, the late and respected University of Chicago sociologist, called what children gain from their parents and their networks "social capital." I do not like this term in discussing humans, but it is much used. Many poor children grow up in primary social networks that are marginal to mainstream institutions and transmit social capital that is different from that needed for school success. School requires mainstream social capital. In a January 2000 New York Times Magazine article, James Traub said that "Coleman consistently pointed out that we now expect the school to provide all the child's human and social capital—an impossibility."

I agree that the school can't do it alone. But schools can do much more than what they now do. Most students, even those from very difficult social conditions, enter school with the potential needed to gain mainstream social capital. But traditional schools—and most reforms—fail such students.

Not long ago I asked approximately 300 experienced teachers and administrators from across the country if they'd taken a child development course; about half had. But when I asked how many had taken a school-based, supervised course in applied child development, only seven hands remained up. This lack of training is why many educators can't discuss the underlying factors involved in a playground fight or how to create social and academic experiences that motivate learning by tapping into the developmental needs and information level of today's students.

Even fewer could construct environments conducive to overcoming racial, ethnic, income, and gender barriers.

But schools can succeed if they are prepared to embrace poor or marginalized families and to provide their children with conditions that promote mainstream skills. And when these conditions are continued throughout the school years, children from low-income backgrounds can do well in school; they will have better life chances. I was first convinced that this was the case for very personal reasons.

My mother was born into the family of a sharecropper in rural Mississippi in 1904. Her father was a good man, but he was killed by lightning when she was six years old. There were no family assistance programs, and a cruel, abusive stepfather came into their lives. He would not allow the children to go to school, and they lived under conditions of extreme poverty. At about eight years of age, as a barefoot child in the cotton fields, my mother realized that education was the way to a better life. When she was 16, she ran away to live with a sister in East Chicago, Indiana, with the hope of getting an education. But that was not possible.

When she had to leave school, my mother declared that if she ever had children, she would make certain they all got a good education. And then she set out—very, very, very carefully—to find my father, a person of like mind and purpose. Her caution paid off. My father, with six or seven years of education, worked as a steel mill laborer; and my mother, with no education, worked as a domestic. The two of them eventually sent the five of us to college, where we earned a total of 13 degrees.

Our family was enmeshed in an African-American church culture that provided the necessary social, ethical, and emotional context. My parents took us to everything educational they could afford; they talked and interacted with us in a way that encouraged learning and promoted overall development. Working for and respected by some of the most powerful people in our community, my mother observed and acquired mainstream success skills and made useful social contacts. Most of the summer jobs that helped us pay our way through college came from those contacts. And I enjoyed caviar brought home after parties before my working-class friends knew that it existed. Indeed, many European, black, and brown immigrants "made it" through similar experiences.

My three best friends were as intelligent as anybody in our family and in the predominantly white working- and middle-class school we attended. On the playground and the street corner, they could think as fast and as well as students who were more successful in school. But all three went on a downhill course: one died early from alcoholism, one spent time in jail, and one was in and out of mental institutions until he died recently. My parents had the same kind of jobs as their parents did, and we all attended the same school. Why the difference? It was the more useful developmental experience we were provided.

This notion was confirmed a few years ago when I visited my mother in the hospital. My spry, 80-plus-year-old first-grade teacher, Ms. Walsh, was a hospital volunteer.

When she saw me, she threw her arms around me and said, "Oh, my little James." I was 55 years old going on six. She stepped back and said, "We just loved the Comer children. You came to school with those bright, eager eyes, and you got along so well with the other children, and you all were so smart," and more. She was describing the outcome of a home and community experience that provided adequate development and school readiness—social capital, if I must use the term.

I acknowledge that my parents, perhaps even my community and school, were not and are not typical. And again, the community conditions that supported family functioning, child rearing, and development to a much greater degree in the past are weaker today. The positive connections that the poor previously had with the more privileged in American society have decreased.

A few scattered programs make good education and life opportunities possible for poor and working-class children. Prep for Prep lays the groundwork for students to attend elite private schools; A Better Chance places students in good suburban schools; the Summer Study Skills Program prepares students for challenging academic courses. These "pull-out" programs provide the social capital, knowledge, and skills needed for mainstream participation. But they do not serve that large body of able young people, like my childhood friends, who are lost in elementary schools. Prepared and supported differently, such children could succeed.

MODELS OF DEVELOPMENT

The Yale Child Study Center's School Development Program has been working with schools for the past 32 years. The outcomes suggest that by basing what we do in schools (and in the education enterprise beyond schools) on what we know about how children develop and learn, we can provide most children with what they need to succeed in school and in life.

I recently visited the Samuel Gompers Elementary School in one of the poorest neighborhoods in Detroit, a school with 97 percent student poverty. The Yale program has been used in this school for the past six years. The neighborhood was a disaster; the school was a pearl. The students were lively, spontaneous, and engaged in their work at appropriate times, yet quiet and attentive when they were supposed to be. They got along well with one another and were eager to demonstrate their skills to their parents and teachers. Eighty percent of the students passed the 1999 fourth-grade Michigan Educational Assessment Program (MEAP) test in reading and science, and 100 percent passed in mathematics. In 2000 they achieved the highest MEAP test scores among elementary schools in their size category in the state. Why here? It is not a mystery.

The Gompers School's success is related as much to the conditions that promote development and learning as it is to curriculum and instruction. How did it create these conditions and achieve good academic outcomes? The Yale program provided the conceptual and operational framework, child development–centered training for staff and parents, and very limited field support. The Skillman Foundation in Detroit, the Detroit Public Schools, Eastern Michigan University College of Education staff members, and parents (key members of the education enterprise) all came together to help the Gompers School and others provide the social capital the students need. The philosophy of the principal, Marilee Bylsma, is an important underpinning: "The school should be a safe haven for children, someplace that inspires learning." The staff, parents, and students did the work.

Committees, operations, and guidelines help schools create a culture of mutual respect and collaboration as well as social and academic programs that enable them to support students' development and learning. The transformation is gradual but frequent in schools that work to form good adult relationships. Good student relationships can follow.

At Gompers there is a 15-minute assembly every morning in which the students say the Pledge of Allegiance and make a school pledge. They sing a patriotic song and the school song. The custodian recognizes the "birthday boys and girls." (Message: It's everybody's school; we all play important roles.) The class with the best previous-day behavior gets "Gator points." Other recognitions take place. During the announcements, the students often discuss what's going on in their lives—the unexpected death of a teacher, problems in the neighborhood, and so on—and the adults help them learn to manage related feelings.

In traditional high schools, teachers are often much more anchored in subject matter than in student development.

When the school basketball team lost a tournament they had expected to win, the principal gave much thought to how to help the players manage their disappointment and grow from the experience. The next morning, she talked about how important it is to try to be number one in all you do. But the team members should celebrate their effort, she explained—they came in third in a large field—and look forward to the next opportunity. The students can tell you that they participate in extracurricular activities to create a good community, a condition that they value.

Activities and interactions like those at Gompers can't be carried out very long, if at all, in a school where the staff members don't like, trust, or respect one another or the parents. And you can't just mandate these conditions. Child

development–oriented structures and processes must operate in a way that brings about these conditions.

Initially, the Yale program's work was just in elementary schools, but it is now being carried out in many middle schools and high schools. Admittedly, middle school is difficult, and high school is even more so. That's when teens are "placing" themselves in the world and establishing their identity. Young people who place themselves and their futures in family and social networks that are dysfunctional are likely to perform in school in ways that lead to similar poor or marginal outcomes for themselves. Additionally, they are physically able to engage in adult behaviors. Only a half-century ago, many teens were married, working, and raising families; but in these more complex times, they often lack the experiences and resultant judgment, personal control, discipline, and problem solving skills needed to manage adult living.

In traditional high schools, teachers are often much more anchored in subject matter than in student development. Peer groups provide belonging and therefore become very powerful. They are sometimes positive, but too often are troublesome—it's the inexperienced and immature leading the inexperienced and immature. Aside from athletic coaches and teachers in the arts and other special areas, too few mature adults can interact with students in sustained and meaningful ways. These are powder keg conditions. And in communities where there are too few constructive supports for good development both inside and outside school, bad things happen—among staff, students, and parents.

In all schools—but particularly in low-income and non-mainstream communities—it is important for the staff to expose students to mainstream work as well as civic activities so that the connection between learning and later expectations is clear. School should help young people to learn what is needed for life success. Social and academic skills, attitudes, management of feelings, and other attributes needed to participate successfully in the mainstream can then be developed.

West Mecklenberg High School in Charlotte, North Carolina, received an additional 222 students in 1992 from a competing high school; its enrollment went from 1,144 to 1,366, precipitating a crisis. The school was almost evenly divided between whites and African Americans. Most of the students were children of blue-collar workers. Fourteen guns and many knives were confiscated during the first year, and parents, teachers, and students were concerned about their safety. Dennis Williams was assigned to the school as principal; Haywood Homsley, then the guidance counselor and coach, became the Yale-program facilitator. Williams and Homsley began to focus on reducing intergroup tensions and creating a climate that enabled staff members to consider and respond to the developmental needs of the students.

The transformation was dramatic. On April 28, 1995, *The Leader*, Charlotte's major newspaper, highlighted the gains seen at West Mecklenberg since the Yale program was introduced: Scholastic Assessment Test (SAT) scores rose by an average of 16 points; the number of students who made the honor roll jumped 75 percent; the number of students enrolled in advanced courses increased 25 percent; and the average daily attendance rate for the year went from 89 percent to almost 94 percent. The process of change at West Mecklenberg was essentially the same as in elementary schools like Gompers except that the students themselves were more involved in the thinking and planning of the programs.

In the 1994–1995 academic year, West Mecklenberg was designated a "school of excellence" by the state of North Carolina for the high level at which it reached its benchmark goals, and it was the only high school of 11 in its district to attain this status. Despite the fact that there have been three principals since 1992, the school has held the "excellence" rating for three of the past five years.

SUSTAINING GAINS

Are the academic gains large enough? Can they be sustained? What about the schools that do not improve? And what about middle- and upper-income young people, who face a more complex world? Even with developmentally based programs and other reform models, it's true that academic gains in schools serving students who are most in need do not quickly and routinely match those of more privileged students. Sometimes they can't be sustained; and sometimes there is no improvement at all. But when the process is well implemented, large gains have been achieved and sustained.

> **Frequent changes in administrators or teachers can undo in several months or less a school culture that took years to create.**

For example, the Norman Weir K-8 school in Paterson, New Jersey, went from 34th to first in academic achievement among eighth-graders in 1995. They equaled or surpassed suburban schools for four consecutive years. A school in Virginia went from 24th to first but fell apart the next year because the principal and several key senior staff members were removed or left and were replaced by untrained staff. Weir escaped the same fate because a group of staff members went to the superintendent and asked for

and were assigned a good principal whose educational philosophy was grounded in child development.

Before a school can experience large, widespread, sustained achievement-test gains and adequately prepare students for adult life, it must be able to promote student development and manage its way to success, as Gompers, West Mecklenberg, and others have done. For this to be possible, we must produce large numbers of adequately prepared and supported staff. The policies and practices of the major players in the education enterprise nationwide—schools of education, legislators at all levels, state and federal departments of education, school districts, businesses—must be coherent by virtue of being based in child-and-youth development.

There are many obstacles to significant school improvement. Five in particular are very troublesome yet more accessible than the seemingly intransigent issues of race, class, and financial equity. These five are the ones that prevent the education enterprise as a whole from empowering school staffs, as in the case of the Gompers School. If these were addressed all at once, the United States could begin to foster widespread, sustained, high-level school improvement—and perhaps, eventually, could even address the most resistant issues.

First, frequent changes in personnel—particularly in districts and schools faced with great challenges—is a major problem. Child development–based strategies require continuity, training, and support of school staff. Frequent changes in administrators or governance at the district or building level, or in teachers—without careful selection and training of new people—can undo in several months or less a school culture that took three to five years to create. Understanding student and organization needs, developing resources and staff, and building community support isn't possible in the two-year tenure of most school superintendents.

Second, education policy is often fragmented rather than prioritized. This is because it is made everywhere—legislatures, state departments, districts, unions, city councils, businesses, and more. Many policy makers have no expertise in child development, teaching, and learning. And when crafting policy, most do not talk to one another, to students, or to school staff. Rarely are these policies guided by what we know about child growth and development and its relationship to learning.

And legislators, businesspeople, state departments, and others are—like school administrators—under great pressure to "Do something!" Because they widely believe that test scores alone can measure school effectiveness, that is what they focus on most. And without well-considered, evidence-based, coherent education policies, equitable funding will be impossible. In one city, eight of the 10 schools listed as "failing" had made the greatest gains in the system over the previous two years. The listing was demoralizing and led to harmful staff turnover and achievement setbacks, but it was the only way to get funds to help those schools.

Third, most schools of education do not provide future teachers or administrators with adequate knowledge or skills to promote a culture supportive of overall student development. Most focus—and in the college classroom, particularly—on curriculum, instruction, assessment, administration, and, sometimes, use of technology.

Sound knowledge of academic disciplines is important but not sufficient. Many schools of education provide courses in abnormal child development but no study of normal development. And the preparation to teach reading is often limited. Yet a child who has difficulty learning to read—the academic task that serves as a foundation for all future learning—is likely to experience feelings that limit emotional, psychological, ethical, and social developmental growth, or that promote troublesome growth.

Fourth, schools of education are seldom involved with other departments of the university in mutually enriching ways. Meaningful interaction between colleges of education and other university departments would be beneficial also to the institutions and the communities around them.

And fifth, there is no vehicle in universities or among research-and-development groups that will enable working educators to update their skills regularly and learn best practices. Also, there is no existing way to address these five most troublesome obstacles simultaneously so that synergy results.

Agricultural extension provides a useful model for educators. The Smith-Lever Act of 1914 created the Agricultural Extension Service to transmit knowledge to a large number of farmers through federal, state, and county partnerships. Farm agents, in addition to changing farmer practice, changed policy makers' and the public's understanding of best practice, as well as the policies needed to promote it. Improved agriculture enriched the economy and made America the breadbasket of the world.

Education is to the information-age economy of today what agriculture was to the economy at the turn of the twentieth century. Schools of education could create centers designed to overcome major obstacles in the education enterprise. Such centers would provide education agents. Schools of education will need to incorporate and institutionalize child development knowledge and expertise. But once this is done, education scholars and agents will be well positioned to share with and learn from colleagues at universities, to help future and current teachers and administrators become more effective practitioners, and to help policy makers and the public better understand and support good schooling.

Few schools of education or university programs are presently prepared to work in this way. We should not rush into such programs without sound pilot and infrastructure work. But knowledge, organization, and support can be acquired. The states—who are legally responsible for educating America's children—should support such efforts. Most, largely through their departments of education, have been involved in standard-setting as well as in regulatory and oversight activities. They are involved in takeovers of failing districts. Yet they have little experience in—and no mechanisms for—correcting the complex problems involved in school improvement.

The decisions we make in the next few years will involve significant amounts of money and will lock us into helpful or harmful directions. A miracle quick fix is not possible. But if we today begin to mount programs that connect to practice and to policy what we know about how children develop and learn, we could soon be well on our way to having better-functioning systems of education in five years and good ones in a decade. If we continue to be guided by tradition, ideology, and power, however, we will reach a point of no return—one where too many young people are undereducated, acting out, and gradually undermining our economy and our democracy.

JAMES P. COMER, M.D., is the Maurice Falk Professor of Child Psychiatry at the Yale University Child Study Center. He founded the Center's School Development Program in 1968.

Seeking Abortion's Middle Ground

Why My Pro-Life Allies Should Revise Their Self-Defeating Rhetoric

Frederica Mathewes-Green

The following article is adapted from a talk the author gave May 31, [1996], in Madison, Wis., at the first national conference of the Common Ground Network for Life and Choice, an organization of antiabortion activists and abortion-rights supporters who are seeking new ways to discuss their differences.

I WAS pro-choice at one point in my life, but I came over to a pro-life position years ago. I've been there ever since. Perhaps because of my background, I think there's a logic to the pro-choice position that deserves respect, even as we engage it critically. It is possible to disagree with somebody without calling them baby-killers, without believing that they are monsters or fiends. It is possible to disagree in an agreeable way.

The abortion argument is essentially an argument among women. It's been a bitter and ugly debate, and I find that embarrassing. For me, that gives a special urgency to this conference.

To reach agreement in any kind of conflict, you need to be able to back up and see far enough into the distance to locate a point you can actually agree on. What the two sides have in common is this: Each of us would like to see a world where women no longer want abortions.

I don't believe that even among the most fervent pro-choice people there is anybody who rejoices over abortion. I think we both wish that there were better solutions that could make abortion unnecessary, or prevent pregnancies in the first place. We'd like to see the demand for the procedure reduced, by resolving women's problems and alleviating the pressure for abortion. We can go along this road together as far as we can, and there will come a time when pro-choicers are satisfied, and pro-lifers want to keep going, but that doesn't mean we can't go together for now.

A few years ago, quite by accident, I discovered an important piece of common ground. Something I wrote in a conservative think-tank journal was picked up and quoted widely. I had written: "There is a tremendous sadness and loneliness in the cry 'A woman's right to choose.' No one wants an abortion as she wants an ice-cream cone or a Porsche. She wants an abortion as an animal, caught in a trap, wants to gnaw off its own leg."

What surprised me was where it appeared: I started getting clips in the mail from friends, showing the quote featured in pro-choice publications. I realized I had stumbled across one of those points of agreement: We all know that no one leaves the abortion clinic skipping. This made me think that there was common ground, that instead of marching against each other, maybe we could envision a world without abortion, a world we could reach by marching together.

The problem thus far, and I believe the pro-life movement has been especially complicit in this, is that we have focused only on abortion, and not on women's needs. We in the pro-life movement have perpetuated a dichotomy where it's the baby against the woman, and we're on the baby's side. You can look over 25 years of pro-life rhetoric and basically boil it down to three words: "It's a baby." We have our little-feet lapel pins, our "Abortion stops a beating heart" bumper stickers, and we've pounded on that message.

In the process we have contributed to what I think is a false concept—an unnatural and even bizarre concept—that women and their unborn children are mortal enemies. We have contributed to the idea that they've got to duke it out, it's going to be a fight to the finish. Either the woman is going to lose control of her life, or the child is going to lose its life.

It occurred to me that there's something wrong with this picture. When we presume this degree of conflict between women and their own children, we're locating the conflict in the wrong place. Women and their own children are not

In news coverage of the abortion controversy, The Washington Post has adopted the terms "anti-abortion" and "abortion rights" as more neutral descriptions of the opposing points of view. Frederica Mathewes-Green's article, however, is drawn from her talk at the network's recent conference and therefore is similar to a quotation; it would change the meaning and context of her remarks to use Post style, so the terms "pro-life" and "pro-choice" appear throughout.
—The Editors

naturally mortal enemies, and the problem is not located inside women's bodies, it's within society. Social expectations make unwanted pregnancy more likely to occur and harder for women to bear. Unwed mothers are supposed to have abortions, to save the rest of us from all the costs of bringing an "unwanted" child into the world.

There are three drawbacks to emphasizing "It's a baby" as the sole message. One is that it contributes to the present deadlock in this debate. We say "It's a baby," and our friends on the pro-choice side say, "No, it's her right," and the arguments don't even engage each other. It's an endless, interminable argument that can go on for another 25 years if we don't find a way to break through.

Second, the "It's a baby" message alienates the woman distressed by a difficult pregnancy. There's a pro-life message that I sometimes hear which makes me cringe: "Women only want abortions for convenience. They do this for frivolous reasons. She wants to fit into her prom dress. She wants to go on a cruise." But this alienates the very person to whom we need to show compassion. If we're going to begin finding ways to live without abortion, we need to understand her problems better.

Of course, there has been a wing of the pro-life movement that has been addressing itself to pregnant women's needs for a long time, and that is the crisis pregnancy center movement. Centers like these have been giving women maternity clothes, shelter, medical care, job training and other help for 30 years. But you wouldn't know that from the things the movement says. I once saw a breakdown of the money and time spent on various sorts of pro-life activities, and over half the movement's energy was going into direct aid to pregnant women. Yet you don't hear this in the rhetoric.

The third problem with this rhetoric is that it enables the people in the great mushy middle, the ones who are neither strongly pro-life or strongly pro-choice, to go on a shrugging off the problem. While both sides know that women don't actually want abortions in any positive sense, the middle is convinced they do. And that's because both sides are telling it they do. Pro-lifers say, "She wants an abortion because she's selfish"; pro-choicers say, "She wants an abortion because it will set her free." No wonder the middle believes us; it's one of the few things we appear to agree on.

But both sides know that abortion is usually a very unhappy choice. If women are lining up by the thousands every day to do something they do not want to do, it's not liberation we've won. But our rhetoric in the pro-life movement, our insistence that "It's a baby and she's just selfish," keeps the middle thinking that abortion really is what women want, so there's no need for change and nothing to fix. I want to recognize my side's complicity in contributing to this deadlock and confusion.

I can understand why my pro-life allies put the emphasis on "It's a baby." It's a powerful and essential message. Visualizing the violence against the unborn was the conversion point for me and many others. But it cannot be the sole message. Polls on American attitudes toward abortion show that between 70 and 80 percent already agree that it's a baby—especially since the advent of sonograms. So when we say, "It's a baby," we're answering a question nobody's asking any more. I believe there is a question they are asking about abortion, and the question is, "How could we live without abortion?"

The abortion rate in this country is about a million and a half a year, a rate that has held fairly stable for about 15 years. Divide that figure by 365 and that equals about 4,100 abortions every day.

Now imagine for a moment that in the middle of the country there is a big abortion store, and outside it 4,100 women got in a long line, one behind the other—and that's just today. It's a sobering image. And the short-sighted pro-life response has been, "Put a padlock on the abortion store." But that's not going to solve the problem. You cannot reduce the demand by shutting off the supply. If 4,100 women were lining up every day to get breast implants, we'd be saying, "What's causing this demand? What's going on here?"

How can we solve the problems that contribute to the demand for abortion? If this were easy, we would have done it by now. It's not easy. There are two obvious components: preventing the unwanted pregnancy in the first place, and assisting women who slip through the cracks and become pregnant anyway.

The obvious tool for pregnancy prevention is contraception, but the pro-life movement has been very reluctant to support the contraceptive option. I come from a religious tradition that permits some forms of contraception, so it's not been a theological problem for me. So when I started considering this, I thought, "This is great! I'll get a helicopter, fill it with condoms, get a snow shovel, and just fly over the country tossing 'em out. We'll close all of the abortion clinics tomorrow!"

But then I began to analyze it a little deeper. While I believe the pro-life movement needs to make a strong stand in favor of preventing these unplanned pregnancies, I became skeptical of the contraceptive solution. For example, there's the recent study showing about two-thirds of births to teenage moms in California involved a dad who was an adult, and another one that found teen mothers had been forced into sex at a young age and that the men who molested them had an average age of 27. Closer to home, a friend of mine was brought to an abortion clinic by her older brother, who molested her when she was 12; they gave her a bag of condoms and told her to be more careful. You're not going to solve problems like these by tossing a handful of condoms at [them].

But leaving aside the question of sexual abuse, I think we need to look hard at the consequences of the sexual revolution that began in the 1960s. When I entered college in the early 1970s, the revolution was in full bloom. It seemed at the time a pretty care-free enterprise. Condoms, pills and diaphrams were readily available and abortion had just been legalized by the Supreme Court. But I gradually began to think that it was a con game being played on women. We were "expected to behave according to men's notions of sexuality," to use author Adrienne Rich's phrase. Instead of gaining respect and security in our bodies, we were expected to be more physically available, more vulnerable than before, with little offered in return.

What women found out is that we have hearts in here along with all our other physical equipment, and you can't put a condom on your heart. So in answering the question, "How do we live without abortion?," I'd say we need to look at restoring respect and righting the balance of power in male-female sexual relationships.

What can we do to help women who get pregnant and would rather not be? For a book I was writing, I went around the country talking to women who have had an abortion and to women who provide care for pregnant women. I had presumed that most abortions are prompted by problems that are financial or practical in nature.

But to my surprise, I found something very different. What I heard most frequently in my interviews was that the reason for the abortion was not financial or practical. The core reason I heard was, "I had the abortion because someone I love told me to." It was either the father of the child, or else her own mother, who was pressuring the woman to have the abortion.

Again and again, I learned that women had abortions because they felt abandoned, they felt isolated and afraid. As one woman said, "I felt like everyone would support me if I had the abortion, but if I had the baby I'd be alone." When

I asked, "Is there anything anyone could have done? What would you have needed in order to have had that child?" I heard the same answer over and over: "I needed a friend. I felt so alone. I felt like I didn't have a choice. If only one person had stood by me, even a stranger, I would have had that baby."

We also must stop thinking about abortion in terms of pregnancy. We harp on pregnancy and forget all about what comes next. Getting through the pregnancy isn't nearly the dilemma that raising a child for 18 years is. In most families, marriage lightens the load, but for some people that isn't the best solution. A neglected option is adoption, which can free the woman to resume her life, while giving the child a loving home.

The numbers on this, however, are shocking. Only 2 percent of unwed pregnant women choose to place their babies for adoptions. Among clients at crisis pregnancy centers, it's 1 to 2 percent. Adoption is a difficult sell to make for a number of complex reasons, but the bottom line is that 80 to 90 percent of the clients who go through pregnancy care centers and have their babies end by setting up single-parent homes. This is very serious. Pregnancy care centers know this, but aren't sure what to do about it. I've been strongly encouraging that there be more emphasis on presenting adoption to clients, and equipping center volunteers so they feel comfortable with the topic and enabled to dis-

cuss it. Adoption is not a one-size-fits-all solution, but it's got to fit more than 1 or 2 percent. More women should try it on for size.

Let me finish with these thoughts. I want to encourage us to view the pregnant woman and child as a naturally-linked pair that we strive to keep together and support. Nature puts the mother and the child together, it doesn't make them enemies, it doesn't set one against the other in a battle to the death. If our rhetoric is tearing them apart, we're the ones who are out of step. The pro-life movement should be answering the question "How can we live without abortion?" by keeping mother and child together, looking into pregnant women's needs and examining how to meet them, and encouraging responsible sexual behavior that will prevent those pregnancies in the first place.

Frederica Mathewes-Green is a columnist for Religion News Service and does commentary on National Public Radio. She is the author of "Real Choices," a book on alternatives to abortion (Questar, 1994). She lives in Baltimore with her husband and three teenaged children.

DEATH STALKS A CONTINENT

In the dry timber of African societies, AIDS was a spark. The conflagration it set off continues to kill millions. Here's why

By Johanna McGeary

IMAGINE YOUR LIFE THIS WAY. You get up in the morning and breakfast with your three kids. One is already doomed to die in infancy. Your husband works 200 miles away, comes home twice a year and sleeps around in between. You risk your life in every act of sexual intercourse. You go to work past a house where a teenager lives alone tending young siblings without any source of income. At another house, the wife was branded a whore when she asked her husband to use a condom, beaten silly and thrown into the streets. Over there lies a man desperately sick without access to a doctor or clinic or medicine or food or blankets or even a kind word. At work you eat with colleagues, and every third one is already fatally ill. You whisper about a friend who admitted she had the plague and whose neighbors stoned her to death. Your leisure is occupied by the funerals you attend every Saturday. You go to bed fearing adults your age will not live into their 40s. You and your neighbors and your political and popular leaders act as if nothing is happening.

Across the southern quadrant of Africa, this nightmare is real. The word not spoken is AIDS, and here at ground zero of humanity's deadliest cataclysm, the ultimate tragedy is that so many people don't know—or don't want to know—what is happening.

As the HIV virus sweeps mercilessly through these lands—the fiercest trial Africa has yet endured—a few try to address the terrible depredation. The rest of society looks away. Flesh and muscle melt from the bones of the sick in packed hospital wards and lonely bush kraals. Corpses stack up in morgues until those on top crush the identity from the faces underneath. Raw earth mounds scar the landscape, grave after grave without name or number. Bereft children grieve for parents lost in their prime, for siblings scattered to the winds.

The victims don't cry out. Doctors and obituaries do not give the killer its name. Families recoil in shame. Leaders shirk responsibility. The stubborn silence heralds victory for the disease: denial cannot keep the virus at bay.

The developed world is largely silent too. AIDS in Africa has never commanded the full-bore response the West has brought to other, sometimes lesser, travails. We pay sporadic attention, turning on the spotlight when an international conference occurs, then turning it off. Good-hearted donors donate; governments acknowledge that more needs to be done. But think how different the effort would be if what is happening here were happening in the West.

By now you've seen pictures of the sick, the dead, the orphans. You've heard appalling numbers: the number of new infections, the number of the dead, the number who are sick without care, the number walking around already fated to die.

But to comprehend the full horror AIDS has visited on Africa, listen to the woman we have dubbed Laetitia Hambahlane in

Durban or the boy Tsepho Phale in Francistown or the woman who calls herself Thandiwe in Bulawayo or Louis Chikoka, a long-distance trucker. You begin to understand how AIDS has struck Africa—with a biblical virulence that will claim tens of millions of lives—when you hear about shame and stigma and ignorance and poverty and sexual violence and migrant labor and promiscuity and political paralysis and the terrible silence that surrounds all this dying. It is a measure of the silence that some asked us not to print their real names to protect their privacy.

HALF A MILLION AFRICAN CHILDREN WERE INFECTED WITH HIV LAST YEAR

Theirs is a story about what happens when a disease leaps the confines of medicine to invade the body politic, infecting not just individuals but an entire society. As AIDS migrated to man in Africa, it mutated into a complex plague with confounding social, economic and political mechanics that locked together to accelerate the virus' progress. The region's social dynamics colluded to spread the disease and help block effective intervention.

We have come to three countries abutting one another at the bottom of Africa—Botswana, South Africa, Zimbabwe—the heart of the heart of the epidemic. For nearly a decade, these nations suffered a hidden invasion of infection that concealed the dimension of the coming calamity. Now the omnipresent dying reveals the shocking scale of the devastation.

AIDS in Africa bears little resemblance to the American epidemic, limited to specific high-risk groups and brought under control through intensive education, vigorous political action and expensive drug therapy. Here the disease has bred a Darwinian perversion. Society's fittest, not its frailest, are the ones who die—adults spirited away, leaving the old and the children behind. You cannot define risk groups: everyone who is sexually active is at risk. Babies too, unwittingly infected by mothers. Barely a single family remains untouched. Most do not know how or when they caught the virus, many never know they have it, many who do know don't tell anyone as they lie dying. Africa can provide no treatment for those with AIDS.

They will all die, of tuberculosis, pneumonia, meningitis, diarrhea, whatever overcomes their ruined immune systems first. And the statistics, grim as they are, may be too low. There is no broad-scale AIDS testing: infection rates are calculated mainly from the presence of HIV in pregnant women. Death certificates in these countries do not record AIDS as the cause. "Whatever stats we have are not reliable," warns Mary Crewe of the University of Pretoria's Center for the Study of AIDS. "Everybody's guessing."

THE TB PATIENT

CASE NO. 309 IN THE TUGELA FERRY HOME-CARE PROGRAM shivers violently on the wooden planks someone has knocked into a bed, a frayed blanket pulled right up to his nose. He has the flushed skin, overbright eyes and careful breathing of the tubercular. He is alone, and it is chilly within the crumbling mud

walls of his hut at Msinga Top, a windswept outcrop high above the Tugela River in South Africa's KwaZulu-Natal province. The spectacular view of hills and veld would gladden a well man, but the 22-year-old we will call Fundisi Khumalo, though he does not know it, has AIDS, and his eyes seem to focus inward on his simple fear.

Before he can speak, his throat clutches in gasping spasms. Sharp pains rack his chest; his breath comes in shallow gasps. The vomiting is better today. But constipation has doubled up his knees, and he is too weak to go outside to relieve himself. He can't remember when he last ate. He can't remember how long he's been sick—"a long time, maybe since six months ago." Khumalo knows he has TB, and he believes it is just TB. "I am only thinking of that," he answers when we ask why he is so ill.

But the fear never leaves his eyes. He worked in a hair salon in Johannesburg, lived in a men's hostel in one of the cheap townships, had "a few" girlfriends. He knew other young men in the hostel who were on-and-off sick. When they fell too ill to work anymore, like him, they straggled home to rural villages like Msinga Top. But where Khumalo would not go is the hospital. "Why?" he says. "You are sick there, you die there."

"He's right, you know," says Dr. Tony Moll, who has driven us up the dirt track from the 350-bed hospital he heads in Tugela Ferry. "We have no medicines for AIDS. So many hospitals tell them, 'You've got AIDS. We can't help you. Go home and die.'" No one wants to be tested either, he adds, unless treatment is available. "If the choice is to know and get nothing," he says, "they don't want to know."

Here and in scattered homesteads all over rural Africa, the dying people say the sickness afflicting their families and neighbors is just the familiar consequence of their eternal poverty. Or it is the work of witchcraft. You have done something bad and have been bewitched. Your neighbor's jealousy has invaded you. You have not appeased the spirits of your ancestors, and they have cursed you. Some in South Africa believe the disease was introduced by the white population as a way to control black Africans after the end of apartheid.

Ignorance about AIDS remains profound. But because of the funerals, southern Africans can't help seeing that something more systematic and sinister lurks out there. Every Saturday and often Sundays too, neighbors trudge to the cemeteries for costly burial rites for the young and the middle-aged who are suddenly dying so much faster than the old. Families say it was pneumonia, TB, malaria that killed their son, their wife, their baby. "But you starting to hear the truth," says Durban home-care volunteer Busi Magwazi. "In the church, in the graveyard, they saying, 'Yes, she died of AIDS.' Oh, people talking about it even if the families don't admit it." Ignorance is the crucial reason the epidemic has run out of control. Surveys say many Africans here are becoming aware there is a sexually transmitted disease called AIDS that is incurable. But they don't think the risk applies to them. And their vague knowledge does not translate into changes in their sexual behavior. It's easy to see why so many don't yet sense the danger when few talk openly about the disease. And Africans are beset by so plentiful a roster of perils—famine, war, the violence of desperation or ethnic hatred, the regular illnesses of poverty, the dangers inside mines or on the roads—that the delayed risk of AIDS ranks low.

A CONTINENT IN PERIL

17 million Africans have died since the AIDS epidemic began in the late 1970s, more than 3.7 million of them children. An additional 12 million children have been orphaned by AIDS. An estimated 8.8% of adults in Africa are infected with HIV/AIDS, and in the following seven countries, at least 1 adult in 5 is living with HIV

1. Botswana

Though it has the highest per capita GDP, it also has the highest estimated adult infection rate—**36%**. 24,000 die each year. 66,000 children have lost their mother or both parents to the disease.

2. Swaziland

More than **25%** of adults have HIV/AIDS in this small country. 12,000 children have been orphaned, and 7,100 adults and children die each year.

3. Zimbabwe

One-quarter of the adult population is infected here. 160,000 adults and children died in 1999, and 900,000 children have been orphaned. Because of AIDS, life expectancy is 43.

4. Lesotho

24% of the adults are infected with HIV/AIDS. 35,000 children have been orphaned, and 16,000 adults and children die each year.

5. Zambia

20% of the adult population is infected, 1 in 4 adults in the cities. 650,000 children have been orphaned, and 99,000 Zambians died in 1999.

6. South Africa

This country has the largest number of people living with HIV/AIDS, about **20%** of its adult population, up from 13% in 1997. 420,000 children have been orphaned, and 250,000 people die each year from the disease.

7. Namibia

19.5% of the adult population is living with HIV. 57% of the infected are women. 67,000 children are AIDS orphans, and 18,000 adults and children die each year.

Source: UNAIDS

THE OUTCAST

TO ACKNOWLEDGE AIDS IN YOURSELF IS TO BE BRANDED AS monstrous. Laetitia Hambahlane (not her real name) is 51 and sick with AIDS. So is her brother. She admits it; he doesn't. In her mother's broken-down house in the mean streets of Umlazi township, though, Laetitia's mother hovers over her son, nursing him, protecting him, resolutely denying he has anything but TB, though his sister claims the sure symptoms of AIDS mark him. Laetitia is the outcast, first from her family, then from her society.

For years Laetitia worked as a domestic servant in Durban and dutifully sent all her wages home to her mother. She fell in love a number of times and bore four children. "I loved that last man," she recalls. "After he left, I had no one, no sex." That was 1992, but Laetitia already had HIV.

She fell sick in 1996, and her employers sent her to a private doctor who couldn't diagnose an illness. He tested her blood and found she was HIV positive. "I wish I'd died right then," she says, as tears spill down her sunken cheeks. "I asked the doctor, 'Have you got medicine?' He said no. I said, 'Can't you keep me alive?' " The doctor could do nothing and sent her away. "I couldn't face the word," she says. "I couldn't sleep at night. I sat on my bed, thinking, praying. I did not see anyone day or night. I ask God, Why?"

Laetitia's employers fired her without asking her exact diagnosis. For weeks she could not muster the courage to tell anyone. Then she told her children, and they were ashamed and frightened. Then, harder still, she told her mother. Her mother raged about the loss of money if Laetitia could not work again. She was so angry she ordered Laetitia out of the house. When her daughter wouldn't leave, the mother threatened to sell the house to get rid of her daughter. Then she walled off her daughter's room with plywood partitions, leaving the daughter a pariah, alone in a cramped, dark space without windows and only a flimsy door opening into the alley. Laetitia must earn the pennies to feed herself and her children by peddling beer, cigarettes and candy from a shopping cart in her room, when people are brave enough to stop by her door. "Sometimes they buy, sometimes not," she says. "That is how I'm surviving."

Her mother will not talk to her. "If you are not even accepted by your own family," says Magwazi, the volunteer home-care giver from Durban's Sinoziso project who visits Laetitia, "then others will not accept you." When Laetitia ventures outdoors, neighbors snub her, tough boys snatch her purse, children taunt her. Her own kids are tired of the sickness and don't like to help her anymore. "When I can't get up, they don't bring me food," she laments. One day local youths barged into her room, cursed her as a witch and a whore and beat her. When she told the police, the youths returned, threatening to burn down the house.

But it is her mother's rejection that wounds Laetitia most. "She is hiding it about my brother," she cries. "Why will she do nothing for me?" Her hands pick restlessly at the quilt covering her paper-thin frame. "I know my mother will not bury me properly. I know she will not take care of my kids when I am gone."

Jabulani Syabusi would use his real name, but he needs to protect his brother. He teaches school in a red, dusty district of KwaZulu-Natal. People here know the disease is all around them, but no one speaks of it. He eyes the scattered huts that make up his little settlement on an arid bluff. "We can count 20 who died just here as far as we can see. I personally don't remember any family that told it was AIDS," he says. "They hide it if they do know."

Syabusi's own family is no different. His younger brother is also a teacher who has just come home from Durban too sick to work anymore. He says he has tuberculosis, but after six months the tablets he is taking have done nothing to cure him. Syabusi's wife Nomsange, a nurse, is concerned that her 36-year-old brother-in-law may have something worse. Syabusi finally asked the doctor tending his brother what is wrong. The doctor said the information is confidential and will not tell him. Neither will his brother. "My brother is not brave enough to tell me," says Syabusi, as he stares sadly toward the house next door, where his only sibling lies ill. "And I am not brave enough to ask him."

Kennedy Fugewane, a cheerful, elderly volunteer counselor, sits in an empty U.S.-funded clinic that offers fast, pinprick blood tests in Francistown, Botswana, pondering how to break through the silence. This city suffers one of the world's highest infection rates, but people deny the disease because HIV is linked with sex. "We don't reveal anything," he says. "But people are so stigmatized even if they walk in the door." Africans feel they must keep private anything to do with sex. "If a man comes here, people will say he is running around," says Fugewane, though he acknowledges that men never do come. "If a woman comes, people will say she is loose. If anyone says they got HIV, they will be despised."

Pretoria University's Mary Crewe says, "It is presumed if you get AIDS, you have done something wrong." HIV labels you as living an immoral life. Embarrassment about sexuality looms more important than future health risks. "We have no language to talk candidly about sex," she says, "so we have no civil language to talk about AIDS." Volunteers like Fugewane try to reach out with flyers, workshops, youth meetings and free condoms, but they are frustrated by a culture that values its dignity over saving lives. "People here don't have the courage to come forward and say, 'Let me know my HIV status,'" he sighs, much less the courage to do something about it. "Maybe one day…"

Doctors bow to social pressure and legal strictures not to record AIDS on death certificates. "I write TB or meningitis or diarrhea but never AIDS," says South Africa's Dr. Moll. "It's a public document, and families would hate it if anyone knew." Several years ago, doctors were barred even from recording compromised immunity or HIV status on a medical file; now

they can record the results of blood tests for AIDS on patient charts to protect other health workers. Doctors like Moll have long agitated to apply the same openness to death certificates.

THE TRUCK DRIVER

HERE, MEN HAVE TO MIGRATE TO WORK, INSIDE THEIR COUNtries or across borders. All that mobility sows HIV far and wide, as Louis Chikoka is the first to recognize. He regularly drives the highway that is Botswana's economic lifeline and its curse. The road runs for 350 miles through desolate bush that is the Texas-size country's sole strip of habitable land, home to a large majority of its 1.5 million people. It once brought prospectors to Botswana's rich diamond reefs. Now it's the link for transcontinental truckers like Chikoka who haul goods from South Africa to markets in the continent's center. And now the road brings AIDS.

Chikoka brakes his dusty, diesel-belching Kabwe Transport 18-wheeler to a stop at the dark roadside rest on the edge of Francistown, where the international trade routes converge and at least 43% of adults are HIV-positive. He is a cheerful man even after 12 hard hours behind the wheel freighting rice from Durban. He's been on the road for two weeks and will reach his destination in Congo next Thursday. At 39, he is married, the father of three and a long-haul trucker for 12 years. He's used to it.

Lighting up a cigarette, the jaunty driver is unusually loquacious about sex as he eyes the dim figures circling the rest stop. Chikoka has parked here for a quickie. See that one over there, he points with his cigarette. "Those local ones we call bitches. They always waiting here for short service." Short service? "It's according to how long it takes you to ejaculate," he explains. "We go to the 'bush bedroom' over there [waving at a clump of trees 100 yds. away] or sometimes in the truck. Short service, that costs you 20 rands [$2.84]. They know we drivers always got money."

Chikoka nods his head toward another woman sitting beside a stack of cardboard cartons. "We like better to go to them," he says. They are the "businesswomen," smugglers with gray-market cases of fruit and toilet paper and toys that they need to transport somewhere up the road. "They come to us, and we negotiate privately about carrying their goods." It's a no-cash deal, he says. "They pay their bodies to us." Chikoka shrugs at a suggestion that the practice may be unhealthy. "I been away two weeks, madam. I'm human. I'm a man. I have to have sex."

What he likes best is dry sex. In parts of sub-Saharan Africa, to please men, women sit in basins of bleach or saltwater or stuff astringent herbs, tobacco or fertilizer inside their vagina. The tissue of the lining swells up and natural lubricants dry out. The resulting dry sex is painful and dangerous for women. The drying agents suppress natural bacteria, and friction easily lacerates the tender walls of the vagina. Dry sex increases the risk of HIV infection for women, already two times as likely as men to contract the virus from a single encounter. The women, adds

Chikoka, can charge more for dry sex, 50 or 60 rands ($6.46 to $7.75), enough to pay a child's school fees or to eat for a week.

UNVANQUISHED

A Fighter in a Land of Orphans

Silence and the ignorance it promotes have fed the AIDS epidemic in Africa perhaps more than any other factors. In Malawi, where until the end of dictator Hastings Banda's rule in 1994 women were barred from wearing short skirts and men could be jailed for having long hair, public discussion of AIDS was forbidden. According to the government, AIDS didn't exist inside Malawi. Catherine Phiri, 38, knew otherwise. She tested positive in 1990, after her husband had died of the disease. Forced to quit her job as a nurse when colleagues began to gossip, she sought refuge with relatives in the capital, Lilongwe. But they shunned her and eventually forced her to move, this time to Salima on beautiful Lake Malawi. "Even here people gossiped," says Phiri, who's brave, open face is fringed by a head of closely cropped graying hair.

Determined to educate her countrymen, Phiri set up a group that offers counseling, helps place orphans and takes blood that can then be tested in the local hospital. "The community began to see the problem, but it was very difficult to communicate to the government. They didn't want to know.

They do now. According to a lawmaker, AIDS has killed dozens of members of Parliament in the past decade. And Malawi's government has begun to move. President Bakili Muluzi incorporates AIDS education into every public rally. In 1999 he launched a five-year plan to fight the disease, and last July he ordered a crackdown on prostitution (though the government is now thinking of legalizing it). At the least, his awareness campaign appears to be working: 90% of Malawians know about the dangers of AIDS. But that knowledge comes too late for the estimated 8% of HIV-positive citizens—800,000 people in 1999—or the 276,000 children under 15 orphaned by the disease.

Last October, Phiri picked up an award for her efforts from the U.N. But, she says, "I still have people who look at me like trash…" Her voice trails off. "Sometimes when I go to sleep I fear for the future of my children. But I will not run away now. Talking about it: that's what's brave."

—By Simon Robinson/Salima

Chikoka knows his predilection for commercial sex spreads AIDS; he knows his promiscuity could carry the disease home to his wife; he knows people die if they get it. "Yes, HIV is terrible, madam," he says as he crooks a finger toward the businesswoman whose favors he will enjoy that night. "But, madam, sex is natural. Sex is not like beer or smoking. You can stop them. But unless you castrate the men, you can't stop sex—and then we all die anyway."

Millions of men share Chikoka's sexually active lifestyle, fostered by the region's dependence on migrant labor. Men desperate to earn a few dollars leave their women at hardscrabble rural homesteads to go where the work is: the mines, the cities, the road. They're housed together in isolated males-only hostels but have easy access to prostitutes or a "town wife" with whom they soon pick up a second family and an ordinary STD and HIV. Then they go home to wives and girlfriends a few times a year, carrying the virus they do not know they have. The pattern is so dominant that rates of infection in many rural areas across the southern cone match urban numbers.

IN SOME AFRICAN COUNTRIES, THE INFECTION RATE OF TEEN GIRLS IS FOUR TIMES THAT OF BOYS

If HIV zeros in disproportionately on poor migrants, it does not skip over the educated or the well paid. Soldiers, doctors, policemen, teachers, district administrators are also routinely separated from families by a civil-service system that sends them alone to remote rural posts, where they have money and women have no men. A regular paycheck procures more access to extramarital sex. Result: the vital professions are being devastated.

Schoolmaster Syabusi is afraid there will soon be no more teachers in his rural zone. He has just come home from a memorial for six colleagues who died over the past few months, though no one spoke the word AIDS at the service. "The rate here—they're so many," he says, shaking his head. "They keep on passing it at school." Teachers in southern Africa have one of the highest group infection rates, but they hide their status until the telltale symptoms find them out.

Before then, the men—teachers are mostly men here—can take their pick of sexual partners. Plenty of women in bush villages need extra cash, often to pay school fees, and female students know they can profit from a teacher's favor. So the schoolmasters buy a bit of sex with lonely wives and trade a bit of sex with willing pupils for A's. Some students consider it an honor to sleep with the teacher, a badge of superiority. The girls brag about it to their peers, preening in their ability to snag an older man. "The teachers are the worst," says Jabulani Siwela, an AIDS worker in Zimbabwe who saw frequent teacher-student sex in his Bulawayo high school. They see a girl they like; they ask her to stay after class; they have a nice time. "It's dead easy," he says. "These are men who know better, but they still do it all the time."

THE PROSTITUTE

THE WORKINGWOMAN WE MEET DIRECTS OUR CAR TO A reedy field fringing the gritty eastern townships of Bulawayo, Zimbabwe. She doesn't want neighbors to see her being interviewed. She is afraid her family will find out she is a prostitute, so we will call her Thandiwe. She looked quite prim and proper in her green calf-length dress as she waited for johns outside 109 Tongogaro Street in the center of downtown. So, for that matter, do the dozens of other women cruising the city's dim street corners: not a mini or bustier or bared navel in sight. Zimbabwe is in many ways a prim and proper society that frowns on commercial sex work and the public display of too much skin.

FINANCIAL AID

A Lending Tree

Getting ahead in Africa is tough. Banks lend money only to the middle class and the wealthy. Poor Africans—meaning most Africans—stay poor. It's even harder if you're sick. Without savings to fall back on, many HIV-positive parents pull their kids out of school. They can't afford the fees and end up selling their few possessions to feed the family. When they die, their kids are left with nothing.

Though not directly targeted at people with AIDS, microcredit schemes go some way toward fixing that problem. The schemes work like minibanks, lending small amounts—often as little as $100—to traders or farmers. Because they lack the infrastructure of banks and don't charge fees, most charge an interest rate of as much as 1% a week and repayment rates of over 99%—much better than that for banks in Africa, or in most places.

Many microcredit schemes encourage clients to set aside some of the extra income generated by the loan as savings. This can be used for medical bills or to pay school fees if the parents get sick. "Without the loans I would have had to look for another way to make money," says Florence Muriungi, 40, who sings in a Kampala jazz band and whose husband died of AIDS four years ago. Muriungi, who cares for eight children—five of her own and three her sister left when she too died of AIDS—uses the money to pay school fees in advance and fix her band's equipment. Her singing generates enough money for her to repay the loans and save a bit.

Seventeen of the 21 women at a weekly meeting of regular borrowers in Uganda care for AIDS orphans. Five are AIDS widows. "I used to buy just one or two bunches of bananas to sell. Now I buy 40, 50, 60," says Elizabeth Baluka, 47, the group's secretary. "Every week I put aside a little bit of money to help my children slowly by slowly."

—By Simon Robinson/Kampala

That doesn't stop Thandiwe from earning a better living turning tricks than she ever could doing honest work. Desperate for a job, she slipped illegally into South Africa in 1992. She cleaned floors in a Johannesburg restaurant, where she met a cook from back home who was also illegal. They had two daughters, and they got married; he was gunned down one night at work.

She brought his body home for burial and was sent to her in-laws to be "cleansed." This common practice gives a dead husband's brother the right, even the duty, to sleep with the widow. Thandiwe tested negative for HIV in 1998, but if she were positive, the ritual cleansing would have served only to pass on the disease. Then her in-laws wanted to keep her two daughters because their own children had died, and marry her off to an old uncle who lived far out in the bush. She fled.

Alone, Thandiwe grew desperate. "I couldn't let my babies starve." One day she met a friend from school. "She told me she was a sex worker. She said, 'Why you suffer? Let's go to a place where we can get quick bucks.'" Thandiwe hangs her head. "I went. I was afraid. But now I go every night."

She goes to Tongogaro Street, where the rich clients are, tucking a few condoms in her handbag every evening as the sun sets and returning home strictly by 10 so that she won't have to service a taxi-van driver to get a ride back. Thandiwe tells her family she works an evening shift, just not at what. "I get 200 zim [$5] for sex," she says, more for special services. She uses two condoms per client, sometimes three. "If they say no, I say no." But then sometimes resentful johns hit her. It's pay-and-go until she has pocketed 1,000 or 1,500 Zimbabwe dollars and can go home—with more cash than her impoverished neighbors ever see in their roughneck shantytown, flush enough to buy a TV and fleece jammies for her girls and meat for their supper.

"I am ashamed," she murmurs. She has stopped going to church. "Every day I ask myself, 'When will I stop this business?' The answer is, 'If I could get a job'..." Her voice trails off hopelessly. "At the present moment, I have no option, no other option." As trucker Chikoka bluntly puts it, "They give sex to eat. They got no man; they got no work; but they got kids, and they got to eat." Two of Thandiwe's friends in the sex trade are dying of AIDS, but what can she do? "I just hope I won't get it."

In fact, casual sex of every kind is commonplace here. Prostitutes are just the ones who admit they do it for cash. Everywhere there's premarital sex, sex as recreation. Obligatory sex and its abusive counterpart, coercive sex. Transactional sex: sex as a gift, sugar-daddy sex. Extramarital sex, second families, multiple partners. The nature of AIDS is to feast on promiscuity.

79% OF THOSE WHO DIED OF AIDS LAST YEAR WERE AFRICAN

Rare is the man who even knows his HIV status: males widely refuse testing even when they fall ill. And many men who suspect they are HIV positive embrace a flawed logic: if I'm already infected, I can sleep around because I can't get it again. But women are the ones who progress to full-blown AIDS first and die fastest, and the underlying cause is not just sex but power. Wives and girlfriends and even prostitutes in this part of the world can't easily say no to sex on a man's terms. It matters little what comes into play, whether it is culture or tradition or the pathology of violence or issues of male identity or the sub-servient status of women.

Beneath a translucent scalp, the plates of Gertrude Dhlamini's cranium etch a geography of pain. Her illness is obvious in the thin, stretched skin under which veins throb with the shingles that have blinded her left eye and scarred that side of her face. At 39, she looks 70. The agonizing thrush, a kind of fungus, that paralyzed her throat has ebbed enough to enable her to swallow a spoon or two of warm gruel, but most of the nourishment flows away in constant diarrhea. She struggles to keep her hand from scratching restlessly at the scaly rash flushing her other cheek. She is not ashamed to proclaim her illness to the world. "It must be told," she says.

Gertrude is thrice rejected. At 19 she bore a son to a boyfriend who soon left her, taking away the child. A second boyfriend got her pregnant in 1994 but disappeared in anger when their daughter was born sickly with HIV. A doctor told Gertrude it was her fault, so she blamed herself that little Noluthando was never well in the two years she survived. Gertrude never told the doctor the baby's father had slept with other women. "I was afraid to," she says, "though I sincerely believe he gave the sickness to me." Now, she says, "I have rent him from my heart. And I will never have another man in my life."

Gertrude begged her relatives to take her in, but when she revealed the name of her illness, they berated her. They made her the household drudge, telling her never to touch their food or their cooking pots. They gave her a bowl and a spoon strictly for her own use. After a few months, they threw her out.

Gertrude sits upright on a donated bed in a cardboard shack in a rough Durban township that is now the compass of her world. Perhaps 10 ft. square, the little windowless room contains a bed, one sheet and blanket, a change of clothes and a tiny cooking ring, but she has no money for paraffin to heat the food that a home-care worker brings. She must fetch water and use a toilet down the hill. "Everything I have," she says, "is a gift." Now the school that owns the land under her hut wants to turn it into a playground and she worries about where she will go. Gertrude rubs and rubs at her raw cheek. "I pray and pray to God," she says, "not to take my soul while I am alone in this room."

Women like Gertrude were brought up to be subservient to men. Especially in matters of sex, the man is always in charge. Women feel powerless to change sexual behavior. Even when a woman wants to protect herself, she usually can't: it is not uncommon for men to beat partners who refuse intercourse or request a condom. "Real men" don't use them, so women who want their partners to must fight deeply ingrained taboos. Talk to him about donning a rubber sheath and be prepared for accusations, abuse or abandonment.

A nurse in Durban, coming home from an AIDS training class, suggested that her mate should put on a condom, as a kind of homework exercise. He grabbed a pot and banged loudly on it with a knife, calling all the neighbors into his house. He pointed the knife at his wife and demanded: "Where was she between 4 p.m. and now? Why is she suddenly suggesting this? What has changed after 20 years that she wants a condom?"

Schoolteacher Syabusi is an educated man, fully cognizant of the AIDS threat. Yet even he bristles when asked if he uses a condom. "Humph," he says with a fine snort. "That question is nonnegotiable." So despite extensive distribution of free condoms, they often go unused. Astonishing myths have sprung up. If you don one, your erection can't grow. Free condoms must be too cheap to be safe: they have been stored too long, kept too hot, kept too cold. Condoms fill up with germs, so they spread AIDS. Condoms from overseas bring the disease with them. Foreign governments that donate condoms put holes in them so that Africans will die. Education programs find it hard to compete with the power of the grapevine.

THE CHILD IN NO. 17

IN CRIB NO. 17 OF THE SPARTAN BUT CROWDED CHILDREN'S ward at the Church of Scotland Hospital in KwaZulu-Natal, a tiny, staring child lies dying. She is three and has hardly known a day of good health. Now her skin wrinkles around her body like an oversize suit, and her twig-size bones can barely hold her vertical as nurses search for a vein to take blood. In the frail arms hooked up to transfusion tubes, her veins have collapsed. The nurses palpate a threadlike vessel on the child's forehead. She mews like a wounded animal as one tightens a rubber band around her head to raise the vein. Tears pour unnoticed from her mother's eyes as she watches the needle tap-tap at her daughter's temple. Each time the whimpering child lifts a wan hand to brush away the pain, her mother gently lowers it. Drop by drop, the nurses manage to collect 1 cc of blood in five minutes.

The child in crib No. 17 has had TB, oral thrush, chronic diarrhea, malnutrition, severe vomiting. The vial of blood reveals her real ailment, AIDS, but the disease is not listed on her chart, and her mother says she has no idea why her child is so ill. She breast-fed her for two years, but once the little girl was weaned, she could not keep solid food down. For a long time, her mother thought something was wrong with the food. Now the child is afflicted with so many symptoms that her mother had to bring her to the hospital, from which sick babies rarely return.

VIRGINITY TESTING IS BACK The practice of virginity testing used to be part of traditional Zulu rites. It is regaining popularity among anxious mothers who believe that if their daughters remain virgins, they won't get AIDS.

She hopes, she prays her child will get better, and like all the mothers who stay with their children at the hospital, she tends her lovingly, constantly changing filthy diapers, smoothing sheets, pressing a little nourishment between listless lips, trying to tease a smile from the vacant, staring face. Her husband works in Johannesburg, where he lives in a men's squatter camp. He comes home twice a year. She is 25. She has heard of

AIDS but does not know it is transmitted by sex, does not know if she or her husband has it. She is afraid this child will die soon, and she is afraid to have more babies. But she is afraid too to raise the subject with her husband. "He would not agree to that," she says shyly. "He would never agree to have no more babies."

Dr. Annick DeBaets, 32, is a volunteer from Belgium. In the two years she has spent here in Tugela Ferry, she has learned all about how hard it is to break the cycle of HIV transmission from mother to infant. The door to this 48-cot ward is literally a revolving one: sick babies come in, receive doses of rudimentary antibiotics, vitamins, food; go home for a week or a month; then come back as ill as ever. Most, she says, die in the first or second year. If she could just follow up with really intensive care, believes Dr. DeBaets, many of the wizened infants crowding three to a crib could live longer, healthier lives. "But it's very discouraging. We simply don't have the time, money or facilities for anything but minimal care."

Much has been written about what South African Judge Edwin Cameron, himself HIV positive, calls his country's "grievous ineptitude" in the face of the burgeoning epidemic. Nowhere has that been more evident than in the government's failure to provide drugs that could prevent pregnant women from passing HIV to their babies. The government has said it can't afford the 300-rand-per-dose, 28-dose regimen of AZT that neighboring nations like Botswana dole out, using funds and drugs from foreign donors. The late South African presidential spokesman Parks Mankahlana even suggested publicly that it was not cost effective to save these children when their mothers were already doomed to die: "We don't want a generation of orphans."

Yet these children—70,000 are born HIV positive in South Africa alone every year—could be protected from the disease for about $4 each with another simple, cheap drug called nevirapine. Until last month, the South African government steadfastly refused to license or finance the use of nevirapine despite the manufacturer's promise to donate the drug for five years, claiming that its "toxic" side effects are not yet known. This spring, however, the drug will finally be distributed to leading public hospitals in the country, though only on a limited basis at first.

The mother at crib No. 17 is not concerned with potential side effects. She sits on the floor cradling her daughter, crooning over and over, "Get well, my child, get well." The baby stares back without blinking. "It's sad, so sad, so sad," the mother says. The child died three days later.

The children who are left when parents die only add another complex dimension to Africa's epidemic. At 17, Tsepho Phale has been head of an indigent household of three young boys in the dusty township of Monarch, outside Francistown, for two years. He never met his father, his mother died of AIDS, and the grieving children possess only a raw concrete shell of a house. The doorways have no doors; the window frames no glass. There is not a stick of furniture. The boys sleep on piled-up blankets, their few clothes dangling from nails. In the room that passes for a kitchen, two paraffin burners sit on the dirt floor alongside the month's food: four cabbages, a bag of oranges and one of potatoes, three sacks of flour, some yeast, two jars of oil

and two cartons of milk. Next to a dirty stack of plastic pans lies the mealy meal and rice that will provide their main sustenance for the month. A couple of bars of soap and two rolls of toilet paper also have to last the month. Tsepho has just brought these rations home from the social-service center where the "orphan grants" are doled out.

Tsepho has been robbed of a childhood that was grim even before his mother fell sick. She supported the family by "buying and selling things," he says, but she never earned more than a pittance. When his middle brother was knocked down by a car and left physically and mentally disabled, Tsepho's mother used the insurance money to build this house, so she would have one thing of value to leave her children. As the walls went up, she fell sick. Tsepho had to nurse her, bathe her, attend to her bodily functions, try to feed her. Her one fear as she lay dying was that her rural relatives would try to steal the house. She wrote a letter bequeathing it to her sons and bade Tsepho hide it.

As her body lay on the concrete floor awaiting burial, the relatives argued openly about how they would divide up the profits when they sold her dwelling. Tsepho gave the district commissioner's office the letter, preventing his mother's family from grabbing the house. Fine, said his relations; if you think you're a man, you look after your brothers. They have contributed nothing to the boys' welfare since. "It's as if we don't exist anymore either," says Tsepho. Now he struggles to keep house for the others, doing the cooking, cleaning, laundry and shopping.

The boys look at the future with despair. "It is very bleak," says Tsepho, kicking aimlessly at a bare wall. He had to quit school, has no job, will probably never get one. "I've given up my dreams. I have no hope."

Orphans have traditionally been cared for the African way: relatives absorb the children of the dead into their extended families. Some still try, but communities like Tsepho's are becoming saturated with orphans, and families can't afford to take on another kid, leaving thousands alone.

Now many must fend for themselves, struggling to survive. The trauma of losing parents is compounded by the burden of becoming a breadwinner. Most orphans sink into penury, drop out of school, suffer malnutrition, ostracism, psychic distress. Their makeshift households scramble to live on pitiful handouts—from overstretched relatives, a kind neighbor, a state grant—or they beg and steal in the streets. The orphans' present desperation forecloses a brighter future. "They hardly ever succeed in having a life," says Siphelile Kaseke, 22, a counselor at an AIDS orphans' camp near Bulawayo. Without education, girls fall into prostitution, and older boys migrate illegally to South Africa, leaving the younger ones to go on the streets.

1 IN 4 SOUTH AFRICAN WOMEN AGES 20 TO 29 IS INFECTED WITH HIV

EVERY DAY SPENT IN THIS PART OF AFRICA IS ACUTELY DEPRESSING: there is so little countervailing hope to all the stories of the dead and the doomed. "More than anywhere else in the world, AIDS in Africa was met with apathy," says Suzanne LeClerc-

Madlala, a lecturer at the University of Natal. The consequences of the silence march on: infection soars, stigma hardens, denial hastens death, and the chasm between knowledge and behavior widens. The present disaster could be dwarfed by the woes that loom if Africa's epidemic rages on. The human losses could wreck the region's frail economies, break down civil societies and incite political instability.

In the face of that, every day good people are doing good things. Like Dr. Moll, who uses his after-job time and his own fund raising to run an extensive volunteer home-care program in KwaZulu-Natal. And Busi Magwazi, who, along with dozens of others, tends the sick for nothing in the Durban-based Sinoziso project. And Patricia Bakwinya, who started her Shining Stars orphan-care program in Francistown with her own zeal and no money, to help youngsters like Tsepho Phale. And countless individuals who give their time and devotion to ease southern Africa's plight.

But these efforts can help only thousands; they cannot turn the tide. The region is caught in a double bind. Without treatment, those with HIV will sicken and die; without prevention, the spread of infection cannot be checked. Southern Africa has no other means available to break the vicious cycle, except to change everyone's sexual behavior—and that isn't happening.

The essential missing ingredient is leadership. Neither the countries of the region nor those of the wealthy world have been able or willing to provide it.

South Africa, comparatively well off, comparatively well educated, has blundered tragically for years. AIDS invaded just when apartheid ended, and a government absorbed in massive transition relegated the disease to a back page. An attempt at a national education campaign wasted millions on a farcical musical. The premature release of a local wonder drug ended in scandal when the drug turned out to be made of industrial solvent. Those fiascoes left the government skittish about embracing expensive programs, inspiring a 1998 decision not to provide AZT to HIV-positive pregnant women. Zimbabwe too suffers savagely from feckless leadership. Even in Botswana, where the will to act is gathering strength, the resources to follow through have to come from foreign hands.

AIDS' grip here is so pervasive and so complex that all societies—theirs and ours—must rally round to break it. These countries are too poor to doctor themselves. The drugs that could begin to break the cycle will not be available here until global pharmaceutical companies find ways to provide them inexpensively. The health-care systems required to prescribe and monitor complicated triple-cocktail regimens won't exist unless rich countries help foot the bill. If there is ever to be a vaccine, the West will have to finance its discovery and provide it to the poor. The cure for this epidemic is not national but international.

The deep silence that makes African leaders and societies want to deny the problem, the corruption and incompetence that render them helpless is something the West cannot fix. But the fact that they are poor is not. The wealthy world must help with its zeal and its cash if southern Africa is ever to be freed of the AIDS plague.

A UGANDAN TALE

Not Afraid to Speak Out

Major Rubaramira Ruranga knows something about fighting. During Idi Amin's reign of terror in Uganda in the 1970s, Ruranga worked as a spy for rebels fighting the dictator. After Amin's ouster, the military man studied political intelligence in Cuba before returning to find a new dictator at the helm and a blood war raging. Hoping for change, Ruranga supplied his old rebel friends with more secrets, this time from within the President's office. When he was discovered, he fled to the bush to "fight the struggle with guns."

The turmoil in Uganda was fueling the spread of another enemy—AIDS. Like many rebel soldiers, Ruranga was on the move constantly to avoid detection. "You never see your wife, and so you get to a new place and meet someone else," he says. "I had sex without protection with a few women." Doctors found he was HIV positive in 1989. "They told me I would die in tow to three years, so I started preparing for when I was away. I told my kids, my wife. Worked on finishing the house for them. I gave up hope." But as he learned about AIDS, his attitude changed. After talking to American and European AIDS activists—some had lived with the disease for 15 years or more—"I realized I was not going to die in a few years. I was reborn, determined to live."

He began fighting again. After announcing his HIV status at a rally on World AIDS Day in 1993—an extraordinarily brave act in Africa, where few activists, let alone army officers, ever admit to having HIV—he set up a network for those living with HIV/AIDS in Uganda, "so that people had somewhere to go to talk to friends." And while Uganda has done more to slow the spread of AIDS than any other country—in some places the rate of infection has dropped by half—"we can always do better," says Ruranga. "Why are we able to buy guns and bullets to kill people and we are not able to buy drugs to save people?" The fight continues.

—By Simon Robinson/Kampala

From *Time*, February 12, 2001, pp. 36-38, 40-42, 44-45. © 2001 by Time, Inc. Magazine Company. Reprinted by permission.

THE FUTURE OF RELIGION IN AMERICA

Andrew M. Greeley

In this year marking the start of a new millennium, there will be many efforts to peer into the fog of the future and predict what will happen in various areas of American life. The purpose of this article will be to attempt to see in the fog what will happen to religion in the United States.

Let me begin by proposing a number of unexceptionable assertions about contemporary religion in this country as we begin the 21st century, assertions which will provide a frame for my remarks. The data I will cite in this presentation are taken from the National Opinion Research Center's General Social Survey (GSS), an annual, more recently biennial, survey of a probability sample of Americans, funded in part by the National Science Foundation. The GSS began in 1972 and has used full probability samples since 1975. Block quotas were used from 1972 to 1974.

Propositions

1) Belief in a supernatural reality will slowly erode as educational levels rise and the impact of scientific thinking expands. Belief in life after death, for example, can be expected to continue to erode.

2) As the possibility of combining rationality and religion declines, the fundamentalist denominations will continue their steady growth in recruits from the mainline denominations.

3) Hence America's religious "exceptionalism" will diminish as American religious belief and practice converges with that of Europe.

4) The destabilization of the Catholic Church launched by the Second Vatican Council will continue to produce substantial losses for the Catholic Church. While dissent in American Catholicism may not lead to an open break with the Vatican, Catholics will increasingly display little difference from American Protestants.

5) Moreover, denominational differences among mainline Protestants will continue to diminish, so that the non-fundamentalist segment of American religion will be increasingly homogenized, save perhaps for those Catholics who might choose to make alliances with the fundamentalists. Religious boundaries are eroding and men and women—a generation of seekers as one author calls them, now make their own religion out of the primal plasma created by the implosion of denominationalism.

6) The political power of the evangelical right will continue to grow in American politics which will mean pressure on abortion rights and gay and lesbian rights.

7) Immigration from Asia will substantially increase the proportions of Americans who belong to religious denominations which are not part of the Jewish and Christian traditions. Hence, as the *New York Times* has reported, serious study of religion in America must consider these "new religions" because they have changed the map of American religion.

8) Like the fundamentalists, the "New Age" religious movements, unique to our time, will continue to grow as more people opt for non-rational religion in a climate of post-modernity.

9) Religion's impact on life in America will continue to decline as the influences of the churches on their membership will become less important.

Now these propositions may seem to be so obvious that to repeat them is trite, not to say trivial. They sum up the not always expressed assumptions of both the academy (including especially many religion and theology departments) and the higher media. How can anyone challenge at least the general picture they present? Are not these the trends we all know about? The only trouble is that none of the nine propositions are true.

1) Belief in life after death has *increased* over the years of the General Social Survey by some five percentage points. When that increase is spread out over age cohorts from the beginning of the century, there has been a twenty percentage point increase in belief in life after death among American Catholics

and a doubling (to over fifty percent) for American Jews. This totally unexpected increase is not the result of increase in fundamentalism or the rise of the "New Age" religion or changes in any of the other "usual suspects" of demographic variables.

As Michael Hout and I have demonstrated in an article in the *American Sociological Review*, the increase for Catholics is a function of generation in America, as the eastern and southern European immigrant groups of the third and fourth generation "catch up" with the Irish orthodoxy. It would appear that this "catching up" is the result of the fierce resistance of the Catholic Church to (as it saw it) attempts at conversion of Catholic immigrants to the host culture. Those who "caught up" were either members of Catholic organizations (which proliferated in the immigrant parishes) or had attended Catholic schools. Despite the mythology, the religion of the immigrants is less orthodox than that of the third and fourth generation. We found that the increase in belief in the life after death (which is taught in the Mishna by the way) among Jews is harder to explain because even in a sample of almost forty thousand respondents there are not all that many Jews. However, the increase seems to occur especially among those who attend services more often, describe themselves as strongly Jewish, and are either Orthodox or conservatives. These findings are obviously counterintuitive. Belief is supposed to go down. In fact belief in this particular (central) item of faith has increased.

2) The increase in fundamentalists which virtually every author has attributed to dissatisfaction with the modernist tendencies of liberal and mainline Protestant denominations is in fact the result of higher levels of fertility among the fundamentalists. Fertility accounts for approximately 75% of the increase in the mainline proportion of American Protestants. There is very little change across denominational lines between the mainline and the fundamentalists. Mainline religious change is mostly either to no religion or to Catholicism. The net flow from mainline to fundamentalism is +4%, to Catholics +6%, and to no religion +10%. We conclude from these findings that one should not indulge in sweeping generalizations about cultural change until one has taken into account demographic factors.

3) Sweeping generalizations about religion in Europe (particularly from scholars who are in the United Kingdom or The Netherlands) do not stand up to the test of data from other countries. Thus, since the fall of socialism in Eastern Europe there has been a significant increase in religious faith in Hungary, Slovenia, East Germany, and the Soviet Union, particularly in matters of religious faith like belief in God, life after death, heaven, hell, and religious miracles. The argument here is not that there are never any changes in religion. Quite the contrary there are constant changes. However, they are not unidirectionally downward. "What about The Netherlands?", one is asked. "What about Russia?", I respond. In some countries religion seems to decrease and in others to increase. Why that is so is a fascinating question but it cannot be answered in a perspective which insists that all religious change is in the direction of decline.

4) Reports of the death of Catholicism in the United States are premature. Catholics continue to be a quarter of the American population. Moreover since the second birth cohort (the 1910s) approximately 2/3 of every cohort of those raised Cath-

olic choose spouses who were also raised Catholic. The Catholic religious imagination, emphasizing the graciousness of God with its components of community, sacramentality, and hierarchy is still strikingly different from that of Protestants (as I have argued in my book, *Religion as Poetry*) and in the years since the council, the difference has significantly *increased*. Catholics, apparently because of this religious imagination, also have sex more often than do other Americans, even as reported by their spouses who are not Catholic. Indeed, their sex is on the average more playful. For Catholics church attendance and fine arts participation is positive, for Protestants it's negative. I do not contend that Catholics have not changed in the last three decades, but only that they are still Catholic and show no signs of not being Catholic.

Indeed, we who are their leaders, despite our best efforts, have not been able to drive them out. Moreover, while the Vatican Council II may be an easy target to blame for the turbulence in Catholicism (and the 1968 birth control encyclical perhaps a more appropriate target), one must ask whether the educational change in the Catholic population might also account for the freedom many Catholics feel to dissent from some of the Church's sexual teaching. In fact education does, but not respondent's education, spouse's education, or father's education. Mother's education, however, accounts for at least a third of the changes on measures of sexual attitudes across the twenty five years of the General Social Survey. Finally there are more Catholic churches in this country than there were in 1968.

5) Denominational affiliation continues to be important in distinguishing among American Protestants. Only eight of the 40,000 respondents cannot give an answer to Will Herberg's famous question of what their religion is (Protestant, Catholic, Jew, other, or none). While over 20% of GSS respondents were raised in mixed marriages, less than 1% cannot give an answer to the question, "In what denomination were you raised?" 70% of Americans continue to belong to the denomination in which they were raised. Denominational affiliation is an important correlate of political, religious, and cultural attitudes and behaviors not only among the broad divisions reaching from fundamentalism to liberalism, but even among the "moderate" denominations.

In particular, statistically significant differences exist among the two large denominational families, Lutherans and Methodists. The latter for example are more likely than the former to support national policies which would spend more money on education, drugs, and African Americans, to believe that you can expect people to be fair, trustworthy and helpful, and to think the lot of the working man is not declining and it is safe to bring children into the world. Lutherans go to church more often, Methodists are more likely to support school prayer and bible reading. Lutherans are more likely to have been confirmed, Methodists are more likely to say that their church attendance lapsed at one time. Lutherans are more afraid of science breaking down morality, Methodists are more likely to be born again and to like Gospel music. Lutherans are more likely to appreciate oldies Rock, to have visited an art museum, to have attended a classic concert or opera, and to have seen a movie during the past year. Methodists are more likely to think that only a few people can judge art. In questions of national policy, then, Methodists are more likely to tilt to the left in comparison with the Lutherans, and in religious and cultural matters more likely to tilt in a fundamentalist direction. Further analysis will be required to sort out these differences in detail. Yet it certainly seems to be true that differences persist among the five major Protestant denominational families—Baptist, Methodist, Lutheran, Presbyterian, and Episcopalian.

One is tempted to say after writing the previous paragraph that we knew about these differences all along—or at least we did if we associated much with Lutherans and Methodists. But the assumption of contemporary social science (and higher media) that Protestants can be divided between fundamentalist and all others misses much of the fine grained but important differences among denominations. Equally important is the strength of denominationalism.

Some writers (Robert Wuthnow, Clark Roof, and Christian Smith) are busily promoting a post-denominational analysis. The observations in the preceding paragraph contradict them. Churches organize religion, and people seem to like them. They need them for ritual devotions, but they are far from indifferent among the choices available. They cling surprisingly strongly to the denominations of their youth. They bring their children to the church they were raised in. Even after moving to a new city or state, when they are most likely to "shop around' they "choose" the denomination they're familiar with.

6) Although the fundamentalist (or evangelical) denominations have increased, Protestants who believe in the literal interpretation of scripture have declined six percentage points since the question was first asked in 1984. Only 57% of the Southern Baptists (who have been unfairly treated by the elite media which persist in identifying statements of the annual Southern Baptist Convention with the actual beliefs of Southern Baptists) believe in the literal interpretation of the bible, as do only 40% of Southern Baptists under 40 who attend church every week. The Evangelical component of American religion has always been substantial, around 20% of the population. Just as Catholics are different from the rest of us, so the evangelicals are different from the rest of us (and the Catholics and the evangelicals are different from one another). However, most evangelicals are not members of the hard line religious right.

Thus if one combines belief in the literal interpretation of the bible, opposition to abortion, belief that premarital sex is always wrong, and belief that abortion is always wrong, one finds that only about 5% of the American people share the agenda of the religious right (even as that is generously defined), as do only 13% of the Southern Baptists. Moreover the religious right is not even the majority or a large minority of committed Republicans, though somehow they have managed to create the illusion that they are. Most of them are hard core Republicans who would vote for a conservative Republican regardless of their religious convictions. Playing the evangelical card is not a wise strategy for the GOP, though it is one that, Irish Catholic Democrat from Chicago that I am, I hope it follows.

7) The impact of Asian migration on American religion has been greatly exaggerated. While Asian American religion is a fascinating subject for study as Asians adjust to American cul-

ture, it does not follow that the map of American religion has changed as greatly as the *New York Times* (with its usual search for the best of the received wisdom on the subject of religion) contends. In the 1998 General Social Survey only 1.1% of Americans report that they are Hindu, Moslem, Buddhist, or "other Eastern."

8) It is hard to know exactly what "New Age" stands for. However, it is very difficult to find traces of membership in the General Social Survey. The proportion of Americans who say that their religion is "other" has hovered around 3% and that includes, for example, Mormons and Eastern Orthodox. Anyone who knows the history of religion in this country, realizes that in addition to various "Great Awakenings," America is always in a state of religious revival and that many interesting movements begin in our "mess" of religious pluralism. Some survive and grow—the Unitarians, the Disciples, the Mormons, the Adventists, and the Christian Scientists for example—most do not. These "new" religions are fascinating subjects for research, but they do not represent a phenomenon on the American religious scene which is radically new.

9) The last assertion—the decline of the influence of religion on American life—is the last refuge of those who think that religion is not as important as it used to be—a classic expression of the so-called "Golden Age" fallacy. Has not the ability of the churches to control sexual behavior almost vanished? Perhaps it has. However, as ought to be patent, religion still strongly influences the civil rights movement, the pro-life movement, the environmental movement, and the volunteer movement. Indeed church membership and church attendance explain completely the higher rates of volunteerism in the United States in comparison with those of European countries.

Reflections

There surely have been changes in American religion in the last thirty years, and there may even be some trends (belief in the literal interpretation of the bible has gone down, for example, but only among Catholics). However none of the phenomena which the received wisdom knows to be true are in fact true. To paraphrase an Irish member of parliament, "The right honorable conventional wisdom has said much that is true and much that is new. Alas, that which is true is not new and that which is new is not true."

Unless and until American social scientists (and their elite media acolytes) are ready to abandon their conviction that there is an overarching religious trend and that it is downward, we will know very little in a systematic way about the religious phenomena in this country or anywhere else. It will be hard for social scientists to abandon this often vague and deep-seated assumption because there is rarely an occasion to question it—and when someone dares to question it, they are dismissed as unworthy of attention. Moreover there still exists in our profession the belief that there are "social laws" which can account for social change—or at least for religious change. William Sewell, Jr. argues convincingly that the search for such laws is illusory:

Sociology's epic quest for social laws is illusory, whether the search is for timeless truths about all societies, ineluctable trends of more limited historical epochs, or inductively derived laws of certain classes of social phenomena. Social processes are inherently contingent, discontinuous, and open-ended. Big and ponderous social processes are never entirely immune from being transformed by small alterations in volatile and local social processes. "Structures" are constructed by human action, and "societies" or "social formations or social systems" are continually shaped and reshaped by the creativity and stubbornness of their human creators.

I believe that such words as modernization, secularization, globalization, etc., etc., (to say nothing of "post-modernity") are labels under which we subsume a wide variety of contrasting and contrary phenomena which are ill served by being lumped together. They may be useful hooks for undergraduate instruction and dinner party conversation, but when they become reified so that they are taken as dynamisms which actually exist in the outside world they are an excuse for thought, indeed a substitute for thought. One who uses such words as if they were realities with an existence of their own may sound profound but actually reveals himself to be shallow and superficial, someone who, for the sake of a convenient labels, loses all sense of the complex realities of social life.

Sewell argues for "well-honed stories," which are perhaps not all that different from Robert K. Merton's "theories of the middle range." You can't tell a well honed story about religion if you believe that the only story to tell is one of decline—particularly of groups you don't happen to like, such as Catholics. All the findings I have reported above are stories told in response to the current conventional wisdom, whether well-honed is not for me to say. At any rate the story of the increase in belief in life after death described above owes nothing to the overarching theory of religious decline. It owes quite a bit to the perspective of a competitive market place in religion, though that theory hardly predicted the finding. If we were not sufficiently immunized to the social law of the decline of religion, I doubt that we would have even noticed the surprising increase in belief in life after death in this country. After considerable struggle we managed to persuade the editor of the *American Sociological Review* that it was sufficiently well-honed to be published.

Why the social law? The answer is easy, religion is not supposed to survive in an age of science and reason. Voltaire said it. Durkheim said it. Most social scientists today, especially those at the elite institutions of higher learning, say it. Therefore, how can it be wrong? It can, patently, be wrong if the data rarely verify it.

The explanation, I think, is fairly easy. The law is more a norm than a law: Religion should be in decline. Those who say it is not are violating the norm. I recall my astonishment when I presented in seminars the findings from ISSP study of religion in Russia which indicated that one of the great religious revivals in history was going on there. Colleagues with indecent haste leaped to their feet to explain why it wouldn't last, even couldn't last—without any data to support their speculations. One young woman from Harvard explained it as a desire by young Russians to have their weddings in church, as though that accounted for everything without having to ask why such weddings were still important after three-quarters of a century of socialist rule. These young Russians, incidentally, also state their firm intention to raise their children in religion).

The social law of the decline of religion is both a dogma and a norm. It is an iron curtain that one can rarely tear open with a well-honed story which either refutes the law or cheerfully ignores it. We will not have good social science study of religion in this country until the anti-religious norms and biases are abandoned. I don't expect that will happen for a long time. I've often wondered why no one thought of studying the thousand Southern Baptists in the GSS to see how the two top executives in our land could both be devout Southern Baptists and still hold the political and social positions to which they are committed. The answer is that the denomination (ten percent of the American people) is pluralistic like every other large religious group) and that the local clergy and members take their orders from the Convention the way Catholic lower clergy and laity take their orders from the Vatican. If pressed Messrs. Clinton and Gore would finesse the question of the literal, word for word interpretation of the bible, in a way similar to the way that Senators Kennedy and Moynihan would finesse questions about how they can be Catholic and not oppose abortion legislation. However, the false myth about Southern Baptists is part of the larger law of the decline of religion. Hence there is no need to question it.

Why has religion survived when everyone knew that it wouldn't? I believe the answer might go something like this. Men and women still want something in which to believe and to which to belong. They aspire to faith and community. Humans are caught between the two possibilities. Perhaps Macbeth was right when he said that life is a tale told by an idiot full of sound and fury and signifying nothing. Or perhaps Pere Teilhard was right when he said that something is afoot in the universe, something that looks like gestation and birth. Uncertain which to believe, they incline to the more hopeful bet proposed by Blaise Pascal and bet on purpose rather than absurdity because in such a bet there seems nothing to lose. They walk on air, in Seamus Heaney's words, against their better judgment.

So they tend, as they always have, to believe with their fingers crossed. For some this is an agonizing decision, to be renewed perhaps every day. Or others it is a minor matter. For most it is something important but not always all-important. There are those who cannot believe and those who believe more or less, and finally, the God haunted who believe fiercely and are haunted by fierce doubts. As Edward Shils once remarked, as long as humans worry seriously about the meaning of life, there will always be some who choose a religious option. One may dismiss religion as wish fulfillment. It may well be that, though it does not follow that because we wish something to be true (e.g., that our beloved really loves us) it is thereby false. Nonetheless, even if we think religion is nothing more than wish fulfillment, we are not thereby excused from objective social science study of religion.

Such an approach is, I would submit, a more useful model than the patient assumption that if one waits long enough religion will disappear—arguably also a form of wish fulfillment. Finally I will repeat a few predictions for the next thirty years that I have made elsewhere.

1. Religion will not lose its adherents.
2. Nor is religion likely to lose its influence on non-religious dimensions of human life.
3. Religious institutions will no more wither away than did the Marxist state.
4. There will be considerably more sympathetic understanding of the wisdom of other religious traditions and of those who profess such traditions.
5. There will be a further understanding both in theory and in practice of the responsibility of the individual as the ultimate religious and ethical agent in the context of the circumstances in which he finds himself and of his personal relationships with those around him.
6. Denominations will not cease to be characteristic of the Western religious scene.
7. The local congregations will not perish.

Not very exciting predictions, are they? Am I not saying that American religion thirty years from now will be pretty much what it's like today? That's indeed what I'm saying and thus arguing for the well-honed story approach to the study of American religion rather then the "mega-trend" approach.

I should add one note. Those predictions were not made this year. Rather they appeared in a book I called *Religion in the Year 2000* and wrote in 1968, around the time it was announced (*Time* magazine Easter Issue 1968) to one and all that God was dead. It turned out that God was not dead but alive and well and living in Moscow! As the French would say, *plus ça change, plus c'est la même chose!* I don't expect to be around, however, to check on the accuracy of these predictions! Nonetheless, I will be watching from somewhere and laughing.

Andrew Greeley is a Catholic priest and best-selling novelist. He is professor of social science at the University of Chicago and a member of its National Opinion Research Center. Greeley is also a visiting professor at the University of Arizona. Among his books are Faithful Attraction, The Denominational Society, Unsecular Man, Death and Beyond, *and* The Church and the Suburbs.

From *Society*, March/April 2001, pp. 32-37. © 2001 by Transaction Publishers. Reprinted by permission.

UNIT 6

Social Change and the Future

Unit Selections

Key Points to Consider

- What are the advantages of slowing world population growth? How can it be done?

- Why are people concerned about current immigration patterns? Do you think their fears are largely imaginary? Explain your answer.

- What dangers does humankind's overexploitation of the environment create?

- What are some of the major problems that technology is creating?

- How bright is America's future? What are the main threats to it? What are some of its main challenges?

- Would you say that both democracy and capitalism are triumphant today? Explain your answer. What kind of problems can democracy and capitalism cause?

 **Links: www.dushkin.com/online/**
These sites are annotated in the World Wide Web pages.

Gil Gordon Associates
http://www.gilgordon.com

National Immigrant Forum
http://www.immigrationforum.org/index.htm

Terrorism Research Center
http://www.terrorism.com/index.shtml

United Nations Environment Program (UNEP)
http://www.unep.ch

William Davidson Institute
http://www.wdi.bus.umich.edu

Fascination with the future is an enduring theme in literature, art, poetry, and religion. Human beings are anxious to know if tomorrow will be different from today and in what ways it might differ. Coping with change has become a top priority in the lives of many. One result of change is stress. When the future is uncertain and the individual appears to have little control over what happens, stress can be a serious problem. On the other hand, stress can have positive effects on people's lives if they can perceive changes as challenges and opportunities.

Any discussion of the future must begin with a look at the interface of population and the environment. Some scholars are very concerned about the impact of population growth on the environment, and others are confident that technological developments will solve most of the problems. Since the debate is about the future, neither view can be "proved." Nevertheless, it is important to understand the seriousness of the problem. Lester Brown, Gary Gardner, and Brian Halweil discuss 16 impacts of population growth. The way that societies are providing for the present 6 billion people is badly damaging Earth's ecosystems and crowding or overshooting environmental limits. Many changes are needed in the next few decades to achieve sustainability, including stabilizing world population.

Another population issue that worries many Americans is the influx of immigrants who compete for scarce jobs with citizens and increase costs for public services. Paul Glastris summarizes the findings of a National Academy of Sciences/National Research Council report and concludes that immigration has only small impacts on average and net positive benefits in the long run. The report concludes that immigrants do impose substantial costs on large numbers of taxpayers—in the short run. But in the long run, when the bills for the baby boomers' retirement come due, immigrants are likely to prove a tax blessing. The report also notes that while the country as a whole benefits from immigrants, a few states, California in particular, bear a steep financial burden for assimilating them.

The next article discusses current scientific thinking about global warming. The environment is in trouble in many ways from overplowing, overgrazing, overfishing, overtimbering, and species loss to resource depletion, toxic wastes, and water shortages, but the focal issue today is global warming. The predictions are scary. The low estimates of warmer world temperatures would cause considerable trouble, but the high estimates "could be disastrous." Michael D. Lemonick reviews many of the possible impacts and urges that the world take steps now to substantially reduce greenhouse gases to prevent these impacts.

The next subsection in unit 6 addresses the linkage between technological change and society. Both articles in this section raise concerns about the possible negative effects of supposedly beneficial technologies. One big technology story concerns genetic engineering, and one of its important areas of application is in agriculture. The crucial question is whether it produces great agricultural advances or ecological nightmares. Madeleine Nash tells the story of the noble efforts to engineer beta-carotene into rice to make children in developing countries more re-

sistant to diseases. Many lives would be saved or improved, but the haunting question is whether this new technology will have harmful unintended consequences. The next article by Eduardo Goncalves evaluates another sophisticated technology—nuclear power. It can win wars and supply useful electrical energy, but it may have already killed 175 million people. Furthermore, the way scientists and governments have acted regarding nuclear energy shows that they cannot always be trusted to pursue the public good in their decisions regarding new technologies.

The next section focuses on the new crisis of terrorism. The first article in this section describes the most likely means that will be used in the next major terrorist attack and identifies the technical difficulties of using them. It is known that operatives of Osama bin Laden's Al Qaeda network are experimenting with biological agents for terrorist uses. The necessary materials for bioterrorism are surprisingly easy to obtain, although weaponizing them may be a greater hurdle. The last article in this subsection examines the motives behind terrorist acts against the United States. Stanley Hoffmann explores the question "Why Don't They Like Us?" Sociologists always analyze the basis for and the bias in selective perceptions that inflame hatreds between groups, and the study of the current hatreds toward the United States by many peoples of the world and especially the terrorists is now crucial to our future.

The final subsection of the last unit looks at the future in terms of some of the most important trends and how to create a good future out of them. Amitai Etzioni describes the trends toward greater inequality and diversity in the United States and asks whether these trends threaten the integration of American society. Since the 1960s, identity politics have succeeded in reducing past injustices but also "have divided the nation along group lines." Then Etzioni draws on sociological theory to propose ways to build community by reducing inequalities, increasing bonds, and generating stronger value commitments. In the final article, Fareed Zakaria celebrates the triumph of capitalism and democracy but also warns that they can cause some troublesome problems. Their strong points are the creativity and productive energy that they generate. However, "they are also forces of destruction. They destroy old orders, hierarchy, tradition, communities, careers, stability and peace of mind itself... They surge forward, changing everything they encounter." Can the world handle the chaos that they create?

16 Impacts of Population Growth

Ongoing global population growth may be THE most critical issue of today.
Here are 16 ways it affects human prospects.

By Lester R. Brown, Gary Gardner, and Brian Halweil

The world's population has doubled during the last half century, climbing from 2.5 billion in 1950 to 5.9 billion in 1998. This unprecedented surge in population, combined with rising individual consumption, is pushing our claims on the planet beyond its natural limits.

The United Nations projects that human population in 2050 will range between 7.7 billion and 11.2 billion people. We use the United Nation's middle-level projection of 9.4 billion (from *World Population Prospects: The 1996 Revision*) to give an idea of the strain this "most likely" outcome would place on ecosystems and governments in the future and of the urgent need to break from the business-as-usual scenario.

Our study looks at 16 dimensions or effects of population growth in order to gain a better perspective on how future population trends are likely to affect human prospects:

Impacts on Food and Agriculture

1. Grain Production

From 1950 to 1984, growth in the world grain harvest easily exceeded that of population. But since then, the growth in the grain harvest has fallen behind that of population, so per-person output has dropped by 7% (0.5% a year), according to the U.S. Department of Agriculture.

The slower growth in the world grain harvest since 1984 is due to the lack of new land and to slower growth in irrigation and fertilizer use because of the diminishing returns of these inputs.

Now that the frontiers of agricultural settlement have disappeared, future growth in grain production must come almost entirely from raising land productivity. Unfortu-

nately, this is becoming more difficult. The challenge for the world's farmers is to reverse this decline at a time when cropland area per person is shrinking, the amount of irrigation water per person is dropping, and the crop yield response to additional fertilizer use is falling.

2. Cropland

Since mid-century, grain area—which serves as a proxy for cropland in general—has increased by some 19%, but global population has grown by 132%. Population growth can degrade farmland, reducing its productivity or even eliminating it from production. As grain area per person falls, more and more nations risk losing the capacity to feed themselves.

The trend is illustrated starkly in the world's four fastest-growing

U.S. AID

Shanty town life in Bangladesh. Countries that fail to reduce population growth will endure the breakdown of their economic and social systems, according to the authors.

large countries. Having already seen per capita grain area shrink by 40%–50% between 1960 and 1998, Pakistan, Nigeria, Ethiopia, and Iran can expect a further 60%–70% loss by 2050—a conservative projection that assumes no further losses of agricultural land. The result will be four countries with a combined population of more than 1 billion whose grain area per person will be only 300–600 square meters—less than a quarter of the area in 1950.

3. Fresh Water

Spreading water scarcity may be the most underrated resource issue in the world today. Wherever population is growing, the supply of fresh water per person is declining.

Evidence of water stress can be seen as rivers are drained dry and water tables fall. Rivers such as the Nile, the Yellow, and the Colorado have little water left when they reach the sea. Water tables are now falling on every continent, including in major food-producing regions. Aquifers are being depleted in the U.S. southern Great Plains, the North China Plain, and most of India.

The International Water Management Institute projects that a billion people will be living in countries facing absolute water scarcity by 2025. These countries will have to reduce water use in agriculture in order to satisfy residential and industrial water needs. In both China and India, the two countries that together dominate world irrigated agriculture, substantial cutbacks in irrigation water supplies lie ahead.

4. Oceanic Fish Catch

A fivefold growth in the human appetite for seafood since 1950 has pushed the catch of most oceanic fisheries to their sustainable limits or beyond. Marine biologists believe that the oceans cannot sustain an annual catch of much more than 93 million tons, the current take.

As we near the end of the twentieth century, overfishing has become the rule, not the exception. Of the 15 major oceanic fisheries, 11 are in decline. The catch of Atlantic cod—long a dietary mainstay for western Europeans—has fallen by 70% since peaking in 1968. Since 1970, bluefin tuna stocks in the West Atlantic have dropped by 80%.

With the oceans now pushed to their limits, future growth in the demand for seafood can be satisfied only by fish farming. But as the world turns to aquaculture to satisfy its needs, fish begin to compete with livestock and poultry for feedstuffs such as grain, soybean meal, and fish meal.

The next half century is likely to be marked by the disappearance of some species from markets, a decline in the quality of seafood caught, higher prices, and more conflicts among countries over access to fisheries. Each year, the future oceanic catch per person will decline by roughly the amount of population growth, dropping to 9.9 kilograms (22 pounds) per person in 2050, compared with the 1988 peak of 17.2 kilograms (37.8 pounds).

5. Meat Production

When incomes begin to rise in traditional low-income societies, one of the first things people do is diversify their diets, consuming more livestock products.

World meat production since 1950 has increased almost twice as fast as population. Growth in meat

175

©PHOTODISC, INC.

The demand for energy will grow faster than population and create even more pollution as developing countries try to become as affluent as industrialized nations.

production was originally concentrated in western industrial countries and Japan, but over the last two decades it has increased rapidly in East Asia, the Middle East, and Latin America. Beef, pork, and poultry account for the bulk of world consumption.

Of the world grain harvest of 1.87 billion tons in 1998, an estimated 37% will be used to feed livestock and poultry, producing milk and eggs as well as meat, according to the U.S. Department of Agriculture. Grain fed to livestock and poultry is now the principal food reserve in the event of a world food emergency.

Total meat consumption will rise from 211 million tons in 1997 to 513 million tons in 2050, increasing pressures on the supply of grain.

Environment and Resources

6. Natural Recreation Areas

From Buenos Aires to Bangkok, dramatic population growth in the world's major cities—and the sprawl and pollution they bring—threaten natural recreation areas that lie beyond city limits. On every continent, human encroachment has reduced both the size and the quality of natural recreation areas.

In nations where rapid population growth has outstripped the carrying capacity of local resources, protected areas become especially vulnerable. Although in industrial nations these areas are synonymous with camping, hiking, and picnics in the country, in Asia, Africa, and Latin America most national parks, forests, and preserves are inhabited or used for natural resources by local populations.

Migration-driven population growth also endangers natural recreation areas in many industrial nations. Everglades National Park, for example, faces collapse as millions of newcomers move into southern Florida.

Longer waiting lists and higher user fees for fewer secluded spots are likely to be the tip of the iceberg, as population growth threatens to eliminate the diversity of habitats and cultures in addition to the peace and quiet that protected areas currently offer.

7. Forests

Global losses of forest area have marched in step with population growth for much of human history, but an estimated 75% of the loss in global forests has occurred in the twentieth century.

In Latin America, ranching is the single largest cause of deforestation. In addition, overgrazing and overcollection of firewood—which are often a function of growing population—are degrading 14% of the world's remaining large areas of virgin forest.

Deforestation created by the demand for forest products tracks closely with rising per capita consumption in recent decades. Global use of paper and paperboard per person has doubled (or nearly tripled) since 1961.

The loss of forest areas leads to a decline of forest services. These include habitat for wildlife; carbon storage, which is a key to regulating climate; and erosion control, provision of water across rainy and dry seasons, and regulation of rainfall.

8. Biodiversity

We live amid the greatest extinction of plant and animal life since the dinosaurs disappeared 65 million years ago, at the end of the Cretaceous period, with species losses at 100 to 1,000 times the natural rate. The principal cause of species extinction is habitat loss, which tends to accelerate with an increase in a country's population density.

A particularly productive but vulnerable habitat is found in coastal areas, home to 60% of the world's population. Coastal wetlands nurture two-thirds of all commercially caught fish, for example. And coral reefs have the second-highest concentration of biodiversity in the world, after tropical rain forests. But human encroachment and pollution are degrading these areas: Roughly half of the world's salt marshes and mangrove swamps have been eliminated or radically altered, and two-thirds of the world's coral reefs have been degraded, 10% of them "beyond recognition." As coastal migration continues—coastal dwellers could account for 75% of world population within 30 years—the pressures on these productive habitats will likely increase.

9. Climate Change

Over the last half century, carbon emissions from fossil-fuel burning expanded at nearly twice the rate of population, boosting atmospheric concentrations of carbon dioxide, the principal greenhouse gas, by 30% over preindustrial levels.

The 20 Largest Countries Ranked According to Population Size (in millions)

1998 Rank	Country	Population	2050 Country	Population
1	China	1,255	India	1,533
2	India	976	China	1,517
3	United States	274	Pakistan	357
4	Indonesia	207	United States	348
5	Brazil	165	Nigeria	339
6	Pakistan	148	Indonesia	318
7	Russia	147	Brazil	243
8	Japan	126	Bangladesh	218
9	Bangladesh	124	Ethiopia	213
10	Nigeria	122	Iran	170
11	Mexico	96	The Congo	165
12	Germany	82	Mexico	154
13	Vietnam	78	Philippines	131
14	Iran	73	Vietnam	130
15	Philippines	72	Egypt	115
16	Egypt	66	Russia	114
17	Turkey	64	Japan	110
18	Ethiopia	62	Turkey	98
19	Thailand	60	South Africa	91
20	France	59	Tanzania	89

SOURCE: UNITED NATIONS, WORLD POPULATION PROSPECTS: THE 1996 REVISION.

Fossil-fuel use accounts for roughly three-quarters of world carbon emissions. As a result, regional growth in carbon emissions tend to occur where economic activity and related energy use is projected to grow most rapidly. Emissions in China are projected to grow over three times faster than population in the next 50 years due to a booming economy that is heavily reliant on coal and other carbon-rich energy sources.

Emissions from developing countries will nearly quadruple over the next half century, while those from industrial nations will increase by 30%, according to the Intergovernmental Panel on Climate Change and the U.S. Department of Energy. Although annual emissions from industrial countries are currently twice as high as from developing ones, the latter are on target to eclipse the industrial world by 2020.

10. Energy

The global demand for energy grew twice as fast as population over the last 50 years. By 2050, developing countries will be consuming much more energy as their populations increase and become more affluent.

When per capita energy consumption is high, even a low rate of population growth can have significant effects on total energy demand. In the United States, for example, the 75 million people projected to be added to the population by 2050 will boost energy demand to roughly the present energy consumption of Africa and Latin America.

World oil production per person reached a high in 1979 and has since declined by 23%. Estimates of when global oil production will peak range from 2011 to 2025, signaling future price shocks as long as oil remains the world's dominant fuel.

In the next 50 years, the greatest growth in energy demands will come where economic activity is projected to be highest: in Asia, where consumption is expected to

Demographic Fatigue

To assess the likelihood that the U.N. population projections will actually occur, it is useful to bear in mind the concept of the demographic transition, formulated by Princeton demographer Frank Notestein in 1945. Its three stages help to explain widely disparate population-growth rates.

The first stage describes pre-industrial societies: Birthrates and death rates are both high, offsetting each other and leading to little or no population growth. In stage two, countries reach an unsustainable state as they begin to modernize: Death rates fall to low levels while birthrates remain high. In the third state, modernization continues: Birth and death rates are again in balance, but at lower levels, and populations are essentially stable. All countries today are in either stage two or stage three.

One key question now facing the world is whether the 150 or so countries that are still in stage two, with continuing population growth, can make it into stage three by quickly reducing births. Governments of countries that have been in stage two for several decades are typically worn down and drained of financial resources by the consequences of rapid population growth, in effect suffering from "demographic fatigue." Such countries are losing the struggle to educate their children, create jobs, and cope with environmental problems such as erosion, deforestation, and aquifer depletion.

Demographic fatigue is perhaps most evident in the inability of many governments to combat the resurgence of traditional diseases, such as malaria or tuberculosis, and new diseases, such as AIDS. If these threats are not dealt with, they can force countries back into stage one. For several African countries with high HIV infection levels, this is no longer a hypothetical prospect. Although most industrialized nations have held infection levels under 1%, governments overwhelmed by population pressures have not.

Zimbabwe, for example, has a 26% adult HIV infection rate and cannot pay for the costly drugs needed to treat the disease. Zimbabwe is expected to reach population stability in 2002 as death rates from the HIV/AIDS epidemic climb to offset birthrates, essentially falling back into stage one. Other African countries that are likely to follow include Botswana, Namibia, Zambia, and Swaziland.

—Lester R. Brown, Gary Gardner, and Brian Halweil

grow 361%, though population will grow by just 50%. Energy consumption is also expected to increase in Latin America (by 340%) and Africa (by 326%). In all three regions, local pressures on energy sources, ranging from forests to fossil fuel reserves to waterways, will be significant.

11. Waste

Local and global environmental effects of waste disposal will likely worsen as 3.4 billion people are added to the world's population over the next half century. Prospects for providing access to sanitation are dismal in the near to medium term.

A growing population increases society's disposal headaches—the garbage, sewage, and industrial waste that must be gotten rid of. Even where population is largely stable—the case in many industrialized countries—the flow of waste products into landfills and waterways generally continues to increase. Where high rates of economic and population growth coincide in

coming decades, as they will in many developing countries, mountains of waste will likely pose difficult disposal challenges for municipal and national authorities.

Economic Impacts and Quality of Life

12. Jobs

Since 1950, the world's labor force has more than doubled—from 1.2 billion people to 2.7 billion—outstripping the growth in job creation. Over the next half century, the world will need to create more than 1.9 billion jobs in the developing world just to maintain current levels of employment.

While population growth may boost labor demand (through economic activity and demand for goods), it will most definitely boost labor supply. As the balance between the demand and supply of labor is tipped by population growth, wages tend to decrease. And in a situation of labor surplus, the quality of

jobs may not improve as fast, for workers will settle for longer hours, fewer benefits, and less control over work activities.

As the children of today represent the workers of tomorrow, the interaction between population growth and jobs is most acute in nations with young populations. Nations with more than half their population below the age of 25 (e.g., Peru, Mexico, Indonesia, and Zambia) will feel the burden of this labor flood. Employment is the key to obtaining food, housing, health services, and education, in addition to providing self-respect and self-fulfillment.

13. Income

Incomes have risen most rapidly in developing countries where population has slowed the most, including South Korea, Taiwan, China, Indonesia, and Malaysia. African countries, largely ignoring family planning, have been overwhelmed by the sheer numbers of young people who need to be educated and employed.

Small families are the key to stabilizing population. Convincing couples everywhere to restrict their childbearing to replacement-level fertility is important enough to warrant a worldwide campaign, according to the authors.

If the world cannot simultaneously convert the economy to one that is environmentally sustainable and move to a lower population trajectory, economic decline will be hard to avoid.

14. Housing

The ultimate manifestation of population growth outstripping the supply of housing is homelessness. The United Nations estimates that at least 100 million of the world's people—roughly equal to the population of Mexico—have no home; the number tops 1 billion if squatters and others with insecure or temporary accommodations are included.

Unless population growth can be checked worldwide, the ranks of the homeless are likely to swell dramatically.

15. Education

In nations that have increasing child-age populations, the base pressures on the educational system will be severe. In the world's 10 fastest-growing countries, most of which

are in Africa and the Middle East, the child-age population will increase an average of 93% over the next 50 years. Africa as a whole will see its school-age population grow by 75% through 2040.

If national education systems begin to stress lifelong learning for a rapidly changing world of the twenty-first century, then extensive provision for adult education will be necessary, affecting even those countries with shrinking child-age populations.

Such a development means that countries which started population-stabilization programs earliest will be in the best position to educate their entire citizenry.

16. Urbanization

Today's cities are growing faster: It took London 130 years to get from 1 million to 8 million inhabitants; Mexico City made this jump in just 30 years. The world's urban population as a whole is growing by just over 1 million people each week. This urban growth is fed by the natural increase of urban populations, by net migration from the country-

side, and by villages or towns expanding to the point where they become cities or they are absorbed by the spread of existing cities.

If recent trends continue, 6.5 billion people will live in cities by 2050, more than the world's total population today.

Actions for Slowing Growth

As we look to the future, the challenge for world leaders is to help countries maximize the prospects for achieving sustainability by keeping both birth and death rates low. In a world where both grain output and fish catch per person are falling, a strong case can be made on humanitarian grounds to stabilize world population.

What is needed is an all-out effort to lower fertility, particularly in the high-fertility countries, while there is still time. We see four key steps in doing this:

Assess carrying capacity. Every national government needs a carefully articulated and adequately supported population policy, one that takes into account the country's carrying capacity at whatever consumption level citizens decide on.

179

Without long-term estimates of available cropland, water for irrigation, and likely yields, governments are simply flying blind into the future, allowing their nations to drift into a world in which population growth and environmental degradation can lead to social disintegration.

Fill the family-planning gap. This is a high-payoff area. In a world where population pressures are mounting, the inability of 120 million of the world's women to get family-planning services is inexcusable. A stumbling block: At the International Conference on Population and Development in Cairo in 1994, the industrialized countries agreed to pay one-third of the costs for reproductive-health services in developing countries. So far they have failed to do so.

Educate young women. Educating girls is a key to accelerating the shift to smaller families. In every society for which data are available, the more education women have, the fewer children they have. Closely related to the need for education of young females is the need to provide equal opportunities for women in all phases of national life.

Have just two children. If we are facing a population emergency, it should be treated as such. It may be time for a campaign to convince couples everywhere to restrict their childbearing to replacement-level fertility.

About the Authors

Lester R. Brown is founder, president, and a senior researcher at the Worldwatch Institute, 1776 Massachusetts Avenue, N.W., Washington, D.C. 20036. Telephone 1-202-452-1999; Web site www.worldwatch.org.

Gary Gardner is a senior Worldwatch researcher and has written on agriculture, waste, and materials issues for *State of the World* and *World Watch* magazine.

Brian Halweil is a Worldwatch staff researcher and writes on issues related to food and agriculture, HIV/AIDS, cigarettes, and biotechnology.

This article is drawn from their report *Beyond Malthus: Sixteen Dimensions of the Population Problem*. Worldwatch Institute. 1998. 98 pages. Paperback. $5.

Originally published in the February 1999 issue of *The Futurist*, pp. 36-41. © 1999, World Future Society, 7910 Woodmont Ave, Bethesda, MD 20814, 301-656-8274. Used with permission.

The alien payoff

The surprising new bottom line on immigration's costs and benefits

BY PAUL GLASTRIS

In the debate over immigration, Francisco Castro could be a Rorschach test. An immigrant from Mexico, Castro supports his wife and three kids by working long hours for minimum wage at Central Market, a Los Angeles fruit and vegetable mart. "I'm always working," he says, "from 7 in the morning until 6 at night, every day but Wednesday." Those who favor immigration would see Castro as a boon to the economy. Those who oppose immigration would see him as undercutting American wages.

These two opposing economic views have played a major role in the debates about immigration for over a decade. Both pro- and anti-immigrant groups have deployed fancy econometric studies to prove that immigration is either hugely costly or hugely beneficial. But there has been no referee trusted by policy makers to decide who is right.

Last week, the respected National Academy of Sciences/National Research Council released a landmark report called *The New Americans: Economic, Demographic, and Fiscal Effects of Immigration.* Commissioned by the federal government as a guide through competing, often contradictory data, the report won't satisfy either the pro- or the anti-immigrant camps—but it does come to clear conclusions about some issues that have seemed murky. The report concludes first that for all the contentious arguments about the impact of immigration on the economy, its actual effect is not that great. "The costs to native-born workers are small, and so are the benefits," notes economist Richard Freeman of Harvard University, one of the report's authors. Second, the report finds that immigrants do impose substantial costs on

large numbers of taxpayers—in the short run. But in the long run, when the bills for baby boomers' retirement come due, immigrants are likely to prove a tax blessing.

The report also notes that while the country as a whole benefits from immigrants, a few states, California in particular, bear a steep financial burden for assimilating them.

Lower fruit prices. There is little dispute about the economic value of highly skilled immigrants. Chinese engineers, Russian physicists, and Indian computer programmers earn high wages, increase the gross domestic product, and, to the extent their skills are not easily matched by those of native-born workers, increase America's per capita income. In other words, they make native-born workers marginally richer.

There has been a great dispute, however, about the economic contribution of low-skilled immigrants like Francisco Castro. The NAS report concludes that their labor does benefit the economy. But the average gain to each native-born American is relatively small. Most of the value of Castro's labor winds up in his own pocket, in the form of the wages he takes home. Those born in this country benefit only to the extent that Castro is willing to work cheaper than someone else. His lower wage translates into greater profit for the fruit vendor he works for, higher fees paid by the vendor to the owners of Central Market, and lower produce prices for shoppers at Central Market.

But for exactly the same reason, Castro's labor also exacts a cost. While the NAS report confirms recent studies showing that immigrants have no negative effects on the wages of most Americans,

there is one exception: the very low skilled. Workers with less than a high school degree (who represent about 15 percent of the work force) earn wages that are somewhat lower (about 5 percent, according to the NAS) than they would be without competition from low-skilled immigrants. Though small, the effect contributes to one of America's more troubling social trends, the growing disparity between rich and poor.

The study found that the other losers are taxpayers in California, Florida, Texas, and a few other states where most immigrants live. The taxes many newcomers pay fall short of covering the costs of the government services they use—primarily health care and public schools for their children. In California, the average household pays an extra $1,178 in taxes because of immigrants.

But the story doesn't end there. Past studies have shown that immigrants generate a growing share of taxes the longer they are here. The NAS report confirms these findings by projecting, in a way never done before, the effects of immigrants and their descendants on tax revenues over decades. According to these projections, each additional immigrant and his or her descendants will provide $80,000 in extra tax revenues over their lifetimes (chart). That's equivalent to about $80 for every American household.

Up the ladder. A good example of the pattern the study found is the Martinez family. Reginaldo Martinez was a migrant worker from Mexico who, in 1954, took a job in a candy factory in Chicago. His wife, Luz, and their six children joined him in this country in the 1960s. The whole family, plus various relatives, lived in a

The bottom line on immigration

Add the taxes that an immigrant and his or her descendants are likely to pay over their lifetimes. Subtract the cost of the government services they're likely to use. The result: Each additional immigrant produces a net revenue gain to government. But the federal government gets most of the benefit. States and localities lose.

Impact on state and local treasuries	Impact on federal Treasury	Total impact
−$25,000	+$105,000	+$80,000

Unless he arrives with little education, an immigrant will pay more in taxes than he costs in services.

Less than high school	High school graduate	More than high school	Overall
−$13,000	+$51,000	+$198,000	+$80,000

Source: National Academy of Sciences/National Research Council report *The New Americans.*

two-bedroom apartment. The parents slept in one bedroom, the four boys in the other, the girls and a cousin in the dining room. The children were envious of an aunt who moved into the pantry, since she had a "private" room.

As the Martinez children advanced up the ladder of affluence, the clan became a fiscal asset. Each sibling earns (with his or her spouse) between $40,000 and $60,000 yearly. Juan is a foreman at a pipe-fitting factory. Javier is a conductor for the Chicago Transit Authority. Reginaldo Jr. joined the Air Force and is now an electrical engineer. Five of the six siblings own homes within blocks of one another in the bustling Mexican-American neighborhood of Little Village in Chicago. The average annual property tax payment per home is $1,300. Each sibling pays an average of $1,705 in Social Security taxes. The family's six kids have had 18 children among them, the oldest of whom are now in college. Alejandro, Juan's eldest, is in graduate school in microbiology at the University of Illinois-Urbana-Champaign. Each generation has done better than the last, contributing that much more in taxes.

But the real tax benefits of immigration, according to the National Academy of Sci-

ences report, won't be seen for a few decades. At that point, future wage earners will have to pay the retirement and medical costs of aging baby boomers. That burden will be split among those working and paying taxes at that time. The burden would fall more lightly on all shoulders if people born here had children at a higher rate than they do now. But if fertility rates remain low, the only way to get more future workers will be through immigration.

Impact aid. The debate over immigration will hardly end with this economic report. Noneconomic questions related to culture, values, and assimilation will play a larger role. Still, Jeff Passel, an immigration policy expert with the Urban Institute in Washington, D. C., predicts that the debate will "move away from the general 'is immigration good or bad?' question toward a focus on specific problem areas." Policy makers might try, for instance, to limit the influx of low-skilled immigrants like the Castro family while boosting the number of those with higher-level skills. That might relieve wage pressures on low-skilled Americans while increasing the overall economic and fiscal benefits of the immigrant population. Having too many high-skilled immigrants, however, might

someday reduce wages for high-skilled native-born workers.

The National Academy of Sciences report might also cause Washington lawmakers to revisit a proposal that almost became law last fall: federal "impact aid" to the handful of states with large immigrant populations. These states have long griped that they have to pay for education, health care, and other government services for immigrants whose entry into the country is controlled by the federal government. The NAS report strengthens these states' claims that they lose out from immigration even as Washington stands to reap a revenue gain in the long run. Pro-immigration forces might concede some of the points made by their opponents and support putting money in places like California. Reducing the costs of immigration to those it hits hardest is the surest way to preserve the benefits to everyone else.

With Warren Cohen in Chicago and Dana Hawkins

SPECIAL REPORT • GLOBAL WARMING

FEELING THE HEAT
LIFE IN THE GREENHOUSE

Except for nuclear war or a collision with an asteroid, no force has more potential to damage our planet's web of life than global warming. It's a "serious" issue, the White House admits, but nonetheless George W. Bush has decided to abandon the 1997 Kyoto treaty to combat climate change—an agreement the U.S. signed but the new President believes is fatally flawed. His dismissal last week of almost nine years of international negotiations sparked protests around the world and a face-to-face disagreement with German Chancellor Gerhard Schröder. Our special report examines the signs of global warming that are already apparent, the possible consequences for our future, what we can do about the threat and why we have failed to take action so far.

By MICHAEL D. LEMONICK

There is no such thing as normal weather. The average daytime high temperature for New York City this week should be 57°F, but on any given day the mercury will almost certainly fall short of that mark or overshoot it, perhaps by a lot. Manhattan thermometers can reach 65° in January every so often and plunge to 50° in July. And seasons are rarely normal. Winter snowfall and summer heat waves beat the average some years and fail to reach it in others. It's tough to pick out overall changes in climate in the face of these natural fluctuations. An unusually warm year, for example, or even three in a row don't necessarily signal a general trend.

Yet the earth's climate does change. Ice ages have frosted the planet for tens of thousands of years at a stretch, and periods of warmth have pushed the tropics well into what is now the temperate zone. But given the normal year-to-year variations, the only reliable signal that such changes may be in the works is a long-term shift in worldwide temperature.

And that is precisely what's happening. A decade ago, the idea that the planet was warming up as a result of human activity was largely theoretical. We knew that since the Industrial Revolution began in the 18th century, factories and power plants and automobiles and farms have been loading the atmosphere with heat-trapping gases, including carbon dioxide and methane. But evidence that the climate was actually getting hotter was still murky.

Not anymore. As an authoritative report issued a few weeks ago by the United Nations-sponsored Intergovernmental Panel on Climate Change makes plain, the trend toward a warmer world has unquestionably begun. Worldwide temperatures have climbed more than 1°F over the

MAKING THE CASE THAT OUR CLIMATE IS CHANGING

From melting glaciers to rising oceans, the signs are everywhere. Global warming can't be blamed for any particular heat wave, drought or deluge, but scientists say a hotter world will make such extreme weather more frequent—and deadly.

EXHIBIT A

Thinning Ice

ANTARCTICA, home to these Adélie penguins, is heating up. The annual melt season has increased up to three weeks in 20 years.

MOUNT KILIMANJARO has lost 75% of its ice cap since 1912. The ice on Africa's tallest peak could vanish entirely within 15 years.

LAKE BAIKAL in eastern Siberia now feezes for the winter 1.1 days later than it did a century ago.

VENEZUELAN mountaintops had six glaciers in 1972. Today only two remain.

EXHIBIT B

Hotter Times

TEMPERATURES SIZZLED from Kansas to New England last May.

CROPS WITHERED and Dallas temperatures topped 100°F for 29 days straight in a Texas hot spell that struck during the summer of 1998.

INDIA'S WORST heat shock in 50 years killed more than 2,500 people in May 1998.

CHERRY BLOSSOMS in Washington bloom seven days earlier in the spring than they did in 1970.

EXHIBIT C

Wild Weather

HEAVY RAINS in England and Wales made last fall Britain's wettest three-month period on record.

FIRES due to dry conditions and record-breaking heat consumed 20% of Samos Island, Greece, last July.

FLOODS along the Ohio River in March 1997 caused 30 deaths and at least $500 million in property damage.

HURRICAN FLOYD brought flooding rains and 130-m.p.h. winds through the Atlantic seabord in September

1999, killing 77 people and leaving thousands homeless.

EXHIBIT D

Nature's Pain

PACIFIC SALMON populations fell sharply in 1997 and 1998, when local ocean temperatures rose 6°F.

POLAR BEARS in Hudson Bay are having fewer cubs, possibly as a result of earlier spring ice breakup.

CORAL REEFS suffer from the loss of algae that color and nourish them. The process, called bleaching, is caused by warmer oceans.

DISEASES like dengue fever are expanding their reach northward in the U.S.

BUTTERFLIES are relocating to higher latitudes. The Edith's Checkerspot butterfly of western North America has moved almost 60 miles north in 100 years.

---

past century, and the 1990s were the hottest decade on record. After analyzing data going back at least two decades on everything from air and ocean temperatures to the spread and retreat of wildlife, the IPCC asserts that this slow but steady warming has had an impact on no fewer than 420 physical processes and animal and plant species on all continents.

Glaciers, including the legendary snows of Kilimanjaro, are disappearing from mountaintops around the globe. Coral reefs are dying off as the seas get too warm for comfort. Drought is the norm in parts of Asia and Africa. El Niño events, which trigger devastating weather in the eastern Pacific, are more frequent.

The Arctic permafrost is starting to melt. Lakes and rivers in colder climates are freezing later and thawing earlier each year. Plants and animals are shifting their ranges poleward and to higher altitudes, and migration patterns for animals as diverse as polar bears, butterflies and beluga whales are being disrupted.

Faced with these hard facts, scientists no longer doubt that global warming is happening, and almost nobody questions the fact that humans are at least partly responsible. Nor are the changes over. Already, humans have increased the concentration of carbon dioxide, the most abundant heat-trapping gas in the atmosphere, to 30% above pre-industrial levels—and each year the

rate of increase gets faster. The obvious conclusion: temperatures will keep going up.

Unfortunately, they may be rising faster and heading higher than anyone expected. By 2100, says the IPCC, average temperatures will increase between 2.5°F and 10.4°F—more than 50% higher than predictions of just a half-decade ago. That may not seem like much, but consider that it took only a 9°F shift to end the last ice age. Even at the low end, the changes could be problematic enough, with storms getting more frequent and intense, droughts more pronounced, coastal areas ever more severely eroded by rising seas, rainfall scarcer on agricultural land and ecosystems thrown out of balance.

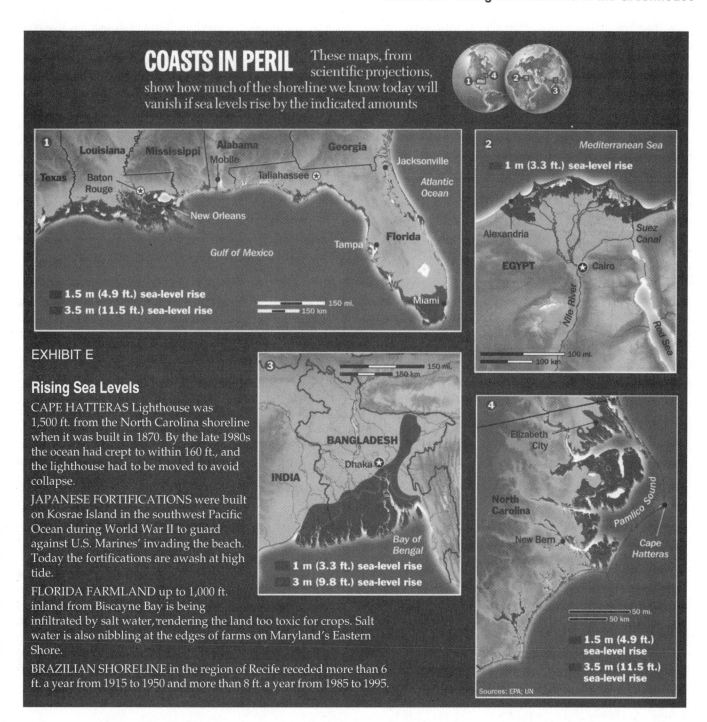

COASTS IN PERIL These maps, from scientific projections, show how much of the shoreline we know today will vanish if sea levels rise by the indicated amounts

EXHIBIT E

Rising Sea Levels

CAPE HATTERAS Lighthouse was 1,500 ft. from the North Carolina shoreline when it was built in 1870. By the late 1980s the ocean had crept to within 160 ft., and the lighthouse had to be moved to avoid collapse.

JAPANESE FORTIFICATIONS were built on Kosrae Island in the southwest Pacific Ocean during World War II to guard against U.S. Marines' invading the beach. Today the fortifications are awash at high tide.

FLORIDA FARMLAND up to 1,000 ft. inland from Biscayne Bay is being infiltrated by salt water, rendering the land too toxic for crops. Salt water is also nibbling at the edges of farms on Maryland's Eastern Shore.

BRAZILIAN SHORELINE in the region of Recife receded more than 6 ft. a year from 1915 to 1950 and more than 8 ft. a year from 1985 to 1995.

But if the rise is significantly larger, the result could be disastrous. With seas rising as much as 3 ft., enormous areas of densely populated land—coastal Florida, much of Louisiana, the Nile Delta, the Maldives, Bangladesh—would become uninhabitable. Entire climatic zones might shift dramatically, making central Canada look more like central Illinois, Georgia more like Guatemala. Agriculture would be thrown into turmoil. Hundreds of millions of people would have to migrate out of unlivable regions.

Public health could suffer. Rising seas would contaminate water supplies with salt. Higher levels of urban ozone, the result of stronger sunlight and warmer temperatures, could worsen respiratory illnesses. More frequent hot spells could lead to a rise in heat-related deaths. Warmer temperatures could widen the range of disease-carrying rodents and bugs, such as mosquitoes and ticks, increasing the incidence of dengue fever, malaria, encephalitis, Lyme disease and other afflictions. Worst of all, this increase in temperatures is happening at a pace that outstrips anything the earth has seen in the past 100 million years. Humans will have a hard enough time adjusting, especially in poorer countries, but for wildlife, the changes could be devastating.

Like any other area of science, the case for human-induced global warming has uncertainties—and like many pro-business lobbyists, President Bush has proclaimed those uncertainties a reason to study the problem further rather than act. But while the evidence is circumstantial, it is powerful, thanks to the IPCC's painstaking research. The U.N.-sponsored group was organized in the late 1980s. Its mission: to sift through climate-related studies from a dozen different fields and integrate them into a coherent picture. "It isn't just the work of a few green people," says Sir John Houghton, one of the early leaders who at the time ran the British Meteorological Office. "The IPCC scientists come from a wide range of backgrounds and countries."

Measuring the warming that has already taken place is relatively simple; the trick is unraveling the causes and projecting what will happen over the next century. To do that, IPCC scientists fed a wide range of scenarios involving varying estimates of population and economic growth, changes in technology and other factors into computers. That process gave them about 35 estimates, ranging from 6 billion to 35 billion tons, of how much excess carbon dioxide will enter the atmosphere.

Then they loaded those estimates into the even larger, more powerful computer programs that attempt to model the planet's climate. Because no one climate model is considered definitive, they used seven different versions, which yielded 235 independent predictions of global temperature increase. That's where the range of 2.5°F to 10.4°F (1.4°C to 5.8°C) comes from.

The computer models were criticized in the past largely because the climate is so complex that the limited hardware and software of even a half-decade ago couldn't do an adequate simulation. Today's climate models, however, are able to take into account the heat-trapping effects not just of CO_2 but also of other greenhouse gases, including methane. They can also factor in natural variations in the sun's energy and the effect of substances like dust from volcanic eruptions and particulate matter spewed from smokestacks.

That is one reason the latest IPCC predictions for temperature increase are higher than they were five years ago. Back in the mid-1990s, climate models didn't include the effects of the El Chichon and Mount Pinatubo volcanic eruptions, which threw enough dust into the air to block out some sunlight and slow down the rate of warming. That effect has dissipated, and the heating should start to accelerate. Moreover, the IPCC noted, many countries have begun to reduce their emissions of sulfur dioxide in order to fight acid rain. But sulfur dioxide particles, too, reflect sunlight; without this shield, temperatures should go up even faster.

The models still aren't perfect. One major flaw, agree critics and champions alike, is that they don't adequately account for clouds. In a warmer world, more water will evaporate from the oceans and presumably form more clouds. If they are billowy cumulus clouds, they will tend to shade the planet and slow down warming; if they are high, feathery cirrus clouds, they will trap even more heat.

Research by M.I.T. atmospheric scientist Richard Lindzen suggests that warming will tend to make cirrus clouds go away. Another critic, John Christy of the University of Alabama in Huntsville, says that while the models reproduce the current climate in a general way, they fail to get right the amount of warming at different levels in the atmosphere. Neither Lindzen nor Christy (both IPCC authors) doubts, however, that humans are influencing the climate. But they question how much—and how high temperatures will go. Both scientists are distressed that only the most extreme scenarios, based on huge population growth and the maximum use of dirty fuels like coal, have made headlines.

It won't take the greatest extremes of warming to make life uncomfortable for large numbers of people. Even slightly higher temperatures in regions that are already drought- or flood-prone would exacerbate those conditions. In temperate zones, warmth and increased CO_2 would make some crops flourish—at first. But beyond 3° of warming, says Bill Easterling, a professor of geography and agronomy at Penn State and a lead author of the IPCC report, "there would be a dramatic turning point. U.S. crop yields would start to decline rapidly." In the tropics, where crops are already at the limit of their temperature range, the decrease would start right away.

Even if temperatures rise only moderately, some scientists fear, the climate would reach a "tipping point"—a point at which even a tiny additional increase would throw the system into violent change. If peat bogs and Arctic permafrost warm enough to start releasing the methane stored within them, for example, that potent greenhouse gas would suddenly accelerate the heat-trapping process.

By contrast, if melting ice caps dilute the salt content of the sea, major ocean currents like the Gulf Stream could slow or even stop, and so would their warming effects on northern regions. More snowfall reflecting more sunlight back into space could actually cause a net cooling. Global warming could, paradoxically, throw the planet into another ice age.

Even if such a tipping point doesn't materialize, the more drastic effects of global warming might be only postponed rather than avoided. The IPCC's calculations end with the year 2100, but the warming won't. World Bank chief scientist, Robert Watson, currently serving as IPCC chair, points out that the CO_2 entering the atmosphere today will be there for a century. Says Watson: "If we stabilize (CO_2 emissions) now, the concentration will continue to go up for hundreds of years. Temperatures will rise over that time."

That could be truly catastrophic. The ongoing disruption of ecosystems and weather patterns would be bad enough. But if temperatures reach the IPCC's worst-case levels and stay there for as long as 1,000 years, says Michael Oppenheimer, chief scientist at Environmental Defense, vast ice sheets in Greenland and Antarctica could melt, raising sea level more than 30 ft. Florida would be history, and every city on the U.S. Eastern seaboard would be inundated.

In the short run, there's not much chance of halting global warming, not even if every nation in the world ratifies the Kyoto Protocol tomorrow. The treaty doesn't require reductions in carbon dioxide emissions until 2008. By that time, a great deal of damage will already have been done. But we can slow things down. If action today can keep the climate from eventually reaching an unstable tipping point or can finally begin to reverse the warming trend a century from now, the effort would hardly be futile. Humanity embarked unknowingly on the dangerous experiment of tinkering with the climate of our planet. Now that we know what we're doing, it would be utterly foolish to continue.

Reported by David Bjerklie,
Robert H. Boyle and
Andrea Dorfman/New York and
Dick Thompson/Washington

GRAINS OF HOPE

GENETICALLY ENGINEERED CROPS could revolutionize farming. Protesters fear they could also destroy the ecosystem. You decide

By J. MADELEINE NASH ZURICH

AT FIRST, THE GRAINS OF RICE that Ingo Potrykus sifted through his fingers did not seem at all special, but that was because they were still encased in their dark, crinkly husks. Once those drab coverings were stripped away and the interiors polished to a glossy sheen, Potrykus and his colleagues would behold the seeds' golden secret. At their core, these grains were not pearly white, as ordinary rice is, but a very pale yellow—courtesy of beta-carotene, the nutrient that serves as a building block for vitamin A.

Potrykus was elated. For more than a decade he had dreamed of creating such a rice: a golden rice that would improve the lives of millions of the poorest people in the world. He'd visualized peasant farmers wading into paddies to set out the tender seedlings and winnowing the grain at harvest time in handwoven baskets. He'd pictured small children consuming the golden gruel their mothers would make, knowing that it would sharpen their eyesight and strengthen their resistance to infectious diseases.

And he saw his rice as the first modest start of a new green revolution, in which ancient food crops would acquire all manner of useful properties: bananas that wouldn't rot on the way to market; corn that could supply its own fertilizer; wheat that could thrive in drought-ridden soil.

But imagining a golden rice, Potrykus soon found, was one thing and bringing one into existence quite another. Year after year, he and his colleagues ran into one unexpected obstacle after another, beginning with the finicky growing habits of the rice they transplanted to a greenhouse near the foothills of the Swiss Alps. When success finally came, in the spring of 1999, Potrykus was 65 and about to retire as a full professor at the Swiss Federal Institute of Technology in Zurich. At that point, he tackled an even more formidable challenge.

Having created golden rice, Potrykus wanted to make sure it reached those for whom it was intended: malnourished children of the developing world. And that, he knew, was not likely to be easy. Why? Because in addition to a full complement of genes from Oryza sativa—the Latin name for the most commonly consumed species of rice—the golden grains also contained snippets of DNA borrowed from bacteria and daffodils. It was what some would call Frankenfood, a product of genetic engineering. As such, it was entangled in a web of hopes and fears and political baggage, not to mention a fistful of iron-clad patents.

For about a year now—ever since Potrykus and his chief collaborator, Peter Beyer of the University of Freiburg in Germany, announced their achievement—their golden grain has illuminated an increasingly polarized public debate. At issue is the question of what genetically engineered crops represent. Are they,

HOW TO MAKE GOLDEN RICE
A four-step process to feed the poor

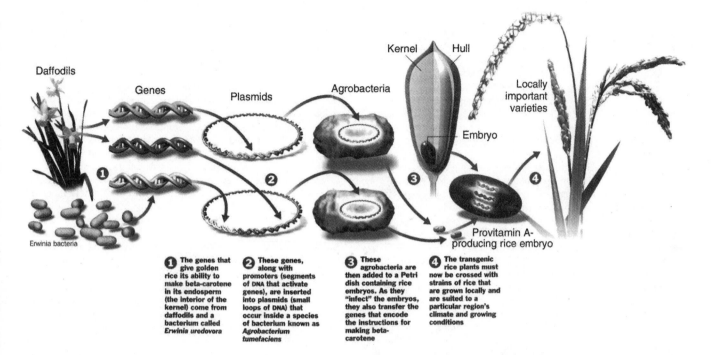

① The genes that give golden rice its ability to make beta-carotene in its endosperm (the interior of the kernel) come from daffodils and a bacterium called *Erwinia uredovora*

② These genes, along with promoters (segments of DNA that activate genes), are inserted into plasmids (small loops of DNA) that occur inside a species of bacterium known as *Agrobacterium tumefaciens*

③ These agrobacteria are then added to a Petri dish containing rice embryos. As they "infect" the embryos, they also transfer the genes that encode the instructions for making beta-carotene

④ The transgenic rice plants must now be crossed with strains of rice that are grown locally and are suited to a particular region's climate and growing conditions

Source: Dr. Peter Beyer, Center for Applied Biosciences, University of Freiburg

as their proponents argue, a technological leap forward that will bestow incalculable benefits on the world and its people? Or do they represent a perilous step down a slippery slope that will lead to ecological and agricultural ruin? Is genetic engineering just a more efficient way to do the business of conventional crossbreeding? Or does the ability to mix the genes of any species—even plants and animals—give man more power than he should have?

The debate erupted the moment genetically engineered crops made their commercial debut in the mid-1990s, and it has escalated ever since. First to launch major protests against biotechnology were European environmentalists and consumer-advocacy groups. They were soon followed by their U.S. counterparts, who made a big splash at last fall's World Trade Organization meeting in Seattle and last week launched an offensive designed to target one company after another (see accompanying story). Over the coming months, charges that transgenic crops pose grave dangers will be raised in petitions, editorials, mass mailings and protest

marches. As a result, golden rice, despite its humanitarian intent, will probably be subjected to the same kind of hostile scrutiny that has already led to curbs on the commercialization of these crops in Britain, Germany, Switzerland and Brazil.

The hostility is understandable. Most of the genetically engineered crops introduced so far represent minor variations on the same two themes: resistance to insect pests and to herbicides used to control the growth of weeds. And they are often marketed by large, multinational corporations that produce and sell the very agricultural chemicals farmers are spraying on their fields. So while many farmers have embraced such crops as Monsanto's Roundup Ready soybeans, with their genetically engineered resistance to Monsanto's Roundup-brand herbicide, that let them spray weed killer without harming crops, consumers have come to regard such things with mounting suspicion. Why resort to a strange new technology that might harm the biosphere, they ask, when the benefits of doing so seem small?

FROM THE TRANSGENIC GARDEN

COTTON
BEAUTIFUL BOLL: This plant has been given a bacterial gene to help it fight off worms that infest cotton crops

CORN
HEALTHY KERNEL: These corn seeds are protected by the same bacterial gene, one that ecologists fear could harm butterflies

PAPAYA
VIRAL RESISTANCE: Fruit carrying a gene from the ringspot virus are better able to withstand ringspot outbreaks

CANOLA
PROBLEM POLLEN: When transgenic seeds contaminated a non-transgenic shipment from Canada, European farmers cried foul

SOYBEANS
ROUNDUP READY: Will crops designed to take frequent spraying with Monsanto's top weed killer lead to Roundup-resistant weeds?

Taking It to Main Street

By MARGOT ROOSEVELT SAN FRANCISCO

IT WAS THE SORT OF KITSCHY STREET THEATER YOU EXPECT IN A city like San Francisco. A gaggle of protesters in front of a grocery store, some dressed as monarch butterflies, others as Frankenstein's monster. Signs reading HELL NO, WE WON'T GROW IT! People in white biohazard jumpsuits pitching Campbell's soup and Kellogg's corn-flakes into a mock toxic-waste bin. The crowd shouting, "Hey, hey, ho, ho—GMO has got to go!" And, at the podium, Jesse Cool, a popular restaurant owner, wondering what would happen if she served a tomato spliced with an oyster gene and a customer got sick. "I could get sued," she says.

But just as the California activists were revving up last week, similar rants and chants were reverberating in such unlikely places as Grand Forks, N.D., Augusta, Maine, and Miami—19 U.S. cities in all. This was no frolicking radical fringe but the carefully coordinated start of a nationwide campaign to force the premarket safety testing and labeling of those GMOs, or genetically modified organisms. Seven organizations— including such media-savvy veterans as the Sierra Club, Friends of the Earth and the Public Interest Research Groups— were launching the Genetically Engineered Food Alert, a million-dollar, multiyear organizing effort to pressure Congress, the Food and Drug Administration and individual companies, one at a time, starting with Campbell's soup.

The offensive represents the seeds of what could grow into a serious problem for U.S. agribusiness, which had been betting that science-friendly American consumers would remain immune to any "Frankenfood" backlash cross-pollinating from Europe or Japan. After all, this is (mostly) U.S. technology, and it has spread so quickly and so quietly that the proportion of U.S. farmland planted in genetically altered corn now stands at nearly 25%. Some 70% of processed food in American supermarkets, from soup to sandwich meat, contains ingredients derived from transgenic corn, soybeans and other plants. Yet all of a sudden, activists are "yelling fire in a movie theater," says Dan Eramian, spokesman for the Biotechnology Industry Organization (BIO).

How widespread is this protest movement? And how deep are its roots? We may soon find out, for it's emergence is a study in the warp-speed politics of the age of the Internet. This is a time when a Web designer named Craig Winters can start an organization called the Campaign to Label Genetically Engineered Food with a staff of one (himself), mount a website and sell 160,000 "Take Action Packets" in nine weeks. Want to know what the Chileans are doing about transgenic grain shipments? How South Korean labeling laws work? Just subscribe to one of the four biotech e-mail lists of the Institute for Agriculture and Trade Policy, based in Minneapolis, Minn.

Even so-called ecoterrorists who have uprooted scores of university test plots across the country in the past year use the Net to organize their lawbreaking protests. In an Internet posting from Santa Cruz last week, Earth First! beckons, "You're all invited to sunny California for a weekend of workshops, training and fun! We also have plenty of [genetically engineered] crops waiting for your night time gardening efforts." Says Carl Pope, the Sierra Club's executive director: "I've never seen an issue go so quickly."

It started about two years ago, when the buzz from European anti-biotech protest groups began to ricochet throughout the Net, reaching the community groups that were springing up across the U.S. Many were galvanized by proposed FDA regulations that would have allowed food certified as "organic" to contain genetically modified ingredients—an effort shouted down by angry consumers. Meanwhile, Greenpeace began to target U.S. companies such as Gerber, which quickly renounced the use of transgenic ingredients, and Kellogg's, which

has yet to do so. With so-called Frankenfoods making headlines, several other companies cut back on biotech: McDonald's forswore genetically engineered potatoes, and Frito-Lay decreed it would buy no more genetically modified corn.

But the issue that is now on the front burner dates back to 1992, when the FDA decided that biotech ingredients did not materially alter food and therefore did not require labeling. Nor, the agency declared, was premarket safety testing required, because biotech additives were presumed to be benign. Last March the Center for Food Safety and 53 other groups, including the Union of Concerned Scientists, filed a petition to force the FDA to change its policy.

Meanwhile, the biotech issue is gathering steam in Congress, where safety and labeling bills have been introduced by Democratic Representative Dennis Kucinich of Ohio and 55 co-sponsors in the House, and by Daniel Patrick Moynihan and Barbara Boxer in the Senate. Similar statewide bills are pending in Maine, Colorado and Oregon. Shareholder resolutions demanding safety testing and labeling have targeted a score of companies from life-science giants to supermarket chains.

Surveys indicate that between two-thirds and three-quarters of Americans want biotech food to be labeled. Then why not do it? Because companies fear such disclosure could spell disaster. "Our data show that 60% of consumers would consider a mandatory biotech label as a warning that it is unsafe," says Gene Grabowski, spokesman for the Grocery Manufacturers of America. "It is easier," BIO's Eramian points out, "to scare people about biotechnology than to educate them."

The labeling threat finally spurred a hitherto complacent industry into action. Last April, Monsanto, Novartis and five other biotech companies rolled out a $50 million television advertising campaign, with soft-focus fields and smiling children, pitching "solutions that could improve our world tomorrow."

But by then the opposition was morphing from inchoate splinter groups into something that looks like a mainstream coalition. In July 1999, some 40 environmentalists, consumer advocates and organic-food activists met in Bolinas, Calif., to map a national campaign. Rather than endorse a total ban on genetically modified foods that Greenpeace was pushing, says Wendy Wendlandt, political director of the state Public Interest Research Groups, "it was more practical to call for a moratorium until the stuff is safety tested and labeled, and companies are held responsible for any harmful effects."

In May the FDA announced that in the fall it would propose new rules for genetically engineered crops and products. Instead of safety testing, it would require only that companies publicly disclose their new biotech crops before they are planted. Labeling would be voluntary.

The critics' response came last week: a campaign to muster public opposition to the FDA's new rules and to target individual companies and their previous trademarks. The mock advertisements for "Campbull's Experimental Vegetable Soup," with the advisory, "Warning: This Product Is Untested," is only the first salvo. Some 18 other brand-name U.S. companies are on a tentative hit list, including General Mills, Coca-Cola and Kraft.

Will the companies succumb to the pressure, as they have in Europe? As of last week, Campbell claimed to be unfazed, with few customers registering concern, despite the spotlight. Even at the San Francisco rally, there was some ambivalence. "I may not eat Campbell's soup as much," offered Shanae Walls, 19, a student at Contra Costa College who was there with her Environmental Science and Thought class. But as the protesters tossed products from Pepperidge Farm—a Campbell subsidiary—into the toxic-waste bin, she had second thoughts. "I love those cookies," she said wistfully. "That might take some time."

THE GLOBAL FOOD FIGHT

① BRUSSELS, 1998 France, Italy, Greece, Denmark and Luxembourg team up to block introduction of all new GM products in the European Union— including those approved by E.U. scientific advisory committees and even a few developed in these five countries. Several E.U. countries have also banned the importation and use of 18 GM crops and foods approved before the blockade went into effect. New safety rules could eventually break this logjam.

② SEATTLE, NOVEMBER 1999 Taking to the streets to protest the spread of "Frankenfoods," among other issues, demonstrators trying to disrupt the World Trade Organization summit are tear-gassed and beaten by police.

③ MIDWESTERN U.S., 1999 A coalition of agricultural groups calls for a freeze on government approval of new GM seeds in light of dwindling markets in anti-GM European countries. Planting of GM corn drops from 25 million acres (10 million hectares) in 1999 to 19.9 million acres (8 million hectares) in 2000.

④ MONTREAL, JANUARY 2000 130 nations, including Mexico, Australia and Japan, sign the Cartagena Protocol on Biosafety, which requires an exporting country to obtain permission from an importing country before shipping GM seeds and organisms and to label such shipments with warnings that they "may contain" GM products.

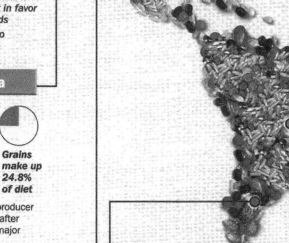

Key

▶ Strongly in favor of GM foods

▷ Somewhat in favor of GM foods

◢ Opposed to GM foods

Canada

POPULATION 31,147,000

ATTITUDE Generally pro, though consumers are wary

Grains make up 24.8% of diet

REASON Second biggest producer of GM products, after the U.S., and a major food exporter.

—By Michael D. Lemonick. With reporting by Yudhijit Bhattacharjee and Max Rust/New York, with other bureaus

U.S.

POPULATION 278,357,000

ATTITUDE Cautiously pro

Grains make up 23.6% of diet

REASON As a major food exporter and home to giant agribiotech businesses, led by Monsanto, the country stands to reap huge profits from GM foods.

Argentina

POPULATION 37,031,000

ATTITUDE Pro

Grains make up 29.5% of diet

REASON Third largest producer of biotech crops in the world, after the U.S. and Canada.

Brazil

POPULATION 170,116,000

ATTITUDE Very cautiously pro

Grains make up 30.9% of diet

REASON The country is eager to participate in the potentially profitable biotech revolution but is worried about alienating anti-GM customers in Europe.

Britain

POPULATION 58,830,000

ATTITUDE Strongly anti

Grains make up 22.8% of diet

REASON "Mad cow" disease in beef and a report that GM potatoes caused immune-system damage in rats have alarmed most Brits. Markets ban GM foods, and experiments are tightly controlled.

France

POPULATION 59,079,000

ATTITUDE Strongly anti

Grains make up 24.3% of diet

REASON Like Britain, France has been stung by incidents with tainted food. Its attitude is also colored by hostility to U.S. imports and a desire to protect French farmers.

(CONTINUED)

(CONTINUED)

⑤ COLOMBO, SRI LANKA, FEBRUARY 2000
The government bans GM foods pending further research.

⑥ RIO DE JANEIRO, FEBRUARY 2000
A U.S. ship suspected of carrying GM corn is turned away by a Brazilian meat producer. The nation as a whole prohibits the importation of GM foods unless they've been proved safe; earlier this month, a federal court upheld that policy despite a statement from the Cabinet that Brazil "cannot be left out of this technology."

⑦ NEW DELHI, MAY 2000
The government approves large-scale field trials of Bollgard, Monsanto's pest-resistant GM cotton. Two years earlier, activists and angry farmers had burned fields planted with transgenic cotton.

⑧ BEIJING, JULY 2000
While still receptive to GM foods, the government passes a law requiring the labeling of GM seeds.

⑨ TOKYO, 2001
New rules will go into effect requiring GM foods to be labeled as such and tested for safety—although the government is also promoting the export of Japanese GM expertise and technology to Third-World nations. Meanwhile, a small anti-GM movement is growing stronger.

India	**China**	**Japan**
POPULATION 1,013,661,000	**POPULATION** 1,277,558,000	**POPULATION** 126,714,000
ATTITUDE Cautiously pro	**ATTITUDE** Pro	**ATTITUDE** Cautiously pro, but heading toward anti
REASON Needs to find the most efficient ways to feed and clothe its enormous, rapidly growing population.	**REASON** Needs to feed and clothe a large population; rural hunger brought about a revolution 50 years ago, and leaders don't want another one.	**REASON** Japan has a national obsession with food quality, enhanced by several recent food-poisoning incidents, and a tradition of protectionism for Japanese farmers.
Grains make up 62.6% of diet	*Grains make up 54.7% of diet*	*Grains make up 40.7% of diet*

Indeed, the benefits have seemed small—until golden rice came along to suggest otherwise. Golden rice is clearly not the moral equivalent of Roundup Ready beans. Quite the contrary, it is an example—the first compelling example—of a genetically engineered crop that may benefit not just the farmers who grow it but also the consumers who eat it. In this case, the consumers include at least a million children who die every year because they are weakened by vitamin-A deficiency and an additional 350,000 who go blind.

No wonder the biotech industry sees golden rice as a powerful ally in its struggle to win public acceptance. No wonder its critics see it as a cynical ploy. And no wonder so many of those concerned about the twin evils of poverty and hunger look at golden rice and see reflected in it their own passionate conviction that genetically engineered crops can be made to serve the greater public good—that in fact such crops have a critical role to play in feeding a world that is about to add to its present population of 6 billion. As former President Jimmy Carter put it, "Responsible biotechnology is not the enemy; starvation is."

Indeed, by the year 2020, the demand for grain, both for human consumption and for animal feed, is projected to go up by nearly half, while the amount of arable land available to satisfy that demand will not only grow much more slowly but also, in some areas, will probably dwindle. Add to that the need to conserve overstressed water resources and reduce the use of polluting chemicals, and the enormity of the challenge becomes apparent. In order to meet it, believes Gordon Conway, the agricultural ecologist who heads the Rockefeller Foundation, 21st century farmers will have to draw on every arrow in their agricultural quiver, including genetic engineering. And contrary to public perception, he says, those who have the least to lose and the most to gain are not well-fed Americans and Europeans but the hollow-bellied citizens of the developing world.

GOING FOR THE GOLD

IT WAS IN THE LATE 1980S, AFTER HE became a full professor of plant science at the Swiss Federal Institute of Technology, that Ingo Potrykus started to think about using genetic engineering to improve the nutritional qualities of rice. He knew that of some 3 billion people who depend on rice as their major staple, around 10% risk some degree of vitamin-A deficiency and the health problems that result. The reason, some alleged, was an overreliance on rice ushered in by the green revolution. Whatever its cause, the result was distressing: these people were so poor that they ate a few bowls of rice a day and almost nothing more.

The problem interested Potrykus for a number of reasons. For starters, he was attracted by the scientific challenge of transferring not just a single gene, as many had already done, but a group of genes that represented a key part of a biochemical pathway. He was also motivated by complex emotions, among them empathy. Potrykus knew more than most what it meant not to have enough to eat. As a child growing up in war-ravaged Germany, he and his brothers were often so desperately hungry that they ate what they could steal.

Around 1990, Potrykus hooked up with Gary Toenniessen, director of food security for the Rockefeller Foundation. Toenniessen had identified the lack of beta-carotene in polished rice grains as an appropriate target for gene scientists like Potrykus to tackle because it lay beyond the ability of traditional plant breeding to address. For while rice, like other green plants, contains light-trapping beta-carotene in its external tissues, no plant in the entire *Oryza* genus—as far as anyone knew—produced beta-carotene in its endosperm (the starchy interior part of the rice grain that is all most people eat).

It was at a Rockefeller-sponsored meeting that Potrykus met the University of Freiburg's Peter Beyer, an expert on the beta-carotene pathway in daffodils. By combining their expertise, the two scientists figured, they might be able to remedy this unfortunate oversight in nature. So in 1993, with some $100,000 in seed money from the Rockefeller Foundation, Potrykus and Beyer launched what turned into a seven-year, $2.6 million project, backed also by the Swiss government and the European Union. "I was in a privileged situation," reflects Potrykus, "because I was able to operate without industrial support. Only in that situation can you think of giving away your work free."

That indeed is what Potrykus announced he and Beyer planned to do. The two scientists soon discovered, however, that giving away golden rice was not going to be as easy as they thought. The genes they transferred and the bacteria they used to transfer those genes were all encumbered by patents and proprietary rights. Three months ago, the two scientists struck a deal with AstraZeneca, which is based in London and holds an exclusive license to one of the genes Potrykus and Beyer used to create golden rice. In exchange for commercial marketing rights in the U.S. and other affluent markets, AstraZeneca agreed to lend its financial muscle and legal expertise to the cause of putting the seeds into the hands of poor farmers at no charge.

No sooner had the deal been made than the critics of agricultural biotechnology erupted. "A rip-off of the public trust," grumbled the Rural Advancement Foundation International, an advocacy group based in Winnipeg, Canada. "Asian farmers get (unproved) genetically modified rice, and AstraZeneca gets the 'gold.'" Potrykus was dismayed by such negative reaction. "It would be irresponsible," he exclaimed, "not to say immoral, not to use biotechnology to try to solve this problem!" But such expressions of good intentions

WEIGHING THE PERILS

BENEATH THE HYPERBOLIC TALK OF Frankenfoods and Superweeds, even proponents of agricultural biotechnology agree, lie a number of real concerns. To begin with, all foods, including the transgenic foods created through genetic engineering, are potential sources of allergens. That's because the transferred genes contain instructions for making proteins, and not all proteins are equal. Some—those in peanuts, for example—are well known for causing allergic reactions. To many, the possibility that golden rice might cause such a problem seems farfetched, but it nonetheless needs to be considered.

Then there is the problem of "genetic pollution," as opponents of biotechnology term it. Pollen grains from such wind-pollinated plants as corn and canola, for instance, are carried far and wide. To farmers, this mainly poses a nuisance. Transgenic canola grown in one field, for example, can very easily pollinate nontransgenic plants grown in the next. Indeed this is the reason behind the furor that recently erupted in Europe when it was discovered that canola seeds from Canada—unwittingly planted by farmers in England, France, Germany and Sweden—contained transgenic contaminants.

The continuing flap over Bt corn and cotton—now grown not only in the U.S. but also in Argentina and China—has provided more fodder for debate. Bt stands for a common soil bacteria, *Bacillus thuringiensis*, different strains of which produce toxins that target specific insects. By transferring to corn and cotton the bacterial gene responsible for making this toxin, Monsanto and other companies have produced crops that are resistant to the European corn borer and the cotton bollworm. An immediate concern, raised by a number of ecologists, is whether or not widespread planting of these crops

will spur the development of resistance to Bt among crop pests. That would be unfortunate, they point out, because Bt is a safe and effective natural insecticide that is popular with organic farmers.

SQUEEZE ME: Scientists turned off the gene that makes tomatoes soft and squishy

Even more worrisome are ecological concerns. In 1999 Cornell University entomologist John Losey performed a provocative, "seat-of-the-pants" laboratory experiment. He dusted Bt corn pollen on plants populated by monarch-butterfly caterpillars. Many of the caterpillars died. Could what happened in Losey's laboratory happen in cornfields across the Midwest? Were these lovely butterflies, already under pressure owing to human encroachment on their Mexican wintering grounds, about to face a new threat from high-tech farmers in the north?

The upshot: despite studies pro and con—and countless save-the-monarch protests acted out by children dressed in butterfly costumes—a conclusive answer to this question has yet to come. Losey himself is not yet convinced that Bt corn poses a grave danger to North America's monarch-butterfly population, but he does think the issue deserves attention. And others agree. "I'm not anti biotechnology per se," says biologist Rebecca Goldberg, a senior scientist with the Environmental Defense Fund, "but I would like to have a tougher regulatory regime. These crops should be subject to more careful screening before they are released."

Are there more potential pitfalls? There are. Among other things, there is the possibility that as transgenes in pollen drift, they will fertilize wild plants, and weeds will emerge that

are hardier and even more difficult to control. No one knows how common the exchange of genes between domestic plants and their wild relatives really is, but Margaret Mellon, director of the Union of Concerned Scientists' agriculture and biotechnology program, is certainly not alone in thinking that it's high time we find out. Says she: "People should be responding to these concerns with experiments, not assurances."

And that is beginning to happen, although—contrary to expectations—the reports coming in are not necessarily that scary. For three years now, University of Arizona entomologist Bruce Tabashnik has been monitoring fields of Bt cotton that farmers have planted in his state. And in this instance at least, he says, "the environmental risks seem minimal, and the benefits seem great." First of all, cotton is self-pollinated rather than wind-pollinated, so that the spread of the Bt gene is of less concern. And because the Bt gene is so effective, he notes, Arizona farmers have reduced their use of chemical insecticides 75%. So far, the pink bollworm population has not rebounded, indicating that the feared resistance to Bt has not yet developed.

ASSESSING THE PROMISE

ARE THE CRITICS OF AGRICULtural biotechnology right? Is biotech's promise nothing more than overblown corporate hype? The papaya growers in Hawaii's Puna district clamor to disagree. In 1992 a wildfire epidemic of papaya ringspot virus threatened to destroy the state's papaya industry; by 1994, nearly half the state's papaya acreage had been infected, their owners forced to seek outside employment. But then help arrived, in the form of a virus-resistant transgenic papaya developed by Cornell University plant pathologist Dennis Gonsalves. In 1995 a team of scientists set up a field trial of two transgenic lines—UH SunUP and UH Rainbow—and by 1996, the verdict had been rendered. As everyone could see, the nontransgenic plants in the field trial were a stunted mess, and the transgenic plants were healthy. In 1998, after negotiations with four patent holders, the papaya growers switched en masse to the transgenic seeds and reclaimed their orchards. "Consumer acceptance has been great," reports Rusty Perry, who runs a papaya farm near Puna. "We've found that customers are more concerned with how the fruits look and taste than with whether they are transgenic or not."

Viral diseases, along with insect infestations, are a major cause of crop loss in Africa, observes Kenyan plant scientist Florence Wambugu. African sweet-potato fields, for example, yield only 2.4 tons per acre, vs. more than double that in the rest of the world. Soon Wambugu hopes to start raising those yields by introducing a transgenic sweet potato that is resistant to the feathery mottle virus. There really is no other option, explains Wambugu, who currently directs the International Service for the Acquisition of Agri-biotech Applications in Nairobi. "You can't control the virus in the field, and you can't breed in resistance through conventional means."

To Wambugu, the flap in the U.S. and Europe over genetically engineered crops seems almost ludicrous. In Africa, she notes, nearly half the fruit and vegetable harvest is lost because it rots on the way to market. "If we had a transgenic banana that ripened more slowly," she says, "we could have 40% more bananas than now." Wambugu also dreams of getting access to herbicide-resistant crops. Says she: "We could liberate so many people if our crops were resistant to herbicides that we could then spray on the surrounding weeds. Weeding enslaves Africans; it keeps children from school."

In Wambugu's view, there are more benefits to be derived from agricultural biotechnology in Africa than practically anywhere else on the planet—and this may be so. Among the genetic-engineering projects funded by the Rockefeller Foundation is one aimed at controlling striga, a weed that parasitizes the roots of African corn plants. At present there is little farmers can do about striga infestation, so tightly intertwined are the weed's roots with the roots of the corn plants it targets. But scientists have come to understand the source of the problem: corn roots exude chemicals that attract striga. So it may prove possible to identify the genes that are responsible and turn them off.

The widespread perception that agricultural biotechnology is intrinsically inimical to the environment perplexes the Rockefeller Foundation's Conway, who views genetic engineering as an important tool for achieving what he has termed a "doubly green revolution." If the technology can marshal a plant's natural defenses against weeds and viruses, if it can induce crops to flourish with minimal application of chemical fertilizers, if it can make dryland agriculture more productive without straining local water supplies, then what's wrong with it?

Of course, these particular breakthroughs have not happened yet. But as the genomes of major crops are ever more finely mapped, and as the tools for transferring genes become ever more precise, the possibility for tinkering with complex biochemical pathways can be expected to expand rapidly. As Potrykus sees it, there is no question that agricultural biotechnology can be harnessed for the good of humankind. The only question is whether there is the collective will to do so. And the answer may well emerge as the people of the world weigh the future of golden rice.

—*With reporting by Simon Robinson/Nairobi*

The secret nuclear war

The equivalent of a nuclear war has already happened. Over the last half-century, millions have died as a result of accidents, experiments, lies and cover-ups by the nuclear industry. **Eduardo Goncalves** pulls together a number of examples, and counts the fearful total cost.

Hugo Paulino was proud to be a fusilier. He was even prouder to be serving as a UN peacekeeper in Kosovo. It was his chance to help the innocent casualties of war. His parents did not expect him to become one.

Hugo, says his father Luis, died of leukaemia caused by radiation from depleted uranium (DU) shells fired by NATO during the Kosovo war. He was one of hundreds of Portuguese peacekeepers sent to Klina, an area heavily bombed with these munitions. Their patrol detail included the local lorry park, bombed because it had served as a Serb tank reserve, and the Valujak mines, which sheltered Serbian troops.

In their time off, the soldiers bathed in the river and gratefully supplemented their tasteless rations with local fruit and cheeses given to them by thankful nuns from the convent they guarded. Out of curiosity, they would climb inside the destroyed Serbian tanks littering the area.

Hugo arrived back in Portugal from his tour of duty on 12 February 2000, complaining of headaches, nausea and 'flu-like symptoms'. Ten days later, on 22 February, he suffered a major seizure. He was rushed to Lisbon's military hospital, where his condition rapidly deteriorated. On 9 March, he died. He was 21.

The military autopsy, which was kept secret for 10 months, claimed his death was due to septicaemia and 'herpes of the brain'. Not so, says Luis Paulino. 'When he was undergoing tests, a doctor called me over and said he thought it could be from radiation.'

It was only then that Luis learnt about the uranium shells—something his son had never been warned about or given protective clothing against. He contacted doctors and relatives of Belgian and Italian soldiers suspected of having succumbed to radiation poisoning.

'The similarities were extraordinary', he said. 'My son had died from leukaemia. That is why the military classified the autopsy report and wanted me to sign over all rights to its release.'

Today, Kosovo is littered with destroyed tanks, and pieces of radioactive shrapnel. NATO forces fired 31,000 depleted uranium shells during the Kosovo campaign, and 10,800 into neighbouring Bosnia. The people NATO set out to protect—and the soldiers it sent out to protect them—are now dying. According to Bosnia's health minister, Boza Ljubic, cancer deaths among civilians have risen to 230 cases per 100,000 last year, up from 152 in 1999. Leukaemia cases, he added, had doubled.

Scientists predict that the use of DU in Serbia will lead to more than 10,000 deaths from cancer among local residents, aid workers, and peacekeepers. Belated confessions that plutonium was also used may prompt these estimates to be revised. But while NATO struggles to stave off accusations of a cover-up, the Balkans are merely the newest battlefield in a silent world war that has claimed millions of lives. Most of its victims have died not in war-zones, but in ordinary communities scattered across the globe.

The hidden deaths of Newbury

Far away from the war-torn Balkans is Newbury, a prosperous white-collar industrial town in London's commuter belt. On its outskirts is Greenham Common, the former US Air Force station that was one of America's most important strategic bases during the Cold War. The base was closed down after the signing of the INF (Intermediate Nuclear Forces) Treaty by Ronald Reagan and Mikhail Gorbachev. The nuclear threat was over. Or so people thought.

In August 1993, Ann Capewell—who lived just one mile away from the base's former runway—died of acute myeloid leukaemia. She was 16 when she passed away, just 40 days after diagnosis. As they were coming to terms with their sudden loss, her parents—Richard and Elizabeth—were surprised to find a number of other cases of leukaemia in their locality.

The more they looked, the more cases they found. 'Many were just a stone's throw from our front door,' says Richard, 'mainly cases of myeloid leukaemia in young people.' What none of them knew was that they were the victims of a nuclear accident at Greenham Common that had been carefully covered up by successive British and American administrations.

> ## 'It is believed that the estimated 1,900 nuclear tests conducted during the Cold War released fallout equivalent to 40,000 Hiroshimas in every corner of the globe.'

On February 28 1958, a laden B-47 nuclear bomber was awaiting clearance for take-off when it was suddenly engulfed in a huge fireball. Another bomber flying overhead had dropped a full fuel tank just 65 feet away. The plane exploded and burnt uncontrollably for days. As did its deadly payload.

A secret study by scientists at Britain's nearby nuclear bomb laboratory at Aldermaston documented the fallout, but the findings were never disclosed. The report showed how radioactive particles had been 'glued' to the runway surface by fire-fighters attempting to extinguish the blazing bomber—and that these were now being slowly blown into Newbury and over other local communities by aircraft jet blast.

'Virtually all the cases of leukaemias and lymphomas are in a band stretching from Greenham Common into south Newbury,' says Elizabeth. However, the British government continues to deny the cluster's existence, whilst the Americans still insist there was no accident.

Yet this was just one of countless disasters, experiments and officially-sanctioned activities which the nuclear powers have kept a closely-guarded secret. Between them, they have caused a global human death toll which is utterly unprecedented and profoundly shocking.

Broken Arrows

In 1981, the Pentagon publicly released a list of 32 'Broken Arrows—official military terminology for an accident involving a nuclear weapon. The report gave few details and did not divulge the location of some accidents. It was prepared in response to mounting media pressure about possible accident cover-ups.

But another US government document, this time secret, indicates that the official report may be seriously misleading. It states that 'a total of 1,250 nuclear weapons have been involved in accidents during handling, storage and transportation', a number of which 'resulted in, or had high potential for, plutonium dispersal.'[1]

Washington has never acknowledged the human consequences of even those few accidents it admits to, such as the Thule disaster in Greenland in 1968. When a B-52 bomber crashed at this secret nuclear base, all four bombs detonated, and a cloud of plutonium rose 800 metres in the air, blowing deadly radioactive particles hundreds of miles. The authorities downplayed the possibility of any health risks. But today, many local Eskimos, and their huskies, suffer from cancer, and over 300 people involved in the clean-up operation alone have since died of cancer and mysterious illnesses.

We may never know the true toll from all the bomb accidents, as the nuclear powers classify these disasters not as matters of public interest but of 'national security' instead. Indeed, it is only now that details are beginning to emerge of some accidents at bomb factories and nuclear plants that took place several decades ago.

Soviet sins

In 1991, Polish film-maker Slawomir Grunberg was invited to a little-known town in Russia's Ural mountains that was once part of a top-secret Soviet nuclear bomb-making complex. What he found was a tragedy of extraordinary dimensions, largely unknown to the outside world, and ignored by post-Cold War leaders.

His film—*Chelyabinsk: The Most Contaminated Spot on the Planet*—tells the story of the disasters at the Soviet Union's first plutonium factory, and the poisoning of hundreds of thousands of people. For years, the complex dumped its nuclear waste—totalling 76 million cubic metres—into the Techa River, the sole water source for scores of local communities that line its banks. According to a local doctor, people received an average radiation dose 57 times higher than that of Chernobyl's inhabitants.

In 1957, there was an explosion at a waste storage facility that blew 2 million curies of radiation into the atmosphere. The kilometre-high cloud drifted over three

The cancer epidemic

Scientists at St Andrew's University recently found that cells exposed to a dose of just two alpha particles of radiation produced as many cancers as much higher doses of radiation. They concluded that a single alpha particle of radiation could be carcinogenic.

Herman Muller, who has received a Nobel Prize for his work, has shown how the human race's continuous exposure to so-called 'low-level' radiation is causing a gradual reduction in its ability to survive, as successive generations are genetically damaged. The spreading and accumulation of even tiny genetic mutations pass through family lines, provoking allergies, asthma, juvenile diabetes, hypertension, arthritis, high blood cholesterol conditions, and muscular and bone defects.

Dr Chris Busby, who has extensively researched the low-level radiation threat, has made a link between everyday radiation exposure and a range of modern ailments: 'There have been tremendous increases in diseases resulting from the breakdown of the immune system in the last 20 years: diabetes, asthma, AIDS and others which may have an immune-system link, such as MS and ME. A whole spectrum of neurological conditions of unknown origin has developed'.[10]

Around the world, a pattern is emerging. For the first time in modern history, mortality rates among adults between the ages of 15 and 54 are actually increasing, and have been since 1982. In July 1983, the US Center for Birth Defects in Atlanta, Georgia, reported that physical and mental disabilities in the under-17s had doubled—despite a reduction in diseases such as polio, and improved vaccines and medical care.

Defects in new-born babies doubled between the 1950s and 1980s, as did long-term debilitating diseases. The US Environmental Protection Agency adds that 23 per cent of US males were sterile in 1980, compared to 0.5 per cent in 1938.

Above all, cancer is now an epidemic. In 1900, cancer accounted for only 4 per cent of deaths in the US. Now it is the second leading cause of premature mortality. Worldwide, the World Health Organisation (WHO) estimates the number of cancers will double in most countries over the next 25 years.

Within a few years, the chances of getting cancer in Britain will be as high as 40 per cent—virtually the toss of a coin.

Soviet provinces, contaminating over 250,000 people living in 217 towns and villages. Only a handful of local inhabitants were ever evacuated.

10 years later, Lake Karachay, also used as a waste dump, began to dry up. The sediment around its shores blew 5 million curies of radioactive dust over 25,000 square kilometres, irradiating 500,000 people. Even today, the lake is so 'hot' that standing on its shore will kill a person within one hour.

Grunberg's film tells of the terrible toll of these disasters on local families, such as that of Idris Sunrasin, whose grandmother, parents and three siblings have died of cancer. Leukaemia cases increased by 41 per cent after the plant began operations, and the average life span for women in 1993 was 47, compared to 72 nationally. For men it was just 45.

The secret nuclear war

Russia's nuclear industry is commonly regarded as cavalier in regard to health and safety. But the fact is that the nuclear military-industrial complex everywhere has been quite willing to deliberately endanger and sacrifice the lives of innocent civilians to further its ambitions.

The US government, for example, recently admitted its nuclear scientists carried out over 4,000 experiments on live humans between 1944 and 1974. They included feeding radioactive food to disabled children, irradiating prisoners' testicles, and trials on new-born babies and pregnant mothers. Scientists involved with the Manhattan Project injected people with plutonium without telling them. An autopsy of one of the victims reportedly showed that his bones 'looked like Swiss cheese'. At the University of Cincinnati, 88 mainly low-income, black women were subjected to huge doses of radiation in an experiment funded by the military. They suffered acute radiation sickness. Nineteen of them died.

'Scientists predict that millions will die in centuries to come from nuclear tests that happened in the 1950s and 1960s.'

Details of many experiments still remain shrouded in secrecy, whilst little is known of the more shocking ones to come to light—such as one when a man was injected with what a report described as 'about a lethal dose' of strontium-89.[2]

In Britain too, scientists have experimented with plutonium on new-born babies, ethnic minorities and the disabled. When American colleagues reviewed a British proposal for a joint experiment, they concluded: 'What is the worst thing that can happen to a human being as a result of being a subject? Death.'[3]

They also conducted experiments similar to America's 'Green Run' programme, in which 'dirty' radiation was released over populated areas in the western states of Washington and Oregon contaminating farmland, crops and water. The 'scrubber' filters in Hanford's nuclear stacks were deliberately switched off first. Scientists, posing as agriculture department officials, found radiation contamination levels on farms hundreds of times above 'safety' levels.

But America's farmers and consumers were not told this, and the British public has never been officially told about experiments on its own soil.

Forty thousand Hiroshimas

It is believed that the estimated 1,900 nuclear tests conducted during the Cold War released fallout equivalent to 40,000 Hiroshimas in every corner of the globe. Fission products from the Nevada Test site can be detected in the ecosystems of countries as far apart as South Africa, Brazil, and Malaysia. Here, too, ordinary people were guinea pigs in a global nuclear experiment. The public health hazards were known right from the beginning, but concealed from the public. A 1957 US government study predicted that recent American tests had produced an extra 2,000 'genetically defective' babies in the US each year, and up to 35,000 every year around the globe. They continued regardless.

Ernest Sternglass's research shows how, in 1964, between 10,000 and 15,000 children were lost by miscarriage and stillbirth in New York state alone—and that there were some 10 to 15 times this number of foetal deaths across America.[4]

> ## 'Over the years, the Harwell, Aldermaston and Amersham plants have pumped millions of gallons of liquid contaminated with radioactive waste into the River Thames.'

Those who lived closest to the test sites have seen their families decimated. Such as the 100,000 people who were directly downwind of Nevada's fallout. They included the Mormon community of St George in Utah, 100 miles away from 'Ground Zero'—the spot where the bombs were detonated. Cancer used to be virtually unheard of among its population. Mormons do not smoke or drink alcohol or coffee, and live largely off their own home-grown produce.

Mormons are also highly patriotic. They believe government to be 'God-given', and do not protest. The military could afford to wait until the wind was blowing from the test site towards St George before detonating a device. After all, President Eisenhower had said: 'We can afford to sacrifice a few thousand people out there in defence of national security.'[5]

When the leukaemia cases suddenly appeared, doctors—unused to the disease—literally had no idea what it was. A nine-year-old boy, misdiagnosed with diabetes,

died after a single shot of insulin. Women who complained of radiation sickness symptoms were told they had 'housewife syndrome'. Many gave birth to terribly deformed babies that became known as 'the sacrifice babies'. Elmer Pickett, the local mortician, had to learn new embalming techniques for the small bodies of wasted children killed by leukaemia. He himself was to lose no fewer than 16 members of his immediate family to cancer.

By the mid-1950s, just a few years after the tests began, St George had a leukaemia rate 2.5 times the national average, whereas before it was virtually non-existent. The total number of radiation deaths are said to have totalled 1,600—in a town with a population of just 5,000.

The military simply lied about the radiation doses people were getting. Former army medic Van Brandon later revealed how his unit kept two sets of radiation readings for test fallout in the area. 'One set was to show that no one received an [elevated] exposure' whilst 'the other set of books showed the actual reading. That set was brought in a locked briefcase every morning.'[6]

Continuous fallout

The world's population is still being subjected to the continuous fallout of the 170 megatons of long-lived nuclear fission products blasted into the atmosphere and returned daily to earth by wind and rain—slowly poisoning our bodies via the air we breathe, the food we eat, and the water we drink. Scientists predict that millions will die in centuries to come from tests that happened in the 1950s and 1960s.

But whilst atmospheric testing is now banned, over 400 nuclear bomb factories and power plants around the world make 'routine discharges' of nuclear waste into the environment. Thousands of nuclear waste dumping grounds, many of them leaking, are contaminating soil and water every day. The production of America's nuclear weapons arsenal alone has produced 100 million cubic metres of long-lived radioactive waste.

The notorious Hanford plutonium factory—which produced the fissile materials for the Trinity test and Nagasaki bomb—has discharged over 440 billion gallons of contaminated liquid into the surrounding area, contaminating 200 square miles of groundwater, but concealed the dangers from the public. Officials knew as early as the late 1940s that the nearby Columbia River was becoming seriously contaminated and a hazard to local fishermen. They chose to keep information about discharges secret and not to issue warnings.

In Britain, there are 7,000 sites licensed to use nuclear materials, 1,000 of which are allowed to discharge wastes. Three of them, closely involved in Britain's nuclear bomb programme, are located near the River Thames. Over the years, the Harwell, Aldermaston and Amersham plants have pumped millions of gallons of liquid contaminated with radioactive waste into the river.

They did so in the face of opposition from government ministers and officials who said 'the 6 million inhabitants of London derive their drinking water from this source. Any increase in [radio-]activity of the water supply would increase the genetic load on this comparatively large group.'[7] One government minister even wrote of his fears that the dumping 'would produce between 10 and 300 severely abnormal individuals per generation'.

Public relations officers at Harwell themselves added: 'the potential sufferers are 8 million in number, including both Houses of Parliament, Fleet Street and Whitehall'. These discharges continue to this day.

Study after study has uncovered 'clusters' of cancers and high rates of other unusual illnesses near nuclear plants, including deformities and Down Syndrome. Exposure to radiation among Sellafield's workers, in northwest England, has been linked to a greater risk of fathering a stillborn child and leukaemia among off-spring. Reports also suggest a higher risk of babies developing spina bifida in the womb.

Although the plant denies any link, even official MAFF studies have shown high levels of contamination in locally-grown fruit and vegetables, as well as wild animals. The pollution from Sellafield alone is such that it has coated the shores of the whole of Britain—from Wales to Scotland, and even Hartlepool in north-eastern England. A nationwide study organised by Harwell found that Sellafield 'is a source of plutonium contamination in the wider population of the British Isles'.[8]

> **'Study after study has uncovered 'clusters' of cancers and high rates of other illnesses near nuclear plants, including deformities and Down Syndrome. Exposure to radiation among Sellafield's workers, in NW England, has been linked to a greater risk of fathering a stillborn child and leukaemia among off-spring.'**

Those who live nearest the plant face the greatest threat. A study of autopsy tissue by the National Radiological Protection Board (NRPB) found high plutonium levels in the lungs of local Cumbrians—350 per cent higher than people in other parts of the country. 'Cancer clusters' have been found around nuclear plants across the globe—from France to Taiwan, Germany to Canada. A joint White House/US Department of Energy investigation recently found a high incidence of 22 different kinds of cancer at 14 different US nuclear weapons facilities around the country.

Meanwhile, a Greenpeace USA study of the toxicity of the Mississippi river showed that from 1968-83 there were 66,000 radiation deaths in the counties lining its banks—more than the number of Americans who died during the Vietnam war.

Don't blame us

Despite the growing catalogue of tragedy, the nuclear establishment has consistently tried to deny responsibility. It claims that only high doses of radiation—such as those experienced by the victims of the Hiroshima and Nagasaki bombs—are dangerous, though even here they have misrepresented the data. They say that the everyday doses from nuclear plant discharges, bomb factories and transportation of radioactive materials are 'insignificant', and that accidents are virtually impossible.

The truth, however, is that the real number and seriousness of accidents has never been disclosed, and that the damage from fallout has been covered up. The nuclear establishment now grudgingly (and belatedly) accepts that there is no such thing as a safe dose of radiation, however 'low', yet the poisonous discharges continue. When those within the nuclear establishment try to speak out, they are harassed, intimidated—and even threatened.

John Gofman, former head of Lawrence Livermore's biomedical unit, who helped produce the world's first plutonium for the bomb, was for years at the heart of the nuclear complex. He recalls painfully the time he was called to give evidence before a Congressional inquiry set up to defuse mounting concern over radiation's dangers.

'Chet Holifield and Craig Hosmer of the Joint Committee (on Atomic Energy) came in and turned to me and said: "Just what the hell do you think you two are doing, getting all those little old ladies in tennis shoes up in arms about our atomic energy program? There are people like you who have tried to hurt the Atomic Energy Commission program before. We got them, and we'll get you."'[9]

Gofman was eventually forced out of his job. But the facts of his research—and that of many other scientists—speak for themselves.

The final reckoning

But could radiation really be to blame for these deaths? Are the health costs really that great? The latest research suggests they are.

It is only very recently that clues have surfaced as to the massive destructive power of radiation in terms of human health. The accident at Chernobyl will kill an estimated half a million people worldwide from cancer, and perhaps more. 90 per cent of children in the neighbouring former Soviet republic of Belarus are contaminated for life—the poisoning of an entire country's gene pool.

Ernest Sternglass calculates that, at the height of nuclear testing, there were as many as 3 million foetal deaths, spontaneous abortions and stillbirths in the US alone. In addition, 375,000 babies died in their first year of life from radiation-linked diseases.[11]

The final reckoning

How many deaths is the nuclear industry responsible for? The following calculations of numbers of cancers caused by radiation are the latest and most accurate:[*]

from nuclear bomb production and testing: 385 million

from bomb and plant accidents: 9.7 million

from the 'routine discharges' of nuclear power plants
(5 million of them among populations living nearby):   6.6 million

likely number of total cancer fatalities worldwide: 175 million

[Added to this number are 235 million genetically damaged and diseased people, and 588 million children born with diseases such as brain damage, mental disabilities, spina bifida, genital deformities, and childhood cancers.]

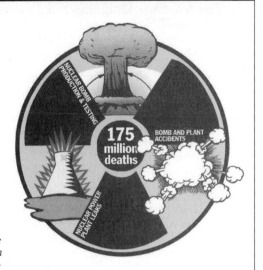

[*]*Calculated by Rosalie Bertell, using the official 'radiation risk' estimates published in 1991 by the International Commission on Radiological Protection (ICRP), and the total radiation exposure data to the global population calculated by the UN Scientific Committee on the Effects of Atomic Radiation (UNSCEAR) in 1993.*

Rosalie Bertell, author of the classic book *No Immediate Danger*, now revised and re-released, has attempted to piece together a global casualty list from the nuclear establishment's own data. The figures she has come up with are chilling—but entirely plausible.

Using the official 'radiation risk' estimates published in 1991 by the International Commission on Radiological Protection (ICRP), and the total radiation exposure data to the global population calculated by the UN Scientific Committee on the Effects of Atomic Radiation (UNSCEAR) in 1993, she has come up with a terrifying tally:

- 358 million cancers from nuclear bomb production and testing
- 9.7 million cancers from bomb and plant accidents
- 6.6 million cancers from the 'routine discharges' of nuclear power plants (5 million of them among populations living nearby).
- As many as 175 million of these cancers could be fatal.

Added to this number are no fewer than 235 million genetically damaged and diseased people, and a staggering 588 million children born with what are called 'teratogenic effects'—diseases such as brain damage, mental disabilities, spina bifida, genital deformities, and childhood cancers.

Furthermore, says Bertell, we should include the problem of nonfatal cancers and of other damage which is debilitating but not counted for insurance and liability purposes'[12]—such as the 500 million babies lost as stillbirths because they were exposed to radiation whilst still in the womb, but are not counted as 'official' radiation victims.

It is what the nuclear holocaust peace campaigners always warned of if war between the old superpowers broke out, yet it has already happened and with barely a shot being fired. Its toll is greater than that of all the wars in history put together, yet no-one is counted as among the war dead.

'It is the nuclear holocaust that peace campaigners always warned of if war between the old superpowers broke out, yet it has already happened and with barely a shot being fired.'

Its virtually infinite killing and maiming power leads Rosalie Bertell to demand that we learn a new language to express a terrifying possibility: 'The concept of species annihilation means a relatively swift, deliberately induced end to history, culture, science, biological reproduction and memory. It is the ultimate human rejection of the gift of life, an act which requires a new word to describe it: omnicide'.[13]

*Eduardo Goncalves is a freelance journalist and environmental researcher. He is author of tile reports **Broken Arrow—Greenham Common's Secret Nuclear Accident** and **Nuclear Guinea Pigs—British Human Radiation Experiments**, published by CND (UK), and was researcher to the film **The Dragon that Slew St George**. He is currently writing a book about the hidden history of the nuclear age.*

Notes

1. 'Report of the safety criteria for plutonium-bearing weapons—summary', US Department of Energy, February 14, 1973, document RS5640/1035.

2. Strontium metabolism meeting, Atomic Energy Division–Division of Biology and Medicine, January 17,1954.

3. memorandum to Bart Gledhill, chairman, Human Subjects Committee. LLNL, from Larry Anderson, LLNL, February 21,1989.

4. see 'Secret Fallout, Low-Level Radiation from Hiroshima to Three-Mile Island'. Ernest Sternglass, McGraw-Hill, New York, 1981.

5. see 'American Ground Zero; The Secret Nuclear War', Carole Gallagher, MIT Press. Boston, 1993.

6. Washington Post, February 24, 1994.

7. see PRO files AB 6/1379 and AB 6/2453 and 3584.

8. 'Variations in the concentration of plutonium, strontium-90 and total alpha-emitters in human teeth', RG. O'Donnell et al, Sd. Tot. Env, 201 (1997) 235–243.

9. interview with Gofman, DOE/OHRE Oral History Project, December 1994, pp 49-50 of official transcripts.

10. 'Wings of Death—nuclear pollution and human health', Dr. Chris Busby, Green Audit, Wales, 1995

11. see 'Secret Fallout, Low-Level Radiation from Hiroshima to Three-Mile Island', Ernest Sternglass, McGraw-Hill, New York, 1981.

12. from 'No Immediate Danger— Prognosis for a Radioactive Earth', Dr Rosalie Bertell. Women's Press. London 1985 (revised 2001)

13. pers. Comm. 4 February 2001

Further reading:

'No Immediate Danger—Prognosis for a Radioactive Earth', Dr Rosalie Bertell, Women's Press, London (revised 2001)

'Deadly Deceit—low-level radiation, high-level cover-up', Dr. Jay Gould and Benjamin A. Goldman, Four Walls Eight Windows, New York, 1991

'Wings of Death—nuclear pollution and human health', Dr. Chris Busby, Green Audit, Wales, 1995

'American Ground Zero: The Secret Nuclear War', Carole Gallagher, MIT Press, Boston, 1993

'Radioactive Heaven and Earth—the health effects of nuclear weapons testing in, on, and above the earth', a report of the IPPNW International Commission, Zed Books, 1991 'Secret Fallout. Low-Level Radiation from Hiroshima to Three-Mile Island', Ernest Sternglass, McGraw-Hill, New York, 1981

'Clouds of Deceit—the deadly legacy of Britain's bomb tests', Joan Smith, Faber and Faber, London, 1985

'Nuclear Wastelands', Arjun Makhijani et al (eds), MIT Press, Boston, 1995 'Radiation and Human Health', Dr. John W. Gofman, Sierra Book Club, San Francisco, 1981

'The Greenpeace Book of the Nuclear Age—The Hidden History, the Human Cost', John May, Victor Gollancz, 1989

'The Unsinkable Aircraft Carrier—American military power in Britain', Duncan Campbell, Michael Joseph, London 1984

Unmasking Bioterror

Terrorists are experimenting with pathogens and poisons.
But they have failed before: daunting technical obstacles
stand in the way of biological and chemical weapons.

By Sharon Begley

Martin Quintino figures he's ready. On the day after the atrocities of Sept. 11, the 22-year-old Miami salesclerk bought one gas mask, one chemical bodysuit, a pair of camouflage gloves and an airtight hood that seals off the head and neck, all for $150. He wasn't alone. After residents of Snellville, Ga., stocked up on flags, they opened their wallets for $50 chemical suits and $100 water-purification kits. On New York's Fifth Avenue, Larry Lopez has been answering the phone of the Army-Navy store he manages, "We're out of gas masks. How can we help you?" In Boston, pharmacies have sold thousands of tablets of Cipro, an antibiotic that can treat anthrax. Miami's Manny Alvarez hasn't a single $38 chemical bodysuit left in his police-supply store—even for himself. But he doesn't care. "They give you a false sense of security," Alvarez says. "Are you going to wear a bodysuit to every Dolphins game you go to? I don't even have a gas mask in my house."

The attacks on the World Trade Center and Pentagon have made an anxious country ask, "What's next?" and for many the worry is: a terrorist assault with biological or chemical weapons. But just as there are panicky Martin Quintinos as well as sanguine Manny Alvarezes among ordinary Americans, so there is a deep divide within the intelligence, national-security, law-enforcement and scientific communities about the risk of attacks with "bugs

or gas," as insiders call germ and chemical weapons. Skeptics point out that the technological hurdles are formidable. Expertise is rare. "There is an underappreciation of the technological obstacles to delivery, particularly with biological agents," says Elisa Harris, a National Security Council official during the Clinton administration. But because terrorists have mounted germ and chemical attacks before, runs the counterargument, they can do so again. This might be just a frustrating standoff among experts, except for one detail. Those with the deepest firsthand knowledge of bugs-and-gas take the threat the most seriously. One is microbiologist Bill Patrick, a leader in America's bioweapons program from 1951 to 1986, an Iraqi weapons inspector in 1994 and now a germ-warfare consultant (his business card shows a skull and crossbones). Unless something is done, says Patrick, the possibility of a bioweapon attack by agents of Osama bin Laden is "highly likely."

What we know for sure is that terrorists are experimenting with chemical and biological weapons. Operatives of bin Laden's Qaeda network have tried (apparently without success) to obtain anthrax and botulinum toxin in Czechoslovakia, an FBI official tells NEWS-WEEK. Dozens of rabbits and dogs have been found fatally poisoned near bin Laden's Jalalabad training camps, according to a foreign intelligence agency. Though U.S. of-

Accessing the Threat of 'Bugs' and 'Gas'

The Sept. 11 terrorist attacks have made a nervous country ask, "What next?" Despite a run on Cipro and gas masks, a terrorist attack with germs, chemicals or nuclear materials would be hugely difficult.

Chemical Agents

While some toxic agents are commercially available and can be dispersed with a simple truck, others are more technically challenging.

MUSTARD GAS First used as a weapon in World War I, it causes blisters and can be fatal if inhaled. The chemical ingredients are hard to obtain.

HYDROGEN CYANIDE A blood agent used worldwide to manufacture acrylic polymers. Reportedly employed during the Iraq-Iran war.

SARIN: A nerve agent developed during World War II, it causes respiratory failure. In 1995 a Japanese cult killed 12 people in a Tokyo subway with it.

CS: Internationally, the most widely used tear gas for riot control. It can be lethal, but only if inhaled in very high concentrations.

SOMAN: This nerve agent made up much of the former Soviet Union's chemical arsenal. Production began in 1967. May be in Iraqi hands.

PHOSGENE: The most dangerous of the group called choking agents, it accounted for 80 percent of all chemical deaths during WWI.

Biological Agents

Certain bacteria, viruses and toxins could be used as weapons, though most agents are difficult to process into lethal forms.

ANTHRAX: Infectious disease that would most likely be spread by aerosol. It causes respiratory failure and death. Antibiotics help only if given early.

PLAGUE: Could be delivered via contaminated vectors (like fleas) or by aerosol. Vaccines exist, but their efficacy against aerosolized plague is unknown.

BOTULINUM: Toxin can cause respiratory failure and death, but lethal strains are hard to grow and 'weaponize.' Not contagious.

BRUCELLOSIS: Mostly a disease found in cattle. Could be spread by aerosol. Not transmittable by humans; antibiotics are ineffective.

CHOLERA: This bacteria is stable in water and could be used to contaminate reservoirs. Can be treated with antibiotics.

SMALLPOX: Eradicated in 1977, this highly contagious virus exists officially in two labs (U.S. and Russia). It's very hard to grow and aerosolize. Limited amounts of the vaccine exist.

Radioactive Agents

Terrorists could resort to smuggled nuclear materials to make crude bombs, but a radioactive release is easier.

PLUTONIUM: A fissile material used to create nuclear weapons.

CESIUM: One of the more commonly smuggled radioactive materials—but is not considered weapons grade.

COBALT: Used in medical laboratories; is relatively easy to smuggle and could be dangerous.

URANIUM 235: Highly enriched uranium—another fissile material—is extremely dangerous and is also used in making nuclear weapons.

What's Being Done

Federal, state and local governments are spending billions to bolster the country's ability to thwart and respond to an attack.

Training: Public-health officials and emergency-response teams run drills simulating how they would respond to an attack.

Medicine: The federal government is strengthening its management of medical stockpiles that could be used to treat victims.

Coordination: The designation of a new cabinet-level position for homeland security aims to integrate governmentwide protection efforts.

SOURCES: FEDERATION OF AMERICAN SCIENTISTS, U.S. GENERAL ACCOUNTING OFFICE, FEMA, CENTERS FOR DISEASE CONTROL, NEWSWEEK RESEARCH CENTER. TEXT AND RESEARCH BY KAREN YOURISH. GRAPHIC BY BONNIE SCRANTON.

ficials adamantly deny that their own satellites spied any such thing, in June CIA Director George Tenet warned, "Terrorists who fly no national flag are trying to acquire chemical and biological weapons." Chilling evidence of that came the following month, when convicted terrorist Ahmed Ressam (he was planning to blow up the Los Angeles airport as 1999 turned into 2000) testified that he had spent six months in 1998 at one of bin Laden's Af-

ghan training camps. There, he said, he learned to release cyanide into the ventilation systems of office buildings. Bin Laden, Ressam told intelligence officials, was also interested in the use of "low-flying aircraft for the distribution of toxic materials."

In light of last month's terror attacks, such evidence looms more ominous for a simple reason: by making the 1993 bombing of the World Trade Center look, in retro-

Suiting Up For Safety

This airtight suit, used regularly by hazardous-material professionals, could protect against a chem-bio terrorist attack.

AIR SUPPLY
A self-contained breathing apparatus is connected to an oxygen tank.

SECOND SKIN
Specially blended materials help seal out harmful contaminants.

GLOVES
Thick Army-issue butyl-rubber gloves attach to the suit arms with locking rings.

TERROR TESTING
Portable chemical detector (an APD 2000) identifies chemical-warfare agents that could be used in an attack.

DOWN BELOW
One-piece suit slips into boots. Splash guard hangs outside, protecting feet.

ROBIN NELSON

spect, like a dry run for Sept. 11, they suggest that recent biological and chemical attacks might also be harbingers of something more horrific. In 1984, followers of Bhagwan Shree Rajneesh contaminated drinking glasses and salad bars in an Oregon town with salmonella. No one died; 751 people came down with the nausea, severe diarrhea, chills, fever and dizziness that mark salmonella poisoning. It was the first, and so far only, biological-weapon attack in the United States. Eleven years later terrorists struck with chemical weapons. Members of the Aum Shinrikyo cult filled plastic bags with the nerve agent sarin, slipped into a Tokyo subway station and punctured the bags with umbrellas. Twelve people died. Though the casualty tolls in Oregon and Tokyo were low, the attacks were a proof of principle: bug and gas terrorism is logistically possible.

But not easy. To mount a germ or chemical assault, terrorists would have to obtain pathogens, culture them in vast quantities and—hardest of all—"weaponize" them, or turn them into a form that remains virulent. And then, of course, the germs have to be released. Weapons experts are understandably reluctant to run down the weak points in the world's system for preventing all this. But this much is known:

Obtaining pathogens: In 1986 the same company that sold the Rajneeshis their salmonella sold the University of Baghdad three types of anthrax and five strains of botulinum, recounts the new book "Germs: Biological Weapons and America's Secret War," by New York Times reporters Judith Miller, Stephen Engelberg and William Broad. (The sales were all legal.) Two years later the company sold anthrax and other pathogens to the Iraqi Ministry of Trade. Deadly pathogens were part of global commerce, and the consequences quickly became clear: from 1990 to 1995, Aum Shinrikyo released anthrax or botulinum around Tokyo up to 12 times. In all likelihood the cult obtained its seed stocks from a rogue government, says Harris. Anthrax can cause fever, respiratory collapse and death within days; botulinum can trigger dizziness, blurred vision, muscle weakening and, ultimately, respiratory failure. None of Aum Shinrikyo's releases caused casualties.

There are other sources of pathogens besides terrorist-friendly states. Anthrax is a relatively common veterinary disease. "It's in Afghanistan," notes molecular biologist Paul Keim of Northern Arizona State University. "If a cow dies of anthrax it will bleed out its nose. All you have to do is scrape up a little blood"—or even get spores from the soil or a carcass—"put it in a petri dish, and you have anthrax." Aum Shinrikyo obtained botulinum organisms from naturally contaminated soil. Bubonic plague is also abundant in nature. "There are little pockets of it in rodents throughout the world," says Stephen Morse of Columbia University. Staphylococcus B enterotoxin comes from foodborne bacteria.

A terrorist would not need to start with rotten chicken, however. The world's supplies of pathogens are ample, their security questionable. In Kazakhstan, site of the old Soviet Union's bioweapons plants, one research center keeps at least 80 strains of anthrax, as well as plague and cholera, at its main facility and eight satellite labs. "Just this year we built a concrete wall and were able to hire a guard who is actually a professional," says lab director Bakhyt Atshabar. "We've put up bars and doors and strengthened security. Of course, before, things were not so well controlled. People got in." At the eight satellite labs, he adds, "there are still problems with security." Smallpox is harder to acquire. After the World Health Organization declared the disease eradicated in 1980, only two repositories of the virus supposedly remained: 451

samples in deep freeze at the U.S. Centers for Disease Control and Prevention in Atlanta, and 120 in Koltsovo, Russia. Both are well secured. But a classified 1998 report by the CIA concluded that clandestine stocks remain, probably in North Korea and Iraq (as well as secret sites in Russia). And China, Cuba, India, Iran, Israel, Pakistan and the former Yugoslavia might have retained smallpox samples from the days when the disease was rampant.

'Weaponizing': A vial of smallpox or a petri dish of anthrax is not a weapon of mass destruction. When Aum piped botulinum into the streets of Tokyo using a truck with a compressor and vents, nobody got sick. It hadn't acquired a virulent strain. And unless your goal is the assassination of a single individual, you need (depending on the pathogen) pounds and pounds to come close to a WTC-level horror. That's a real obstacle to weaponizing smallpox: viruses grow only in live cells, not on dishes of nutrients as, say, staph does. And even if you reap a bumper crop, the germs must still be turned into respirable powder that can be blown into a building's HVAC system or a crowd in a closed space. (Although cholera thrives in water, other pathogens do not. Both anthrax spores and smallpox must reach the lungs to do damage.) "Making a powder is a huge hurdle for the bad guys," says retired Col. David Franz, former commander of the U.S. Army Medical Research Institute of Infectious Diseases. "It's hard to dry stuff without killing it. And the material needs other treatments as well." Grains larger than about 10 microns do not reach the lungs; those smaller than a micron are exhaled right back out. If you skip the powder step, as Aum apparently did, simply scraping anthrax off their culture dishes and spraying it, you will likely have relatively harmless glop. Weaponizing germs, says Sergei Popov, a Soviet biowarfare scientist who defected in 1992, "is not a basement production."

It requires expertise. But there is, unfortunately, more of that on the loose than anyone dreamed. At Stepnogorsk in northern Kazakhstan, in what was once the world's largest bioweapons plant, "many of the specialists are unemployed now, and some have disappeared," says Dastan Eleukenov, head of the Monterey Institute of International Studies' office in Kazakhstan. "We are concerned that some could be working in Iraq or Iran. When you're talking about bioweapons, the brain drain is more important than the material."

Dispersal: Aum Shinrikyo's failures show that the greatest obstacle to bioterrorism is disseminating the pathogen. Aerosolizing germs and spewing a powder through a tiny nozzle poses severe engineering problems, says Franz. Powders are hard to work with. Pumps with powders are hard to work with. Nozzles clog, jam, sputter and backfire. That applies to crop-dusters, too—fears of which, said an FBI source at the weekend, had "gotten out of hand." Because anthrax is not contagious, only people who inhale the airborne spores get sick. But that has to happen fast: ultraviolet light in sunshine degrades anthrax spores within minutes.

The Nagging Fear of Nukes

By Fred Guterl

Anyone who doubts the threat of nuclear terrorism should ask the Russians about it. In 1993 Chechen saboteurs left a package of highly radioactive cesium in Moscow's Izmailovo Park. Authorities managed to avert disaster, but the incident is one of the real-world events prompting security experts to review the odds on a terrorist nuclear attack. Scott Parrish of the Monterey Institute for Nonproliferation Studies says such an assault is still highly unlikely. But as he says, "a month ago, I would've thought flying a jetliner into a building was a pretty low probability."

Experts fear that a suicide attack by plane on a nuclear power plant could damage the dome and trigger a meltdown

The bad news is that Osama bin Laden has been trying to obtain nuclear weapons since the mid-1990s. The good news is that, as far as we know, he hasn't been able to get them. But the United States faces risk from two crude but effective terror stratagems. One is a "dirty bomb," or radioactivity dispersal device (RDD). An RDD consists of conventional explosives wrapped in a shroud of radioactive material that creates fallout when the bomb explodes. Intelligence officials think Al Qaeda has already obtained black-market cesium-137 and cobalt-60 and may be experimenting with RDDs in Afghanistan.

The other gambit would be a suicide attack on a nuclear power plant, most likely using an airplane. "A crop-duster wouldn't have any effect," says Elisa Harris, a National Security Council staffer during the Clinton years. "But a 747 would do the job." Although chances of a nuclear blast are remote, such an attack could breach the containment dome and set off an unshielded meltdown. That could create a Chernobyl-like radioactive disaster with widespread fallout and many casualties.

The bomb itself remains the biggest fear. Essentially, terrorists can either build a bomb or steal one. Making a nuclear weapon is relatively easy if you have the basic design, a good machine shop and enough weapons-grade uranium. But U-235 and plutonium aren't easy to get. Although there have been many reports of uranium trafficking in recent years, there is no evidence that weapons-grade material has leaked out.

That leaves theft. Since the breakup of the Soviet Union, the overriding concern of many nuclear-arms experts has been the diversion of atomic weapons into the wrong hands. Dr. William Potter, director of the Monterey Institute's nonproliferation program, worries about nukes on Russian Air Force bases. Potter says many impoverished former military officers still live on the bases, and some have been caught trying to steal conventional weapons. "I don't want to suggest the weapons on these bases aren't secure," Potter says, "but they're the ones I'd be most concerned about."

Then there's Pakistan, which by most estimates now has 30 to 50 nuclear bombs. Pakistan's leader, Gen. Pervez Musharraf, must contend with a sizable minority of Muslim extremists, including some within the military. A coup could put Pakistan's nuclear arsenal under their control, or a bin Laden sympathizer in the armed forces could steal one of the bombs. Potter says it's "crucial" for Pakistan to plan for either contingency. It's equally crucial for U.S. planners to consider the awful what-ifs.

Chemical agents are easier in every way but are generally less lethal. Many are in wide industrial use (cyanide is used to clean metals, for instance) and thus easier to steal than, say, smallpox. Toxic chemicals are already weaponized. Although you need more of a chemical than of a biological agent to kill people (probably thousands of pounds dropped over a city), delivery is an even lower-tech task than turning 767s into missiles. A truck, perhaps smashed into a concrete barrier, would do fine. Or, "just put an odorless poison into a building's ventilation system," says chemist Igor Revelsky, who helped develop the Soviets' chemical weapons. "You could take out half the Pentagon and you wouldn't need to learn how to fly or train kamikazes."

All of this—the availability of bugs and gas, the "missing" Soviet weapons scientists, the history of bug-and-gas attacks by terrorists—was well known before Sept. 11.

Just last year the CIA's Tenet told the Senate Select Committee on Intelligence that bin Laden was training agents to use biological and chemical weapons. So although such warnings were not always taken seriously, the United States has already launched a multibillion-dollar effort to thwart biochem terrorism, ranging from assistance to local governments in planning for an attack to disease-surveillance systems. Later this year the Department of Energy will test an early warning system for toxic chemicals in subway systems. Detectors have already been secretly installed at the test site, a D.C. Metro station, NEWSWEEK has learned, though nationwide implementation is years away. DoE is also launching a project to install biodetectors in stadiums, convention halls and other large areas. Later this year the biotech company Cepheid expects to deliver to the Army a DNA-based, breadbox-size detector that can identify the presence of anthrax,

Q-fever, staph B enterotoxin and other weaponizable pathogens. The research firm Arthur D. Little expects to market a badge-size detector for nerve gas next year.

Since last month's attacks, federal and state agencies have gone on alert for signs of biochem terrorism. The U.S. Department of Agriculture is stepping up checks on meat at processing plants. The Environmental Protection Agency has ordered every municipal water system on a "heightened state of alert" for bioterrorism. The Department of Health and Human Services is checking canned goods.

So far, there is only limited pressure for quick strikes. 63% say we should wait as long as necessary to develop an effective plan.

And if prevention fails? "We are simply not prepared to respond to a biological or chemical attack," says Columbia's Morse. In a computer-aided simulation this June, a dozen experts including former senator Sam Nunn and Oklahoma Gov. Frank Keating tried to contain a simulated smallpox attack. They failed. No central authority collected information from hospitals, so the extent, speed and even the existence of the epidemic was unknown: patients diagnosed with flu, whose symptoms resemble those of early stage smallpox, traveled long distances and infected hundreds of people. Hospitals were overwhelmed. Americans have not been vaccinated against smallpox since the 1970s, and immunity lasts only about 20 years. There is no drug treatment. Three months after the outbreak, simulated smallpox killed 1 million simulated people.

To protect real Americans requires more than is now in place. We need a system to deliver vaccines, which can act as a firewall against the spread of smallpox. (Anthrax vaccine would hardly staunch a terror attack: you may need as many as six doses over 18 months for full protection.) The United States has some 12 million doses of smallpox vaccine stockpiled and 40 million more on order for 2004.

Drugs and antibiotics can treat cyanide poisoning and staph infection, while atropine counters the effects of the nerve gases VX and sarin. Despite its newfound popularity, however, the antibiotic Ciprofloxacin has to be taken before anthrax symptoms appear. Otherwise, anthrax has a fatality rate of more than 90 percent. To put in place and maintain a bugs-and-gas response system, estimates Dr. Margaret Hamburg of the Nuclear Threat Initiative, would cost $500 million to $1 billion annually.

Is it worth the cost? Many experts argue that Al Qaeda operatives simply do not possess the scientific knowledge to weaponize germs, produce toxic chemicals in quantity or engineer an effective delivery system. After all, Aum Shinrikyo, with a war chest of more than $300 million, half-a-dozen labs and a stable of biologists, got nowhere with bioweapons and killed only a dozen people with sarin. But recent history shows the peril of underestimating the abilities of terrorists. If the 1993 bombing of the World Trade Center was a bungled first attempt, then the attacks on America's embassies in East Africa, on the USS Cole and on the WTC and Pentagon showed that terrorists have a steep learning curve. Edward Szeliga, formerly of the Army Nuclear and Chemical Agency, compares the threat of biological and chemical terrorism today to that of nuclear attack in the 1950s. "Were the Soviets able to launch a massive nuclear strike (then)? No. But they continued to improve (until they) could launch multiple nuclear weapons at us. The real concern about bioterrorism is not the capabilities of terrorists today, but over time."

Biological or chemical terrorism still seems highly improbable in the near term; the gas masks and Cipro bought in the panicky aftermath of Sept. 11 may have long since deteriorated before such an attack becomes more likely than being struck by lightning. Bugs-and-gas is a problem for the long term, for the time when the memory of recent horrors has dulled—in short, the kind of threat that we're not very good at addressing. But in the new world created by the attacks on the World Trade Center and Pentagon, we would do well to be ready.

With ADAM ROGERS, MICHAEL ISIKOFF, DANIEL KLAIDMAN *and* DEBRA ROSENBERG *in Washington,* ERIKA CHECK *and* FRED GUTERL *in New York,* EVE CONANT *in Moscow,* JOSEPH CONTRERAS *in Miami and* SARAH DOWNEY *in Chicago.*

Why Don't They Like Us?

How America Has Become the Object of Much of the Planet's Genuine Grievances—and Displaced Discontents

BY STANLEY HOFFMANN

It wasn't its innocence that the United States lost on September 11, 2001. It was its naïveté. Americans have tended to believe that in the eyes of others the United States has lived up to the boastful clichés propagated during the Cold War (especially under Ronald Reagan) and during the Clinton administration. We were seen, we thought, as the champions of freedom against fascism and communism, as the advocates of decolonization, economic development, and social progress, as the technical innovators whose mastery of technology, science, and advanced education was going to unify the world.

Some officials and academics explained that U.S. hegemony was the best thing for a troubled world and unlike past hegemonies would last—not only because there were no challengers strong enough to steal the crown but, above all, because we were benign rulers who threatened no one.

But we have avoided looking at the hegemon's clay feet, at what might neutralize our vaunted soft power and undermine our hard power. Like swarming insects exposed when a fallen tree is lifted, millions who dislike or distrust the hegemon have suddenly appeared after September 11, much to our horror and disbelief. America became a great power after World War II, when we faced a rival that seemed to stand for everything we had been fighting against—tyranny, terror, brainwashing—and we thought that our international reputation would benefit from our standing for liberty and stability (as it still does in much of Eastern Europe). We were not sufficiently marinated in history to know that, through the ages, nobody—or almost nobody— has ever loved a hegemon.

Past hegemons, from Rome to Great Britain, tended to be quite realistic about this. They wanted to be obeyed or, as in the case of France, admired. They rarely wanted to be loved. But as a combination of high-noon sheriff and proselytizing missionary, the United States expects gratitude and affection. It was bound to be disappointed; gratitude is not an emotion that one associates with the behavior of states.

THE NEW WORLD DISORDER

This is an old story. Two sets of factors make the current twist a new one. First, the so-called Westphalian world has collapsed. The world of sovereign states, the universe of Hans Morgenthau's and Henry Kissinger's Realism, is no longer. The unpopularity of the hegemonic power has been heightened to incandescence by two aspects of this collapse. One is the irruption of the public, the masses, in international affairs. Foreign policy is no longer, as Raymond Aron had written in *Peace and War*, the closed domain of the soldier and the diplomat. Domestic publics—along with their interest groups, religious organizations, and ideological chapels—either dictate or constrain the imperatives and preferences that the governments fight for. This puts the hegemon in a difficult position: It often must work with governments that represent but a small percentage of a country's people—but if it fishes for public support abroad, it risks alienating leaders whose cooperation it needs. The United States paid heavily for not having had enough contacts with the opposition to the shah of Iran in the 1970s. It discovers today that there is an abyss in Pakistan, Saudi Arabia, Egypt, and Indonesia between our official allies and the populace in these countries. Diplomacy in a world where the masses, so to speak, stayed indoors, was a much easier game.

The collapse of the barrier between domestic and foreign affairs in the state system is now accompanied by a disease that attacks the state system itself. Many of the "states" that are members of the United Nations are pseudo-states with shaky or shabby institutions, no basic consensus on values or on procedures among their heterogeneous components, and no sense of national identity. Thus the hegemon—in addition to suffering the hostility of the government in certain countries (like Cuba, Iraq, and North Korea) and of the public in others (like, in varying degrees, Pakistan, Egypt, and even France)—can now easily become both the target of factions fighting one another in disintegrating countries and the pawn in their quarrels (which range over such increasingly borderless issues as drug trafficking, arms trading, money laundering, and other criminal enterprises). In addition, today's hegemon suffers from the volatility and turbulence of a global system in which ethnic, religious, and ideological sympathies have become transnational and in which groups and individuals uncontrolled by states can act on their own. The world of the nineteenth century, when hegemons could impose their order, their institutions, has been supplanted by the world of the twenty-first century: Where once there was order, there is now often a vacuum.

What makes the American Empire especially vulnerable is its historically unique combination of assets and liabilities. One has to go back to the Roman Empire to find a comparable set of resources. Britain, France, and Spain had to operate in multipolar systems; the United States is the only superpower.

But if America's means are vast, the limits of its power are also considerable. The United States, unlike Rome, cannot simply impose its will by force or through satellite states. Small "rogue" states can defy the hegemon (remember Vietnam?). And chaos can easily result from the large new role of nonstate actors. Meanwhile, the reluctance of Americans to take on the Herculean tasks of policing, "nation building," democratizing autocracies, and providing environmental protection and economic growth for billions of human beings stokes both resentment and hostility, especially among those who discover that one can count on American presence and leadership only when America's material interests are gravely threatened. (It is not surprising that the "defense of the national interest" approach of Realism was developed for a multipolar world. In an empire, as well as in a bipolar system, almost anything can be described as a vital interest, since even peripheral disorder can unravel the superpower's eminence.) Moreover, the complexities of America's process for making foreign-policy decisions can produce disappointments abroad when policies that the international community counted on—such as the Kyoto Protocol and the International Criminal Court—are thwarted. Also, the fickleness of U.S. foreign-policy making in arenas like the Balkans has convinced many American enemies that this country is basically incapable of pursuing long-term policies consistently.

NONE OF THIS MEANS, OF COURSE, THAT THE UNITED STATES has no friends in the world. Europeans have not forgotten the liberating role played by Americans in the war against Hitler and in the Cold War. Israel remembers how President Harry Truman sided with the founders of the Zionist state; nor has it forgotten all the help the United States has given it since then. The democratizations of postwar Germany and Japan were huge successes. The Marshall Plan and the Point Four Program were revolutionary initiatives. The decisions to resist aggression in Korea and in Kuwait demonstrated a commendable far-sightedness.

But Americans have a tendency to overlook the dark sides of their course (except on the protesting left, which is thus constantly accused of being un-American), perhaps because they perceive international affairs in terms of crusades between good and evil, endeavors that entail formidable pressures for unanimity. It is not surprising that the decade following the Gulf

War was marked both by nostalgia for the clear days of the Cold War and by a lot of floundering and hesitating in a world without an overwhelming foe.

STRAINS OF ANTI-AMERICANISM

The main criticisms of American behavior have mostly been around for a long time. When we look at anti-Americanism today, we must first distinguish between those who attack the United States for what it does, or fails to do, and those who attack it for what it is. (Some, like the Islamic fundamentalists and terrorists, attack it for both reasons.) Perhaps the principal criticism is of the contrast between our ideology of universal liberalism and policies that have all too often consisted of supporting and sometimes installing singularly authoritarian and repressive regimes. (One reason why these policies often elicited more reproaches than Soviet control over satellites was that, as time went by, Stalinism became more and more cynical and thus the gap between words and deeds became far less wide than in the United States. One no longer expected much from Moscow.) The list of places where America failed at times to live up to its proclaimed ideals is long: Guatemala, Panama, El Salvador, Chile, Santo Domingo in 1965, the Greece of the colonels, Pakistan, the Philippines of Ferdinand Marcos, Indonesia after 1965, the shah's Iran, Saudi Arabia, Zaire, and, of course, South Vietnam. Enemies of these regimes were shocked by U.S. support for them—and even those whom we supported were disappointed, or worse, when America's cost-benefit analysis changed and we dropped our erstwhile allies. This Machiavellian scheming behind a Wilsonian facade has alienated many clients, as well as potential friends, and bred strains of anti-Americanism around the world.

A second grievance concerns America's frequent unilateralism and the difficult relationship between the United States and the United Nations. For many countries, the United Nations is, for all its flaws, the essential agency of cooperation and the protector of its members' sovereignty. The way U.S. diplomacy has "insulted" the UN system—sometimes by ignoring it and sometimes by rudely imposing its views and policies on it—has been costly in terms of foreign support.

Third, the United States' sorry record in international development has recently become a source of dissatisfaction abroad. Not only have America's financial contributions for narrowing the gap between the rich and the poor declined since the end of the Cold War, but American-dominated institutions such as the International Monetary Fund and the World Bank have often dictated financial policies that turned out to be disastrous for developing countries—most notably, before and during the Asian economic crisis of the mid-1990s.

Finally, there is the issue of American support of Israel. Much of the world—and not only the Arab world—considers America's Israel policy to be biased. Despite occasional American attempts at evenhandedness, the world sees that the Palestinians remain under occupation, Israeli settlements continue to expand, and individual acts of Arab terrorism—acts that Yasir Arafat can't completely control—are condemned more harshly than the killings of Palestinians by the Israeli army or by Israeli-sanctioned assassination squads. It is interesting to note that Israel, the smaller and dependent power, has been more successful in circumscribing the United States' freedom to maneuver diplomatically in the region than the United States has been at getting Israel to enforce the UN resolutions adopted after the 1967 war (which called for the withdrawal of Israeli forces from then-occupied territories, solving the refugee crisis, and establishing inviolate territorial zones for all states in the region). Many in the Arab world, and some outside, use this state of affairs to stoke paranoia of the "Jewish lobby" in the United States.

ANTIGLOBALISM AND ANTI-AMERICANISM

Those who attack specific American policies are often more ambivalent than hostile. They often envy the qualities and institutions that have helped the United States grow rich, powerful, and influential.

The real United States haters are those whose anti-Americanism is provoked by dislike of America's values, institutions, and society—and their enormous impact abroad. Many who despise America see us as representing the vanguard of globalization—even as they themselves use globalization to promote their hatred. The Islamic fundamentalists of al-Qaeda—like Iran's Ayatollah Khomeini 20 years ago—make excellent use of the communication technologies that are so essential to the spread of global trade and economic influence.

We must be careful here, for there are distinctions among the antiglobalist strains that fuel anti-Americanism. To some of our detractors, the most eloquent spokesman is bin Laden, for whom America and the globalization it promotes relentlessly through free trade and institutions under its control represent evil. To them, American-fueled globalism symbolizes the domination of the Christian-Jewish infidels or the triumph of pure secularism: They look at the United States and see a society of materialism, moral laxity, corruption in all its forms, fierce selfishness, and so on. (The charges are familiar to us because we know them as an exacerbated form of right-wing anti-Americanism in nineteenth- and twentieth-century Europe.) But there are also those who, while accepting the inevitability of globalization and seem eager to benefit from it, are incensed by the contrast between America's promises and the realities of American life. Looking at the United States and the countries we support, they see insufficient social protection, vast pockets of poverty amidst plenty, racial discrimination, the large role of money in politics, the domination of the elites—and they call us hypocrites. (And these charges, too, are familiar, because they are an exacerbated version of the left-wing anti-Americanism still powerful in Western Europe.)

On the one hand, those who see themselves as underdogs of the world condemn the United States for being an evil force because its dynamism makes it naturally and endlessly imperialistic—a behemoth that imposes its culture (often seen as debased), its democracy (often seen as flawed), and its conception of individual human rights (often seen as a threat to more communitarian and more socially concerned approaches) on other societies. The United States is perceived as a bully ready to use all means, including overwhelming force, against those

who resist it: Hence, Hiroshima, the horrors of Vietnam, the rage against Iraq, the war on Afghanistan.

On the other hand, the underdogs draw hope from their conviction that the giant has a heel like Achilles'. They view America as a society that cannot tolerate high casualties and prolonged sacrifices and discomforts, one whose impatience with protracted and undecisive conflicts should encourage its victims to be patient and relentless in their challenges and assaults. They look at American foreign policy as one that is often incapable of overcoming obstacles and of sticking to a course that is fraught with high risks—as with the conflict with Iraq's Saddam Hussein at the end of the Gulf War; as in the flight from Lebanon after the terrorist attacks of 1982; as in Somalia in 1993; as in the attempts to strike back at bin Laden in the Clinton years.

Thus America stands condemned not because our enemies necessarily hate our freedoms but because they resent what they fear are our Darwinian aspects, and often because they deplore what they see as the softness at our core. Those who, on our side, note and celebrate America's power of attraction, its openness to immigrants and refugees, the uniqueness of a society based on common principles rather than on ethnicity or on an old culture, are not wrong. But many of the foreign students, for instance, who fall in love with the gifts of American education return home, where the attraction often fades. Those who stay sometimes feel that the price they have to pay in order to assimilate and be accepted is too high.

WHAT BRED BIN LADEN

This long catalog of grievances obviously needs to be picked apart. The complaints vary in intensity; different cultures, countries, and parties emphasize different flaws, and the criticism is often wildly excessive and unfair. But we are not dealing here with purely rational arguments; we are dealing with emotional responses to the omnipresence of a hegemon, to the sense that many people outside this country have that the United States dominates their lives.

Complaints are often contradictory: Consider "America has neglected us, or dropped us" versus "America's attentions corrupt our culture." The result can be a gestalt of resentment that strikes Americans as absurd: We are damned, for instance, both for failing to intervene to protect Muslims in the Balkans and for using force to do so.

But the extraordinary array of roles that America plays in the world—along with its boastful attitude and, especially recently, its cavalier unilateralism—ensures that many wrongs caused by local regimes and societies will be blamed on the United States. We even end up being seen as responsible not only for anything bad that our "protectorates" do—it is no coincidence that many of the September 11 terrorists came from America's protégés, Saudi Arabia and Egypt—but for what our allies do, as when Arabs incensed by racism and joblessness in France take up bin Laden's cause, or when Muslims talk about American violence against the Palestinians. Bin Laden's extraordinary appeal and prestige in the Muslim world do not mean that his apocalyptic nihilism (to use Michael Ignatieff's term) is fully endorsed by all those who chant his name. Yet to many, he plays the role of a bloody Robin Hood, inflicting pain and humiliation on the superpower that they believe torments them.

Bin Laden fills the need for people who, rightly or not, feel collectively humiliated and individually in despair to attach themselves to a savior. They may in fact avert their eyes from the most unsavory of his deeds. This need on the part of the poor and dispossessed to connect their own feeble lot to a charismatic and single-minded leader was at the core of fascism and of communism. After the failure of pan-Arabism, the fiasco of nationalism, the dashed hopes of democratization, and the fall of Soviet communism, many young people in the Muslim world who might have once turned to these visions for succor turned instead to Islamic fundamentalism and terrorism.

One almost always finds the same psychological dynamics at work in such behavior: the search for simple explanations—and what is simpler and more inflammatory than the machinations of the Jews and the evils of America—and a highly selective approach to history. Islamic fundamentalists remember the promises made by the British to the Arabs in World War I and the imposition of British and French imperialism after 1918 rather than the support the United States gave to anticolonialists in French North Africa in the late 1940s and in the 1950s. They remember British opposition to and American reluctance toward intervention in Bosnia before Srebrenica, but they forget about NATO's actions to save Bosnian Muslims in 1995, to help Albanians in Kosovo in 1999, and to preserve and improve Albanians' rights in Macedonia in 2001. Such distortions are manufactured and maintained by the controlled media and schools of totalitarian regimes, and through the religious schools, conspiracy mills, and propaganda of fundamentalism.

WHAT CAN BE DONE?

Americans can do very little about the most extreme and violent forms of anti-American hatred—but they can try to limit its spread by addressing grievances that are justified. There are a number of ways to do this:

- First—and most difficult—drastically reorient U.S. policy in the Palestinian-Israeli conflict.
- Second, replace the ideologically market-based trickle-down economics that permeate American-led development institutions today with a kind of social safety net. (Even *New York*

Times columnist Thomas Friedman, that ur-celebrator of the global market, believes that such a safety net is indispensable.)
- Third, prod our allies and protégés to democratize their regimes, and stop condoning violations of essential rights (an approach that can only, in the long run, breed more terrorists and anti-Americans).
- Fourth, return to internationalist policies, pay greater attention to the representatives of the developing world, and make fairness prevail over arrogance.
- Finally, focus more sharply on the needs and frustrations of the people suffering in undemocratic societies than on the authoritarian regimes that govern them.

America's self-image today is derived more from what Reinhold Niebuhr would have called pride than from reality, and this exacerbates the clash between how we see ourselves and foreign perceptions and misperceptions of the United States. If we want to affect those external perceptions (and that will be very difficult to do in extreme cases), we need to readjust our self-image. This means reinvigorating our curiosity about the outside world, even though our media have tended to downgrade foreign coverage since the Cold War. And it means listening carefully to views that we may find outrageous, both for the kernel of truth that may be present in them and for the stark realities (of fear, poverty, hunger, and social hopelessness) that may account for the excesses of these views.

Terrorism aimed at the innocent is, of course, intolerable. Safety precautions and the difficult task of eradicating the threat are not enough. If we want to limit terrorism's appeal, we must keep our eyes and ears open to conditions abroad, revise our perceptions of ourselves, and alter our world image through our actions. There is nothing un-American about this. We should not meet the Manichaeanism of our foes with a Manichaeanism of self-righteousness. Indeed, self-examination and self-criticism have been the not-so-secret weapons of America's historical success. Those who demand that we close ranks not only against murderers but also against shocking opinions and emotions, against dissenters at home and critics abroad, do a disservice to America.

STANLEY HOFFMANN *is the Paul and Catherine Buttenwieser University Professor at Harvard University.*

COMMUNITY BUILDING
STEPS TOWARD A GOOD SOCIETY

AMITAI ETZIONI

Well-formed national societies are not composed of millions of individuals but are constituted as communities of communities. These societies provide a framework within which diverse social groups as well as various subcultures find shared bonds and values. When this framework falls apart, we find communities at each other's throats or even in vicious civil war, as we sadly see in many parts of the world. (Arthur Schlesinger Jr. provides an alarming picture of such a future for our society in his book, *The Disuniting of America*.)

Our community of communities is particularly threatened in two ways that ought to command more of our attention in the next years. First, our society has been growing more diverse by leaps and bounds over recent decades, as immigration has increased and Americans have become more aware of their social and cultural differences. Many on the left celebrate diversity because they see it as ending white European hegemony in our society. Many on the right call for "bleaching out" ethnic differences to ensure a united, homogenous America.

A second challenge to the community of communities emanates from the fact that economic and social inequality has long been rising. Some see a whole new divide caused by the new digital technologies, although others believe that the Internet will bridge these differences. It is time to ask how much inequality the community of communities can tolerate while still flourishing. If we are exceeding these limits, what centrist corrections are available to us?

DIVERSITY WITHIN UNITY

As a multiethnic society, America has long debated the merit of unity versus pluralism, of national identity versus identity politics, of assimilation of immigrants into mainstream culture versus maintaining their national heritages. All of these choices are incompatible with a centrist, communitarian approach to a good society. Assimilation is unnecessarily homogenizing, forcing people to give up important parts of their selves; unbounded ra-

cial, ethnic, and cultural diversity is too conflict-prone for a society in which all are fully respected. The concept of a community of communities provides a third model.

The community of communities builds on the observation that loyalty to one's group, to its particular culture and heritage, is compatible with sustaining national unity as long as the society is perceived not as an arena of conflict but as a society that has some community-like features. (Some refer to a community of communities as an imagined community.) Members of such a society maintain layered loyalties. "Lower" commitments are to one's immediate community, often an ethnic group; "higher" ones are to the community of communities, to the nation as a whole. These include a commitment to a democratic way of life, to a constitution and more generally to a government by law, and above all to treating others—not merely the members of one's group—as ends in themselves and not merely as instruments. Approached this way, one realizes that up to a point, *diversity can avoid being the opposite of unity and can exist within it.*

Moreover, sustaining a particular community of communities does not contradict the gradual development of still more encompassing communities, such as the European Union, a North American community including Canada and Mexico, or, one day, a world community.

During the last decades of the 20th century, the U.S. was racked by identity politics that, in part, have served to partially correct past injustices committed against women and minorities, but have also divided the nation along group lines. Other sharp divisions have appeared between the religious right and much of the rest of the country. One of the merits of the centrist, communitarian approach has been that it has combined efforts to expand the common ground and to cool intergroup rhetoric. Thus communitarians helped call off the "war" between the genders, as Betty Friedan—who was one of the original endorsers of the Communitarian Platform—did in 1997.

New flexibility in involving faith-based groups in the provision of welfare, health care, and other social services, and even allowing some forms of religious activities in public schools, has defused some of the tension between the religious right and the rest of society. The national guidelines on religious expression in public schools, first released by the U.S. Department of Education on the directive of President Clinton in August of 1995, worked to this end. For example, in July of 1996, these guidelines spurred the St. Louis School Board to implement a clearly defined, districtwide policy on school prayer. This policy helped allay the confusion—and litigation—that had previously plagued the role of religion in this school district.

The tendency of blacks and whites not to dialogue openly about racial issues, highlighted by Andrew Hacker, has to some degree been overcome. The main, albeit far from successful, effort in this direction has been made by President Clinton's Advisory Board on Race. And for the first time in U.S. history, a Jew was nominated by a major political party for the post of vice president.

In the next years, intensified efforts are called for to balance the legitimate concerns and needs of various communities that constitute the American society on one hand, and the need to shore up our society as a community of communities on the other. Prayers truly initiated by students might be allowed in public schools as long as sufficient arrangements are made for students who do not wish to participate to spend time in other organized activities. There are no compelling reasons to oppose "after hours" religious clubs establishing themselves in the midst of numerous secular programs. Renewed efforts for honest dialogues among the races are particularly difficult and needed. None of these steps will cause the differences among various communities—many of which serve to enrich our culture and social life—to disappear. But they may go a long way toward reinforcing the framework that keeps American society together while it is being recast.

UNIFYING INEQUALITY

Society cannot long sustain its status as a community of communities if general increases in well-being, even including those that trickle down to the poorest segments of the society, keep increasing the economic distance between the elites and the common people. Fortunately, it seems that at least by some measures, economic inequality has not increased in the United States between 1996 and 2000. And by several measures, the federal income tax has grown surprisingly progressive. (The opposite must be said about rising payroll taxes.) About a third of those who filed income tax returns in 2000 paid no taxes or even got a net refund from the Internal Revenue Service (IRS). However, the level of inequality in income at the end of the 20th century was substantially higher than it was in earlier periods. Between 1977 and 1999, the after-tax income of the top 1 percent of the U.S. population increased by 115 percent, whereas the after-tax income of the U.S. population's lowest fifth decreased by 9 percent. There is little reason to expect that this trend will not continue.

SOCIAL JUSTICE

We may debate what social justice calls for; however, there is little doubt about what community requires. If some members of a community are increasingly distanced from the standard of living of most other members, they will lose contact with the rest of the community. The more those in charge of private and public institutions lead lives of hyper-affluence—replete with gated communities and estates, chauffeured limousines, servants and personal trainers—the less in touch they are with other community members. Such isolation not only frays social bonds and insulates privileged people from the moral cultures of the community, but it also blinds them to the realities of the lives of their fellow citizens. This, in turn, tends to cause them to favor unrealistic policies ("let them eat cake") that backfire and undermine the trust of the members of the society in those who lead and in the institutions they head.

The argument has been made that for the state to provide equality of outcomes undermines the motivation to achieve and to work, stymies creativity and excellence, and is unfair to those who do apply themselves. It is also said that equality of outcomes would raise labor costs so high that a society would be rendered uncompetitive in the new age of global competition. Equality of opportunity has been extolled as a substitute. However, to ensure equality of opportunity, some equality of outcome must be provided. As has often been pointed out, for all to have similar opportunities, they must have similar starting points. These can be reached only if all are accorded certain basics. Special education efforts such as Head Start, created to bring children from disadvantaged backgrounds up to par, and training for workers released from obsolescent industries are examples of programs that provide some equality of results to make equality of opportunity possible.

Additional policies to further curb inequality can be made to work at both ends of the scale. Policies that ensure a rich basic minimum serve this goal by lifting those at the lower levels of the economic pyramid. Reference is often made to education and training programs that focus on those most in need of catching up. However, these work very slowly. Therefore, in the short run more effects will be achieved by raising the Earned Income Tax Credit and the minimum wage, and by implementing new inter-community sharing initiatives.

The poor will remain poor no matter how much they work as long as they own no assets. This is especially damaging because people who own assets, especially a place of residence (even if only an apartment), are most likely to "buy" into a society—to feel and be part of a community. By numerous measures, homeowners are more involved in the life of their communities, and their children are less likely to drop out of school. Roughly one-third of Americans do not own their residence; 73 percent of whites do, compared to 47 percent of African Americans and Hispanics.

MORTGAGES

Various provisions allowing those with limited resources to get mortgages through federally chartered corporations like Fannie Mae, which helps finance mortgages for many lower-income people, have been helpful in increasing ownership. More needs to be done on this front, especially for those of little means. This might be achieved by following the same model used in the Earned Income Tax Credit in the U.S. and the Working Families Tax Credit in the United Kingdom: providing people who earn below a defined income level with "earned interest on mortgages," effectively granting them two dollars for every dollar set aside to provide seed money for a mortgage. And sweat equity might be used as the future owner's contribution—for instance, if they work on their own housing site. (Those who benefit from the houses that Habitat for Humanity builds are required to either make some kind of a financial contribution themselves or help in the construction of their homes.) Far from implausible, various ideas along these lines were offered by both George W. Bush and Al Gore during the 2000 election campaign, as well as by various policy researchers.

Reducing hard core unemployment by trying to bring jobs to poor neighborhoods (through "enterprise zones") or by training the long-unemployed in entrepreneurial skills is often expensive and slow, and is frequently unsuccessful. The opposite approach, moving people from poor areas to places where jobs are, often encounters objections by the neighborhoods into which they are moved, as well as by those poor who feel more comfortable living in their home communities. A third approach should be tried much more extensively: providing ready transportation to and from places of employment.

Measures to cap the higher levels of wealth include progressive income taxes, some forms of inheritance tax, closing numerous loopholes in the tax codes, and ensuring that tax on capital is paid as it is on labor. Given that several of these inequality curbing measures cannot be adopted on a significant scale if they seriously endanger the competitive state of a country, steps to introduce many of them should be undertaken jointly with other Organization for Economic Cooperation and Development (OECD) countries, or better yet, among all the nations that are our major competitors and trade partners.

One need not be a liberal—one can be a solid communitarian—and still be quite dismayed to learn that the IRS audits the poor (defined as income below $25,000) more than the rich (defined as income above $100,000). In 1999, the IRS audited 1.36 percent of poor taxpayers, compared to 1.15 percent of rich taxpayers. In 1988, the percentage for the rich was 11.4. In one decade, there was thus a decline of about 90 percent in auditing the rich. This oc-

curred because Congress did not authorize the necessary funds, despite the General Accounting Office's finding that the rich are more likely to evade taxes than are the poor. This change in audit patterns also reflects the concern of Republican members of Congress that the poor will abuse the Earned Income Tax Credit that the Clinton administration has introduced. It should not take a decade to correct this imbalance.

Ultimately, this matter and many others will not be properly attended to until there is a basic change in the moral culture of the society and in the purposes that animate it. Without such a change, a major reallocation of wealth can be achieved only by force, which is incompatible with a democratic society and will cause a wealth flight and other damage to the economy. In contrast, history from early Christianity to Fabian socialism teaches us that people who share progressive values will be inclined to share their wealth voluntarily. A good society seeks to promote such values through a grand dialogue rather than by dictates.

THE NEW GRAND DIALOGUE

The great success of the economy in the 1990s made Americans pay more attention to the fact that there are numerous moral and social questions of concern to the good society that capitalism has never aspired to answer and that the state should not promote. These include moral questions such as what we owe our children, our parents, our friends, and our neighbors, as well as people from other communities, including those in far away places. Most important, we must address this question: What is the ultimate purpose our personal and collective endeavors? Is ever greater material affluence our ultimate goal and the source of meaning? When is enough—enough? What are we considering the good life? *Can a good society be built on ever increasing levels of affluence? Or should we strive to center it around other values, those of mutuality and spirituality?*

The journey to the good society can benefit greatly from the observation, supported by a great deal of social science data, that ever increasing levels of material goods are not a reliable source of human well-being or contentment—let alone the basis for a morally sound society. To cite but a few studies of a large body of findings: Frank M. Andrews and Stephen B. Withey found that the level of one's socioeconomic status had meager effects on one's "sense of well-being" and no significant effect on "satisfaction with life-as-a-whole." Jonathan L. Freedman discovered that levels of reported happiness did not vary greatly among the members of different economic classes, with the exception of the very poor, who tended to be less happy than others. David G. Myers reported that although per capita disposable (after-tax) income in inflation-adjusted dollars almost exactly doubled between 1960 and 1990, 32 percent of Americans reported that they were "very happy" in 1993, almost the same proportion as did in 1957 (35 percent). Although economic growth slowed after the mid-1970s, Americans' reported happiness was remarkably stable (nearly always between 30 and 35 percent) across both high-growth and low-growth periods.

HAPPINESS

These and other such data help us realize that the pursuit of well-being through ever higher levels of consumption is Sisyphean. When it comes to material goods, enough is never enough. This is not an argument in favor of a life of sackcloth and ashes, of poverty and self-denial. The argument is that once basic material needs (what Abraham Maslow called "creature comforts") are well sated and securely provided for, additional income does not add to happiness. On the contrary, hard evidence—not some hippie, touchy-feely, LSD-induced hallucination—shows that profound contentment is found in nourishing ends-based relationships, in bonding with others, in community building and public service, and in cultural and spiritual pursuits. Capitalism, the engine of affluence, has never aspired to address the whole person; typically it treats the person as *Homo economicus.* And of course, statist socialism subjugated rather than inspired. It is left to the evolving values and cultures of centrist societies to fill the void.

Nobel laureate Robert Fogel showed that periods of great affluence are regularly followed by what he calls Great Awakenings, and that we are due for one in the near future. Although it is quite evident that there is a growing thirst for a purpose deeper than conspicuous consumption, we may not have the ability to predict which specific form this yearning for spiritual fulfillment will take.

There are some who hold firmly that the form must be a religious one because no other speaks to the most profound matters that trouble the human soul, nor do others provide sound moral guidance. These believers find good support in numerous indicators that there was a considerable measure of religious revival in practically all forms of American religion over the last decades of the 20th century. The revival is said to be evident not merely in the number of people who participate in religious activities and the frequency of their participation in these activities, but also in the stronger, more involving, and stricter kinds of commitments many are making to religion. (Margaret Talbot has argued effectively that conservative Christians, especially fundamentalists, constitute the true counterculture of our age; they know and live a life rich in fulfillment, not centered around consumer goods.) Others see the spiritual revival as taking more secular forms, ranging from New Age cults to a growing interest in applied ethics.

PRIORITIES

Aside from making people more profoundly and truly content individuals, a major and broadly based upward shift on the Maslovian scale is a prerequisite for being able to better address some of the most tantalizing problems plaguing modern societies, whatever form such a shift may take. That is what is required before we can come into harmony with our environment, because these higher priorities put much less demand on scarce resources than do lower ones. And such a new set of priorities may well be the only conditions under which those who are well endowed would be willing to support serious reallocation of wealth and power, as their personal fortunes would no longer be based on amassing ever larger amounts of consumer goods. In addition, transitioning to a knowledge-based economy would free millions of people (one hopes all of them, gradually) to relate to each other mainly as members of families and communities, thus laying the social foundations for a society in which ends-based relationships dominate while instrumental ones are well contained.

The upward shift in priorities, a return to a sort of moderate counterculture, a turn toward voluntary simplicity—these require a grand dialogue about our personal and shared goals. (A return to a counterculture is not a recommendation for more abuse of controlled substances, promiscuity, and self-indulgence—which is about the last thing America needs—but the realization that one can find profound contentment in reflection, friendship, love, sunsets, and walks on the beach rather than in the pursuit of ever more control over ever more goods.) Intellectuals and the media can help launch such a dialogue and model the new forms of behavior. Public leaders can nurse the recognition of these values by moderating consumption at public events and ceremonies, and by celebrating those whose achievements are compatible with a good society rather than with a merely affluent one.

But ultimately, such a shift lies in changes in our hearts and minds, in our values and conduct—what Robert Bellah called the "habits of the heart." We shall not travel far toward a good society unless such a dialogue is soon launched and advanced to a good, spiritually uplifting conclusion.

Mr. Etzioni is editor of The Responsive Community. *From "Next: Three Steps Towards A Good Society," by Amitai Etzioni,* The Responsive Community, *Winter 2000–01, pages 49–58.*

Reprinted from *Current,* January 2001, pp. 29-33. Originally printed in *The Responsive Community,* Vol. II, No. 1, Winter 2000/01, pp. 49-58 which was adapted from the author's book *Next: The Road to the Good Society* (New York: Basic Books, 2001).

Across the Great Divide

Our world: Capitalism and democracy are the two great forces of the age. They unleash creativity and human potential. But they can be destructive too; they challenge the old order. Are we ready for the wild ride of tomorrow?

By Fareed Zakaria

December 6, 1999 It has been only 10 years since the fall of the Berlin wall, but we are in a new age. In 1986 people would have seen their world of Reagan and Thatcher and Gorbachev as closely linked to the world of 1976 or, for that matter, of 1966 or 1956 or 1946. But today events, just 10 years old, are dim and quaint memories—remember the Nicaraguan contras? Having crossed a great historical divide, events on the other side of that chasm are like ancient history.

For almost a half century, the West has struggled mightily to spread capitalism and democracy around the world. Now it has gotten what it wanted—unbridled market and people power—and they will prove harder to handle than anyone imagined. Capitalism and democracy are the two dominant forces of modern history; they unleash human creativity and energy like nothing else. But they are also forces of destruction. They destroy old orders, hierarchy, tradition, communities, careers, stability and peace of mind itself. Unsentimental about the world as it exists, they surge forward, changing everything they encounter. The challenge of the West in the next century will be to find ways to channel the sweeping power of these two—the last surviving big ideas—as they reorganize all human activity. Otherwise for much of the world, it may be too fast a ride.

Things seem so different now because they are so different. For three genera-

tions, the world was defined by great political struggles: the Depression, World War II, the cold war, decolonization. Politics and diplomacy held center stage. Today the air is filled with a new sort of energy. "To get rich is glorious," goes a famous, recent tag line. It is the perfect sound bite for our age—because it was said by the leader of China's Communist Party. The heroes of the past may have been soldiers and statesmen, artists and writers: today they are entrepreneurs. Even countries like China, India and Brazil that once scoffed at the crass commercialism of the West now search desperately for ways to create export zones and high-tech corridors. Napoleon once derided England for being "a nation of shopkeepers." We are now a world of shopkeepers.

Intellectuals like to remind us that globalization is actually not that new. At the turn of the 20th century, free trade, free markets and democratic politics flourished. Today one does not need a visa to travel through much of Europe; then you did not even need a passport.

The point of this comparison is, of course, how it ended—badly. In the early 20th century prominent liberal thinkers believed that prosperity and interdependence had made war unthinkable. And yet it happened. World War I brought an end to the first great age of globalization.

But there are crucial differences between this turn of a century and the last one. Globalization today describes a far

more pervasive and deep phenomenon than has ever existed before. Thousands of goods, services and even ideas are manufactured globally, creating complex interconnections between states. A book, for example, can be written in New York, copy-edited in India, typeset in the Caribbean, printed in Singapore and then shipped worldwide. The Internet has made global manufacturing, distribution and communication simple and cheap.

There is another crucial difference between the last round of globalization and this one: the nature of the superpower. An open world economy rests upon the broad edifice of peace, which usually requires a great global hegemony—Britain in 1900, America in 2000. But in 1900 Britain was a declining power; World War I simply accelerated that trend. The picture today could not be more different. Not only is the United States securely the leading power in the world, its advantage is widening. For the past decade, American journalists, politicians and scholars have been searching for a new way to describe the post-cold-war world. It has been staring us in the face: we are living in the American Age.

The American economy has become the envy of the world, spearheading a series of technological breakthroughs that have defined a new post–Industrial Revolution. America's military outpaces any other by leaps and bounds. The Pentagon spends more on defense than the next five great powers combined. It spends more on defense research than *the rest of the world* put together. And Washington has no grand illusions that war is obsolete or that globalization does not require political stability. Whatever Bill Clinton's polemical rhetoric might suggest, there is no groundswell for isolationism in America.

America's edge is as visible in other sectors of society. The gap between American universities and foreign ones is fast widening. Harvard University recently announced that it had completed its $2 billion fund-raising drive months ahead of schedule. Oh, and by the way, it missed its target, overshooting by $0.3 billion. That's $300 million of spare change, which is more than the endowment of many of the best foreign universities. The World Bank recently calculated that the three richest men in America had a combined net worth that exceeds the total GDP of the 48 poorest countries in the world.

Of course, today's tranquil times could be upset by war. A stock-market crash could unnerve the booming economy. Bad foreign policy could bungle many of these extraordinary advantages. But none of these crises is likely to throw up a new superpower. In fact, when a crisis hits, America only becomes more indispensable—think of the East Asian economic collapse, or the Balkan wars. Even in lands where the backlash against America has deep roots, Americanization is pervasive. Listen to a 21-year-old woman, forced to attend an anti-American rally in Tehran: "It's a joke," she told *The New York Times*, pointing at the women clad in black chadors with bright blue colors flashing underneath. "How can you shout, 'Death to America!' when you're wearing blue jeans?" Or consider China. In November, Beijing compromised its gradual approach to economic

reform when it agreed to join the World Trade Organization, largely under U.S. terms.

What can we expect in this new era? The short answer is, more of the same. More of global capitalism but also more of that other distinctive American export, democracy and popular power. Over the last 30 years, a great wave of democratization has swept the world. From Portugal and Greece in the 1970s to Latin America in the 1980s and Central Europe in the 1990s, elections have become a global phenomenon. The pressure will only get more intense. These two forces—capitalism and democracy—will hurl societies into modernity with all its glories and seductions. The companies of tomorrow will be efficient, but will also face brutal competition. Citizens will be able to enjoy culture from all over the world—from opera to Jerry Springer. Teenagers, at the click of a mouse, already have access to great encyclopedias—and racist propaganda.

It is a heady mix and it will only keep getting headier. The forces of creative destruction are beginning to operate at warp speed, creating new companies, careers and communities—but wrecking old ones at an equally dizzying pace. America has gotten used to this high-speed ride. Americans accept the chaos that comes from an ever-changing economy and a chaotic political system. They believe that in the end, it all works out for the best. But will the rest of the world be so understanding? Some countries will close themselves off from this world and stagnate. The wisest will find a balance between their own values and the requirements of modernity.

Most countries recognize the need to tame the fires of capitalism—in fact, they probably do so too much. It will be harder for them to determine how best to

handle democratic populism. Some countries have already begun to see its dangers. They recognize that democracy without the rule of law, minority protections, property rights—what I have called illiberal democracy—can be a hollow shell. It was elections that fueled the fires of nationalism that still rage in the Balkans. It has been elections that have legitimized all manner of thugs from Venezuela to Belarus to Pakistan. In Russia, a well-functioning democracy has been combined with the wholesale corruption of economic reform, law, liberty and political institutions. The result: most Russians now dislike capitalism. They may soon come to dislike democracy.

The United States, the world's greatest democracy, has always kept its own popular pressures on a leash. Its court system is free from public oversight, its Bill of Rights designed to thwart majority rule and its regulatory apparatus keeps tabs on rogue traders and large corporations. Indeed, one could argue that the American way is so successful because both capitalism and democracy are tightly regulated by the rule of law. If the world wishes to learn a lesson about America, this should be the one it takes to heart.

Most difficult of all, societies must make these adjustments as the forces of change swirl around with gathering fury. Whatever the balance countries arrive at, they will still be riding farther, faster than they have ever done. The only advice one can give as we enter a brave new world is this: fasten your seat belts. It's going to be a bumpy ride.

Zakaria is managing editor of Foreign Affairs and author of a forthcoming book on the past, present and future of democracy.

Index

Index

Frankenfood, 188, 190
Fukuyama, Francis, 4
funding, issues on, welfare reform and, 106

G

gangs, 70
gender differences: in child development, 26–29; in morality, 30
gender-based violence, 121, 122, 123
genetically engineered crops, farming and, 188–195
"get tough" policies, 33
Gibson, J. Lockhart, 133
Gilligan, Carol, 27–28, 29, 31
Gini coefficient, 97, 100
global warming, special report on, 183–187
globalization, 211, 217; of communication, 5
government, power elite and, 128
grain production, impact of population growth on, 174
"Green Run" program, 198–199
Greenspan, Alan, 99
grievances, against America, 209–212
Grossman, Dave, 39
gun violence, in America, secrets of, 38–42
gun-buyback programs, 34

H

harm-reduction strategies, for addiction, 44, 45
health care, income inequality and, 97
health, lessons from success stories in, 133–139
"hedonic region," of the brain, addictions and, 43
hegemony, 209–212
HELP (Handgun Epidemic Lowering Plan), 41
high schools, teachers in, student development and, 152
Highway Safety Act, 135
Hiroshima, nuclear war at, 199
HIV, 158, 163; transmission from mother to infant, 165
homicides, guns and, 39
homosexuality, 64–65, 66
honesty, as a virtue, 21
housing; affordable, 100; costs, in cities, 79; impact of population growth on, 179
Human Rights Watch, 121–122
Huntington, Samuel, 4

I

idea-based city, 78–79
Ik people, of Uganda, 8–16
immigration, 181–182, 213; from Asia, impact on American religion, 167, 169
income, impact of population growth on, 178–179
income inequality, in the U.S., 90–95, 96–101, 214
India, female infanticide in, 121
INF (Intermediate Nuclear Forces) Treaty, 197
infanticide, female, 121

interest groups, pluralism and, 127–128
Internet, community and, 81–87
interpersonal trust, 6

J

job training, for ex-offenders, 34
jobs, impact of population growth on, 178
Johnson, Gary, 45
Journal of the American Medical Association (JAMA), 137

K

Kagan, Elizabeth, 40
Kant, Immanuel, 21, 23
Keynes, John Maynard, 142
King, Martin Luther, Jr., 108, 109–110
Kinsey, Alfred, 63–67
Kohlberg, Lawrence, 30–31
Kolata, Gina, 64, 66
Koop, C. Everett, 137
Kosovo war, 196
Kvaerner ASA, 103
Kyoto Protocol, 183, 187, 210

L

labeling, of genetically engineered crops, 190
language, variations of, race relations and, 108
Laumann, Edward, 63
lead poisoning, 133–137
Lesotho, AIDS in, 160
leukemia, due to radiation, 196, 197, 198, 199
Lewis, Julia, 58–59
liberal-labor coalition, 127, 129
life after death, belief in, 167–168
Lightner, Candy, 136
lobbying, 131; by transnational corporations, 141
Locke, John, 21
Lott, Trent, 130, 131
love, among the Ik people of Uganda, 14
low-level radiation, 198
Lutherans, 168–169
Lyme disease, 185
lymphoma, due to radiation, 197
Lynd, Robert and Helen, 51

M

Making Democracy Work (Putnam), 4
malaria, 185
Manhattan Project, 198
married couples, sex and, 63
Marvin, Carolyn, 81–82
Marx, Karl, 3–4
masculinity crisis, 68–76
Maslow, Abraham, 216
masturbation, 65–66
MBA programs, women and, 117, 118
meat product, impact of population growth on, 175–176
men: careers and, 117, 118; in the U.S., 75
Mercedes-Benz, 103

mergers, of corporations, 144
meritocracy, 91–92
Merton, Robert K., 170
Methodists, 168–169
minimum wage, 99–100
minorities, income inequality and, 93
monitoring, of ex-offenders, 34
Monteith, Margo, 114, 115
moonlighting, 147
moral freedom, 20–23
morality: non-decline of, in the U.S., 17–19; psychology of, 30–32
mortgages, low-income people and, 215
mosquitoes, climate change and, 185
Mother Teresa, 19
Mothers Against Drunk Driving (MADD), 136
Moynihan, Daniel Patrick, 190
Multilateral Agreement on Investment (MAI), 143
Muncie, Indiana, research in, on families, 51
murder, violence against women and, 121

N

Nader, Ralph, 135
Namibia, AIDS in, 160
National Academy of Sciences, 181–182
National Center for Injury Prevention and Control, 41
National Health and Nutrition Examination Survey (NHANES), 134
National Institute of Justice, 33, 36
national parks, impact of population growth on, 176
Neighborhood Watch, 34
neurological damage, lead poisoning and, 133
"New Age" religious movements, 167, 169
New York City, crime prevention in, 36
Nietzsche, Friedrich, 3–4
No Immediate Danger (Bertell), 201
nuclear war, secret of, 196–202

O

Office of Juvenile Justice and Delinquency Prevention, 35
online groups, 82–83
oral sex, 63, 66
Organization for Economic Cooperation and Development (OECD), 143, 215
Organization of American States (OAS), 123
ornamental culture, men and, 73–75
orphans, AIDS and, 162, 165
outcasts, AIDS and, 160–161
out-of-wedlock childbearing, 53, 94–95, 105, 106

P

Paglia, Camille, 64, 66
paint, lead in, 133, 134, 138
Pataki, George, 45
patents, lobbying and, 131
peer groups, in high schools, student development and, 152

Test Your Knowledge Form

We encourage you to photocopy and use this page as a tool to assess how the articles in *Annual Editions* expand on the information in your textbook. By reflecting on the articles you will gain enhanced text information. You can also access this useful form on a product's book support Web site at *http://www.dushkin.com/online/*.

NAME: _____ DATE: _____

TITLE AND NUMBER OF ARTICLE: _____

BRIEFLY STATE THE MAIN IDEA OF THIS ARTICLE: _____

_____

LIST THREE IMPORTANT FACTS THAT THE AUTHOR USES TO SUPPORT THE MAIN IDEA:

_____

WHAT INFORMATION OR IDEAS DISCUSSED IN THIS ARTICLE ARE ALSO DISCUSSED IN YOUR TEXTBOOK OR OTHER READINGS THAT YOU HAVE DONE? LIST THE TEXTBOOK CHAPTERS AND PAGE NUMBERS:

_____

LIST ANY EXAMPLES OF BIAS OR FAULTY REASONING THAT YOU FOUND IN THE ARTICLE:

_____

LIST ANY NEW TERMS/CONCEPTS THAT WERE DISCUSSED IN THE ARTICLE, AND WRITE A SHORT DEFINITION:

We Want Your Advice

ANNUAL EDITIONS revisions depend on two major opinion sources: one is our Advisory Board, listed in the front of this volume, which works with us in scanning the thousands of articles published in the public press each year; the other is you—the person a ctually using the book. Please help us and the users of the next edition by completing the prepaid article rating form on this page and returning it to us. Thank you for your help!

ANNUAL EDITIONS: Sociology 02/03

ARTICLE RATING FORM

Here is an opportunity for you to have direct input into the next revision of this volume.
We would like you to rate each of the articles listed below, using the following scale:

1. **Excellent: should definitely be retained**
2. **Above average: should probably be retained**
3. **Below average: should probably be deleted**
4. **Poor: should definitely be deleted**

Your ratings will play a vital part in the next revision.
Please mail this prepaid form to us as soon as possible.
Thanks for your help!

RATING	ARTICLE
	1. Modernization's Challenge to Traditional Values: Who's Afraid of Ronald McDonald?
	2. The Mountain People
	3. More Moral
	4. The Final Freedom
	5. Boys Will Be Boys
	6. Born to Be Good?
	7. Preventing Crime: The Promising Road Ahead
	8. The Secrets of Gun Violence in America
	9. The War on Addiction
	10. The American Family
	11. Should You Stay Together For the Kids?
	12. Now for the Truth About Americans and Sex
	13. The Betrayal of the American Man
	14. Demand for Density? The Functions of the City in the 21st Century
	15. Does the Internet Strengthen Community?
	16. Still the Land of Opportunity?
	17. Are the Rich Cleaning Up?
	18. Corporate Welfare
	19. From Welfare to Work
	20. Racism Isn't What It Used to Be
	21. Where Bias Begins: The Truth About Stereotypes
	22. The Past and Prologue
	23. Violence Against Women
	24. Who Rules America?
	25. How the Little Guy Gets Crunched
	26. Where the Public Good Prevailed
	27. Twilight of the Corporation
	28. Work, Work, Work, Work!
	29. Schools That Develop Children
	30. Seeking Abortion's Middle Ground
	31. Death Stalks a Continent
	32. The Future of Religion in America
	33. Sixteen Impacts of Population Growth
	34. The Alien Payoff
	35. Feeling the Heat: Life in the Greenhouse
	36. Grains of Hope
	37. The Secret Nuclear War

RATING	ARTICLE
	38. Unmasking Bioterror
	39. Why Don't They Like Us?
	40. Community Building: Steps Toward a Good Society
	41. Across the Great Divide

(Continued on next page)

NO POSTAGE
NECESSARY
IF MAILED
IN THE
UNITED STATES

BUSINESS REPLY MAIL
FIRST-CLASS MAIL PERMIT NO. 84 GUILFORD CT

POSTAGE WILL BE PAID BY ADDRESSEE

McGraw-Hill/Dushkin
530 Old Whitfield Street
Guilford, Ct 06437-9989

III....II..I.I..II.I..II.I..II.I.I..I.I.I...I.I..I.I..I.I.I

- -

ABOUT YOU

Name   Date

Are you a teacher? ☐   A student? ☐
Your school's name

Department

Address   City   State   Zip

School telephone #

YOUR COMMENTS ARE IMPORTANT TO US!

Please fill in the following information:
For which course did you use this book?

Did you use a text with this ANNUAL EDITION?   ☐ yes ☐ no
What was the title of the text?

What are your general reactions to the *Annual Editions* concept?

Have you read any pertinent articles recently that you think should be included in the next edition? Explain.

Are there any articles that you feel should be replaced in the next edition? Why?

Are there any World Wide Web sites that you feel should be included in the next edition? Please annotate.

May we contact you for editorial input?   ☐ yes ☐ no
May we quote your comments? ☐ yes ☐ no